Chronotropics

Odile Ferly • Tegan Zimmerman
Editors

Chronotropics

Caribbean Women Writing Spacetime

Editors
Odile Ferly
Language, Literature & Culture
Clark University
Worcester, MA, USA

Tegan Zimmerman
Women and Gender Studies
Saint Mary's University
Halifax, NS, Canada

ISBN 978-3-031-32110-8   ISBN 978-3-031-32111-5 (eBook)
https://doi.org/10.1007/978-3-031-32111-5

© The Editor(s) (if applicable) and The Author(s) 2023. This book is an open access publication.
Open Access This book is licensed under the terms of the Creative Commons Attribution 4.0 International License (http://creativecommons.org/licenses/by/4.0), which permits use, sharing, adaptation, distribution and reproduction in any medium or format, as long as you give appropriate credit to the original author(s) and the source, provide a link to the Creative Commons licence and indicate if changes were made.

The images or other third party material in this book are included in the book's Creative Commons licence, unless indicated otherwise in a credit line to the material. If material is not included in the book's Creative Commons licence and your intended use is not permitted by statutory regulation or exceeds the permitted use, you will need to obtain permission directly from the copyright holder.

The use of general descriptive names, registered names, trademarks, service marks, etc. in this publication does not imply, even in the absence of a specific statement, that such names are exempt from the relevant protective laws and regulations and therefore free for general use.

The publisher, the authors, and the editors are safe to assume that the advice and information in this book are believed to be true and accurate at the date of publication. Neither the publisher nor the authors or the editors give a warranty, expressed or implied, with respect to the material contained herein or for any errors or omissions that may have been made. The publisher remains neutral with regard to jurisdictional claims in published maps and institutional affiliations.

Cover illustration: Ethan Daniels/Stocktrek Images/Getty Images

This Palgrave Macmillan imprint is published by the registered company Springer Nature Switzerland AG.
The registered company address is: Gewerbestrasse 11, 6330 Cham, Switzerland

*I wish to dedicate this volume to Caribbean women writers of the past,
present and future and to the next generations of Caribbean women.
I also dedicate this volume to my daughter and thank her for her patience.*
—Odile Ferly

ACKNOWLEDGMENTS

We wish to express our gratitude to the contributors to this volume, who joined us on this intellectual journey with graciousness and commitment. We are particularly grateful to Joshua R. Deckman for collaborating on the Introduction.

We also would like to extend our thanks to Pace University, the University of Indiana at Bloomington, the College of Charleston, as well as the Higgins School of Humanities at Clark University, the Barbera Faculty Fellowship fund for the Language, Literature and Culture department at Clark University, and the Clark University Provost's Office for their financial support towards Open Access. We especially want to recognise the contributors, whose financial commitment made it happen, and NeMLA (Northeast Modern Language Association) for giving us a platform to germinate and disseminate this work.

Finally, Odile wishes to thank Molly Beck at Palgrave Macmillan, who believed in this project.

—Odile Ferly and Tegan Zimmerman

CONTENTS

1   Poetics and Politics of the Chronotropics: Introduction   1
Odile Ferly, Tegan Zimmerman, and Joshua R. Deckman

Part I   Archival Disruption   25

2   Chronotopal Slave Ships, Corporeal Archives: *Devoir de mémoire* in Fabienne Kanor's *Humus* and Yolanda Arroyo Pizarro's *las Negras*   27
Odile Ferly

3   Wreckognition: Archival Ruins in Dionne Brand's *The Blue Clerk*   47
Erica L. Johnson

4   Past Histories and Present Realities: The Paradox of Time and the Ritual of Performance in Mayra Santos Febres' *Fe en disfraz*   65
Nicole Roberts

5   A Site of Memory: Revisiting (in) Gisèle Pineau's *Mes quatre femmes*   83
Renée Larrier

x CONTENTS

Part II Radical Remapping   101

6 Connecting Diasporas: Reading Erna Brodber's *Nothing's Mat* through African Fractal Theory   103
A. Marie Sairsingh

7 Writing "In Transit": Literary Constructions of Sovereignty in Julia Alvarez's *Afterlife*   121
Megan Jeanette Myers

8 When the Tout-Monde Is Not One: Maryse Condé's Problematic 'World-in-Motion' in *Les belles ténébreuses* (2008) and *Le fabuleux et triste destin d'Ivan et Ivana* (2017)   139
Valérie K. Orlando

9 Re-mapping the Caribbean Gothic in Nalo Hopkinson's *Sister Mine* and Shani Mootoo's *He Drown She in the Sea*   157
Vivian Nun Halloran

10 Imagining Beyond Division, an Environmental Future: Pauline Melville's *The Ventriloquist's Tale* and Elizabeth Nunez's *Prospero's Daughter.*   173
Elaine Savory

Part III Epistemic Marronnage   193

11 Spiritual Crossings: Olokun and Caribbean Futures Past in *La Mucama de Omicunlé* by Rita Indiana   195
Joshua R. Deckman

12 Creolizing Science in Mayra Montero's *Palm of Darkness*   213
Carine M. Mardorossian and Angela Veronica Wong

CONTENTS xi

13 Monstrous Genealogies: Indo-Caribbean Feminist Reckonings with the Violent Past   233
Lisa Outar

14 At the Crossroads of History: The Cohabitation of Past and Present in Kettly Mars's *L'Ange du patriarche*   251
Robert Sapp

15 Fiction as a Spider's Web? Ananse and Gender in Karen Lord's Speculative Folktale *Redemption in Indigo*   271
Tegan Zimmerman

16 Chronotropic Visions: Conclusion   291
Odile Ferly and Tegan Zimmerman

Index   303

Notes on Contributors

Joshua R. Deckman is Assistant Professor of Hispanic Studies in the Department of World Languages and Cultures at Stetson University, Florida, United States. His research and teaching center on contemporary Afro-Latinx and Caribbean literatures and cultural studies. He is a coeditor of the volume *Oxala: Afro-Latinx Futures, Imaginings, and Engagements* and the author of *Feminist Spiritualities: Conjuring Resistance in the Afro-Caribbean and Its Diasporas* (SUNY Press, 2023).

Odile Ferly is Associate Professor of Francophone Studies at Clark University, Massachusetts, United States. Author of *A Poetics of Relation: Caribbean Women Writing at the Millennium* (Palgrave, 2012) and a coeditor of *Chronotropics: Caribbean Women Writing Spacetime*, she examines contemporary literature, especially by women, from a pan-Caribbean perspective (anglophone, francophone, and hispanophone areas). Her current research focuses on culture and politics in the French Caribbean.

Vivian Nun Halloran is Professor of English and Associate Dean for Diversity and Inclusion in the College of Arts and Sciences at Indiana University. She's the author of *Caribbean American Narratives of Belonging* (Ohio State University Press 2023), *The Immigrant's Kitchen: Food, Ethnicity, and Diaspora* (Ohio State University Press 2016), and *Exhibiting Slavery: The Caribbean Postmodern Novel as Museum* (University of Virginia Press, 2009). Her research areas include Caribbean studies, food studies, popular culture, and postmodernism. Her new area of research involves Caribbean diaspora literature in Canada.

xiv NOTES ON CONTRIBUTORS

Erica L. Johnson is a professor of English at Pace University in New York City. Her scholarly fields include Caribbean literature and cultural memory studies, and she is the author of *Cultural Memory, Memorials, and Reparative Writing; Caribbean Ghostwriting;* and *Home, Maison, Casa.* She has coedited a number of volumes, including *Wide Sargasso Sea at 50* with Elaine Savory, *Memory as Colonial Capital* with Éloïse Brezault, and *The Female Face of Shame* and *Jean Rhys: Twenty-First-Century Approaches* with Patricia Moran.

Renée Larrier is a professor emerita, and has taught in the French Department at Rutgers University for more than 30 years and served as chair. Author of *Autofiction and Advocacy in the Francophone Caribbean* and *Francophone Women Writers of Africa and the Caribbean,* she co-coedited *L'Esprit Créateur* "His Legacy Relates: Edouard Glissant's Thought in Literature and Culture" with Georgette Mitchell and *Writing Through the Visual and Virtual: Inscribing Language, Literature, and Culture in Francophone Africa and the Caribbean* with Ousseina D. Alido. She has contributed dozens of articles to essay collections and scholarly journals and shares editing duties of CARAF Books with Mildred Mortimer.

Carine M. Mardorossian is Professor of Global Gender Studies and English at the University at Buffalo, SUNY, where she specializes in Caribbean studies, feminist studies, and narrative nonfiction. Her books include *Reclaiming Difference: Caribbean Women Rewrite Postcolonialism* and *Framing the Rape Victim,* which finds in Caribbean literature the answer to the impasse that has defined approaches to sexual violence. Her 2020 book *Death is but a Dream* is a work of creative nonfiction coauthored with Christopher Kerr, MD. With Professor Wong, she is completing a manuscript on Caribbean literature and the environment entitled *Creolized Ecologies.*

Megan Jeanette Myers is Associate Professor of Spanish and Director of the Languages and Cultures for Professions program at Iowa State University. Myers is the author of *Mapping Hispaniola: Third Space in Dominican and Haitian Literature* (University of Virginia Press, 2019), and has recently published in journals such as *CARIBE, The Journal of Haitian Studies,* and *Latino Studies.* Myers is a co-founder and organizer of Border of Lights (borderoflights.org). She is also the coeditor of *The*

Border of Lights Reader: Bearing Witness to Genocide in the Dominican Republic (Amherst College Press, 2021).

Valérie K. Orlando is Professor of French and Francophone Literatures at the University of Maryland, College Park. She is the author of six books, the most recent of which include: *The Algerian New Novel: The Poetics of a Modern Nation, 1950–1979* (2017), *New African Cinema* (2017), and *Screening Morocco: Contemporary Film in a Changing Society* (2011). Recently, she published with Cécile Accilien *Teaching Haiti: Strategies for Creating New Narratives* (2021).

Lisa Outar is an independent scholar who publishes in the fields of Indo-Caribbean literature, feminist writing, and the connections between the Caribbean and other post-indentureship spaces. She serves as acting editor in chief of the *Journal of West Indian Literature*, and is at work on a manuscript about feminist engagements with religion and folkore in Indo-Caribbean women's writing. She is coeditor of *Indo-Caribbean Feminist Thought: Genealogies, Theories, Enactments*, published in 2016 by Palgrave Macmillan.

Nicole Roberts is a senior lecturer in Spanish at The University of the West Indies (UWI), St. Augustine campus. Her research work mainly explores race thinking and identity in the Afro-Hispanic Caribbean (Cuba, Puerto Rico, and the Dominican Republic). She is currently working on two book-length studies; one on *Our Caribbean: Cuba and Anglophone Caribbean Relations* and another on Caribbean identity and integration in the narrative of the Puerto Rican author Mayra Santos Febres.

A. Marie Sairsingh is Professor in English Studies at the University of the Bahamas and teaches a range of Composition and Literature courses. Dr. Sairsingh is co-editor of *Zoe International Journal of Social Transformation* and Advisory Editor for *College Language Association Journal*; she serves on the editorial boards of the *International Journal of Bahamian Studies* and *Tout Moun: Caribbean Journal of Cultural Studies*. Her areas of research and publication include Literatures of the African Diaspora, the intersection of Literature and Africana Philosophy, Caribbean Literary and Cultural Theory, and Gender and Cultural Studies.

Robert Sapp is Associate Professor in the Department of French, Francophone, and Italian Studies at the College of Charleston specializing in literature from the Francophone Caribbean and Québec. His current research focuses on the expression of the past in contemporary Haitian novels. His work appears in *French Review, Women in French Studies, Contemporary French and Francophone Studies, The Journal of Haitian Studies, The Journal of West Indian Literature, Romance Notes,* and *The New Zealand Journal of French Studies.*

Elaine Savory has published widely on Caribbean and African literatures, including women's writing, theater and drama, poetry and literary history, and especially Jean Rhys (*Jean Rhys; The Cambridge Introduction to Jean Rhys; Wide Sargasso Sea at Fifty*, coedited with Erica Johnson) as well as Kamau Brathwaite. She coedited *Out of the Kumbla: Women and Caribbean Literature*, with Carole Boyce Davies, and has published a poetry collection, *flame tree time*. Recent work pertains to the fields of postcolonial ecocriticism and environmental humanities. She is Emeritus Professor (The New School, NYC).

Angela Veronica Wong holds a Ph.D. in English from the University at Buffalo, SUNY, and is currently revising her dissertation, "Women, Cultural Labor, and Internationalist Networks in the U.S., U.K, and Caribbean, 1910-1960," for publication. She has published on Edwidge Danticat's novels, and is currently collaborating with Carine Mardorossian on a book about Caribbean fiction and ecocriticism. She has taught literature, composition, and creative writing at UB, Marymount Manhattan College, and NYU. A former Humanities New York Public Humanities Fellow, she was a 2021–2022 ACLS/Mellon Public Fellow.

Tegan Zimmerman is an adjunct professor in Women and Gender Studies at Saint Mary's University, Halifax, Canada, and the chair of the International Comparative Literature Association's Comparative Gender Studies Research Committee. She specializes in contemporary gender theory and women's writing, with a concentration on Caribbean women's historical fiction. She is the author of *Matria Redux: Caribbean Women Novelize the Past* (The University Press of Mississippi, 2023).

CHAPTER 1

Poetics and Politics of the Chronotropics: Introduction

Odile Ferly, Tegan Zimmerman, and Joshua R. Deckman

Twenty-first-century literature by women from across the Caribbean and its diaspora evidences an urge to start afresh. It frequently points to the lingering legacy of enslavement, coloniality, and patriarchy as it denounces the pernicious effects of an inequitable global economic order premised on exploitative relationships and unsustainable practices that have ushered in ecological cataclysms. The present collection examines these matters through the prism of what we term "chronotropics." Stemming from *chronos* (time) and *tropos*, both in reference to the geographical area under study and in its etymological acceptation of "a turn," we use this neologism to designate a poetics that calls for a turning point, a revolution in

O. Ferly (✉)
Clark University, Worcester, MA, USA
e-mail: oferly@clarku.edu

T. Zimmerman
Saint Mary's University, Halifax, NS, Canada
e-mail: tegan.zimmerman@smu.ca

J. R. Deckman
Stetson University, DeLand, FL, USA

© The Author(s) 2023
O. Ferly, T. Zimmerman (eds.), *Chronotropics*,
https://doi.org/10.1007/978-3-031-32111-5_1

the social, economic, and political spheres, but also of an epistemic and ethical order. The narratives included here are chronotropic in that they actively challenge the anthropocentric and androcentric logic propelled by European capitalism according to which space is delimited, privatized,[1] tamed, and subject to extraction and time is measured, linear, singular, arbitrarily standardized,[2] and teleological.

Bringing together Julia Alvarez, Yolanda Arroyo Pizarro, Vashti Bowlah, Dionne Brand, Erna Brodber, Maryse Condé, Nalo Hopkinson, Rita Indiana, Fabienne Kanor, Karen Lord, Kettly Mars, Pauline Melville, Mayra Montero, Shani Mootoo, Elizabeth Nunez, Ingrid Persaud, Gisèle Pineau, Krystal M. Ramroop, and Mayra Santos Febres, *Chronotropics: Caribbean Women Writing Spacetime* proposes novel interpretations of the region's landscapes and history that are anticolonial, gender inclusive, and pluralistic. Attuned to autochthonous modes of being, ancestral cosmologies, and an indigenous relation to terrains and temporalities, the theoretical and literary projects discussed in this pan-Caribbean volume gesture towards justice and social change through archival disruption, radical remapping, and epistemic *marronnage*. Our collection is articulated around these three converging approaches to Caribbean women's spacetime.

The writers gathered here, each speaking from a particular site of enunciation grounded in various linguistic and cultural contexts, all invoke a need for solidarity from which to re-think geopolitical boundaries, racialized histories, and ethno-phallogocentric appropriations of spacetime. Each of them persists in challenging the contours of gender and the body as constructed within and by spacetime, in its physical, biological, and psychological materiality as much as its sociocultural, historical, and political manifestations. These writers' dispersed, yet collective, locus of creation and activism invites us to pause and ask how we might break the cycle of violence and trauma repeated from generation to generation by forging new alliances and political coalitions, generating new myths, and remapping and reimagining our spatiotemporal relationship to the landscape, that is, space through time: *isla, monte y mar*.

The chronotropics uses Caribbean women's creative interpretations of spacetime as its theoretical foundation to acknowledge their role in contemporary discourse and politics. By recognizing these authors as philosophers, public intellectuals and social activists, our conceptual framework redresses the frequent scholarly neglect of such vital contributions.[3] Drawing on the theories of several women writers featured in this volume,

1 POETICS AND POLITICS OF THE CHRONOTROPICS: INTRODUCTION 3

this Introduction establishes the chronotropics along the axes of ontologies, cosmogonies, and epistemologies; it then proceeds to outline how each critical perspective engages with our gender-inflected paradigm of spacetime. "Charting the Chronotropics," the opening section, defines and then situates the chronotropics as expanding current philosophical and literary discourses on human being such as those put forth by Mayra Santos Febres and Sylvia Wynter; the second section, "Inhabiting the Chronotropics of Ancestral Knowledge," guided by the work of Lydia Cabrera, articulates the spiritual dimension of Caribbean epistemologies (belief systems, philosophies, wisdom, folktales, oral histories) like those espoused by Yolanda Arroyo Pizarro, Erna Brodber, Rita Indiana, Fabienne Kanor, Mayra Montero, and Mayra Santos Febres. The third section, "(Im)Possible Subjects of the Chronotropics" reflects on identity, agency, and positionality politics in Dionne Brand, Maryse Condé, and Shani Mootoo. "Reengineering Community," concludes our discussion by emphasizing writing and activism as political praxis.

This collection pays particular homage to three seminal edited volumes that have endured for decades: *Her True, True Name: An Anthology of Women's Writing from the Caribbean*, by Pamela Mordecai and Betty Wilson (1990); *Out of the Kumbla: Caribbean Women and Literature*, by Carol Boyce Davies and Elaine Savory Fido, a contributor to this volume (1990); and Selwyn R. Cudjoe's *Caribbean Women Writers: Essays from the First International Conference* (1990). Our pan-Caribbean approach likewise brings together several generations of authors and critics to argue that gendered perspectives on spacetime must be apprehended from a reevaluated and redefined notion of human being.

CHARTING THE CHRONOTROPICS

Contemporary Caribbean women's writing displays an array of innovative approaches to spacetime. This collection uncovers what will be characterized as a poetics and politics of the chronotropics. A paradigm referring to a vision informed by idiosyncrasies of being and knowing that have shaped distinctive approaches to space and time in the area, the chronotropics undermines the hegemonic perspectives steeped in Newtonian and quantum physics that are inherent to the novelistic chronotope of western modernity, as first popularized by literary critic Mikhail Bakhtin in 1930s Russia.[4] The narratives herein therefore participate in the epistemic resistance characteristic of what Derek Lee (2020) designates the postquantum novel, or "speculative ethnic fiction" (1) whose main imperative is to question the supremacy of science and debunk Occidental pretension to universality. In these chronotropic narratives that work to destabilize debilitating colonial patterns, space can shift, contract, or expand to encompass the region as a whole, its multiple points of origin, and its diaspora, while representations of time convey how little structural reform these societies have truly undergone. The complex, multidimensional textual interventions of the creative writers-theorists-activists included here draw attention to gender to revitalize regional discourses such as Antonio Benítez Rojo's repeating island (1989), E. Kamau Brathwaite's articulation of creolization (1971), Paul Gilroy's black Atlantic, or Édouard Glissant's Relation (1981, 1990, 1997).

Chronotropics seeks to amplify the dialogue Paul Gilroy (1993) initiated as he reformulated Mikhail Bakhtin's chronotope for his black Atlantic (see Odile Ferly's opening chapter in this volume). David W. Hart (2004) also resorts to Bakhtin and specifically his chronotope of the threshold (in which time is measured by the events of collective life) to discuss how the past functions in Caribbean literature to claim cultural (and, we might add, political) agency in the present. Isabel Hoving (2001) and Clarisse Zimra (1993) accentuated the postcolonial turn by examining the chronotope as the house in Beryl Gilroy and as Africa in Simone Schwarz-Bart. In Njelle Hamilton's analysis of what she coins *chronotrope* (2018, 2019, see also her *Caribbean Chronotropes*, in progress), time supersedes space. Returning to an equal emphasis on both, chronotropics places gender at the core of the conversation.

Despite their significant material impact on our daily reality, Mikhail Bakhtin's chronotopes largely belong to the abstract domain of narratives, ideologies, and the imaginary. In this they differ from Michel Foucault's heterotopias, which exist and operate within the physical world, although they remain on the margin (Foucault 1984 [1967], 47). By contrast, the chronotropics is a vision in the process of being (but rarely fully) realized. Chronotopes and to a large extent heterotopias are inherently conservative insofar as they act as a pressure relief mechanism that helps maintain "the order of things" (Foucault 1966). The poetics and politics of the chronotropics, on the other hand, have an avowed vocation for revolutionary change: it is intentional about undoing the status quo. While it is made of the fabric of dreams and ideals, it is anchored in the real and frequently translates as social activism. This sets the chronotropics apart from the utopia, which is more firmly entrenched in the realm of the imaginary, the unreal (Foucault 1984 [1967], 47).

Our approach also builds on transformative developments in philosophy such as those undertaken by Sylvia Wynter, Paget Henry, and Linda Martín Alcoff. Alcoff (2003) in particular has argued against the discipline's assumptions that Western man and his experience constitute universality and truth. Alcoff has advocated for feminist epistemologies that legitimize the status of women and marginalized figures as authoritative knowers and that consider, in conjunction with other political markers such as race and culture, the implications of the "sexed body of the knower upon the production of knowledge" (Alcoff and Potter 1993, 2). The emphasis on community as the "primary agent of knowledge" (9) over the "isolated individual subject" (8) in Caribbean and feminist philosophies likewise often finds echo in the creative outputs that concern *Chronotropics*. The women authors examined here therefore reimagine the ontological and ontic in leading philosophical-political-poetic traditions. The result is that our collection emphasizes a sense of gendered solidarity embracing what Mayra Santos Febres, inspired by Erna Brodber (2014), has deemed a Caribbean fractality, one that conjures the concept of the *uno múltiple*, that is, the many-in-one.

Santos Febres (2019) expands on her concept in an unpublished lecture titled "The Fractal Caribbean." For the Puerto Rican writer and scholar, feminist movements across the Caribbean underscore the ways in which African diasporic epistemological systems offer a space where we might reimagine solidarity practices beyond the geopolitical borders of the nation-state. She draws from teachings of Yoruba-Ifá traditions that claim *Yo soy yo y mis santos* (I am myself and my saints/spirits) as well as Vodou tradition which all understand the body as an open vessel. She likens it to the bodily experience of listening to jazz "a set of repetitions that are never the same, [...] an improvisational solo from each and every instrument that composes melody, cacophony, but also rhythm ... Improvisation lets different phrases reach for the manifestation of the message, the energy, the One that is Multiple" (translation Joshua R. Deckman's). In this way, the atavistic drive towards the singular root or any claim of truth becomes obsolete, as each element within the totality is given the space to intervene, to interrupt, to demand a voice. She continues: "Time as rhythm becomes multi-layered. Each individual enters a system of relations that creates a reality that is both One and Multiple. Since we live in a world organized by linear movement of time and narratives, history is propelled by binary oppositions, black versus white, poor versus rich, native versus immigrant, male versus female, past versus present ... or future." Santos Febres urges us to break with this linear thinking in order to usher in new modes of relations, in which the stories and lived experiences of Caribbean women from across the diaspora combine with those of the archipelago to disrupt a violent history of colonial, heteropatriarchal power.

Remarking that theories of the Western Self (and by corollary its oppositional Others) developed in the age of colonialism and capitalism, foundational critic Sylvia Wynter takes a gendered anticolonial look at historically contingent epistemes or discursive frameworks and their conceptual schemas (Henry 2000, 126–128). Wynter (2003, 322–323) shows how epistemes, dependent on semiotically derived hierarchical binaries, schematize sameness/difference categories which, in turn, order and make social life intelligible. According to this tradition, first "Christian becomes Man1 (as political subject), then ... Man1 becomes Man2 (as a bio-economic subject)" (318). Deemed as "isomorphic with the being of being human itself" (266), whiteness, Europeanness, and maleness become the dominant referents in this "matrix of colonial power" (Quijano 2000; Mignolo 2009, 3). The Caribbean woman exists discursively as "lack": anti-reason, anti-civility, anti-culture, and as sub-human. Calvin L. Warren (2018) thus argues against a specific tradition of European philosophy that resulted in what he calls a "metaphysical holocaust" that enforced "the nonexistence of black being" (144) and obliterated their "place of representation" (145); he conveys the (in)ability to represent lack visually on the page by repeatedly crossing out the word "being" after "black" throughout his book. Wynter (1990) in her earlier work demonstrates the above by calling attention to the absence of "Caliban's Woman," a physiognomic partner for Shakespeare's infamous racialized character in *The Tempest*. This volume engages with Wynter's directive to decolonize spheres of intellectualism, especially the overdetermination of "Man."

New postcolonial theories of Caribbeanness will only unfold, Wynter argues, after an "epistemological break" with the prevailing western logic/ideology (1984, 40), a mandate we call epistemic *marronnage* that the writers included here all take to heart, as illustrated most notably through their approaches to spacetime. Wynter and David Scott (2000) argue that "something else [besides the dominant cultural logic] constituted another—but also transgressive—ground of understanding ... not simply a sociodemographic location but the site both of a form of life and of possible critical intervention" (164). Such sites of intervention are the "demonic" spaces and temporal pauses opened by each writer. The chronotropics articulates a new Caribbean, where bodies and imaginations come together to propose other modes of being in the world, ways that dissolve and break through the sediment of colonial-heteronormative patriarchy. Wynter's move to apprehend ontology and epistemology from space and place opens critical paths towards "reengineering"—to borrow the term by Erna Brodber (1997)—an archipelago of woman's thought which this volume begins to explore.

INHABITING THE CHRONOTROPICS
OF ANCESTRAL KNOWLEDGE

Resonating with Wynter's work, the authors studied here outline alternative ways of inhabiting Caribbean spacetime. Their writings reconstitute an expanded Caribbean space and actively push back at the legacy of colonialism that has been at the heart of the ongoing marginalization of women's voices and (hi)stories. Many of these women tap into a deep *feeling* of solidarity with their kin, intellectual peers, and/or long line of ancestors to access "other" types of knowledge and creolize, as Henry argues, "aspects of shattered Amerindian, Indian, and African worldviews" (2000, 15). For example, Yolanda Arroyo Pizarro, discussed in the opening chapter, pays tribute to her rebellious enslaved female forebears, whose spirits—much like Danticat's in "Women Like Us" from *Krik? Krak!* (1995)—inhabit her and compel her to write "como si ... estuviera en trance" (as if [she] were in a trance): "*They* direct my hands for me to write ... for me to write them into being" (Arroyo Pizarro 2018, 48, translation Deckman's). Among Arroyo Pizarro's literary precursors is Santos Febres, whose novel *Fe en disfraz* (examined by Nicole Roberts) she credits as an inspiration for her own short stories in *las Negras* ([2012] 2013). Denouncing the official history of Puerto Rico "por habernos dejado fuera" (for leaving us out, translation Ferly's) in her epigraph, Arroyo Pizarro *restitutes* the memory of enslaved women by illuminating their acts of resistance and contributions to humankind; reclaiming the woman-centered transgenerational knowledge in her fiction further advances her goal of "narr[ar] el devenir de las antepasadas" (Arroyo Pizarro 2018, 53) [telling the becoming of our forebears, Deckman's translation], Arroyo Pizarro's formulation evidences a chronotropic vision of time that merges past, present, and future: all happen and can be acted upon simultaneously. This applies to

8   O. FERLY ET AL.

many works discussed in this collection, most prominently those that use time travelling as a central feature: Hopkinson's *Sister Mine* (2013), Indiana's *La mucama de Omicunlé* (2015), Lord's *Redemption in Indigo* (2010), Pineau's *Mes quatre femmes* (2007), and Santos Febres's *Fe en disfraz* (2009).

Thus, Arroyo Pizarro (like all the authors discussed in this volume) engage with "imaginación y creatividad" (Arroyo Pizarro 2018, 13) to forge a *sense* of community among black women across the archipelago and the black Atlantic who might see themselves in her fictional tales, in her archive of ancestral memories, and in the political project that emerges from her engagement with them. In Ferly's chapter on Arroyo Pizarro and Kanor, this space of remembrance is re-articulated through the chrono-tope of the slave ship (in dialogue with Gilroy, Glissant, and Saidiya Hartman) and the immaterial archive of the body on which both writers draw to envision a future of renewed potential. Erna Brodber, Rita Indiana, Mayra Montero, and Gisèle Pineau utilize this same chronotope of ances-tral knowledge to advocate for their own collective archives (biographies, histories, contemplated futures) in which women occupy a central place. Meanwhile, Nalo Hopkinson, Karen Lord, and Kettly Mars respectively outline a reliance on African and Hindu pantheons and folktales as well as the Bois Caïman Vodou ceremony in order to communicate a state of cohabitation with the spirits and a different metaphysics. Lisa Outar's chapter expands the conversation to examine Indo-Caribbean representa-tions that negotiate both vulnerable and powerful spaces of femininity to challenge the boundaries between the human and the non-human as well as conventional historiography and trauma narratives. This, in turn, opens a space for critical thought that may make room for women whose own beliefs, spiritual practices, oral traditions, and experiences have been sys-tematically silenced or denigrated by the hegemonic history of their home-lands. As such, this involves what Yomaira Figueroa (2020) has outlined as "worlds/otherwise," or the enunciation of what has been rendered invis-ible by coloniality (2).

These women point to an "ancestor"—explicitly and implicitly—of trans-Caribbean identity and epistemologies: Lydia Cabrera, whose eth-nographic studies on Ñáñigo people and Afro-Caribbean beliefs chart sto-ries of gender, sexuality, and race that lay the groundwork for an intra-Caribbean immaterial archive. This archive—whether spiritual or corporeal—is elaborated as certain spiritual traditions, customs, nonmate-rial entities, and ancestors are invoked, engaged, or given cultural value to make sense of lived experience. It is encoded in the practices that surround its construction—in the memories, feelings, and yearnings that mark its emergence. While for Kanor (2006, 2009) this archive grounded in the body encompasses more than the spiritual, Cabrera, specifically in her books *Yemayá y Ochún* and *El monte*, encounters a space of freedom and becoming within the realm of religiosity in which women in particular are empowered to follow the spirits to experiment with gender expression and sexual desire. She calls upon the spiritual archive of Afro-Cuban deities to document how her interlocutors engage with them, emulate them, and draw knowledge. In a similar way, Rita Indiana recurs to the work of Cabrera and her engagement with these religious practices—particularly in the blurring of gender and sexual boundaries through the deity Yemayá-Olokún, as noted by Joshua R. Deckman in his chapter on *La mucama de Omicunlé*.

Echoing other writers of the collection such as Nalo Hopkinson, Mayra Montero, or Pauline Melville (1997) in relation to Indigenous cosmologies in Guyana, Indiana returns to Afro-Indigenous ontologies to reject the idolatrous Cartesian mind/body dichotomy so central to European thought; in doing so, she breathes life back into old ways of knowing to produce new knowledges. Indiana thereby represents a particularly pan-Caribbean approach to these categories, anchoring herself firmly in the syncretic gaps between the islands of Cuba and Hispaniola. Born in the Dominican Republic and influenced by systems of Haitian Vodou that are prevalent in her musical productions (e.g., the song "Da' pa' lo' do'"), she is an initiate in Afro-Cuban rites who resides in Puerto Rico. Her move to engage Yoruba systems developed in Cuba to make sense of Caribbean environmental disasters and colonial destruction specifically on the island of Hispaniola therefore performs a critical intervention that exceeds imposed colonial, linguistic, temporal, and epistemological boundaries. Indiana's non-binary protagonist is the *uno múltiple* of African spiritual traditions—that is, they are themself, but they are also informed by multiple entities from the past and the future simultaneously. In this way, Indiana reconfigures how we might comprehend several Caribbean presents, by engaging with what Brodber would call a fractal timeline—or what we call a chronotropic mindset—whereby the here and now is disclosed through a continuous negotiation of what has come before and what may come to be.

Furthermore, Rita Indiana looks to her Afro-Cuban pantheon to envision an alternative textual-sacred space for gender fluidity and queerness.

The author underscores the *pataki* of Yemayá-Olokún, a spirit of multiple *caminos* who can take on "male" and "female" attributes depending on the need of the moment. Indiana reconstructs gender by merging spirituality and storytelling; this resonates with several other writers such as Karen Lord, whose speculative folktale *Redemption in Indigo* disrupts sexual difference. As Tegan Zimmerman's closing chapter argues, Lord updates the African-Caribbean Ananse figure by exploring the maternal/feminine and portraying the storyteller as non-binary. Other folkloric reimaginings within this collection, like the churile or the diablesse, strongly suggest that such stories can function as chronotopes capable of not only breaking through modern desires of (dis)embodiment but also destabilizing understandings of time that subscribe to linearity, that is to say, history.

For example, in *L'Ange du patriarche* (2018), Kettly Mars—much like Montero, Indiana, and Cabrera—opens a space to reflect on history within the transcorporeal realm of African-derived religious practices imbued with Christianity. In her novel, Mars (discussed by Robert Sapp) constructs an imaginary archive that resists the restrictive silences of the State archive. Ancestral remembrance enables the protagonist to open herself and her community to close communion with those who came before her, thus also opening the door to new ways of being Caribbean. Likewise, Mars stresses the role of women in Haitian history, shifting the spotlight from Boukman to Marinette pye chèch, the lesser-known mambo said to have assisted at the Bois Caïman ritual. This work underscores the oppressive, inescapable nature of history against which Mars positions her protagonist Emmanuela and her concept of cohabitation, whereby seemingly irreconcilable views of the past and ways of inhabiting the present coexist. Making possible an intervention into the future, cohabitation maintains the tension of the dialectic, preserving the mystery: it is resistance.

Resistance, in particular when spiritual, is at the core of Erna Brodber's work too (Sharpe 2012). A trained historian and sociologist as well as a creative writer, Brodber decries the colonizers as "spirit thieves" whose onslaught on potentially subversive African religious practices "stymied the spiritual growth and development of transported Africans" (Brodber 2012a, xii), resulting in a region-wide psychic amputation that leaves Caribbean people, especially the most educated, "torn by the experience of living with two systems of thought that are difficult to reconcile" (xi), or, to use Mars's terminology, a state of cohabitation that is excruciating because it is not assumed. Brodber responds to the existential threat of epistemic erasure by centering Afro-diasporic practices (see, for instance,

Brodber 1974, 2012b, and 2013). Foregrounding Jamaican and African epistemologies such as myalism and fractals (the focus of A. Marie Sairsingh's chapter in this volume), Brodber's fiction, scholarship, and community activism thus emerge out of a sense of retribution and can be seen as a set of restorative practices or "sovereign acts," to use the theoretical frame deployed by Megan Jeanette Myers in her chapter on Julia Alvarez, that empower Afrodescendants to counter colonial denigration and neoliberal assimilation; the reclamation of the 1838 Emancipation in Jamaica is one such sovereign act. Similarly, Hanétha Vété-Congolo (2018) shows how the enslaved were sustained in their resistance to dehumanization by Muntu, a concept from ancestral Bantu philosophy disseminated throughout sub-Saharan Africa that maintains that "everyone is a person" (rendered by the French Caribbean Creole aphorism *tout moun sé moun*), thereby positing equality as the fundamental basis of interpersonal relations.

In an interview in *Bomb Magazine*, Mayra Montero likewise claims to have "a great aesthetic, even philosophic affinity" with syncretic belief systems for which she maintains an altar in her house; "this wonderful mixture," she adds, "gives us depth and spirituality as a people" (Prieto 2000, 2). Montero points to "we" as a community of Caribbean women who are brought together in difference through African diasporic beliefs. Montero (1995) makes an implicit argument for creolizing epistemologies, urging the reader to take into consideration what we can gather from traditions that have been demonized and made invisible, as Carine M. Mardorossian and Angela Veronica Wong's chapter emphasizes. In a move similar to that of Yolanda Arroyo Pizarro, Mayra Montero therefore builds upon the potential of the spiritual archive of rebellious being; this epistemological shift reveals the extent to which the subordination and marginalization of non-Western gnosis, ecology, and femininity proves ethically and logically untenable. Perspectives like Montero's seek to redefine humans as stewards of the planet. These eco-conscious worldviews, in which spaces and times are infused with sacred meaning, pursue sustainable and reciprocal relations both intra and inter species, and between humans and nature. In her call to embrace the altar, Montero suggests that the first step towards retributive justice for these women's histories is to recuperate, amplify, and insert ancient traditions of thought into contemporary Western epistemology. The authors analyzed in *Chronotropics* therefore reject this Anthropocene era by recuperating cosmogonies which de-center Man.

12 O. FERLY ET AL.

Indeed, the authors examined here challenge positivism with the metaphysical and other-worldly, existential and phenomenological, social and political. Several works discussed in this collection, e.g., Hopkinson's *Sister Mine*, provide a lens through which to apprehend diaspora and sacred spaces of not only imagined histories but also as Afrofuturistic divine systems that radically affect women's twenty-first-century visions of the Caribbean canon. Lord's cosmological reconstruction of Ananse's web, Indiana's reformulations of traditional *patakís*, or Brodber's reconfiguration of African fractals into a familial mat similarly affirm the validity of autochthonous conceptions of space, time, and humanity. The blurring of geopolitical and spiritual borders within African/Indigenous/Indo and other cosmovisions, however, also conjures into being a longer history of dispossession and forced displacement—from which many souls are unable to recover. Other forms of ancestral knowledge, most notably alternative histories, are therefore invoked by the writers gathered here. Thus, Brodber's scholarly and literary work centers Afro-diasporic epistemes—in her words, the Alternative Tradition (Brodber 1997, 72)—by unearthing and preserving Jamaican narratives from the perspective of the enslaved and their descendants, "the half [that] has never been told"—as one character in *Myal* puts it.[5] A. Marie Sairsingh's chapter discusses how in *Nothing's Mat* Brodber advocates to remap the oral tradition (represented by the family history for which the mat stands) in the production of academic knowledge (as illustrated in Princess's scholarly pursuit to understand the Caribbean family). The same is true of Brodber's scholarship (1990, 2013).

Deeply invested in oral history projects, Brodber delineates how for local historians "the research process begins, not with the archives of documents but with the very large archive of our minds, imagination and memory" (Brodber 2000, 119). Pointing to "the paucity of records for a conventional history of us [Black Jamaicans]," she further contends that "imagination and meditation" may well be the only avenue to self-discovery for Black people, a point illustrated by her own fiction that also echoes other Caribbean writers, most notably E. Kamau Brathwaite (another historian), Alejo Carpentier, Édouard Glissant, and Derek Walcott, as well as Dionne Brand, discussed by Erica L. Johnson in this volume. Brodber and Brathwaite (1975), however, uniquely apply this methodology and their Afrocentric conception of time to the discipline of history. Brodber's multidisciplinary research in sociology, history, social psychology, and Afro-diasporic belief systems strives to instil in post-Independence Jamaicans a knowledge of their past and vision of themselves unfiltered by the neo/colonial lens from which can emerge "a new definition of the possibilities of our collective selves" (Brodber 1997, 72). Seeking to "re-engineer blackspace," Brodber tasks "the intellectual worker" with "the development of philosophy, of creeds, of myths, of ideologies, of pegs on which to hang social and spiritual life, the construction of frames of reference" (73).

To this end, Brodber conceived Blackspace, where what she terms "blackspace reasoning" (John 2012, 74) is collectively generated and circulates far beyond the readership of her fiction and scholarship. Indeed, Brodber's multidisciplinary research steadfastly promotes what literary critic Rae Ann Meriwether (2012) has called "learning from below" (118), that is, to refrain from over analysis and let the collected data (oral testimonies, questionnaires) speak for itself. Despite its name ostensibly pointing to space, Blackspace is equally, if not primarily, concerned with the survival of the African legacy through time. This makes Brodber's project a truly chronotropic endeavour. Occurring in the same place (the rural community of Woodside in Jamaica) at the same time (over the two weeks leading to the Emancipation of 1838 celebration) every year, including during the COVID-19 pandemic, Blackspace has emerged since around 2000 as a landmark in its own right for segments of the Jamaican community and the African diaspora (Brodber and Ellis Russel 2001; John 2012; Nixon 2015). During the events that integrate art, lectures, a play by Brodber, a religious service, and youth educational workshops, time is transformed: the past and present are explored from various interdisciplinary scholarly, educational, and artistic angles and the future is optimistically envisioned. Blackspace thus solidifies as a chronotope the 1838 Emancipation, whose status as a realm of memory subsisted among Jamaican folks but had been considerably eroded among the educated middle class subject to a Eurocentric policy of forgetting carried out in the name of national harmony.

For their part, Fabienne Kanor and Mayra Santos Febres insist on the corporeality of the collective memory and transgenerational trauma inherited by Caribbean people and more specifically, women. Ferly discusses in her chapter Kanor's notion of *corps-fossile*, or fossil body, which echoes sociologist Roger Bastide's corporeal geography, or his contention that the epistemic disruption caused by the sudden disappearance with the Middle Passage of the topographical markers that anchored collective memory was palliated with the partial *incorporation* of this memory into religious rituals and dances (Francis 2016, 280; Bastide 1970). The term "fossil body" points to a layered memory made up of disjunctions and dislocations that resulted in abrupt epistemic shifts for peoples of the black Atlantic. Similarly, the tropes of scars, bodily pain, and—in the case of Santos Febres's *Fe en disfraz*—sadomasochistic love, accentuate the imprint left by a violent past on black women's bodies and psyche, distorting their very essence, as manifested in their intimate relationships. In this sense, while in Arroyo Pizarro's *las Negras* and Kanor's *Humus* the slave ship emerges as a chronotope of the black Atlantic, as is also true in Dionne Brand (*A Map to the Door of No Return*, *The Blue Clerk*), in Santos Febres's novel the very body, most notably when it is black and female, becomes the chronotope. Fe's personal chronotope—the titular disguise, or the dress from the past—also features in the text as the avatar of the body. However, donned by Fe every year on Halloween and, centuries earlier, by a light mulatto woman striving to assimilate into Brazilian white society, this time travelling "mask" (understood both in its Caribbean meaning of full carnival disguise and in the way Frantz Fanon uses it in *Black Skin, White Masks*) turns out to be both illusory and particularly damaging to the black psyche.

Polyphonic neoslavery texts such as Arroyo Pizzaro's and Kanor's resonate with Pineau's memoir *Mes quatre femmes* (see Renée Larrier's chapter). Pineau subverts the genre's standard parameters by recounting the lives and voices of four asynchronous female ancestors imprisoned in the jail of her own memory. This "psychic map of the past" (Zimra 1993, 60) attempts to confront the history of enslavement and its legacy, personally and collectively. Pineau's memory jail thus figures as a chronotope that Larrier identifies as a distinctly gendered *lieu de mémoire*. Like in many of the works under study here, Pineau's chronotropic approach to the historically gendered trope of domesticity reflects not only the irrevocable implications of coloniality, migration, and capitalism but also the complicated dynamics of race and color as they intersect with spacetime, not least of which includes women's struggles for independence and rooms of their own. The narratives and scholarly chapters in *Chronotropics* are a testament to the fact that bringing Caribbean women into being through literature is "no longer simply or only a practice of resistance or of counter-discursivity but an assertion of subjectivity, agency—in short, of autonomy" (Chancy 2020, 2), an autonomy with the power to disrupt the discursive and sociopolitical hegemonies of "Man's" time and space.

(Im)Possible Subjects of the Chronotropics

Many of the creative outputs studied in *Chronotropics* participate in the "geographical and conceptual de/reterritorialization" (Huggan 2008, 26) of the region. Maryse Condé's entire oeuvre was pioneering in deterritorializing Caribbeanness, expanding spacetime beyond the strictly physical boundaries of the Caribbean and critically examining its historical connection with Africa through the interrogation of the continent's chronotopal status in the intellectual discourses of the decolonization era. For Condé, redefining collective identity should entail transcending "origin, ethnicity, language or colour" (Condé 2014, 152). Condé's sobering portrayals of black life, aptly captured in *Le fabuleux et triste destin d'Ivan et Ivana* and *Les belles ténébreuses*, call for a reassessment of Caribbean identity and the subject's position in an age of hyper-capitalism. The author's depiction of disempowered nomads who often take their frustrations out on women, for instance, cautions us against a chaotic, heedless future fueled by technology and globalization that begets exacerbated poverty, exploitation, intensified violence, as well as religious fundamentalism and militarization, as shown in Valérie K. Orlando's chapter.

Beyond a serious reflection on geopolitically displaced individuals, Condé, like Julia Alvarez (discussed by Megan Jeanette Myers), evokes "other" types of Caribbean communities, which are not tied to any particular land, but are expanding, archipelagic, and diasporic in their conceptualization. This chronotropic vision anticipates Yolanda Martínez-San Miguel's call to imagine archipelagos and islands otherwise in her use of the term "terripelagoes": "it is only when the regional and the diasporic are activated in dialogue and tension that we can fully grasp the multiplicity of dimension of occupied spaces, and how central imagination is to unleashing their many meanings" (Martínez-San Miguel 2021, 120). Through migrant literature we become witness to Martinez-San Miguel's "dialogue and tension" and how this opens space for the emergence of new modalities of (un)belonging and being.

As Derek Gladwin (2014) indicates, "to map" is not only "to claim territory and ultimately define ownership" but "also a way to experience landscape through memory and imagination" (161). A geographical concentration therefore underscores notions of space as ongoing hybrid productions that shift through time, "for while the closed system is the foundation for the singular, universal opening that makes room for a genuine multiplicity of trajectories, and thus potentially of voices, it also posits a positive discrete multiplicity against an imagination of space as the product of negative spacing, through the abjection of the other" (Massey 2005, 67). Here Doreen Massey highlights the critical position that space-making occupies as a "locus of the generation of new trajectories," while also positing that an open understanding of space leads to an equally open understanding of time. This heterogeneity stemming from the convergence of multiple narratives rather than an intrinsically coherent site that predetermines human experience thus allows for the concepts of Caribbean time and history to be questioned and reapprehended. Identity and belonging are configured as a process that must be negotiated in the here-and-now, a process that must take place within and between existing spaces, places, and temporalities (140). Thus, in engaging questions of spacetime, the Caribbean women of this volume shift from a historical narrative that seeks to delimit Caribbean space and restrict the movements of certain bodies, towards a new spatio-temporal future, one of "loose ends and missing links," in Massey's words (3). This future becomes a heterogeneous space where one is simultaneously able to uncover the past, take power in the present, and forge a new kind of future.

Considering identity as a simultaneous breaking and braiding in relation to mobility and space is also a major preoccupation of Indo-Trin-Can writer, filmmaker, and visual artist Shani Mootoo (2008, 83). Like Ingrid Persaud, Mootoo regards the Kala Pani as "an opportunity [for her Indian foremothers] to reinvent themselves in new landscapes where their histories were unknown, where caste, for instance, could be shed or, for the enterprising and daring, changed" (83). Indeterminism thus leads Mootoo to emphasize women's agency during the indentureship period. In the open, fluid, and undefined future, women can redefine not only their being-in-the-world but also "dis- or re-order" the world itself (Mootoo 2000, 109). Mapping onto her personal experiences, Mootoo's literary works routinely take up queerness as a means to interrogate heteronormative spaces such as the street, the restaurant, or the family home. In both the region and the diaspora, she has sought "Permission to exist as a woman, a woman of color, as a lesbian, within–not on the out-side of–the everyday world of society" (110). Accordingly, one finds across Mootoo's artistic productions examples of exile or debilitating trauma, when one cannot escape the prejudices of her time and place, especially rigid national demarcations or identity markers that are either seemingly immutable or hierarchized according to traditional binaries that Other women and minorities.[6]

Mootoo's fiction *He Drown She in the Sea* (discussed by Vivian Nun Halloran) suggests there might be a radical potential for reinventing the self if one is unknown and/or unmappable. This contrasts with several of the works studied in this collection such as Condé's, Pineau's, and Indiana's that illustrate the link between enslavement and present-day immigrants and refugees, both legal and undocumented. Mootoo, on the other hand, advances a cartography that seeks neither a return to nor a romanticizing of an ancestral homeland, the Caribbean, or its diaspora (Mootoo 2008, 83). Instead, hybridizing factual and fictional spaces with past and possible temporalities, Mootoo explores how new opportunities for a transnational identity and community might be coordinated. The intense focalization of Othered, queer, or monstrous selves further demonstrates the writer's desire for a Caribbean that might not exist in facticity or even its mimetic copy, but in italics, just beyond the horizon, in the achronotopic, outside physical spacetime, those pages left blank at the end of the text.

As Gladwin contends, "Historically European countries perceived and steadily charted so-called 'blank spaces' of the globe" in an attempt to extend their empires and to solidify power (Gladwin 2014, 160); thus, topographical blank spaces reflect an official discursive absence that as many of the writers in our collection affirm cannot always be revived, not even by literature. Critic Kaya Fraser suggests in connection to Dionne Brand that "To believe that [one can make a new space through language, that is, the writer's 'own shadow'] is to swallow another myth, created in and by language, which effectively forgets 'the history of harm,' the truth of suffering" (Fraser 2005, 16, quoting Brand's *No Light to Land On*, 45). This "own shadow" is precisely the relation Brand develops through her eponymous blue clerk and her poem's speaker—reinforced by the inclusion of several blank pages throughout the text. One of Brand's chief concerns is to explore how the black woman's being is (un)realizable through language. As with many of Brand's texts, in *The Blue Clerk* (2018) black bodies in the archipelago and its diaspora are simultaneously made and unmade. Paraphrasing Makeda Silvera, Leslie C. Sanders poignantly asserts: "History resides in language, which in turn inscribes it on to landscape, translating space and place into lived genealogy" (Sanders 2009, xi). Resonating with Condé's cynicism, Brand offers a bleak vision of the world, one in which racialized, gendered bodies are violently displaced: "Our inheritance in the Diaspora is to live in this inexplicable space. That space is the measure of our ancestors' step through the door toward the ship. One is caught in the few feet *in between*. The frame of the doorway is the only space of true existence" (Brand 2001, 20, emphasis Zimmerman's). Brand and the other authors examined in *Chronotropics* routinely return to the question of how literature might be redeployed to navigate identity and inhabit spacetime differently. Their work signals new ways of Caribbean knowing and being and in doing so directly challenges "Man's" ever-increasingly dystopian, imperialistic, and secularized future.

Re-engineering Community

Literature serves as a vehicle to annihilate borders and construct a region that seeks to address the legacy of genocide, ethnic discrimination, and ecosystem tampering while countering centuries of imperialist capitalism and Western notions of the self. Yet beyond their creative and intellectual productions, the writers gathered in *Chronotropics* suggest that also central to these goals is a commitment to community, cooperation, and social justice. They actively engage in efforts to create a sense of "we" (or in the Rastafari formulation, "I and I") rather than "I." For example, the assertion of Caribbean epistemologies is an important political aim for Erna Brodber, Yolanda Arroyo Pizarro, and Mayra Santos Febres. Brodber is invested in her grassroots educational project Blackspace, while Arroyo Pizarro works to uncover hidden histories of Black women from the archives of enslavement and reconstruct their lives in literature through her groundbreaking oral history project, the collective *Cátedra de mujeres negras ancestrales*; for her part, Santos Febres was instrumental in formalizing the first program in Afro-Diasporic and Racial Studies at the University of Puerto Rico, Río Piedras, inaugurated in 2021. Santos Febres sees the *uno múltiple* harnessed in the creative response to hurricane María in Puerto Rico in 2017 seeking to re-engineer community: the artists "told [their] stories together in camps" and "proposed dialogues of multiple agencies," while "publishing books alongside videos and movies, and editorial practices and artistic political interventions, and community-based programs that reinscribe knowledge" (Santos Febres 2019). These voices ruptured the official narrative of María, the death count as publicized by governments both on the island and in the US, and pointed out how the environmental disaster was manufactured by years of imperial capitalism. They created together a complex, mangrove-like web of relations in which each participant worked from a specific contextual space to add their voice to the larger movement—a singularity that became multiple, encompassing contradiction while demanding a new type of future. This artist collective fully aligns with the activism of many women authors featured here; in this sense, Caribbean fractality shares deep affinities with mangrove poetics (Ferly 2012) and the chronotropics.

Echoing Shani Mootoo's multidisciplinary artistic projects, Rita Indiana is an outspoken advocate for LGBTQ PLUS_SPI rights in the Dominican Republic, Puerto Rico, and other Caribbean nations, and created an anthem of protest through her album *Mandinga Times* (Indiana 2020). Likewise, Fabienne Kanor's journalistic, scholarly and creative work, most notably her film *Des pieds, mon pied* and her novels *Humus* and *Faire l'aventure* (Kanor 2009, 2006, and 2014, respectively) document and convey the psychic cost of human trafficking across space and time. The works studied in this volume thus recuperate and revise local stories, cosmologies, and philosophies to defy totalizing notions of time and space and to conceive Caribbean women in the twenty-first century anew. Whether revisiting the past or envisioning the future, the possibility for social change, resistance, and/or new homelands therefore remains powerfully present in the pluriverse of the Caribbean and beyond. *Chronotropics* calls and responds to the need for a turn toward new spacetimes and towards solidarity and reparation through archival disruption, radical remapping, and epistemic *marronnage*.

NOTES

1. For the Indigenous populations, confinement on reservations quickly followed dispossession; by contrast, maroon camps defied colonial control and its concomitant spatial logic.
2. A case in point is the Western calendar, which purports to impose the birth of Christ as the universal origin; the compression of time zones in countries as extensive as Canada, Russia, or the United States, for instance, also sheds light on the artificial nature of the time we live by.
3. In her *Mayaya Rising*, Dawn Duke cites Yolanda Arroyo Pizarro as an example among others of Caribbean and Latin American Afrodescendant women who are "both creative and philosophical producers... driven to design discourses that highlight the deeper ideological agendas behind such poetic production" (Duke 2023, 8, 12). Fabienne Kanor's essays *La poétique de la cale: Variations sur le bateau négrier* (2022) share the same intention. Duke further discusses the theoretical positioning of Mayra Santos Febres in detail (22–24).
4. Most often credited for coining the term, Bakhtin defines the chronotope as "intrinsic connectedness of temporal and spatial relationships that are artistically expressed in literature" (Bakhtin 1981, 84). For a contemporary adaptation of the chronotope, see, for instance, Vaara and Pedersen 2013.

20   O. FERLY ET AL.

5. This spin on Bob Marley's lyrics in "Get Up Stand Up" is a good illustration on how Brodber fuses the vernacular and oral popular culture with the written intellectual tradition. See also O'Callaghan (2012, p. 65).
6. Having been born in Ireland, Mootoo inadvertently lost her Trinidadian citizenship when she became Canadian.

REFERENCES

Alcoff, Linda. 2003. Philosophy in/and Latino and Afro-Caribbean Studies: Introduction. *Nepantla: Views from South* 4(1): 133–137. *Project MUSE* muse. jhu.edu/article/40195.

Alcoff, Linda and Elizabeth Potter. 1993. Introduction: When Feminisms Intersect Epistemology. *Feminist Epistemologies*, 1–14. New York: Routledge.

Arroyo Pizarro, Yolanda. 2013 [2012]. *las Negras*. Cabo Rojo, PR: Editora Educación Emergente. Originally published by Boreales.

———. 2018. *Afrohistoria: Ensayos*. San Juan, PR: Isla Negra.

Bakhtin, Mikhail M. 1981 [1937]. Form of Time and Chronotope in the Novel. In *The Dialogic Imagination: Four Essays*, ed. Michael Holquist, 84–258. Austin: University of Texas Press. Translated by Caryl Emerson and Michael Holquist.

Bastide, Roger. 1970. Mémoire collective et sociologie du bricolage. *L'Année Sociologique* 21: 65–108.

Benítez Rojo, Antonio. 1989. *La isla que se repite: el Caribe y la perspectiva posmoderna*. Hanover, NH: Ediciones del Norte.

Boyce Davies, Carole, and Elaine Savory Fido. 1990. *Out of the Kumbla: Caribbean Women and Literature*. Trenton: Africa World Press, Inc.

Brand, Dionne. 2001. *A Map to the Door of No Return: Notes to Belonging*. Toronto: Vintage Canada.

———. 2018. *The Blue Clerk. Ars Poetica in 59 Versos*. Durham: Duke University Press.

Brathwaite, Edward Kamau. 1971. *The Development of Creole Society in Jamaica, 1770–1820*. Kingston: Ian Randle.

———. 1975. Caribbean Man in Space and Time. *Savacou* 11–12 (September): 1–11.

Brodber, Erna. 1974. Social Psychology in the English-Speaking Caribbean – A Bibliography and Some Comments. *Social and Economic Studies* 23.3 (September): 398–417.

———. 1990. Fiction in the Scientific Procedure. In *Caribbean Women Writers: Essays from the First International Conference*, ed. Selwyn R. Cudjoe, 164–168. Amherst, MA: University of Massachusetts Press.

———. 1997. Re-engineering Blackspace. *Caribbean Quarterly* 43.1-2, *The Plenaries: Conference on Caribbean Culture in Honour of Professor Rex Nettleford* (March–June): 70–81.

———. 2000. Myths are Us Too. *Caribbean Quarterly* 46.3–4, The Sir Philip Sherlock Lectures (Sept.–Dec.): 118–32.

———. 2012a. Foreword. In *Obeah and Other Powers: The Politics of Caribbean Religion and Healing*, ed. Diana Paton and Maarit Forde, ix–xii. Durham: Duke University Press.

———. 2012b. Reggae as Black Space. In Carolyn Cooper, ed. *Global Reggae*, 21–36. Kingston: Canoe Press, The University Press of the West Indies.

———. 2013. Oral History and the Other Perspective. *Caribbean Quarterly* 59.1 (March): 20–30.

———. 2014. *Nothing's Mat*. Kingston: UWI Press.

Brodber, Erna and Nadia Ellis Russell. 2001. Crossing Borders: An Interview with Writer, Scholar, and Activist Erna Brodber. *Inthefray*, 7 May, n. pag. Web. 8 March 2010. https://inthefray.org/joomla/images/stories/mpn/issues/200105/imagine/brodber2/brodber2-page2.html. Accessed 17 July 2022.

Chancy, Myriam J.A. 2020. *Autochthonomies: Transnationalism, Testimony, and Transmission in the African Diaspora*. Champaign: University of Illinois Press.

Condé, Maryse. 2014. *The Journey of a Caribbean Writer*. Trans. Richard Philcox. Calcutta: Seagull Press.

Cudjoe, Selwyn R., ed. 1990. *Caribbean Women Writers: Essays from the First International Conference*. Amherst, MA: University of Massachusetts Press.

Danticat, Edwidge. 1995. *Krik? Krak!* New York: Soho Press.

Duke, Dawn. 2023. *Mayaya Rising: Black Female Icons in Latin America and Caribbean Literature and Culture*. Lewisburg, PA: Bucknell University Press.

Ferly, Odile. 2012. *A Poetics of Relation: Caribbean Women Writing at the Millennium*. New York: Palgrave.

Figueroa, Yomaira. 2020. *Decolonial Diasporas: Radical Mappings of Afro-Atlantic Literatures*. Evanston: Northwestern University Press.

Foucault, Michel. 1966. *Les mots et les choses. Une archéologie des sciences humaines*. Paris: Gallimard.

———. 1984 [1967]. Des Espace Autres. *Conférence au Cercle d'études architecturales*, 14 mars 1967. Architecture, Mouvement, Continuité 5 (October): 46–49. https://foucault.info/documents/heterotopia/foucault.heteroTopia.fr/. Accessed 30 July 2022.

Francis, Gladys. 2016. Entretien avec Fabienne Kanor, "L'Ante-llaise par excellence": Sexualité, corporalité, diaspora et créolité. French. Forum 41.3 (Winter): 273–288.

Fraser, Kaya. 2005. Language to Light On: Dionne Brand and the Rebellious Word. *Studies in Canadian Literature* 30 (1) Retrieved from https://journals.lib.unb.ca/index.php/SCL/article/view/15283.

Gilroy, Paul. 1993. *The Black Atlantic: Modernity and Double Consciousness.* Cambridge, MA: Harvard University Press.

Gladwin, Derek. 2014. The Literary Cartographic Impulse: Imagined Island Topographies in Ireland and Newfoundland. *The Canadian Journal of Irish Studies*, 38.1-2: 158–83. *JSTOR*, www.jstor.org/stable/43410727. Accessed 15 Aug 2021.

Glissant, Édouard. 1981. *Le Discours antillais.* Paris: Gallimard.

———. 1990. *Poétique de la Relation.* Paris: Gallimard.

———. 1997. *Traité du Tout-Monde.* Paris: Gallimard.

Hamilton, Njelle. 2018. "Jah Live": Messianic Time and Post-Traumatic Narrative Disorder in Marlon James's *A Brief History of Seven Killings. Journal of West Indian Literature* 26 (2): 80–95.

———. 2019. Jamaican String Theory: Quantum Sounds and Postcolonial Spacetime in Marcia Douglas's *The Marvellous Equations of the Dread. Journal of West Indian Literature* 27 (1): 88–105.

Hart, David W. 2004. Caribbean Chronotopes: From Exile to Agency. *Anthurium: A Caribbean Studies Journal* 2 (2): 1–22.

Henry, Paget. 2000. *Caliban's Reason: Introducing Afro-Caribbean Philosophy.* New York: Routledge.

Hopkinson, Nalo. 2013. *Sister Mine.* New York and Boston: Grand Central Publishing.

Hoving, Isabel. 2001. *In Praise of New Travelers: Reading Caribbean Migrant Women Writers.* Redwood City: Stanford University Press.

Huggan, Graham. 2008. *Interdisciplinary Measures: Literature and the Future of Postcolonial Studies.* Liverpool: Liverpool University Press.

Indiana, Rita. 2015. *La mucama de Omicunlé.* Cáceres: Periférica.

———. 2020. After School. *Mandinga Times.* YouTube, https://www.youtube.com/watch?v=jvyZEEGCYRM.

John, Catherine. 2012. Caribbean Organic Intellectual: The Legacy and Challenge of Erna Brodber's Life Work. *Small Axe* 16.3 (39, November): 72–88.

Kanor, Fabienne. 2006. *Humus.* Paris: Gallimard.

———. 2009. Director. *Des pieds, mon pied.* Cifap.

———. 2014. *Faire l'aventure.* Paris: Lattès.

———. 2022. *La poétique de la cale: Variations sur le bateau négrier.* Paris: Payot & Rivages.

Lee, Derek. 2020. Postquantum: *A Tale for the Time Being, Atomik Aztex*, and Hacking Modern Space-Time. *Melus* 45.1 (Spring), 1–26. doi: https://doi.org/10.1093/melus/mlz057.

Lord, Karen. 2010. *Redemption in Indigo.* Easthampton, MA: Small Beer Press.

Mars, Kettly. 2018. *L'Ange du patriarche.* Paris: Mercure de France.

Martínez-San Miguel, Yolanda. 2021. Terripelagoes: Archipelagic Thinking in Culebra (Puerto Rico) and Guam. In *Caribbean Migrations: The Legacies of*

Colonialism, ed. Anke Birkenmaier. New Brunswick, NJ: Rutgers University Press.

Massey, Doreen. 2005. *For Space*. London: Sage.

Melville, Pauline. 1997. *The Ventriloquist's Tale*. London: Bloomsbury.

Meriwether, Rae Ann. 2012. The Blues Matrix: Cultural Discourses and Community in Erna Brodber's *Louisiana*. *Small Axe* 16.3 (39, November): 103–18.

Mignolo, Walter D. 2009. Epistemic Disobedience, Independent Thought and De-Colonial Freedom. *Theory, Culture and Society* 26 (7–8): 159–181. https://doi.org/10.1177/0263276409349275.

Montero, Mayra. 1995. *Tú, la oscuridad*. Barcelona: Tusquets. English edition: Montero, Mayra 1997. *In the Palm of Darkness* (trans: Grossman, Edith). New York: HarperCollins.

Mootoo, Shani. 2000. Shani Mootoo: An Interview with Lynda Hall. *Journal of Lesbian Studies* 4 (4): 107–113.

———. 2008. On Becoming an Indian Starboy. *Canadian Literature* 196 (Spring): 83–94.

Mordecai, Pamela, and Betty Wilson, eds. 1990. *Her True, True Name: An Anthology of Women's Writing from the Caribbean*. London: Heinemann.

Nixon, Angelique. 2015. *Resisting Paradise*. University Press of Mississippi.

O'Callaghan, Evelyn. 2012. Play It Back a Next Way: Teaching Brodber. Teaching Us. *Small Axe* 39: 59–71.

Pineau, Gisèle. 2007. *Mes quatre femmes: récit*. Paris: Philippe Rey.

Prieto, José Manuel. 2000. Mayra Montero by José Manuel Prieto. *BOMB Magazine*, 1 Jan, https://bombmagazine.org/articles/mayra-montero. Accessed 17 July 2022.

Quijano, Anibal. 2000. Coloniality of Power, Eurocentrism, and Latin America. *Nepantla: Views from South* 1 (3): 533–580.

Santos-Febres, Mayra. 2009. *Fe en disfraz*. Doral, FL: Alfaguara.

Santos Febres, Mayra. 2019. *The Fractal Caribbean*. Unpublished lecture. https://www.youtube.com/watch?v=8tFlLkUSr84

———. 2021. Afroepistemologías: Fractalidad vs fragmentación en las identidades afrolatinoamericanas y caribeñas. *Aproximaciones Teóricas* 12.

Sharpe, Jenny. 2012. When Spirits Talk: Reading Erna Brodber's *Louisiana* for Affect. *Small Axe* 39: 90–102.

Sanders, Leslie C. 2009. Introduction. In *Fierce Departures: The Poetry of Dionne Brand*, ix–xv. Waterloo, ON: Wilfrid Laurier University Press.

Vaara, Eero, and Anne Reff Pedersen. 2013. Strategy and Chronotopes: a Bakhtinian Perspective on the Construction of Strategy Narratives. *Management* 16 (2013/5): 593–604.

Vété-Congolo, Hanétha. 2018. Caribbean French-African Creole and African Metaphysics. In *Tracing Language Movement in Africa*, ed. Ericka A. Albauh and Kathryn M. de Luna, 366–386. New York: Oxford University Press.

Warren, Calvin L. 2018. *Ontological terror: blackness, nihilism, and emancipation.* Durham: Duke University Press.

Wynter, Sylvia. 1990. Beyond Miranda's Meanings: Un/silencing the 'Demonic Ground' of Caliban's 'Woman'. In *Out of the Kumbla: Caribbean Women and Literature*, ed. Carole Boyce Davies and Elaine Savory Fido, 355–370. Trenton, NJ: Africa World Press, Inc.

———. 2003. Unsettling the Coloniality of Being/Power/Truth/Freedom: Towards the Human, After Man, Its Overrepresentation—An Argument. *CR: The New Centennial Review* 3 (3): 257–337. https://doi.org/10.1353/ncr.2004.0015.

———. 1984. The Ceremony Must Be Found: After Humanism. *Boundary 2* (12–13): 19–70. www.jstor.org/stable/302808. Accessed 15 Aug 2021.

Wynter, Sylvia, and David Scott. 2000. The Re-Enchantment of Humanism: An Interview with Sylvia Wynter. *Small Axe* 8: 119–207.

Zimra, Clarisse. 1993. In the Name of the Father: Chronotopia, Utopia, and Dystopia in *Ti Jean l'horizon*. *L'Esprit Créateur* 33(2) (Summer): 59–72.

Open Access This chapter is licensed under the terms of the Creative Commons Attribution 4.0 International License (http://creativecommons.org/licenses/by/4.0/), which permits use, sharing, adaptation, distribution and reproduction in any medium or format, as long as you give appropriate credit to the original author(s) and the source, provide a link to the Creative Commons licence and indicate if changes were made.

The images or other third party material in this chapter are included in the chapter's Creative Commons licence, unless indicated otherwise in a credit line to the material. If material is not included in the chapter's Creative Commons licence and your intended use is not permitted by statutory regulation or exceeds the permitted use, you will need to obtain permission directly from the copyright holder.

PART I

Archival Disruption

CHAPTER 2

Chronotopal Slave Ships, Corporeal Archives: *Devoir de mémoire* in Fabienne Kanor's *Humus* and Yolanda Arroyo Pizarro's *las Negras*

Odile Ferly

Fabienne Kanor's and Yolanda Arroyo Pizarro's accounts of transatlantic enslavement in *Humus* (2006) and *las Negras* (2013 [2012]) are a form of epistemic *marronnage* whose intent is to excavate the acts of resistance by Africans and Afro-diasporic people, especially women, systematically expunged from official records.[1] The Martiniquan and Puerto Rican authors' gendered perspectives thus fill in a gap left by male predecessors such as E. Kamau Brathwaite, Alejo Carpentier, Edouard Glissant, and Derek Walcott, whose iconic poem "The Sea Is History" actually figures as an epigraph to *Humus*. Aligned with what could be characterised as mangrove poetics (Ferly 2012), their narratives draw instead on immaterial fragments stored in the explicitly sexed body, a dynamic corporeal archive that unsettles the authority of the annals upholding dominant

---

O. Ferly (✉)
Clark University, Worcester, MA, USA
e-mail: oferly@clarku.edu

© The Author(s) 2023
O. Ferly, T. Zimmerman (eds.), *Chronotropics*,
https://doi.org/10.1007/978-3-031-32111-5_2

chronicles.[2] Both authors seek to fulfil their *devoir de mémoire* (literally, "memory duty" or obligation to remember) by elaborating a tangible though fictional alternative archive that withstands erasure.

Moreover, the leitmotif of the slave ship in *Humus* and *las Negras* illustrates Paul Gilroy's contention that for people of the black Atlantic, the slave ship is a chronotope—understood here as an artefact combining space and time that constitutes a landmark for a given community—and the bedrock of modernity (Gilroy 1993).[3] Yet in the African diasporic discourse and imaginary, this trope is pervaded by a gender symbolism fraught with troubling implications for black women. A liminal site both catalyst and witness to the collision between distinct worlds, the slave ship became for the Africans a new point of origin marked by colonial attempts of ontological and epistemic annihilation. Nevertheless, this motif features in both narratives as a locus of regeneration through a reconfiguration of spacetime that forges unforeseen alliances and fuels sociopolitical struggle.

"THE FIRST MEMORY COULD BE THE SHIP": CHRONOTOPES AND SHIP SISTERS

At the inception of Fabienne Kanor's *Humus* was a 1774 note from the French colonial archives in Nantes in which the attempted collective suicide of fourteen female captives was reported by a slave ship captain as partial "cargo" loss. From this business statement that relegates an unfolding human tragedy of unprecedented magnitude to a footnote, the novel sets out to reconstruct the history of the Middle Passage. Revisiting the official narrative around transatlantic enslavement, *Humus*, perhaps a misnomer, is set at sea, aboard the vessel *Le Soleil*, for the core of the action. The triangular trade likewise appears prominently in *las Negras*, whose opening words in the first story "Wanwe" set the tone for the entire collection: "El primer recuerdo pudiera ser el barco. Una barriga de maderos unidos y flotantes [...] Tanta enormidad, tanto espacio" (19) [The first memory could be the ship. A belly made of timber tied together that floats [...] Such enormity, so much space].[4] The slave ship thus becomes the new point of origin. The metaphor of the belly recalls the Biblical sea monster that swallowed Jonah: it signifies an ending, implying that the peoples of Africa will never be the same.

Yet *barriga* (or *ventre* in French) also means womb, so that in both languages the term can designate the end of life, but also where life originates. In this second acceptation, dear to many Caribbean thinkers, just like the entrails of the fish for Jonah, so does the vessel stand for a new beginning, a matrix that will literally scatter the seeds of Africa across the New World.[5] The outcome of extreme dispersion was not extinction, but rather, regeneration, hence the evocative title of Kanor's novel, *Humus*.[6] Nevertheless, as Kanor and Arroyo Pizarro suggest, the children of the black Atlantic did not emerge from the process unscathed. This harsh reality prompts Edouard Glissant to state in his *Traité du Tout-Monde* that for Creole societies, the mythical night of origin has been substituted with an austere darkness of historical making, the ship hold, designated as "[le] ventre du bateau négrier," or the belly of the slave ship (Glissant 1997, 36). Glissant calls this inauspicious origin "une digenèse" or digenesis.

This particular gendering of the trope of the slave ship, literally envisioned as a matrix, is not unique to Glissant (see also 2007, 107–108); rather, it permeates the black Atlantic discourse. Saidiya Hartman points to W. E. B. DuBois's conception of the slave ship as a "matrix of black death and dispossession" that was succeeded by the plantation, the ghetto, and then the prison (Hartman 2016, 169). European traffickers, Hartman notes elsewhere, extended this metaphor to the cells holding Africans captive prior to the journey. To them, "the dungeon was a womb in which the slave was born," it was a place where alchemy took place, where what they held as waste—other human beings—was "transformed into capital" (Hartman 2007, 111). For her part, contesting Glissant, Hanétha Vété-Congolo argues that Kanor's work is evidence to the importance of "telling one's word, activating and enacting one's memory" in order to "pre-empt digenesis and enable genesis": "Ainsi, dire sa *pawòl*, faire exister et agir sa mémoire, c'est contre-dire la digenèse et permettre la genèse" (Vété-Congolo 2014, 14). In this sense, Kanor's fiction, just like Arroyo Pizarro's, may be understood as foundational.[7] Arguably, the ubiquity of the ship-matrix metaphor has run the risk of eclipsing the ship's concomitant role as the primary tool that begot the African *diaspora*, a term understood here in its etymological meaning. This duality and the inherent gender bias of the trope prompt me to postulate instead the slave ship as an indomitable hermaphrodite machine capable of at once scattering the seed and nurturing it in its matrix.

Fundamentally, the slave ship figures in *las Negras* and *Humus* as a spacetime machine that literally dis-locates the captives on board, displacing their myths of origins and eroding their collective memory to become "the first memory" (to cite Arroyo Pizarro), thereby shattering their sense of self.[8] Compressing space, the ship is what Foucault calls a heterotopia, in that it becomes a microcosm of pre-colonial Africa, bringing together nations that previously scarcely interacted. It further transmutes space through simultaneous concentration and expansion, subjecting its shackled passengers, entrapped but in motion, to a double process of extreme confinement and antipodal displacement, two treatments that are seemingly incompatible. The vessel also distorts time, stretching it, fragmenting it, and looping it through the physical and psychological effects of captivity, trauma, and post traumatic memory, all the while transporting the enslaved towards an uncertain future that will soon catapult them into the unfamiliar, accelerated pace of early capitalism, also commonly known as "modernity." Astonishingly, Foucault (1984 [1967], 49) pictures the ships of the era of European colonialism as "the heterotopia *par excellence*": a parallel world with the appeal of freedom (from Europe's authoritarianism, land scarcity, or limited opportunities) that offers aspiring settlers a conduit for self-reinvention through expatriation. Yet to those who fell prey to the triangular trade, ships on the contrary are tantamount to dyschronotopias. At a more symbolic level, the slave ship enables the two authors to reconfigure Caribbean spacetime. As a site that foments (or nurtures) spontaneous or organised resistance, it holds the promise of renewal.

Indeed, Gilroy remarks that, beyond their economic role, slave ships functioned as "cultural and political units" that provided "a means to conduct political dissent and possibly a distinct mode of cultural production" (Gilroy 1993, 17). Thus, the pattern of alliances and rivalries among the captives in *Humus* reflects the continent's diversity while conveying the "divisions in the imagined community of the race" (24). Still, the women's pact aboard *Le Soleil* also suggests "the means to comprehend or overcome" these divisions (24), even though their radical, fatal gesture signals the inherent difficulty of the task. The novel, Renée Larrier notes, details "their coalescing into a group, the emergence of a leader, the planning of the escape" (Larrier 2011, 107). Jamaican scholar and writer Erna Brodber further underscores the binding potential of transoceanic crossings when she refers to members of the black diaspora as "shipmates" (Brodber 1990, 168; Josephs 2013, 134). The Trinidadian-Canadian writer David Chariandy likewise glosses on the corresponding phenomenon among the Indo-Caribbean population, *jahaji bhai*, or "ship brothers," as "new types of kinship and identification among indentured South Asian migrants that broke down previously existing divisions between ethnic groups and castes" (Josephs and Chariandy 2014, 123). Facilitated by the Kala Pani, the gender-based alliances *jahaji bhai* and *jahaji bahin* (or "ship sisterhood," Mehta 2020) therefore supersede formerly inescapable social divides. *las Negras* too recounts the emergence of a people for which kinship no longer relies on bloodlines. In a scene from the opening story, women hitherto strangers to each other spontaneously unite in a chant of lamentation to accompany the last moments of a rebellious "ship sister" during her public execution (Arroyo Pizarro 2013, 36). The "army of midwives" (42) who risk their own lives by taking those of newborns they wish to spare from enslavement likewise constitutes a mighty support network in the second story "Matronas." Finally, in "Saeta," enslaved women display sorority and kinship in daily reciprocal gestures intended to restore dignity.

Solidarity is symbolised in "Wanwe" by the rhizome. In an unspecified region evocative of today's Namibia, women rely on whistling signals for hunting. When they are preyed upon by enslavers, the alarm raised by one of them is compared to a rhizomic plant: "El pitido se alarga como una liana de árbol gigante, interminable. Como un helecho adornado de musgos rizomatosos, sin principio ni fin" (26) [The whistle stretches on like a gigantic, endless liana. Like fern adorned with rhizomic moss, with no beginning or end]. The striking metaphor of lianas and rhizomes to refer to the women's form of communication underlines the ties that bind them. It points to the larger web of the mangrove, a flexible, inclusive network endowed with the capacity to expand in all directions. This ecosystem is an apt paradigm to theorise the black Atlantic and Caribbean diasporas, in that it encapsulates the ability to forge new alliances to compensate for the loss of kinship that the Middle Passage, Kala Pani, and other forms of coercive crossings entailed. Furthermore, I posit the mangrove, a "webbed network" of rhizomic roots that aligns with Gilroy's black Atlantic, as a useful frame to examine the literary expressions of a more explicitly gendered African and South or East Asian diasporic experience. As Arroyo Pizarro illustrates, it provides a powerful metaphor for the solidarity network among Caribbean women.[9] Thus the mangrove mindset already at work among the female hunters described in "Wanwe" can be detected in the midwives' rebellious spirit in "Matronas," the avenging spectre in "Saeta," or in the wind of sedition onboard *Le Soleil* that urges the fourteen women to jump together in Kanor. Female solidarity and the woman-centred praxis portrayed in these texts can therefore be regarded as a kind of proto womanism, or in its French Caribbean version, *femmisme* (Vété-Congolo 2017, 135) or *fanmisme* (Francis 2016).[10]

Certainly, Arroyo Pizarro's and Kanor's emphasis on female solidarity, fortitude, and resistance is a source of inspiration for contemporary women of the black Atlantic. Yet their most radical proposition lies in the archival disruption and in the engagement with collective memory carried out in their works. From the outset, Arroyo Pizarro's and Kanor's narratives openly challenge hegemonic historiographic and documenting practices. *las Negras* is defiantly dedicated "To the historians/for leaving us out" (Arroyo Pizarro 2013 [2012], 7). Animated by a similar desire to amend the records and eager to "barter technical jargon for speech" and "[t]he sailors' elusive utterances for the captives' screams," Kanor asks in *Humus*: "Comment dire, comment redire, cette histoire-là des hommes?" (Kanor 2006, 13) [How to tell, again and again, this story of mankind?]. In addition to recuperating and revising the chronotopal slave ship, Kanor and Arroyo Pizarro undermine the cornerstone of Eurocentric historiography when they posit the black Atlantic body (the body of those subjected to the triangular trade and its multiple incarnations in Afrodescendants of the past and present), as a chronotope in its own right; more still, an archive.

Corporeal Archives and *Devoir de Mémoire*

Mikhail Bakhtin, who is most often credited for popularising the term "chronotope," defines it as "the intrinsic connectedness of temporal and spatial relationships that are artistically expressed in literature" (Bakhtin 1981 [1937], 84). Elaborating on Bakhtin's concept, linguistic anthropologist Keith Basso remarks in relation to Western Apaches: "Chronotopes thus stand as monuments to the community itself, as symbols of it, as forces operating to shape its members' images of themselves" (Basso 1984, 44–45).[11] While Europe, and the West more broadly, is fond of memorials and commemorations, such materiality is sorely lacking to the black Atlantic experience. Unlike holding barracks spread along the West African coast or the more problematic plantation ruins, slave ships did not remain as tangible *lieux de mémoire* (sites of memory, Nora 1984). Derek Walcott regards the absence of vestiges in the Americas, this "world without monuments and ruins" (Walcott 1998 [1974], 38), as an invitation to shed burdensome elements of tradition; he urges writers and artists of the region to look ahead and not back. "The Sea Is History" likewise underscores the lack of material records on the African diasporic experience:

"Where are your monuments, your battles, martyrs?/Where is your tribal memory? Sirs, / in that gray vault. The sea. The sea/has locked them up. The sea is History" (Walcott 1980, 25). This oft-cited opening of the poem finds echo in Glissant's conviction in *Le Discours antillais* that the landscape is its own monument, as well as the sole witness of Caribbean history (Glissant 1981, 11). Indeed, forced displacement turned Africans into what Glissant (2007, 108–109) aptly describes as "migrants nus" (naked migrants). Coupled with centuries of ethnocentric archival practices, this has resulted in most black Atlantic chronotopes being immaterial. And yet this collective memory loss can be liberating, as it grants people of the black Atlantic the freedom to fashion their future by digging in their own archives. Furthermore, as Kanor argues, the fragmentary nature of the records and memory presents an opportunity for reinvention: "Ne pas tout savoir permet aux héritiers que nous sommes de réinventer l'histoire, de combler les trous à la mesure de nos moyens (artistiques, politiques). [...] Si nous nous souvenions de tout, sans doute cette mémoire finirait-elle par nous asphyxier, sa douleur nous maintiendrait dans un éternel ressentiment" (Herbeck 2013, 975) [Not knowing everything allows us, the heirs, to reinvent history, to fill in the holes according to our artistic or political talents. If we remembered everything, this memory would no doubt eventually stifle us, its pain would maintain us in a state of eternal resentment]. Kanor signals the potential of creative writing to palliate the gaps in history in the Prologue of *Humus,* where she stresses the interplay between history and story (both *histoire* in French): "Cette histoire n'est pas une histoire. Mais un poème. [...] une tentative de glissement, là où il n'est plus de témoins pour dire, là où l'homme [...] affronte la pire épreuve qui soit: la mort de la parole, l'aporie" (14) [This story is not a story. It is a poem. [...] an attempt to dive where nobody is left to bear witness, where man [...] faces the greatest ordeal of all: the death of speech, aporia.]

The opening "The first memory could be the ship" in *las Negras* likewise highlights the connection between memory, history, and the Middle Passage (Arroyo Pizarro 2013, 19). Insofar as they figure in the collective consciousness as immaterial "monuments to the community itself" (Basso), slave ships are indeed quintessential chronotopes of the black Atlantic (Gilroy). The primary focus in Arroyo Pizarro's and Kanor's poetics, however, is the black Atlantic body, which functions as an archive. Rather than seeing in the "amnesia [of the slave] the true history of the New World" (Walcott 1998 [1974], 39), the two authors point to the

34   O. FERLY

traumatic memory transmitted along generations, what could be called postmemory (van Alphen 2006; Hirsch 2008).

Sociologist Roger Bastide (1970) details the processes of *bricolage* that operate in African diasporic cultures following the partial loss of collective memory due to enforced dispersion. He also shows in relation to religious rites how this collective memory originally reliant on topography has largely been inscribed in rhythms that are now tied to what he calls a corporeal geography (such as ritualised moves and dances).[12] Consequently, much of the broader collective memory of the African diaspora is recorded in oral stories, songs, ceremonies, or even body language in addition to dances, rites, and rituals. For this reason, Kanor calls the black Atlantic body a *corps-fossile*, a fossil-body where memory is stored and history is engraved: "il est le lieu qui dit l'histoire. [...] Il est, ce corps-fossile où sont déposés chagrins, victoires, deuils, où sont stockés les grands chapitres de notre histoire" (Francis 2016, 280) [it is the locus that tells history. [...] It is the fossil-body where pains, victories, mourning are deposited, where the great chapters of our history are archived]. Departing from the common understanding of fossils as *body remains* used in science to reconstruct the history of the natural world, Kanor's notion of fossil-body actually refers to the body of flesh and blood as a *living fossil*, an archive that can "tell history." Whereas fossils are artefacts that illuminate foregone origins, the fossil-body *relates* (in its Glissantian double acceptation of "linking" and "telling") past, present, and future; it highlights the continuity, thereby enabling the genesis that counters digenesis, according to Vété-Congolo. Thus, the fossil-body of the present still feels or reacts to the suffering and emotions experienced generations ago; in many ways, the oppression is ongoing. The layered memory deposited in the corporeal archive is at once individual—a compilation of personal pains, victories, and mourning—and collective—a transgenerational record of the trauma of the transatlantic trade and its impact on black women's bodies that have been uniquely (though not exclusively) subject to sexual violence.

Yet in *Humus*, the ultimate violation of the black Atlantic body appears to be confinement. The insistence on the captives' immobility in the novel underlines the physical restraint they endure on the journey: they cross the Atlantic in shackles, crowded in the ship hold, and unable to stand onboard, let alone move around, for weeks or months. Running against the grain of the traditional slave narrative packed with action, movement, and excitement, the Prologue calls attention to the affective charge of the novel and warns that this account of history will compel the reader to

2 CHRONOTOPAL SLAVE SHIPS, CORPOREAL ARCHIVES: *DEVOIR DE...* 35

vicariously experience enslavement: "*Vous serez pris. Enchaînés* bien malgré vous aux mots. *Enfermés* dans cette histoire qui comme chant se répète, préfère au point final les suites, aux conclusions radicales le plus sûr des bégaiements" (Kanor 2006, 14, emphasis mine) [You will be *trapped.* Unwillingly chained to the words. *Locked up* in this story that, like a chant repeating itself, prefers sequels to a final period, the most certain stammering to radical conclusions]. The "stammers" triggered by the denial of physical freedom announce the loss of speech, the "aporia" quoted earlier, which figures as the obliteration of the self. It is therefore no accident that the opening chapter of the novel should focus on "La muette," or the silent one. *las Negras* too focuses on physical restraint: the rebellious captive in "Wanwe" is tied by the neck, her hands immobilised behind her back (Arroyo Pizarro 2013, 19); in "Matronas," the ship hold is substituted by the prison cell—one of Foucault's negative heterotopias—where Ndizi is held and where the entirety of the action is set. Yet here again, recollecting, or in Vete-Congolo's words, "activating and enacting one's memory," is a tool to resist incarceration: as Ndizi muses over her six escapes and numerous acts of sedition (35), she evades once more, breaking out of the narrow confines of her cell by travelling through spacetime via memory.[13]

The fossil-bodies of the peoples of the black Atlantic archive intangibles like memory and habitus (culture, language, personal and collective history, genealogy); as such, they were invested with liberatory power for those faced with enslavers set on obliterating their past, civilisation, and episteme in addition to their personhood. Today, the potential of the corporeal archive remains critical in the face of continued oppression, debasement, and erasure of Afrodescendants and everything that pertains to them. With its opening "The first memory could be the ship" (19), a phrase later modified as "the first memory could also be the village" (23) that then morphs into "It is also possible that the first memory could be the day of the rapt" (25), the story "Wanwe" signals that, however malleable, memory is a powerful tool to counter digenesis. In "Matronas," the characterisation of Ndizi as a true polyglot further illustrates the archival function of the body, mind, and spirit that is used as a form of resistance. In fact, in the enslavement era, Arroyo Pizarro (2016) reminds us, the body, specifically female hair, literally served as a geographical archive, albeit temporary, as braiding was used to map the topographical terrain to assist fugitives. Similarly, Ndizi's multilingualism traces back her personal history, as each tongue is acquired at a given stage of her life: her childhood in an unspecified African region, her service under enslavers from distinct European countries, her successive episodes of *marronnage* accompanying different ethnic groups (35). Like a fossil, Ndizi's personal reminiscences and language acquisition figure as a register of the era, an imprint bearing testimony to the wide gamut of ethnicities across Africa that were targeted by transatlantic enslavement, the various European colonial powers that profited from it, and the competing imperial interests of the period. The various cultural practices archived in Ndizi's body thus constitute an immaterial historical record in and of themselves.[14] In particular, Ndizi's polyglossia is revealed as a linguistic fossil that parallels Kanor's fossil-body. When Ndizi, shielding herself with the enslavers' prejudice by faking ignorance, pretends not to understand the priest who visits her daily in her cell, or when she refuses to confess to the crimes she is accused of, she uses silence as an act of dissidence. In "Matronas," aporia takes on another meaning than in *Humus*: it becomes protection. Arroyo Pizarro therefore transforms fictional personal memory into archival material.

The preoccupation with the records is certainly palpable throughout the collection, as apparent from the epigraph, a provocative short poem dedicated to historians:

> A los historiadores,
> por habernos dejado fuera.
> Aquí estamos de nuevo …
> cuerpo presente, color vigente,
> declinándonos a ser invisibles …
> rehusándonos a ser borradas.
>
> [To the historians,
> for leaving us out.
> Here we are again …
> present, fully fleshed and coloured,
> declining to be made invisible …
> refusing to be erased.]

Here content matches form, as the poetic cadence of the lines "declinándonos a ser invisibles… /rehusándonos a ser borradas," with the atypical stress on the antepenultimate syllable, conveys the restive spirit and combative nature of black Atlantic women, whose stories are about to be told in the collection. For the author, then, writing these stories was an act of epistemic *marronnage*.

"Matronas" most directly addresses the question of archives and historiography through the character of Petro, the northern European priest who befriends Ndizi and whose ulterior motive is to seditiously chronicle the era of transatlantic enslavement to denounce its atrocities and inhumanity. Moreover, that Ndizi gradually forgets her native tongue and especially the word for "freedom" in some of the languages she knows (37) underscores the process of erasure and dehumanisation instituted by enslavement as well as the substantial loss in collective memory resulting from the dispersion, what Bastide calls *trous de mémoire* or "memory holes." To some extent, syncretism is a mechanism that emerged to palliate for this collective memory loss: forgetting, therefore, is intrinsic to creolisation. Thus, Ndizi is an archetypally syncretic Afrodescendant. Stolen as a child, she is left with a fading recollection of her origin and mother tongue. She fulfills her *devoir de mémoire* by actively summoning up scenes of her childhood to trigger her remembrance. Yet despite hints that she may be from Congo, in adulthood her ethnicity has become barely identifiable, to the extent that Ndizi can stand for the entire African diaspora. Her strategy to conceal her extensive linguistic knowledge as a mode of survival has further eroded her memory. Ndizi's syncretism or loss of ethnic markers represents black Atlantic cultures, which emerged out of partial forgetting.

Like Ndizi, the protagonists in *Humus* counter the dehumanising effects of confinement, uprooting, dis-location, and eventual collective amnesia induced by uprooting and enslavement with a range of stratagems drawn from the immaterial corporeal archive that allows them to cross back the Atlantic: reminiscence, imagination, and the supernatural. Thus *la volante*, or "the flying one," the Vodun priestess from Ouidah (in today's Benin) aboard the Saint Domingue-bound *Le Soleil*, enjoys remarkable freedom of movement: she can fly to Nantes (France) and later Badagry (Nigeria). *La volante* also travels across time, living through the turbulent period between 1750 and 1804 in Saint-Domingue, to reappear in the twenty-first century. Moving across spacetime, both *la volante* and *l'héritière*, or "the heiress," retrace the contours of the black Atlantic and over two centuries of its history. *L'héritière*, the author's alter ego, considers *la volante* to be "the sole survivor, really" (Kanor 2006, 241). The ability to survive the trauma of the Middle Passage is thus intimately linked to the agency exerted by *la volante* through movement, a strategy replicated by *l'héritière*, who "walks the world," to use Kanor's own self-description (Kanor 2015). The phrase "la seule survivante, en vérité," however, could suggest that the contemporary narrator does not view herself as a survivor, but rather as someone who remains scarred by trauma and has yet to overcome the history of the black Atlantic.

Such an interpretation is further supported by the structure of the novel, which reproduces the effect of "a song repeating itself" (14). Nearly each of the fourteen defiant captives has her own chapter, and their mutinous jump overboard is repeated every time. Despite the different perspectives, there eventually arises a feeling of *déjà lu* in the reader, like a scratched vinyl record or a song looping on replay. An impactful tribute to each of the tens of millions of deported, these repetitions also point to the socioeconomic legacy of the triangular trade and enslavement, and its psychological imprint on the African diaspora to this day. While the author asserts that for sure, "[she] was not there" ("je n'y étais pas"), the artistry with which she manages to convey the forced exodus hints at a collective postmemory handed down from one generation to the next.

Set in contemporary times, the final chapter features "the heiress" grappling with her black Atlantic past, which she tries to overcome through writing. Haunted by this harrowing legacy, *l'héritière* travels to Badagry and Ouidah. There she retraces the Slave Route, attempts to remember by turning seven times around the Tree of Forgetting in reverse, and suffers hallucinations of the slave ship *Le Soleil*. The affect generated by the weight of this transgenerational trauma is palpable. Unlike most people around her in Nigeria and Benin, *l'héritière* wishes to dwell on her history, to piece it together, like "a seamstress of pain assembles, piece by piece, a history to be recomposed" (243: "je songeai avec effroi aux couturières de la douleur ... L'histoire à assembler pièce par pièce, à passer-recomposer"). This sentence and the final words of the novel "Je me levai. Face au livre à venir. A ces murs où nichaient les fantômes et qui bientôt s'effaceraient" (247) [I stood up. Facing the book to come. These walls nestling ghosts that would soon fade away], make explicit the author's project to not only recover the past, but to *recompose* it and imagine a different present and future through creative writing.[15] Whereas the spectral figure of *la volante* exhorts *l'héritière* to continue her search for meaning as a form of healing, the phantoms of history that assail the narrator-protagonist in the final chapter are overwhelming and paralysing.[16] On the individual level, writing becomes the best way to dispel these phantoms; on the collective level, creative works such as *Humus* and *las Negras* also represent a way out of the lingering effects of this haunting history, an escape from digenesis, in short, a foundation, or perhaps modest sketches, to build a new future.

Kanor and Arroyo Pizarro fulfil their *devoir de mémoire* by drawing on the intangible corporeal archives of the black Atlantic to redress the monolithic, partial narratives propped up by the materiality of colonial records. If in fact the archive is a "discursive system" invested with the power to validate or invalidate particular accounts of the past (Foucault 1969), then the dynamic record that is the collective memory stored in fossil-bodies, however fragmented, still provides essential protection against colonial ontological and epistemic erasure. Made of "multiple layers sedimenting together like a palimpsest" from which resistance and new societies can arise (Douglas 2022, 18), this collective memory is primarily activated in *Humus* and *las Negras* via the chronotope of the slave ship, whose problematic gender symbolism is deconstructed through a focus on female-centred solidarity networks metaphorically represented by the mangrove; the two texts thus succeed in inscribing contemporary Afro-diasporic women into a genealogy of combatants. The authors themselves, having embarked on the task of unearthing and re/writing the past, can be conceived as epistemic maroons whose work parallels what René Depestre (1980) calls *marronnage intellectuel.* Moreover, the reconfiguration of spacetime in both works facilitates the emergence of versions of the past that counter the digenesis of the Middle Passage and empowers people throughout the African diaspora to imagine alternative futures, be they sovereign or nonsovereign. Therefore, these are chronotropic narratives in which past, present, and future are in continuous dialogue, attesting to Kanor's belief that "the dialogue between Africa and the Americas must be reinvented; the voices of yesteryear are still speaking to us" (Herbeck 2013, 967).

NOTES

1. Arroyo Pizarro's atypical lower and upper case in the title of the original edition is respected.
2. Initially referring in the 1970s to the demand to memorialise the Shoah and for official recognition by the French State of its own responsibility in the deportation of French Jews during World War II, the expression *devoir de mémoire* surfaced in the field of French Caribbean Studies in the years leading up to 1998, when the 150 years commemoration of the second abolition in French colonies gave impetus for a number of specific initiatives and scholarly research on the history and memory of French transatlantic enslavement. See, for instance, Cottias 1997, 1998, and 2000, and Chivallon 2012.

3. Gilroy, a disciple of Stuart Hall, is indebted to his non-essentialist conception of identity as dynamic and cultural identities as "the different ways we are positioned by, and position ourselves within, the narratives of the past" (Hall 2003 [1990], 236).

    See note 11 for Basso's adaptation of Bakhtin's 1937 literary concept of the chronotope to linguistic anthropology.

4. Translations of all works cited are mine, unless otherwise stated.

5. See numerous writings by Glissant, including *Mémoires des esclavages*, where he states that the deported African was stripped of culture, knowledge, and measurement and appreciation of spacetime, "all of which was engulfed and digested in the belly of the slave ship" ("tout cela s'est englouti et a été digéré dans le ventre du bateau négrier"). Glissant's phrase casts the slave ship as simultaneously the ocean and a sea monster that ingests all elements of African cultures and epistemologies through ship wrecks, collective drownings, and the amnesia induced by enslavement. Thus stripped naked, Glissant continues, the African is now tasked with "recomposing the *traces* of their cultures of origin" ("recomposer, avec la toute-puissance de la mémoire désolée, les *traces* de ses cultures d'origine") to combine them with the enslavers' cultural impositions, thus creating "considerable creole cultures" (Glissant 2007: 108–109, italics his; gender inclusive pronouns in the English translation are mine).

    Saidiya Hartman too recurs to the ambiguous symbolic womb/belly, picturing the Middle Passage as the "birth canal that spawned the tribe" of a generic black people that supplanted all ethnic distinctions (Hartman 2007, 103), while likening the trail of dungeons along the West African coast to "a large intestine" and imagining the captives as "inching [their] way along the entrails of power." Hartman sees in ingestion and cannibalism "vivid" metaphors for "the relation between the haves and the have-nots, the rulers and the ruled, the parasite and the host" at play in the African and transatlantic enslavement systems (112).

6. Conversation with the author, March 2016. Herbeck (2013) also notes that the considerable interval required for organic debris to become fertile soil or humus mirrors the time lag before deported Africans can adapt to their new environment and cohere into a social body.

7. Doris Sommer, *Foundational Fictions: The National Romances of Latin America*, 1991.

8. Jacinth Howard (2019) notes the recurrence of space ships represented as slave ships in Caribbean speculative fiction. Moreover, Cuban author Antonio Benítez Rojo (1989) understands the slave ship as one piece in

the system of machines (in Deleuze and Guattari's acceptation) that comprises the triangular trade and the plantation economy.

9. A unique, underappreciated biotope that is essentially a diffuse Third Space, the mangrove, an extension of Edouard Glissant's paradigmatic rhizome and his Relation (Glissant 1990, 44–47), stands as a creative matrix or incubator for the poetics and aesthetics of many regional writers and artists, especially women. Thus, while Guadeloupean Maryse Condé parodies the trope of the mangrove-matrix through her protagonist Mira in *Traversée de la mangrove* (1989), she nonetheless endows the ecosystem with rich symbolism throughout her acclaimed novel. Resonances with the trope of the slave ship in the black Atlantic imaginary notwithstanding, this network of rhizomic roots is attuned to Gilroy's black Atlantic, a "webbed network, between the local and the global" simultaneously constituted by roots (or the impulsive fascination for ethnic origins) and routes (the impetus to incorporate multiple diasporic cultural strands) that challenges "all narrow nationalist perspectives" (Gilroy 1993, 29).

10. Vété-Congolo coins the term "femmisme" to designate "une éthique de la transcendance" (ethics of transcendence) that women enslaved on plantations throughout the Americas elaborated to counter the denial of their humanity and femininity and overcome the multiples traumas inflicted (Vété-Congolo 2017, 135).

11. Basso's adaption of Bakhtin's definition of the chronotope reads in full: "[Chronotopes are] points in the geography of a community where time and space intersect and fuse. Time takes on flesh and becomes visible for human contemplation; likewise, space becomes charged and responsive to the movements of time and history and the enduring character of a people. Chronotopes thus stand as monuments to the community itself, as symbols of it, as forces operating to shape its members' images of themselves" (Basso 1984, 44–45).

12. See Roger Bastide 1970, p. 88: "Or, pour bien comprendre la survie des religions africaines dans le Nouveau Monde, il faut passer [...] de l'espace topique [...] à un espace moteur – de la géographie des 'pierres de la cité' à une autre géographie, corporelle." [To understand the survival of African religions in the New World [...] we must go from topical space [...] to a motor space – from the geography of "city stones" to another, a corporeal one].

    See also Jan Assmann 1995 on the link between rituals and collective memory.

13. Significantly, Johan Galtung (1969, 174–175) lists the deprivation of both movement and speech as forms of "personal somatic violence."

Galtung identifies two forms of personal somatic violence: "denial of input (sources of energy in general, air, water, and food in the case of the body), and denial of output (movement)," including "movements of vocal chords" (175). He notes the imprecise borderline between somatic and psychological violence, and the "mental implications" of physical constraints. Furthermore, Galtung's pioneering notion of structural violence is a useful lens through which to look at Caribbean societies of the past and present. These societies have emerged from a brutality historically enshrined in a succession of institutions aiming to support the plantation economy (and its subsequent avatars) such as codified enslavement and indentured servitude; the Church; the colonial school system; and, increasingly so after World War II, the more discreet violence of state-sponsored mass labour migration schemes, notably the French Caribbean BUMIDOM or its Puerto Rican equivalent Operation Boot Straps, that amount to contemporary, albeit less brutal, iterations of the Middle Passage. Today this characteristic violence persists, for instance through the perpetuation of a carefully crafted economic dependency and under-development, a school system that sustains an adherence to the untenable sociopolitical status quo, starker social injustices than in the metropole, and laxed regional enforcement of, if not patent disregard for, national or federal laws intended to protect civilians.

14. Rachel Douglas makes a very similar argument in relation to Haiti, arguing that: "Resistance and a new society ... [rest on] decolonial histories, like the Kreyòl language and popular Vodou practices, [which] should be seen as contributing to the communal alternative archives that continue to be woven together" (Douglas 2022, 18).

15. Emmanuel Bruno Jean-François (2017, 87) likewise notes how in *Humus* Kanor gathers the fragments of black Atlantic history. The term "recompose" echoes Glissant's description of the cultural syncretism that occurred in the Americas (Glissant 2007, 108–109, see note 5); it seems to hold strong positive evocations of creolisation for the two Martiniquans. Recomposing is central to Glissant's *pensée archipélique* (archipelagic thinking), which is, in John Drabinski's words, an "embrace of fragmentation" that, unlike French or U.S. poststructuralism, is rooted "in the specificity of the Caribbean experience of the Americas" (Drabinski 2019, xv).

16. Here I draw on the distinction made by Colin Davis (2005, 373) between Nicolas Abraham's phantom, or the internalisation of somebody else's crime or trauma that can eventually be exteriorised, and Jacques Derrida's spectre, who represents what can never be fully apprehended and therefore cannot totally disappear.

References

Arroyo Pizarro, Yolanda. 2013 [2012]. *las Negras*. Cabo Rojo: Editora Educación Emergente. Original edition: Boreales.

———. 2016. *Y tu abuela, dónde está?* TEDxUPR. 20 July. https://www.youtube.com/watch?v=EB0hQEvXgDM

Assmann, Jan. 1995. Collective Memory and Cultural Identity. Trans. by John Czeplicka. *New German Critique* 65: 125–133.

Bakhtin, Mikhail M. 1981 [1937]. *The Dialogic Imagination: Four Essays*. Trans. by Caryl Emerson and Michael Holquist, U of Texas P.

Basso, Keith. 1984. "Stalking with Stories": Names, Places and Moral Narratives Among the Western Apache. In *Text, Place and Story*, ed. Edward Bruner, American Anthropological Association.

Bastide, Roger. 1970. Mémoire collective et sociologie du bricolage. *L'Année Sociologique* 21: 65–108.

Benítez Rojo, Antonio. 1989. *La isla que se repite: el Caribe y la perspectiva posmoderna*. Hanover, NH: Ediciones del Norte.

Brodber, Erna. 1990. Fiction in the Scientific Procedure. In *Caribbean Women Writers: Essays from the First International Conference*, ed. Selwyn R. Cudjoe, 164–168. Amherst, MA: University of Massachusetts Press.

Chivallon, Christine. 2012. *L'esclavage, du souvenir à la mémoire*. Paris: Karthala/CIRESC.

Condé, Maryse. 1989. *Traversée de la mangrove*. Paris: Mercure de France.

Cottias, Myriam. 1998. La politique de l'oubli. *France-Antilles: Supplément-Edition* (Guadeloupe, 25 mai): 38–40.

———. 1997. "L'oubli du passé" contre la "citoyenneté": troc et ressentiment à la Martinique (1848-1946). In *1946–1996: Cinquante ans de départementalisation outre-mer*, ed. Fred Constant and Justin Daniel, 293–313. Paris: L'Harmattan.

———. 2000. Le triomphe de l'oubli ou la mémoire tronquée? In *De l'esclavage aux Réparations*, ed. Serge Chalons, 95–103. Paris: Karthala.

Davis, Colin. 2005. Hauntology, Spectres, and Phantoms. *French Studies* 59.3 (July): 373–379.

Depestre, René. 1980. *Bonjour et adieu à la négritude*. Paris: Robert Laffont.

Douglas, Rachel. 2022. Futures in the Present: Decolonial Visions of the Haitian Revolution. *Interventions: International Journal of Francophone Studies*. https://doi.org/10.1080/1369801X.2022.2080574.

Drabinski, John E. 2019. *Glissant and the Middle Passage: Philosophy, Beginning, Abyss*. Minneapolis and London: University of Minnesota Press.

Ferly, Odile. 2012. *A Poetics of Relation: Caribbean Women Writing at the Millennium*. New York: Palgrave.

Foucault, Michel. 1969. *L'archéologie du savoir*. Paris: Gallimard.

―――. 1984 [1967]. Des Espace Autres. Conférence au Cercle d'études architecturales, 14 mars 1967. *Architecture, Mouvement, Continuité* 5 (October): 46–49.

Francis, Gladys. 2016. Entretien avec Fabienne Kanor, "L'Ante-llaise par excellence": Sexualité, corporalité, diaspora et créolité. *French. Forum* 41.3 (Winter): 273–288.

Galtung, Johan. 1969. Violence, Peace, and Peace Research. *Journal of Peace Research* 6 (3): 167–191.

Gilroy, Paul. 1993. *The Black Atlantic: Modernity and Double Consciousness.* Cambridge, MA: Harvard University Press.

Glissant, Edouard. 1981. *Le Discours antillais.* Paris: Gallimard.

―――. 1990. *Poétique de la Relation.* Paris: Gallimard.

―――. 1997. *Traité du Tout-Monde.* Paris: Gallimard.

―――. 2007. *Mémoire des esclavages: la fondation d'un centre national pour la mémoire des esclavages et de leurs abolitions.* Paris: Gallimard.

Hall, Stuart. 2003 [1990]. Cultural Identity and Diaspora. In *Theorizing Diaspora. A Reader*, eds. Jana Evans Braziel and Anita Mannur, 233–246. Oxford: Blackwell.

Hartman, Saidiya. 2007. *Lose Your Mother: A Journey along the Atlantic Slave Route.* New York: Farrar, Straus and Giroux.

―――. 2016. The Belly of the World: A Note on Black Women's Labors. *Souls* 18.1 (January–March): 166–173. https://doi.org/10.1080/1099994 9.2016.1162596.

Herbeck, Jason. 2013. Entretien avec Fabienne Kanor. *The French Review* 86.5 (April): 964–976.

Hirsch, Marianne. 2008. The Generation of Postmemory. *Poetics Today* 29 (1): 103–128.

Howard, Jacinth. 2019. Black Technologies: Caribbean Visions and Versions in the Speculative Narratives of Tobias Buckell and Karen Lord. *Journal of West Indian Literature* 27(2): 1–14, 81.

Jean-François, Emmanuel Bruno. 2017. Espace océanique, parole archipélique, et polyphonie mémorielle dans *Humus* de Fabienne Kanor. *Women in French Studies* 25: 77–92.

Josephs, Kelly Baker. 2013. Beyond Geography, Past Time: Afrofuturism, *The Rainmaker's Mistake*, and Caribbean Studies. *Small Axe* 17 (2): 123–135. https://doi.org/10.1215/07990537-2323355.

Josephs, Kelly Baker and David Chariandy. 2014. Straddling Shifting Spheres: A Conversation with David Chariandy. *Transition* 113, *What is Africa to me now?*, 111–27.

Kanor, Fabienne. 2006. *Humus.* Paris: Gallimard.

―――. 2015. Interview by Consulat Général de France à la Nouvelle Orléans. *"Cinq questions pour Fabienne Kanor."* 08 mars. https://nouvelleorleans.consulfrance.org/Cinq-Questions-pour-Fabienne-Kanor. Accessed 22 Oct 2022.

Larrier, Renée. 2011. Histoire engagée, histoire occultée: Fabienne Kanor's *Humus*. *Women in French Studies* (Special Issue): 103–11.

Mehta, Brinda. 2020. *Jahaji-bahin* Feminism: a Decolonial Indo-Caribbean Consciousness. *South Asian Diaspora* 12 (2): 179–194. https://doi.org/10.1080/19438192.2020.1765072.

Nora, Pierre. 1984. Entre Mémoire et Histoire: La problématique des lieux. In *Les lieux de mémoire*, ed. Pierre Nora, xv–xlii. Paris: Gallimard.

van Alphen, Ernst. 2006. Second-Generation Testimony, the Transmission of Trauma, and Postmemory. *Poetics Today* 27: 473–488.

Vété-Congolo, Hanétha. 2014. L'humus de la "memidentité" ou la métaphysique de la *pawòl* contre l'oubli: l'exemple de *Humus* de Fabienne Kanor. *Présence francophone* 82: 114–130.

———. 2017. Le Douboutisme dans les sociétés caribéennes créolophones. In *Féminisme: (en)jeux d'une théorie*, ed. N'Gussan Kouadio Germain. Abidjan: Inidaf.

Walcott, Derek. 1998 [1974]. The Muse of History. *What the Twilight Says. Essays by Derek Walcott*. New York: Farrar, Straus and Giroux, 36–64.

———. 1980. The Sea Is History. *The Star-Apple Kingdom*. London: Jonathan Cape, 25–28.

Open Access This chapter is licensed under the terms of the Creative Commons Attribution 4.0 International License (http://creativecommons.org/licenses/by/4.0/), which permits use, sharing, adaptation, distribution and reproduction in any medium or format, as long as you give appropriate credit to the original author(s) and the source, provide a link to the Creative Commons licence and indicate if changes were made.

The images or other third party material in this chapter are included in the chapter's Creative Commons licence, unless indicated otherwise in a credit line to the material. If material is not included in the chapter's Creative Commons licence and your intended use is not permitted by statutory regulation or exceeds the permitted use, you will need to obtain permission directly from the copyright holder.

CHAPTER 3

Wreckognition: Archival Ruins in Dionne Brand's *The Blue Clerk*

Erica L. Johnson

Sitting among a rapt audience at a conference in 2013, I listened to Dionne Brand's incantatory reading of her manuscript in progress, which she invited us to picture as a book printed only on the right-hand pages; the left pages, left blank.[1] Even as she sketched this mental image, Brand acknowledged that her proposed book would be too expensive to find acceptance with any publishing board and yet, five years later when *The Blue Clerk: Ars Poetica in 59 Versos* appeared in print it contained seemingly equal parts of inscribed and blank page. The format is not that of empty left-hand pages but the versos vary in length from a single word to several pages of text with the result that many pages are lightly touched by text and, in fact, several left-hand pages remain blank by coincidence as well as design. This gesture toward the blank page is one that other Caribbean women writers including M. NourbeSe Philip and Michelle Cliff have explored in their use of scattered text across the white space of the page, most notably in Philip's *Zong!* in which she leaves intentional blankness around words and their fragments, and Cliff uses lists and

---

E. L. Johnson (✉)
Pace University, New York, NY, USA
e-mail: ejohnson@pace.edu

© The Author(s) 2023
O. Ferly, T. Zimmerman (eds.), *Chronotropics*,
https://doi.org/10.1007/978-3-031-32111-5_3

fragments in several of her short stories and novels. In the most recent example of poetic use of "blank" left-hand pages, Claudia Rankine preserves the left-hand pages of *Just Us* (2020) for annotation of the prose and poetry that appear on the right-hand pages; on the few occasions where the right-hand page requires no annotation, the left-hand page is left blank.[2] The blank page is a reflection of the absent archive, the paucity of record, and the literal and figurative white space surrounding Black histories. In Brand's book the blank spaces illustrate the structuring debate of the book between the blue clerk, the archivist, and keeper of bales of paper, and the author, the keeper of memory and experience. It may seem contradictory that the archivist's bales are full of blank pages but that is precisely the point: in a Caribbean context and in postcolonial contexts more generally, archival records are not so much historical evidence as they are remains and ruins of histories untold.[3] Their internal logic privileges presence—the presence of newspaper articles, court records, property deeds, letters, photographs, and so forth; however, to read these items as a record of *absence*, as material remains of what has chipped away from history, is to defy their power. Remnants, ruins, and wrecks, colonial archives prompt authors to engage in counter-archival writing that dives into the wreck, as does *The Blue Clerk*.

In her engagement with the wreckage of the archive, I want to argue that Brand practices a strategy of wreckognition, an idea that plays with a metaphorical understanding of the colonial archive as a site of ruin in the sense that Ann Laura Stoler explores in both *Duress* and in her edited volume *Imperial Debris: Reflections on Ruins and Ruination*. She argues that the tensions of imperial history chaff against one another, doing inevitable damage: "To speak of colonial ruination," she says, "is to trace the visible and visceral senses in which the effects of empire are reactivated and remain" (Stoler 2013, 196). It is noteworthy that her explanation is indebted to Caribbean literature: she draws from Derek Walcott's line, "the rot remains," spinning out both the materiality of "rot" and the temporality of "remains," and she sums up her line of inquiry as one of "how empire's ruins contour and curve through the psychic and material space in which people live and what compounded layers of imperial debris do to them" (Stoler 2016, 2).[4] In addition to the kind of historical connectivity that Stoler stipulates here, archival ruination is as Saidiya Hartman puts it, an episteme: for all that researchers are drawn to records from the past, colonial archives are evidence of occlusion, violence, and absence from those very records. Writing specifically of the colonial archive surrounding slavery, Hartman observes, "This silence in the archive in combination with the robustness of the fort or barracoon, not as a holding cell or space of confinement but as an episteme, has for the most part focused the historiography of the slave trade on quantitative matters and on issues of markets and trade relations" (Hartman 2008, 3–4). Hartman's characterization of the archive as silent and blinded by its own *raison d'être*, of underwriting capital, describes its wreckage, or the extent to which records lie in shards of representation from the moment of their inscription.

To return to the metaphor of ruination, a structure is deemed a ruin when it starts to go missing, when it crumbles into its own absence. Cliff presents the concept of ruination in its Caribbean specificity through not only her aesthetic but also her attention to the word itself throughout her oeuvre; in a prominent example, she opens *No Telephone to Heaven* (1996 [1987]) with a chapter entitled "Ruinate" and a footnote about its distinctive Jamaican creole use to refer to colonial structures—in the metaphor of the receding agricultural landscape—growing back into the wilderness that preceded them.[5] The status of the archive as a crumbling colonial structure prompts writers like Hartman and Brand to read these texts through a method of wreckognition, or a tacit acknowledgment that the act of research must expand upon an academic tradition of discovering and marshaling evidence; rather, they recognize from the outset that the material with which they engage is itself a wreck of history replete with repressed voices and unrecorded experiences. Again, Hartman leads the way on this kind of counter-archival mode of inquiry across her body of work engaging the scant evidence of enslaved people's experiences and lives. In *Wayward Lives, Beautiful Experiments*, she brings her methodology to bear on the lives of Black girls and women at the turn of the century who "refused the terms of visibility imposed on them" (Hartman 2019, 18) by the social workers, sociologists, and police who compiled the extant archive of records and photographs of their resistant subjects. Hartman engages this material in all of its failure to represent its subjects, writing frequently in the subjunctive and in interrogative sentences and proposing stories that directly challenge the "notebooks, monographs, case files, and photographs" that compel her to "speculate, listen intently, read between the lines, attend to the disorder and mess of the archive, and to honor silence" (34).

This messy disorder is in keeping with the metaphor of archival ruination and wreckage. In a Caribbean context, such wreckage is not confined to metaphor in the sense that record keeping in the region is beset by material forces of ruination that run the gamut from sparse and dehumanizing record keeping in the first place to the fact that most Caribbean countries were under a succession of imperial powers that leeched even these limited records out of local contexts and hid them away in different European institutions, to the fact that the climate of the Caribbean works on printed and other material records with a distinct power of heat, damp, and other sources of destruction.[6] In an important address to the status of Caribbean archives, Jeannette Bastian establishes the paradox of their power: she cites the importance of "a community of records" to community itself in that "archives can be both physical spaces and memory spaces ... containers of the collective memory of their creators as well as their users and interpreters" (Bastian 2003, 13). At the same time, the graphomania surrounding archives is central to their power to corroborate colonial endeavor. Whatever lies in the archive (including cryptic fragments and violent forms of representation), as a discipline it props up exclusive forms of citizenship and imperial identities in a variety of contexts. Moreover, the removal of Caribbean archives to European libraries imposes a geopolitical form of forgetting on Caribbean societies, as Bastian and the dozens of contributors to her volume, *Decolonizing the Caribbean Record: An Archives Reader*, demonstrate in their approach to archival materials as deeply problematic yet essential building blocks of cultural memory and identity.

As complicit and foundational colonial materials and valuable sources of counter-discourse alike, archives are not a discreet body of materials but rather an idea in ongoing construction as *The Blue Clerk* demonstrates in its iterative practices. While issues of archival absence and erasure have long been central to postcolonial studies (and arguably the field's primary impetus by way of Subaltern Studies), once again the notion of archival absence is not only metaphorical in a Caribbean context. In a fascinating study of the archival records pertaining to Dionne Brand's childhood home, Trinidad and Tobago, Roma Wong Sang explains the role of archives in the cultural memory of postcoloniality, arguing that "a community of records [...] may be pivotal in recasting an inclusive past that may lay a foundation for forging a strong national identity and democratizing heritage in Trinidad and Tobago" (2018, 594). Such records are particularly important for a diverse nation like Trinidad and Tobago, whose two major islands, annexed to one another in 1889, have distinct histories and demographics that give rise to a complex narrative of nationhood. Rita Pemberton (2018) describes how Tobago staged effective resistance against a series of colonizers for centuries with the result that it changed colonial hands some fourteen times, with each transfer of power divesting the colony of more of its historical records and scattering them to sites as far flung as London, Stockholm, Madrid, and, thanks to the Moravian missionary presence, Pennsylvania.[7] Thus the colonial archive of the Caribbean is not just a body of misrepresentative records but its state of ruin is such that it is not even accessible as a sum of its remaining parts, spread out as it is across the hemisphere.

Brand plays with the disjointed, ruinous state of this archive in *The Blue Clerk*, which Hartman describes in an interview with Brand as an address to "the economy of the colonial archive."[8] Indeed, the recurring image of the clerk waiting on a dock, standing guard over bales of paper, invokes the impression of records and the recording of information. Aside an unnamed sea: "There are bales of paper on a wharf somewhere; at a port, somewhere. There is a clerk inspecting and abating them. She is the blue clerk" (Brand 4). These are the left-hand pages that Brand theorized in her conception of her book and that she realized in an approximated presentation of blank pages throughout her versos. As left-hand pages, the bales of paper are blank and not blank in the sense that they hold all that is "withheld," "all that is left out," as Brand puts it in the conversation with Hartman (2018). This intermingling of absence and presence in the metaphor of the archive theorizes its power of record and its failure to record. The clerk approaches the bales' "abilities" that she "is forever curtailing and marshalling" (4), a line that implies that they contain information or evidence of some kind. They are also "brightly scored, crisp and cunning" (4) though, which speaks to the deceptive nature of whatever evidence they hold.

From this opening presentation of the clerk, Brand offers a gendered twist on the archive, the vast majority of which would have been written by white men. The author's clerk, however, is identified as "she" from the beginning of the text, as is the author later on. In the clerk's first appearance, "She is dressed in a blue ink coat, her right hand is dry, her left hand is dripping; she is expecting a ship. She is preparing [...] She keeps account of cubic metres of senses, perceptions, and resistant facts" (4). The gendered affiliation that underscores the tensions between author and clerk point the reader toward possible alliance between creativity and the archive even as the book explores the impasse between them as well. This alliance is a foundational source of the wreckognition that exists between the clerk and author in that they often mirror one another even as they struggle with missing or false histories. As a feminist collective of artists and writers noted in a recent roundtable, archivists are not only attached to national collections but are also librarians, mothers, and gardeners (Belle et al. 2020); moreover, to the extent that cultural memory is embodied, there is such a thing as an affective archive that runs counter to the records created over centuries by men. The reference to the clerk's dripping hand emphasizes her embodiment even beyond gender and makes the body a significant factor in archival engagement; in a later verso, she remembers having lived a previous life with a boyfriend who "slapped her and left her without her clothes in a motel" (137) and a subsequent encounter with another man seeking to attack her. Not only is the clerk's female embodiment illustrated in all of its vulnerabilities here, but her memory runs through her body as, turning her attention back to the bales on the dock, she does so with a "shiver" (138). Because of their embodiment, the clerk is both an adversary and an intimate of the author. Moreover, even though the colonial archive was scripted primarily by white men, Brand claims that power for Black artists by noting that only they have a clerk. She refers to dozens of writers but the only other writer and artist with a clerk are Ralph Ellison and Wynton Marsalis, whose clerks attach in singular relationships. She observes that Marsalis has a fearsome and demanding clerk while Ellison and his clerk share such depths of understanding that they are the only team to have written a book entirely of left-hand pages. The prominent embodiment and gendering of the blue clerk opens a line of possibility that flows counter to the abstract tensions between author and archivist and suggests at least the potential of mutual productivity between them. Brand emphasizes their embodied perspective in several passages including one in which the two of them condemn the anti-Black racism of canonical Western writers including Charles Baudelaire, Walter Benjamin, T. S. Eliot, and John Locke, who "when he wrote 'An Essay Concerning Human Understanding,' in 1689 he had already been the Secretary of the Board of Trade and Plantations [...] I cannot get past this" (168); they also discuss the "micro-abrasions" of Gertrude Stein's *Melanctha* and her dismissive comments about African art (116). Whatever the clerk's blind spots, she and the author find some reciprocity in the implicit embodied alliances of race and gender.

And yet, Brand sustains the tension between the archivist's obsessive watchfulness over the crisp and cunning pages and the author's frustration with having to constantly negotiate with the clerk over her artistic vision. She does this in both the poetry and the structure of her book. While the

3 WRECKOGNITION: ARCHIVAL RUINS IN DIONNE BRAND'S *THE BLUE...*

empty left-hand pages did not make it to production, Brand nonetheless incorporates the principle of the partial and ruined archive into the structure of her book as Hartman notes in her mention of what she terms the book's "wayward index." As Brand prefaces the index, "*Every listing generates a new listing. Every map another road*" (233, italics in original). Like the iterative nature of her deeply intraconnected oeuvre, *The Blue Clerk* draws on intertextual references to the characters of Bola, Maya, and Kamena in her 1999 novel *At the Full and Change of the Moon* (albeit without naming them) and is a poetic version of the otherwise entirely unique genre of memoir/history/archival intervention she created with *A Map to the Door of No Return: Notes on Belonging* (2001). The index of *The Blue Clerk* presents the arbitrary nature of documentation in graphic form. Speaking of the book in an interview with Dionne Brand and Canisia Lubrin (2018), Brand remarks on the endeavor of collecting documents, saying, "This collecting is involuntary on the part of the clerk. And the clerk would rather not. The author has an archive; the clerk has a living library whose records are always undone, always changing. That living, breathing, elliptical, complicated, undone thing is [the subject of] the actual discussion that they're having."[9] The clerk's work is not methodical but random, and as Brand says in her interview with Hartman, "all coloniality is order" with the result that the disruption of referentiality both with regard to the archive and with regard to the contents of the versos and their index goes against the grain of coloniality.

Emphasizing the iterative dynamic of the book, Brand explains to Hartman how she wrote a poem that "could go on forever" and indeed the index illustrates this by weaving referentiality back and forth between the versos and their catalogued contents in the index—contents that range from the primary colors of the book (blue, violet, and lemon) to typical index content such as references to musicians, writers, and Brand's other books. As a wayward index, though, it also repeats such seemingly random points of reference as aphids, ladybirds, and the act of furrowing. In a note in the index, the clerk asks, "Why do you have this fetish with bibliography? It's the fever of coloniality, the author answers honestly for once" (238). Brand seems to be invoking Derrida's *Archive Fever* in this exchange, a foundational text on the pathology of compiling and endowing archival material with power.[10] As a feverish symptom, the wayward index to the versos creates a loop of referentiality that does not privilege either poetry or its catalogue as a primary versus secondary source.[11] Similarly, archival materials are not, in effect, "sources" so much as they are texts in play with the literary texts that invoke, interrogate, and challenge them in much the same way that Brand's index and poems both highlight and hide from one another. For example, the index draws attention to the frequent appearance of aphids in the poem, a detail that might go as unnoticed as the tiny creature to which it refers. And yet, the indexing and highlighting of aphids underscores that which is not indexed; of the seven versos indexed for aphids, one of them, verso 25.1, presents one of the most extended stories/memories in the entire book, a tale of an epic relay race among schoolgirls. The verso describes the drama of the race during which one of the girls drops the baton, and then the team's joy at a recovery and second-place finish. The clerk is witness to the race and celebration, and while her focus, too, is on the girls she at one point gives a sidelong glance at "the bales and the aphids and the midges and all the insects who had gathered on her papers" (146). Of this ecstatic memory, what is indexed, what is archived, is the aphid in the story's marginalia. The closing sentence of the verso comes from the clerk, who reflects on her appreciation of obituaries because "there was a lengthy life crushed into a few sentences as the author and the author's family would crush hers into parentheses" (148). The index crushes the verso's emotions and experiences into a small detail that, while not an inaccurate reference to the verso, absents the poem's meaning.

The interplay of index and text forms an element of what Beth A. McCoy and Jasmine Y. Montgomery (2019) have identified as an important dimension of Brand's work, her "peritext, Genette's term for authorial elements inserted into the interstices of the text" (McCoy and Montgomery 2019, 137). *The Blue Clerk* is of a pair with Brand's *A Map to the Door of No Return* in its peritextual strategies and in its interrogation of archives.[12] In their reading of *A Map to the Door of No Return*, McCoy and Montgomery look at the object of the book through Brand's concept of "the cognitive schema [of] captivity" (McCoy and Montgomery 131). They offer a reading of Brand's methods of leveraging the peritext to disrupt the "closure and containment" (McCoy and Montgomery 134) that a book's boundaries offer a reader. They point to her use of numbers as well as words for chapter titles, observing the way that in *A Map to the Door of No Return* Brand creates small anti-patterns of numerical series, some of which "stop at 4; at other times the series stops at 13. At 2. At 6 or at 10" (McCoy and Montgomery 137). *The Blue Clerk*'s peritext is all about numbers starting with its subtitle, *Ars Poetica in 59 Versos*. And yet it includes an additional, free-standing poem placed after the wayward index, a poem labeled as verso 33.1 that appears without context well after the 59th verso of the "59 Versos." The lingering poem breaks the progress from the opening "stipules" and first numbered verso, 1.1.01 to a concluding endpoint—particularly in light of the fact that verso 59 is followed by 59.1 and 59.2, indicating a continuing series that might or might not end at any point in spite of the given framework of 59 versos. Moreover, Brand breaks down many (but not all) of the verso numbers with iterative decimals in much the same way that she arranges number series in *A Map* to disorient rather than orient her reader.[13] Her 59 versos technically include 178 distinct prose poems including the introductory verses that are not numbered. McCoy and Montgomery, writing before the publication of *The Blue Clerk* but drawing on their notes from the same presentation with which I opened, turn to Brand's theorization of a book composed of inscribed right-hand pages and blank left-hand pages that pile up next to them (with all that is withheld) as a means of wrecking the cognitive schema of the book, its episteme.

Indeed, unlike the cognitive schema of most books, *The Blue Clerk* dispenses with narrative as an organizing principle. One way in which Brand does this is to explore the extent to which the archive is not a scaffolding for narrative but rather an element in shifting and changeable versions of the past. In 1.1.01 she interrogates another childhood memory about the local library "in a town by the sea," which she plays out against her grandfather's "logs and notebooks." She recalls "the white library with wide steps, but when I ask, there is no white library with wide steps, they tell me, but an ochre library at a corner with great steps leading up. What made me think it was a white library?" (8). This wonderful interrogation of the library, the very architectural vessel of records and texts—of cultural capital and power—is presented as a misremembered fragment from when the author was "agile and small" (9).[14] She free-associates her memory of the library with that of her grandfather and his extensive collection of notebooks in which he tracked purchases and merchandise as well as the sea and the rain: "he filled many logbooks with rain and its types: showers, sprinkles, deluges, slanted, boulders, pebbles, sheets, needles, slivers, pepper … *Relief rain* he wrote in his logbook in his small office, and the rain came in from the sea like pepper, then pebbles, then boulders" (10). The strands of memory and documentation come together at the end of the verso when the author "walked into the library and it was raining rain and my grandfather's logs were there, and the wooden window was open" (11). This verso captures Bastian's point that a "community of records" can be integral to the lived experience of community and communal memory in that the grandfather's records provide the author with a prompt for childhood memories. The dynamic between the logs and the memories is one of equivocation and not that of primary and secondary source material. The verso's closing line affirms this: "Now you sound like me, the clerk says. I am you, the author says" (11).

This expression is one of mutual wreckognition between the clerk and the author. Both work with the ruins of historical evidence, the clerk that of cunningly inscribed, crisp pages and the author with that of faulty memory. In a verso that includes multiple moments of mirroring between the author and the clerk, 16.3, the clerk brings the conversation to bear on the body as an archival site, musing, "I do know that the bodies that we inhabit now are corpses of the humanist narrative" (91). Casting the narrators themselves as figures in a state of decay, the clerk addresses the false wholeness attributed to bodies under the rubric of humanism, a school of thought that Europeans developed in the same historical moment that they institutionalized dehumanization during the height of the trans-Atlantic slave trade. Brand refers to bodies in terms of parts that do not make a sum, detailing feet, arms, legs, mouths, and vaginas along with muscle, fat, and bones. The author, referred to also as the poet in this verso, picks up on this gesture to say, "Well, I can only give you a glimpse of these bits and pieces of a body that has been deconstructed as itself, and reconstructed as a set of practices in un-freedom" (93). Their shared vision is one that perceives a lack of wholeness, the failure of humanism in the face of the history of slavery with its trade in and destruction of humans. In the face of the humanistic conceit that bodies map onto contained, sovereign individuals, the clerk scoffs at this "ethical development of a certain subject whom is not we" (91). Throughout the verso, the clerk and poet address what Julietta Singh, in *No Archive Will Restore You*, names "the body archive." She defines her own "body archive" as "an assembly of history's traces deposited in me" (Singh 2018, 29). Her discussion of the body archive focuses on the disintegration of bodily wholeness under the weight of affective flows anchored in but also in excess of the body. Singh also seems to invoke liberal humanism when she remarks, "the body archive is an attunement, a hopeful gathering, an act of love *against the foreclosure of reason*. It is a way of knowing the body-self as a becoming and unbecoming thing, of scrambling time and matter [...] of thinking-feeling the body's unbounded relation to other bodies" (Singh 2018, 29, emphasis mine). Similarly, the author and the clerk explore the affective interconnectivity of bodies in their exposure of "the death of a certain set of narratives, the death of the aesthetic of imperialism. It is an aesthetic that contains narratives of the body" (92) based in humanistic concepts. Their shared vision is one of wreckognition as they glance back at imperial and intellectual history and the "body that has been deconstructed as itself." Brand also emphasizes their bodily interconnectivity in the language of mirroring in this verso as when, "My job, it seems, is to notice, the clerk says. My job it seems is to notice, the author says" (91); "That is when I left you, the clerk says, that is when I created you, the author says, that is when I created you, the clerk says, that is when you left me, the author says" (91–2).

Beyond the verso's theme of bodily ruins and embodied archives, that of mutual wreckognition provides an exceptional depiction of how an archivist and an author might regard one another. The relationship between the archive and archivist is an active one. What is saved, and why, and by whom? What materials are catalogued and where are they kept? How is the material organized and labeled? Hartman makes this point in her reflections on how young Black women's lives "were under surveillance and targeted not only by the police but also by the sociologists and the reformers who gathered the information and made the case against them, forging their lives into tragic biographies of crime and pathology" (Hartman 2019, 236) from which she, as an author, had to wrest their stories, their subjectivity. An alliance between such an author and the pathologizing archival material with which she has to work seems unlikely. However, Brand's clerk is wreckognizable by her author because although she claims that "I can only collect" (53), she collects *that which is withheld*—a working subtitle Brand used for the book prior to its publication.[15] The blue clerk can be a genuine interlocuter because of her own powers of wreckognition: although she guards them closely and fusses over them, she sees that the bales of archival material are composed of blankness, that they are unwritten. In this way, the author's writing and the clerk's unwritten pages enter into a mutual production of memory. What is more, this mutual regard between author and clerk is a counter-archival move in the sense that it displaces archival material as a primary source, one that artistic engagements interpret or challenge secondarily. Along the same lines of the wayward index (Hartman) that reconfigures referentiality between primary and secondary sourcing in the format of the book as a whole, the wreckognition between author and clerk forms a relationship that does inherently counter-archival work by undoing the primary power of archival contents.

In Brand's eschewal of narrative arc in *The Blue Clerk*, she embraces an iterative vision of art and archiving as ongoing negotiations and processes. The porous, open-ended nature of the archive is something that Belle emphasizes in referring to it as "pastpresentfuture" (Belle et al. 2020, 35) and Singh speaks of envisioning a "future-archive" (35), both concepts that expand upon the archive's attachment to and ability to represent the past. As when: "the clerk climbs out, looks back at the dock, the freight, the whole enterprise, the temblous archive. When I was, ... the author begins. I hate the past, the clerk concludes that sentence" (180). Not only does the clerk reject any emphasis on the past in this passage, but Brand's neologism, temblous, points to the archive's impossibility, its partial existence, and its non-referentiality. The word also conjures the tremendous, tremulous, trembling waves of the sea in the stanza. Brand's deep engagement in *The Blue Clerk* with the relationship between archive and art, on both theoretical and poetic levels, redefines this crucial conversation within Caribbean art and literature.

At that 2013 presentation of her work in progress, Brand asked those of us in her audience to envision her book as an art object. The book's structure with its blank left-hand pages was meant to signify visually as well as poetically. I have thus always thought of *The Blue Clerk* as a work of visual art and its appearance in print corroborated its status as such: the book is so beautiful that it became my first ever coffee-table book along with Brand's similarly stunning novel *Theory*, both of which were designed by C. S. Richardson, who won a major book design award for *The Blue Clerk* in 2018.[16] Given the ontological significance of the book as an object, as demonstrated by McCoy and Montgomery, the design schema of Brand's book aptly mirrors its conversations and debates about the role of archives in art. The cover indicates bound paper—paper that may be inscribed or, depending on how you look at it, may provide a blank background image on which the publisher stamped the title, subtitle, and author's name. Given *The Blue Clerk*'s multi-tiered and comprehensive engagement with its own artistry, I was astonished and thrilled to see it on the wall of the Whitney Museum in a painting by Cauleen Smith.[17] Part of her series entitled *Mutualities*, in which Smith reflects on memory and African diasporic histories, the painting is of a copy of *The Blue Clerk* being held up and cradled in strong brown hands. As a further iteration of Brand's endlessly iterative poetry, the painting archives the book in an ongoing project of citing Black and Indigenous women's work and creating an interconnected body of referentiality, an open-ended wayward index that exceeds any single text. Entitled "Natalie holds Dionne Brand," the painting is one in a series, *Firespitters*, of writers holding up a work that inspires them, and Brand's book is held by Mojave American poet Natalie Diaz. The Whitney catalogue describes this image as the essence of Smith's exhibition in that it is designed to witness "the embodied labor of literary production" and "the notion of mutuality that is at the crux of this exhibition."[18] *The Blue Clerk* arises from mutualities as well—mutual mistrust, mutual frustration, mutual commitments, and mutual wreckognition of the pastpresentfuture (Belle) nature of counter-archival art. This is a comment that Brand has made in several interviews, that the clerk lives in time—in the perpetual present—exclusive of place. Indeed, she includes no geographical references in *The Blue Clerk* in contrast to the narrative position she creates in *A Map to the Door of No Return* of the perpetual traveler, the visitor to multiple continents. These two works explore an underlying crossroads of Caribbean space and time insofar as the earlier memoir maps out geographies and draws heavily on the archives to trace journeys both imperial and decolonial. Brand's emphasis on global routes and passageways in *A Map* shifts in the later book with the inclusion of the clerk, for "The clerk lives in time like this, several and simultaneous. The author lives in place and not in time. Weighted. In place" (135). The recognition between the clerk, who states "I would like therefore, to live in time, and not in space," (135) and the "weighted" author occurs at a Caribbean axis that Brand explores in much of her work. If *A Map* is Brand's memoir about how history is a place on the map, *The Blue Clerk* is about how a haunting past occupies our ever-unfolding present moment in time.

Acknowledgments I would like to thank Cauleen Smith for her generosity in sharing her work and allowing me to publish a photo of her beautiful painting.

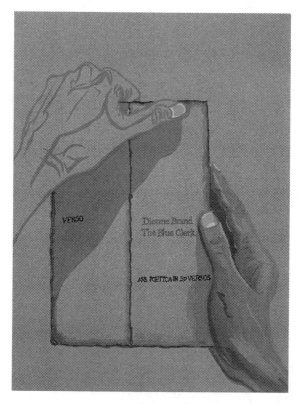

Artist/copyright holder: Cauleen Smith. Photo credit: Matthew Sherman

Notes

1. Conference of the Northeast Modern Language Association, Keynote address: "The Versos of the Blue Clerk, or What is Withheld," Boston, March 2, 2013.
2. Christina Sharpe argues in *In the Wake: On Blackness and Being* that annotation (along with redaction) is an "anagrammatical" strategy essential to disrupting the "dysgraphia" of anti-Blackness (Sharpe 2016, 123). Her practice of redaction also demonstrates how to read the archive as a body of non-representation, as she cuts away at archival photographs and contemporary journalism alike to try to excavate Black experience and expression.

3. This is true only of institutionalized archives—materials logged in libraries and government buildings. Archival material can manifest in any number of affective or embodied forms as well as in cultural praxis that far exceeds written record.
4. I am grateful to Odile Ferly for her prompt to connect what Stoler says about colonial "debris" with the topic of monuments, for one of the ways in which imperial ruins "contour" contemporary life is through their imprint in public space in the form of monuments and memorials. Confederate and colonial monuments that have been torn down in the U.S., Canada, the Caribbean, and Europe in 2020 when they became widely recognized as the emblems of white supremacy that they are, figure as debris left over from violent regimes; the fact that several of them were literally broken by those who tore them down—reduced to a state of physical ruin—reiterates their status as such.
5. In some other examples of Cliff's presentation of the creolized etymology of ruination/ruinate, she opens *Into the Interior* with a description of "the landscape, real and imagined, ordered and ruinate, kept it so. Traces of heresies overcome with green" (Cliff 2010, 3) and she refers to the surroundings of Annie Christmas's secretive dwelling in *Free Enterprise* as "strung with escaped, ruinate green, gray-green, blue-green, river-nourished green" (Cliff 1993, 185).
6. European nations usually took any colonial records they had generated to Europe upon exiting a colony, whether because they did not want their successor colonial power to have access to information or, as Bastian argues in the case of England, to avoid embarrassment over the slave societies they had established and perpetrated for centuries. The British removed over 20,000 administrative files from 37 colonies at the end of their imperial reign and sent them to England to be literally hidden away in closed archives on the eve of Caribbean and African nations' independence in the mid-twentieth century (Bastian et al. 2018, 22). Bastian points out that many of these materials were not only removed from the Caribbean but they were made unavailable to researchers for decades. By her count, over 1000 items are still closed to the public and other records have been destroyed (Bastian et al. 2018, 22).
7. Tobago was among the Caribbean countries, including the Virgin Islands, Antigua, and St. Kitts, where the Moravian Church established significant settlements in the eighteenth century.
8. Dionne Brand and Saidiya Hartman in conversation, Barnard University, October 30, 2018.
9. https://quillandquire.com/omni/qa-canisia-lubrin-speaks-to-dionne-brand-about-her-two-new-books-the-blue-clerk-and-theory/

10. Brand (2018) also riffs on another canonical theorist synonymous with archival work, Foucault: in verso 16.7 she writes, "If you say Foucault here, the clerk arrives brimming, you will be understood. By whom, says the author. By those you want to understand, says the clerk" (97).

11. This dynamic also theorizes the large body of Caribbean literature that engages the archive by exploring artistic and imaginative pathways through the past that flow from and around sparse and dehumanizing records.

12. I argue elsewhere that Brand draws upon archival materials from the trans-Atlantic slave trade in order to break them open to the ongoing production of knowledge occurring in literary texts and contemporary journalism alike ("Building the Neo-Archive in Dionne Brand's *A Door to the Map of No Return*," *Meridians: race, class, transnationalism* 12.1 [2014]).

13. A thank you to Tegan Zimmerman for the great point that, as per Brand's emphasis on the intertextual nature of her non-fiction in *The Blue Clerk* and *A Map*, this deliberate disorientation is something that she explores in her fiction as well. Kamena, in *At the Full and Change of the Moon*, attempts to retrace a path he once took to a Maroon settlement that eludes him later on. He returns from his reconnaissance journeys not with more, but with less and less information, asking his daughter to "hold" whatever details he gleans after each try; his last request to "hold this: '---'."

14. Brand's misremembered library also resonates with Jamaica Kincaid's ruined library in *A Small Place* (1988), in which the local library is closed off and neglected for years after an earthquake and labeled with a seemingly permanent sign saying "repairs pending." The presentation of libraries as unreliable or broken structures has the effect of questioning their colonial contents.

15. Brand shared this subtitle with her audience during the reading I mention at the top of this piece, at the 2013 Northeast Modern Language Association meeting.

16. Richardson won the Alcuin Society Award for Excellence in Book Design in Canada in 2018 for his design of *The Blue Clerk*.

17. Whitney Museum of American Art, New York, NY, February 23, 2020.

18. https://whitney.org/exhibitions/cauleen-smith?section=3&subsection=1#exhibition-artworks

References

Bastian, Jeannette A., John A. Aarons, and Stanley H. Griffin, eds. 2018. *Decolonizing the Caribbean Record: An Archives Reader*. Sacramento: Library Juice Press.

Bastian, Jeanette Allis. 2003. *Owning Memory: How a Caribbean Community Lost Its Archives and Found Its History*. Santa Barbara: Libraries Unlimited.

Belle, La Vaughn, Zayaan Khan, Holly A. Smith, and Julietta Singh. 2020. Experimentations with the Archive: A Roundtable Conversation. *Feminist Review* 125: 17–37.

Brand, Dionne. 1999. *At the Full and Change of the Moon*. New York: Grove Press.

———. 2001. *A Map to the Door of No Return: Notes to Belonging*. New York: Doubleday.

———. 2018. *The Blue Clerk: Ars Poetica in 59 Versos*. Durham: Duke University Press.

Brand, Dionne and Canisia Lubrin. 2018. Q and A: Canisia Lubrin Speaks to Dionne Brand about her two new books. *The Blue Clerk* and *Theory. Quill and Quire*. n. p. 13 September.

Cliff, Michelle. 1993. *Free Enterprise*. San Francisco: City Lights Publishers.

———. 1996 [1987]. *No Telephone to Heaven*. New York: Plume Press.

———. 2010. *Into the Interior*. Minneapolis: University of Minnesota Press.

Hartman, Saidiya. 2008. Venus in Two Acts. *Small Axe* 12 (2): 1–14.

———. 2018. "Reading of *The Blue Clerk* by Dionne Brand Followed by a Conversation with Saidiya Hartman." Barnard Institute for Research on Women, Barnard College, October 30, 2018.

———. 2019. *Wayward Lives, Beautiful Experiments: Intimate Histories of Riotous Black Girls, Troublesome Women, and Queer Radicals*. New York: Norton.

McCoy, Beth A., and Jasmine Y. Montgomery. 2019. Dionne Brand's *A Map to the Door of No Return* and the Antiblackness of the Book as an Object. In *Against a Sharp White Background*, ed. Brigitte Fielder and Jonathan Senchyne, 131–146. Madison: University of Wisconsin Press.

Pemberton, Rita. 2018. Distant, Damaged, Destroyed and/or Disappearing: The Archival Records of Tobago. In *Decolonizing the Caribbean Record: An Archives Reader*, ed. Jeannette A. Bastian et al., 271–92, ibid.

Sang, Roma Wong. 2018. Building an Inclusive Past, Democratizing Heritage: An Evaluation of Community Record Keeping and Its Potential for Shaping Identity in Trinidad and Tobago. In *Decolonizing the Caribbean Record: An Archives Reader*, ed. by Jeannette Bastian et al., 585–616, ibid.

Sharpe, Christina. 2016. *In the Wake: On Blackness and Being*. Durham: Duke University Press.

Singh, Julietta. 2018. *No Archive Will Restore You*. Santa Barbara: Punctum Press.

Stoler, Ann Laura. 2016. *Duress: Imperial Durabilities in Our Time*. Durham: Duke University Press.

———, ed. 2013. *Imperial Debris: On Ruins and Ruination*. Durham: Duke University Press.

Open Access This chapter is licensed under the terms of the Creative Commons Attribution 4.0 International License (http://creativecommons.org/licenses/by/4.0/), which permits use, sharing, adaptation, distribution and reproduction in any medium or format, as long as you give appropriate credit to the original author(s) and the source, provide a link to the Creative Commons licence and indicate if changes were made.

The images or other third party material in this chapter are included in the chapter's Creative Commons licence, unless indicated otherwise in a credit line to the material. If material is not included in the chapter's Creative Commons licence and your intended use is not permitted by statutory regulation or exceeds the permitted use, you will need to obtain permission directly from the copyright holder.

CHAPTER 4

Past Histories and Present Realities: The Paradox of Time and the Ritual of Performance in Mayra Santos Febres' *Fe en disfraz*

Nicole Roberts

Afro-Puerto Rican author Mayra Santos Febres' novel *Fe en disfraz* (2009) presents a bold examination of the consequences of sexual exploitation and abuse on black women during enslavement and the implications for contemporary society, a topic which continues to be under-explored in Puerto Rican and Latin American narrative. In the novel, Santos Febres invokes historical memory so as to re/present ideas surrounding time and the way in which black women's lives were systemically eclipsed from the Puerto Rican landscape. In just 115 pages, and set in twenty-first-century USA, the story recounts the tale of Fe Verdejo, an Afro-Venezuelan historian who, while researching in a Chicago library, encounters several documents that connect the reader to black, female, Latin-American enslaved women of the eighteenth century. Indeed, despite its brevity and although

N. Roberts (✉)
The University of the West Indies, St. Augustine, Trinidad and Tobago
e-mail: Nicole.Roberts@sta.uwi.edu

© The Author(s) 2023
O. Ferly, T. Zimmerman (eds.), *Chronotropics*,
https://doi.org/10.1007/978-3-031-32111-5_4

65

it makes no specific mention of the history of enslavement in Puerto Rico, the novel manages to faithfully document the lived experiences of the enslaved (particularly women and children) across Latin America and the Caribbean.

This chapter argues that through an analysis of Santos Febres' imagined (or re/invented) historical past as well as Fe's life story, we are able to understand the brutal and dehumanizing nature of enslavement and the inherited sense of powerlessness among blacks which in turn redound to an understanding of the present-day realization of Caribbean societies, specifically Puerto Rico. In addition, this chapter examines the way in which Santos Febres' play with time reveals the black female body to be a site of cultural inscription while at the same time one of resilience, thus foregrounding the centrality of this black female writer to contemporary Puerto Rican society.

Much of Santos Febres' work centers on gender and sexuality, and this novel is no exception. However, *Fe en disfraz* distinguishes itself from her other works because it makes clear the history of blacks, that is, the African history of blacks in Latin America and in so doing, it foregrounds the positionality of blackness to the Puerto Rican landscape. This type of imaginative memorializing of the past is important today not simply because of the gaps in historical and official records regarding enslaved persons, but also because it provokes the reader to question official representations of blackness. Ultimately, this lacuna in the documentation of atrocities during enslavement is precisely what the novel seeks to remediate.

Fe en disfraz recounts the brief, intense relationship between the first-person narrator Martín Tirado, a white Puerto Rican, and the Afro-Venezuelan historian María Fernanda Verdejo, whose lives come together at the University of Chicago. Race is a constant concern in the novel although it is also true to state that Santos Febres does not specifically center it above other concerns such as gender, violence, and trauma. Martín Tirado is a computer scientist who leads a typically mundane life, and has a white Puerto Rican girlfriend, Agnes, who is a linguist in Madrid. However, Martín's life changes radically and irrevocably following his move to work on a project in Chicago, which is where he meets the Afro-Venezuelan scholar. They begin a somewhat sordid relationship based on pain and passion. Their intense relationship serves to painfully reconstruct the lives of black enslaved women and thus underscore their impact on society. We can argue that Fe and Martín's relationship is founded on historical relations, their love itself an historical experience while at the same time, the sexual sadism of their union highlights the repressive background of enslavement which they seek to document in an exhibition. Their sexual acts are described in great detail throughout the novel and their ritualistic nature serves to evoke the original trauma experienced by many enslaved black women. For Santos Febres, the erotic is intertwined with history in the present and in past time. In an echo of T.S. Eliot's poem "Burnt Norton" the first of *The Four Quartets*, in which all time is eternally present, Santos Febres consistently blurs time in the novel. Similarly, she also blurs geographical boundaries. By presenting Fe as Afro-Venezuelan and not Puerto Rican, she removes the memory of the specific Puerto Rican past and later as Fe's research uncovers Venezuelan, Brazilian, Puerto Rican, and Costa Rican women, Santos Febres forces the reader to reflect on the legacy of enslavement across the entire Latin American region, including Puerto Rico.

Through the work in Chicago, and following the finding of the various documents which relate to eighteenth-century, black, Latin American, enslaved women, the research trail takes Fe to Brazil where she makes the biggest find of all; the luxurious dress which Xica da Silva, a woman enslaved at birth who later gained her freedom, wore in an attempt to assimilate into the powerful white society of the time. The dress is a pale yellow with decorative lace trimming. It is a dress for a mulatto woman who wants to blend in as a white woman in society. Irresistibly attracted to the beautiful outfit, da Silva thinks that using it is the only way to be able to relate to others but more importantly to accept herself. Fe had found the dress in a convent and the Mother Superior had warned her to never wear it because it had witnessed many sorrows. However, Fe puts on the dress in Chicago on every Halloween. Adorned with the dress, Fe's body becomes an allegory for the colonial past. And so it is that Fe's relationship with Martín changes every 31 October when she dons the disguise of a formerly enslaved black woman striving to be accepted into white Brazilian society. This is the point when Fe Verdejo and Xica da Silva become one and the same woman. Like Xica da Silva and all black women past and present, Fe displays the collective pain of generations of black women, the history of violence wreaked upon them, and internalized by them. As Valladares-Ruiz (2016) acknowledges, "Fe—conocedora de estos antecedentes y desatendiendo las recomendaciones de la monja—se apropia del traje y hace de él un *lugar de memoria*" (601). [Fe—aware of the background and disregarding the nun's recommendations—appropriates the dress and makes it a site of memory]. In the narration, Santos Febres constantly plays with the momentary blurred space which exists in between pain and pleasure.

Ironically it is in the darkness of Halloween that Fe brings the stories of enslavement to light. Interestingly too, the novel's title *Fe en disfraz* is metaphoric as it presents the idea of skin as a costume. Skin (specifically skin color) is what connects the protagonist Fe Verdejo to the ancestors. But Xica has a dual identity: her connection is not solely to the enslaved black ancestors but also to the white enslavers.

However, when Fe puts on the dress, she assimilates into the night, she becomes one with the carnivalesque masquerade. Santos Febres describes in great detail the beauty of the golden yellow silk dress adorned with rhinestones and pearls. The dress becomes costume and masks Fe's real self. It is as if Xica's spirit possesses her. At the same time, we also learn that the wires of the harness in place to keep the shape of the dress are corroded and scrape and slice small cuts into Fe's skin as she walks. The pain inflicted by the movement of the dress is a constant reminder to Fe that she can never fully blend in, in much the same way that Xica da Silva was ultimately unable to assimilate despite her love for her former enslaver. Fe's Halloween masquerade moves us back in time to see the history of various enslaved women over the decades who struggled to overcome the exploitative laboring conditions and sexual abuse, to surmount the male enslavers whose attraction to them came at all costs, and to disguise and hide their skin which ultimately became a symbol of pain. Through the dress, Santos Febres shows us that these narratives of pain are intergenerational and again reinforces the notion that traumatic remnants from the past continue to affect black women's lives today.

At the same time, by making Martín Tirado a white Puerto Rican man and the narrator of the tale, Santos Febres sets him up to be the "official" source of information for the reader. The novel is told from Martín's point of view and this reinforces the notion that history is told from specific perspectives (white, male, upper class, heteronormative). Santos Febres' choice of Martín as the narrator of the story is a critique of the bias of official historical narratives in Puerto Rico and across Latin America. Through Martín, we realize the author's play with narrative and her subtle questioning of who precisely gets to tell official stories, and how they are told, especially where Afro-Puerto Ricans are concerned. In a similar vein, in his essay "Desiring Colonial Bodies in Mayra Santos Febres' *Fe en disfraz*," Victor Figueroa points out:

the text insists, history is never evoked from a neutral, objective position. Even historians write—or, to use Hayden White's now classic formulation, "emplot" their historical narratives—from specific locations and moments, with their concomitant political agendas and ideological compromises or commitments. (Figueroa 2017, 56)

In the novel Santos Febres does not make a direct statement about blacks in Puerto Rico but rather she forces the reader to consider the ways in which blackness has been essentialized as negative across Latin America and in so doing, she reminds the reader that this association of blackness with negativity also exists in Puerto Rico. Moreover, official narratives traditionally silence black history and represent slavery as milder in Puerto Rico and indeed throughout the Hispanic world (Godreau et al. 2008, 119). Jamaican critic Erna Brodber critically reflects on the relationship between the white master and the black enslaved female. She posits that:

Our question here is not whether there is genuine affection between slave and master or whether the relationship was crassly developed with ulterior motives; the issue is, what the relationship does to the liberation process. (Brodber, 28)

Here Brodber points out that the effects of slavery and slave/master relationships are not just difficult to understand in part because the black is psychically debilitated by being forced to negate her blackness but also that these relationships must be examined if we are to recognize the pain of degradation and dehumanization that is the legacy of the enslavement of blacks across the Caribbean.

Santos Febres centers the reader on the absence of information surrounding enslaved Africans. In fact, at the end of the novel Santos Febres leaves a poignant Nota de la autora (Author's note) in which she describes everything in her narrative as a mixed bag of sources. She tells the reader:

Fe en disfraz es muchas cosas, pero, también, es una novela acerca de la memoria, de la herida que es recordar. Está montada sobre documentos falsos, falsificados, reescritos con retazos de declaraciones de esclavos que recogí de múltiples fuentes primarias y secundarias; que recombiné, traduje o que, francamente, inventé. (Nota de la autora)

[*Faith in Disguise* is many things, but it is also a novel about memory, of the wound that is to remember. It is mounted on false, falsified documents, rewritten with snippets of statements of slaves that I collected from multiple primary and secondary sources; that I reassembled, translated or, frankly, invented.] (Author's note.)

The author's machinations with the material found in her research, tantamount to archival disruption, underscore the thorny issue of the lacuna in historical documentation regarding enslaved blacks but perhaps also serve to remove any direct confrontation with the Puerto Rican public. At the same time, this could show how Santos Febres may herself be grappling with the harshness of black history in her own interrogation as a black woman.

Additionally, there is a possible parodic intent behind the author's choice of job for Martín, as a digital archivist. She explicitly tasks this white man with digitizing and preserving the records of black enslaved women in the twenty-first century when mere decades earlier, Puerto Rico's clear embracing of *mestizaje* as the way forward for the Puerto Rican nation was meant to rid it of its black past (Godreau 2006, 182). Thus, a previously erased past is not simply being re-written but is being documented and digitized so as to make a permanent record of these enslaved women and ironically, this is being done by a white male. Martín's role is not merely to liberate Fe, but it is also to rewrite and to right history, by making a permanent record. The ancestral pain of slavery is remembered, and the wound is sealed by the very act of reminding us that the past is not dead. It is only through remembrance that we learn to accept the past. Martín tells us:

Soy algo así como un investigador virtual. Hago la mismísima tarea del monje escribe, pero en tiempos cibernéticos. Recompongo (e ilustro) fragmentos del pasado. Los ofrezco al presente en tiempo hiperreal, un tiempo que pretende burlar la muerte de lo orgánico, la quietud del papel, la lentitud de los hechos (17).

[I am a kind of virtual researcher. I do the same work as a scribe, but in cyber times. I recompose (and illustrate) fragments of the past. I offer them to the present in hyper-real time, a time that aims to circumvent the death of the organic, the stillness of paper, the slow pace of events.]

4 PAST HISTORIES AND PRESENT REALITIES: THE PARADOX OF TIME... 71

During the time that Martín is assisting Fe in digitizing the legal papers and manuscripts which she has found at the library in Chicago, they find documents which reveal information about the history of enslavement in Latin America. In the exhibition and on the website, Martín serves to give direction and, in a way, imparts value to the documents and the artifacts in the digitizing process. He rewrites history in much the same way that Santos Febres herself invents the narrative of the novel, both working to impart significance and meaning to the historical events described. For the exhibition, Martín writes explanatory notes and illustrations. He seeks to add in music and in this way rewrite the narrative by injecting his own white perspective. He says to Fe: "Quizás sea bueno armar algo con movimiento: un hipertexto con animación y música de Liszt o, quizás música de cámara" (51–52). [Perhaps it would be good to include movement: a hypertext with animation and music by Liszt, or maybe Chamber music.]

Through the inclusion of the sound effects and specifically classical music, Martín subtly shifts the audience's thinking away from the brutality effected on the black enslaved subjects, to one of soothing entertainment but through a westernized framing of the world. So that the harshness of slavery is not memorialized through the exhibition but rather, the lack of sensitivity clearly shows the reader the ways in which white, European privilege continues to dehumanize blacks till today. Contradictorily, Santos Febres' most interesting bid to positively reconstitute the image of enslaved Africans occurs when Martín, in seeking to find some images of the enslaved, is told by Fe that these were few and occurred either in the event of a necessary sale, or when a crime had been committed, or in a few pornographic photos. Despite Fe's comments, Martín repeatedly reflects aloud on what the women would have looked like. It is only with Fe's cryptic response indicating that the enslaved women would have looked exactly like her, that Martín connects the past and the present. According to Joy De Gruy (2017) it is at this point that the cognitive dissonance that is associated with slavery comes to the fore as Martín regains a sense of humanity. He says:

> Me quedé mirando a Fe, en silencio. Curiosamente, nunca antes me había detenido a pensar que sus esclavas se le parecieran. Que ella, presente y ante mí, tuviera la misma tez, el mismo cuerpo que una esclava agredida hace más de doscientos años. Que el objeto de su estudio estuviera tan cerca de su piel. (53)

[I remained looking at Fe, in silence. Curiously, I had never before stopped to think that her slaves would have resembled her. That she, present before me, would have had the same skin, the same body as an abused slave over two hundred years ago. That the object of her research would have been so close to her skin.]

In these few words, Martín acknowledges that as a white man, he experiences the world in a very different manner to Fe, a black woman. His life experience has separated him from her. He would not have had to strive for acceptance as did Fe at the convent that she attended. His whiteness would have assured him full inclusion at school while earning him a certain privilege.

Clearly the novel's main thrust is the comprehensive documentation of the experiences of the enslaved blacks (particularly women and children) across Latin America and the Caribbean. This seems to contrast ironically with Santos Febres' choice of digitizing the records. In the twenty-first century, digital records most definitely suggest permanence yet this notion is at odds with the records of enslavement and the trade which have been destroyed, lost, or were never properly recorded. Santos Febres underscores the idea that it is impossible to comprehensively, faithfully, and/or truthfully re-create the experience of the enslaved. In critically thinking about issues surrounding the abuse of enslaved women, Santos Febres is forced to re-create history given the lacuna of information which she (much like Fe, the character) finds when researching the black experience of the era. Interestingly, throughout the novel she seeks to correct ideas and long-held, false assumptions of the past and of these enslaved black women by constantly playing with notions of past and present realities. As Patricia Valladares-Ruiz points out:

En la novela de Santos-Febres el acto liberador no ocurre en el espacio colonial—como consecuencia de la abolición—, sino en el presente, como resultado de la reinterpretación de las relaciones de poder definidas por el sistema de jerarquías raciales. (Valladares-Ruiz 2016, 599)

[In Santos Febres' novel, the liberating act does not occur in the colonial space—as a result of abolition—, but rather in the present, as a result of the reinterpreting of the relations of power defined by the system of racial hierarchies.]

In her seminal study *Common Threads: Themes in Afro-Hispanic Women's Literature*, Clementina R. Adams (1998) suggests: "What is important in labeling a writer Afro-Hispanic is the degree to which she finds the African roots and their influence to be an important part of her humanity" (21). The manifestation of this humanism is evident in *Fe en disfraz*. From the start, Fe Verdejo's fortuitous encounter with Martín Tirado and similarly her chance finding of the historical documents relating to the enslaved empowers her as an historical agent and presents the reader with a more humanistic view of the liberation of Afro-Puerto Ricans. Santos Febres does not suggest that this is unique to Puerto Rico. But as a black woman, and given the paucity of information in terms of documented historical records, she sets about making these enslaved women more real to the reader through Fe's eyes. And through her narrative, Santos Febres ensures that the reader grasps the vast importance of Fe's project specifically to black people in the Hispanic Caribbean in the twenty-first century. The project at the museum brings a deep level of consciousness to their humanity. In this, Santos Febres seems to concur with other Caribbean thinkers, for example Hall (1999), who speaks of the self that is constructed by narratives (16). Erna Brodber (2003) also distinctively presents the case of Jamaica where she argues that slaves were "denied their humanity and this unto perpetuity" (13) but that this wrong can be made right through re-representations and interrogations of the myths of slavery which currently exist.

There can be no doubt that her own identity markers as black and female influence Santos Febres' presentation of the positive recuperation and reconstruction of black identity among the women who populate the story, chief among them Fe Verdejo. It is through her character that Santos Febres presents the black female bodyscape. From the inception of the tale, Fe is performing identity. It is the 31st October and Halloween marks the remembrances of the dead, a liminal time when pagans felt that the souls of the dead revisited the earth. Santos Febres uses this notion of pagan ritual to demonstrate identity as performative. Specifically, she describes the moments of performance as comparative with resistance and she further captures the ways in which Fe's black female body is consumed. Martín, Fe's white lover, must carry out the acts of cleansing, as mandated by Fe, before his trysts with her. She demands it. Martín's rituals are described in minute detail and in a way, they challenge the notion of the patriarchy as he is in fact performing for Fe in a strange reversal of patriarchal and colonial logic. That is, as Radost A. Rangelova (2012) signals, Fe "fashions her relationship with Martín to invert, physically and symbolically, the gender and racial hierarchies of power revealed through slave narratives. In this way, she becomes a model of black feminine agency" (154). Sex is realized throughout the novel as an extraordinary primal force. Santos Febres uses carnal desire in an attempt to articulate an historical vision of the erotic and at the same time effect a significant liberation. Martín says:

> Alcanzo la navaja toledana, la que me regaló Fe durante aquel distante viaje. La acerco a mi pubis. Afeito primero las comisuras de la ingle; después, sobre el monte enmarañado que la cubre. Paso a librar de vellos la base, halo para estirar la piel aún más. Boca de Fe llegando hasta esa piel doblemente desnuda, sensible por el roce de la navaja. (15)

> [I reach for the Toledo knife, the one that Faith gave me during that distant trip. I bring it closer to my pubis. I shave the corners of my groin first; later, the tangled mound that covers it. I move on to rid the base of hair, I pull down to stretch the skin even more. Fe's mouth reaching that doubly naked skin, sensitive from the brush of the knife.]

The eroticism in Santos Febres' novel affirms Martín as the object of desire and endows Fe at all times with dominance and at the same time a level of dignity. This is significant as Fe, a contemporary, black woman is finally able to recuperate some worth. Through the symbolism of the title as well as its theme, *Fe en disfraz* plays with the reader's understanding of the idea of the purity of love and that of the erotic. Santos Febres uses an almost gothic element to describe the relationship between Fe and Martín. She discards any sense of abstractness normally related to love conventions in the European tradition and presents the total carnality of the human experience of love. Fe is all woman and is always presented in the context of the materiality of a real woman. In a twisting of history, Fe is always fiercely empowered. As Figueroa cogently argues:

> For sexuality in the novel is not merely a metaphor or symbol for something else that needs to be brought up to the light. Sexuality and other affects are themselves, in Deleuzian fashion and by virtue of their being forms of desire, vehicles in the struggle for liberation, and spheres that need to be liberated in their own right. (Figueroa 2017, 59)

In a sense this highlights again Brodber's questioning of the impact of the relationship. Fe is central to the liberation process because unlike enslaved women such as Diamantina (described in chapter III) or even free blacks such as Xica, she holds power. As a result of her performances in the sex acts with Martín, Fe is not seeking integration to his group. Rather, Fe's use of Martín's body is an effort to undo past trauma. At the psychic level, she remains grounded in her blackness as much as in her sexuality. Fe does more than simply show resistance to patriarchal structures of oppression. From childhood she is acutely aware of her role as a black woman. She chooses education as her route to success and a sure way out of the constraints of the past. She was not going to repeat the errors of her mother with an early pregnancy. Through her choice of education, Fe alters her historical path out of poverty and into success. Fe's body represents the past history of her African ancestry while at the same time her intellect stands for the future. Although it is Martín who narrates, we see clearly that Fe is the mind behind the exhibition who will rewrite the historical, colonial representation of black enslaved women in much the same way that Santos Febres has chosen to rewrite this history. At the same time, as we have previously indicated, by demanding certain role play of Martín in terms of their relationship and especially his submission during the sex act, Fe is able to shed the domination enacted on black bodies for centuries.

As with time, the notion of personal identity also becomes tremendously blurred in the novel as Fe comes to represent all black women. While in Chicago, she prepares for the exhibition about enslaved women, she notes the abuses inflicted on them. They are beaten, violently assaulted, raped, and their psychological damage ranging from loneliness to psychotic trauma is documented. This documentation occurs through the artifacts found of the enslaved women themselves which are central to an understanding of the historical relevance of the stories especially as Fe is unable to find pictorial evidence. Notably, Santos Febres appears to point out that the Anglophone Caribbean seems to have extremely well-documented historical testimonies, unlike the absence in the Hispanic Caribbean. Martín reveals:

> En inglés, existen miles de declaraciones de esclavos que dan su testimonio en contra de la esclavitud. Mujeres educadas que formaban parte de sociedades abolicionistas les enseñaban a leer y a escribir, recogían sus palabras y, luego, financiaban la publicación de esos testimonios para que el público

conociera los terrores de la trata. Oludah Equiano, Harriet Jacobs, Mary Prince, Frederich Douglass, esclavos con nombres y apellidos, contaron el infierno de sus vidas bajo el yugo de la esclavitud. En español, por el contrario, fuera de las memorias del cubano Juan Manzano o del testimonio *Cimarrón* de Miguel Barnet, no existe ninguna narrativa de esclavos; menos aún, de esclavas. (22–23)

[In English, there are thousands of statements by slaves giving their testimony against slavery. Educated women who were part of abolitionist societies taught them to read and write, collected their words, and then financed the publication of those testimonies so that the public knew the terrors of trafficking. Oludah Equiano, Harriet Jacobs, Mary Prince, Frederick Douglass, slaves with first and last names, told of the hell of their lives under the yoke of slavery. In Spanish, on the contrary, apart from the memoirs of the Cuban Juan Manzano or the *Cimarrón* testimonio of Miguel Barnet, there is no narrative of slaves; even less so, of slave women.]

In this, Martín signals a time and a place where slaves had names and surnames, that is to say, their own identities. Paradoxically, their personal situations are no less difficult but the suggestion is that there was a spirit of resistance among the enslaved in the English Caribbean and the US that was not to be found in the Spanish Caribbean. This notion tallies with the idea commonly found in Puerto Rico that the institution of slavery in the Hispanic Caribbean was somehow more benign than that experienced in territories of other colonial powers.

Intriguingly, the collection that Fe finds carries no title. This also centers the idea of naming, or lack thereof and forces the reader to consider history's inability to ever fully represent the vicissitudes of enslavement. Nevertheless, Fe and Martín's ability to create the exhibition and website presents a way in which to share enslaved experiences despite the weight of historical erasure. Santos Febres not only documents the treatment and suffering of these enslaved persons but she is able to force the reader to actively engage in the lives of these persons in a more powerful manner than the reader of a testimony such as the very descriptive *Biografía de un cimarrón* (1993) by Miguel Barnet. And even though one might contest the accuracy of the account, the images evoked present a clear picture of the brutality, the violence, and the trauma in the lives of the black enslaved women but perhaps more importantly, Fe documents the very existence of these women, many of whom were erased from historical records. Thus,

4 PAST HISTORIES AND PRESENT REALITIES: THE PARADOX OF TIME... 77

she manages to fill the gaps left by the Eurocentric, openly racist historiography which abound in the New World.

In historical scholarship, there is a tendency to essentialize the enslaved African. She/he is seen either as victim or as rebel. This type of categorization does not capture the experiences or indeed the at-times difficult choices that enslaved people have been forced to make. Santos Febres centers on the effects of exploitation of the black female body. Indeed, the erotic description of the torrid relationship between the two characters of Martín and Fe presents almost phantasmatic accounts of bodily being. Martín describes: "Tirados en el suelo, yo le curaba con mi lengua un rasguño en el hombro. La sangre de Fe sabía a minerales derretidos. Acabábamos de hacer el amor" (24). [Lying on the ground, I would cure a scratch on her shoulder with my tongue. Fe's blood tasted of melted minerals. We had just made love.] Here Martín's power and domination as a white male are shed as he becomes a part of the healing process. Martín's desire for Fe and Santos Febres' emphasis on the various body parts both serve to emphasize the past injustices which endure to today. They echo the idea of the body and blood of remembrance of Christ's suffering which of course constantly reaffirm our very existence, that is, the present:

> Los ancestros son la duplicidad y la contradicción. Los ancestros (y el acopio de sus saberes) son lo que nos fija en el tiempo. Esas largas genealogías de muertos intentan trazar una línea que, atravesando una masa informe de cuerpos, se desplaza por el espacio infinito. Eso es la Historia, una tenue línea que va uniendo en el aire a los ancestros —a esos pobres animales sacrificados en la pira del tiempo—. (92)

> [The ancestors are duplicity and contradiction. The ancestors (and the sum of their knowledge) are what fixes us in time. These long genealogies of the dead try to draw a line that, crossing a shapeless mass of bodies, travels through infinite space. That is History, a thin line that unites the ancestors in the air—those poor animals sacrificed on the pyre of time—.]

Santos Febres repeatedly appears to be more concerned with characterizing the experiences of the many Afro-Hispanic women throughout history to contemporary times. The female subjects in the short vignettes in the novel reveal thoughts, accusations of sexual abuse, and actions carried out by enslaved women (in some cases young girls), against their masters.

Throughout the novel, Santos Febres describes their lives, situations of abuse, and also the female psyche and the reader comes to understand the ways in which there were attempted erasures of black female identity. Fe comes to symbolize all black enslaved Caribbean women and this novel is more a testimony to that strength. The novel moves from the traditional depiction of the slave/master paradigm to the broader contemporary focus which includes the perspectives of the enslaved female characters. Thus, the text alludes to the ironic fact that black enslaved women and young girls who did not enjoy any official state rights were astute enough to be aware of the ways in which the system worked or could be manipulated to their advantage or usefulness of purpose. For example, one of the documents which Fe found recounts the story of Ana María (chapter VIII), a 12-year-old slave girl who goes to court seeking the state's protection as she denounces her master's nephew don Manuel Joseph García. The young girl testifies:

> "García me dio un pescozón por el rezongo que traía. Por este motivo, le contesté que les pegase a sus criados y a sus esclavos, pero que yo no era su esclava. García me volvió a golpear, pero esta vez, tomó un zapato de mujer y, con el tacón me dio muchos golpes en la cabeza y me hirió en varias partes, mientras mi ama, doña Manuela, miraba y se reía", aseguró la niña. (49)

> ["Garcia gave me a hard slap because of the annoyance that he felt. For this reason, I replied that he beat his servants and his slaves, but that I was not his slave. García hit me again, but this time, he took a woman's shoe and, with the heel, he gave me many blows on the head and wounded me in several places, while my mistress, doña Manuela, looked on and laughed", said the child.]

Young women and girls would go to the tribunals or the master in attempted spaces of negotiation. But this close up, still-frame-like, graphic description presented by Santos Febres of the beating of the child ties in with her intention to point out to the reader the ways in which black female bodies were defiled, framed as unworthy of care, and violently mistreated. Reading through the description, one almost forgets that this is a child until Santos Febres' reiteration at the end "aseguró la niña." In addition, by naming the women, Santos Febres humanizes them by allowing us to hear specific voices. The details of their abuses clearly provide us with a record, albeit a fictional one, where previously no such details existed in

4 PAST HISTORIES AND PRESENT REALITIES: THE PARADOX OF TIME...

official documents. In scripting their stories, Santos Febres underscores the idea of the black female bodyscape, a site of inscription of historical violence. In this intimate and subjective space, Santos Febres describes the pain, mistreatment, the wounds, and scars of these women: a trajectory over generations. She also presents their will, ambition, and the strength of their love and desire in their interactions when negotiating the power relations of the societies in which they lived. Although Brodber is more scathing in her analysis, indicating clearly that "double loyalty" (2003, 28) ensues from the white master-black enslaved woman relationship and that the resulting confusion would be debilitating for the enslaved blacks, Santos Febres sees more optimism in the course of time. By the end of the novel, when Fe's dress is in Martín's hands, we realize the potentiality of the mask. Martín now comes to represent love across all ages. His hands rewrite the historic wrongs to Fe, to Xica, and indeed to all women of color. Through the relationship, Fe is reconciled to her history. By the end of the novel, Fe is reborn in Martín's healing hands:

> En la memoria de mi dueña, sonarán latigazos y carimbos. Se desvanecerán cicatrices y humillaciones. Entonces, Fe, liberada, entenderá y se abrirá para mí. Ella misma lo ha querido. Me lo ha pedido todo este tiempo "Rompe el traje, desgárralo, sácame de aquí." (114–115)

> [In the memory of my owner [Fe], lashes and carimbos will sound. Scars and humiliations will fade. Then Faith, freed, will understand and open up for me. She herself wanted it. She constantly asks me to "Rip the dress, tear it apart, get me out."]

In the dress, Fe's skin is perforated and pierced. Wracked by the pain of the past, she knows that she must destroy the dress if she is to extirpate the past pain and the trauma that she continues to mentally experience as a result of her blackness. Martín here and now becomes representative of a Puerto Rico that saves her, that recuperates her story. Fe now understands that her socio-psychological peace lies in remembering and in accepting her blackness. The novel ends: "Abandonarse es, a veces, la única manera de comenzar" (115) [Giving in, is sometimes the only way to begin].

Deeply rooted in this story, as with memory, is Santos Febres' insistent agenda to rewrite history. The past she tells the reader is not that far away from the present and perhaps even from the future. Through the theme of enslavement, she systematically rewrites in a profoundly eroticized manner the history which has traveled through time to confront the contemporary negotiation of male-female desire and identity and which finds roots in the intersection between an imaginary and imagined past and an opaque present. Santos Febres was forced to re-create this memory of enslavement given the absence discovered when she sought to research these black women. The novel ends before the opening of the exhibition. But by the end and through the note to the reader by the author, we come to realize that, much like Fe has sought to honor the memory of the enslaved African women, so too Santos Febres through the novel seeks to rewrite the lives of these women in the Hispanic Caribbean and to write them into history. She makes a significant and commanding representation of the black female subject. Weighed down by colonization, racialization, labor exploitation, as well as gender and sexual regulation, Santos Febres voices the black enslaved women's right to social transformation. What appears most fascinating is that her assertions in this novel open the way to social development at both the psychic and corporeal levels. It is about Puerto Rican society being able to afford dignity to all of its members. That is to say, not just the dignity of body for blacks and whites alike but also the internalization of dignity among blacks themselves. The brevity of the novel also signals the author's continued grappling with the burden of this history. Through the brief text, she forces the reader to confront, to know our past in all of its fullness; the trauma of violence, shared silence, suffering, and bodily harm.

For Santos Febres, taking on issues such as race, gender, and sexuality is an intellectual obligation for black women. As Victor Figueroa concludes, Santos Febres manages to "re-territorialize spaces, practices and affects colonized by power" (Figueroa 2017, 67). Through the use of alternative archives, Santos Febres presents the paradox of enslavement and forces us to understand its consequences on the black lives affected. Additionally, she aids with aspects of generational healing as she presents the reader with hope for a future of resilience and self-affirmation. Thus, to return to the Brodber quotation earlier cited, true liberation comes when, like Martín, the reader acknowledges his/her own uncomfortable desires and the role that they play in the liberation process. In *Fe en disfraz*, Santos Febres re-engineers the records found on the lives of black enslaved women so as to comprehensively describe the nature of their enslavement, and to ensure that in present-day Puerto Rico and across the Caribbean, we understand the notion of transgenerational trauma while necessarily raising our level of black consciousness.

References

Adams, Clementina R. 1998. *Common Threads: Themes in Afro-Hispanic Women's Literature*. Miami: Ediciones Universal.

Barnet, M. 1993. *Biografía de un Cimarrón*. La Habana: Letras Cubanas.

Brodber, Erna. 2003. *The Continent of Black Consciousness: On the History of the African Diaspora from Slavery to the Present Day*. London: Beacon Books.

De Gruy, Joy. 2017. *Post Traumatic Slave Syndrome*. Portland, OR: Joy Degruy Publications Inc.

Figueroa, Victor. 2017. Desiring Colonial Bodies in Mayra Santos-Febres' *Fe en disfraz*. *Ciberletras: Revista de crítica literaria y de cultura* 38: 56–83.

Godreau, Isar P., et al. 2008. The Lessons of Slavery: Discourses of Slavery, Mestizaje, and Blanqueamiento in an Elementary School in Puerto Rico. *American Ethnologist* 35 (1): 115–135.

Godreau, Isar P. 2006. Folkloric "Others:" Blanqueamiento and the Celebration of Blackness as an Exception in Puerto Rico. In *Globalization and Race: Transformations in the Cultural Production of Blackness*, ed. Kamari Maxine Clarke and Deborah A. Thomas, 171–187. Durham: Duke University Press.

Hall, Stuart. 1999. Thinking the Diaspora: Home-Thoughts from Abroad. *Small Axe* 3 (2): 1–18.

Rangelova, Radost A. 2012. Writing Words, Wearing Wounds: Race and Gender in a Puerto Rican Neo-Slave Narrative. *Tinkuy: Boletín de Investigación y Debate* 18: 150–158.

Santos Febres, Mayra. 2009. *Fe en disfraz*. Doral, FL: Santillana.

Valladares-Ruiz, Patricia. 2016. El cuerpo sufriente como lugar de memoria en *Fe en disfraz*, de Mayra Santos-Febres. *Cuadernos de literatura XX* 40: 596–616.

Open Access This chapter is licensed under the terms of the Creative Commons Attribution 4.0 International License (http://creativecommons.org/licenses/by/4.0/), which permits use, sharing, adaptation, distribution and reproduction in any medium or format, as long as you give appropriate credit to the original author(s) and the source, provide a link to the Creative Commons licence and indicate if changes were made.

The images or other third party material in this chapter are included in the chapter's Creative Commons licence, unless indicated otherwise in a credit line to the material. If material is not included in the chapter's Creative Commons licence and your intended use is not permitted by statutory regulation or exceeds the permitted use, you will need to obtain permission directly from the copyright holder.

CHAPTER 5

A Site of Memory: Revisiting (in) Gisèle Pineau's *Mes quatre femmes*

Renée Larrier

Guadeloupean writer Gisèle Pineau (born in 1956) asserts: "We carry within ourselves forever the people we have lost, loved" (Pineau qtd. in Veldwachter 2004). These are the voices that made her write, that saved her from the racism, alienation, and isolation that she faced as a young student in France (Pineau 2002, 222). In her 2007 autobiographical narrative *Mes quatre femmes: récit*, Pineau identifies the ghosts of her female relatives whose constant presence she senses, and who are instrumental in shaping her identity: her paternal ancestor Angélique, who was born in 1792, and grandmother Julia; and on the maternal side, her mother Daisy and her aunt Gisèle, after whom the author is named. Representing different generations, historical moments, classes, complexions, life experiences, and comportments over a period of 200 years, they form a distinct female genealogy residing in her memory, in what she calls a "geôle obscure de la mémoire" [dark memory jail], which in this chapter, I read as an oral archive. My analysis of the dark memory jail as an alternative, oral archive, replete with "leur dictée, … la cendre, la boue et le sang" (Pineau 2010,

R. Larrier (✉)
Rutgers University, New Brunswick, NJ, USA
e-mail: rlarrier@french.rutgers.edu

© The Author(s) 2023
O. Ferly, T. Zimmerman (eds.), *Chronotropics*,
https://doi.org/10.1007/978-3-031-32111-5_5

84 R. LARRIER

171–2) [their words … ash, mud and blood] expands Betty Wilson's assertion that a closed space in Caribbean women's texts can function as both a prison and a refuge.[1] I argue that not only does this inherent paradox operate in *Mes quatre femmes*, but also that inseparable tensions between death/life and official/unofficial histories define Pineau's memory archive and justify her need to reinvent the inner lives of her foremothers through writing.

THE MEMORY JAIL

When meditating on the relationship between the living and the dead, some Francophone Caribbean women writers subvert conventional representations of haunting—of which, "the intention [is] to frighten readers by exploiting their fears, both conscious and subconscious: fears of supernatural forces, alien visitations, madness, death, dismemberment, and other terrifying notions,[2] fashioning instead haunting as reconciliatory or as possessing the power of ancestral healing. For instance, Maryse Condé's "invisibles"—Abena, Man Yaya, and Yao—appear several times unexpectedly to offer advice to Tituba in *Moi, Tituba sorcière, Noire de Salem* (1986), before she becomes one herself at the end of the novel.[3] Emma communicates with her enslaved ancestor in Marie-Célie Agnant's *The Book of Emma* (2006): "sometimes I call on Kilima, Cécile, the Emmas before me, then Rosa, all those eternal marrons for help. I invoke their memory; they will know how to guide me, I tell myself; but I don't see them" (Agnant 190). Healer Man Cia, transformed into a faithful dog, greets Télumée in Simone Schwarz-Bart's *Pluie et vent sur Télumée Miracle* (1972b). In these texts, the authors defy conventional spatio-temporal boundaries so that their characters can offer knowledge, guidance, and companionship to members of the younger generation. What distinguishes *Mes quatre femmes* is that the four women are confined to the author's memory as primary characters co-creating a Caribbean women's archive.[4]

Accordingly, the "geôle obscure de la mémoire" is a dark, windowless four-walled space, reminiscent of the hold of a slave ship on the one hand, or, on the other, a plantation *cachot* in which rebellious enslaved persons, like Solitude, were imprisoned.[5] Though not necessarily revolutionary heroines in the official sense, e.g., the feminist politician Gerty Archimède or the legendary stalwart *femme-matador* (Thomas 2004), Pineau shows that her ancestors can still be considered what Kaiama L. Glover calls "disorderly women," as they navigate life's challenges (Glover 2021, 5–33).

As opposed to enslaved women who were detained in a "geôle de l'oubli où l'histoire les avait emmurées," (Pineau and Abraham 1998, 11) [jail of oblivion where history had confined them], that silenced them and made them invisible to society and history, the four women recuperated by Pineau are unquestionably speaking subjects, claiming their place in the world.

The walls of this *geôle* are permeable, allowing characters conjured up by memory to appear, perform, and then vanish. As Glissant reminds us: "La mémoire dans les oeuvres n'est pas celle du calendrier; notre vécu du temps ne fréquente pas seulement les cadences du mois et de l'an … [la mémoire] parle plus haut et plus loin que les chroniques et les recensements" (Glissant 1990, 86) [memory in texts isn't like a calendar; our experience of time doesn't follow only the cadences of month and year … it speaks louder and farther than chronicles and censuses]. In addition, collective memory in this text operates in its simplest form as the sum of what the four women relate and in its more complex form coalesce as shared intergenerational memory (Halbwachs 1997) and "intergenerational trauma" (Thomas 2010). Pineau suggests that these "transgenerational traumas" (Thomas 2010), including her own, began with Angélique, whose emancipation and marriage did not solve her personal challenges.[6] Julia Roman, born seventy years later in 1898, ironically, the year of the fiftieth anniversary of the second abolition, also experiences a form of servitude, when she, a naive nineteen-year-old cane field worker, is chosen as a wife by a handsome, mixed-race, army veteran who is discharged due to a head injury and hired as a plantation guard.

Over the centuries, women from both sides of the family experience the impact of (colonial) patriarchal systems: raised without their fathers in the home, Angélique and Julia lacked reliable and trustworthy role models for partners; Gisèle, Angélique, Julia, and Daisy remain in unhappy, unhealthy relationships and fall into a depression; Julia and Daisy suffer the effects of their husbands' post-traumatic stress disorder resulting from their military service; Angélique and Gisèle become young widows, with the former gaining status, protection, and agency, while the latter succumbs to despair; at one point, Angélique, Gisèle, and Julia even withdraw to become invisible in response to their difficult situations. *Mes quatre femmes'* memory archive therefore shows how "Trauma profoundly disorders one's experience of one's body, creating the sensation of being both out of one's mind and outside of one's body" (Hamilton 2018, 83) but sees women's writing as a means toward psychic-physical reparation.

86   R. LARRIER

Through (re)writing these trauma narratives and the women's lives and voices in the singular and plural, Pineau begins to convert the *geôle* into a nurturing, womb-like space of storytelling. Recognizing how "trauma disorders linear and horological time consciousness" (Hamilton 2018, 84) Pineau gives prominence to the gender dimension, illustrating Wilson's contention that a closed space in Caribbean women's novels can indeed function as a refuge: "The closed space can function generally as both a positive and a negative image. In later West Indian novels, it is a trap which forces a confrontation with self, a confrontation often too painful to endure. It is a prison which is accepted and transformed by an effort of the woman's imagination into a refuge from a reality perceived as intolerable" (Wilson 1990, 49).[7] The women share Pineau's memory space as if it were a communal room for them to support each other through talking, listening, questioning each other, singing, sighing, laughing, and sleeping. With the exception of Daisy, who chooses to join the others in this memory prison, the others are deceased.

FAMILY ARCHIVE: A RHIZOMATIC GENEALOGY

Subtitled "récit," which accentuates the narrative's oral, testimonial core, *Mes quatre femmes* contains numerous autobiographical details—Pineau appears briefly as a young child in Julia's and Daisy's chapters. Pineau admits that the narrative "is about the four women who have made me who I am [...]. This book tells my intimate family history." The possessive adjective "mes" further suggests belonging, kinship, and gratitude. The gathering of these female relatives in the memory jail reconstructs a rhizomatic genealogy, one that rejects the notion of a single-root ancestry as well as linear history. For example, the voice of the speaking subject relates past events spanning the late eighteenth to the twenty-first century in the present tense making the text a kind of prequel to and expansion of Pineau's *Un papillon dans la cité* (1992) and *L'Exil selon Julia* (1996), both of which focus on the relationship between Man Ya and her young granddaughter. Space and time coalesce as memories resurface in a tangle of voices; contemporaries Daisy and her sister Gisèle interact with Julia, whom sister Gisèle had never met in life, and Angélique—a witness to slavery, its first abolition in 1794, and its definitive abolition in 1848—shares space with all of them as temporal distinctions are erased. The narrative moves back and forth across several locations and eras, for example, from a colonial plantation in Guadeloupe to the Cité Kremlin-Bicêtre, the

Paris-area housing project where many BUMIDOM families, like the Pineaus, settled, and back to Guadeloupe.

The often-repeated sentence "elles sont quatre" [there are four of them] and the individual accounts—each chapter carries the name of a single character and unfolds in non-chronological order—imply the randomness of memory and its enduring transiency as an archive. While each chapter privileges one person's recollections, it also contains verbatim fragments from the others' stories, creating the effect of a chorus in which each voice has a chance to solo or what could be characterized as a polyphonic call-and-response dynamic. For example, the author traces her surname back to Angélique, who reverses the dispossession of enslavement through wedlock by marrying her owner's son with whom she has had a coercive thirty-year arrangement. Julia, who also married into the Pineau family, survives a hard life, finding happiness back in her hometown, where she makes the decision to stand up to her spouse's abuse. The author's maternal kin, sisters Daisy and Gisèle, who are separated from her by only one generation, are aspirational like Angélique; they conform to gender norms in exchange for social status and financial security. Nevertheless, by naming her daughter in honor of her older sister, Daisy acknowledges her struggle and assures that she will not be forgotten. The convergence of "Gisèle Pineau" then is more than the juxtaposition of two separate family lines coming together; rather its strands intertwine and interlock, like a rhizome, exposing a complex lineage. Furthermore, while the women on her father's side are the ones whose decisions are somewhat more constructive, the generational trajectory is uneven, as upward mobility is accompanied by significant setbacks. Time does improve these women's material lives, but in other ways, their condition regresses.

Thus, Julia endures physical and verbal abuse at the hands of her fear-inspiring husband Astrubal, nicknamed Le Bourreau, who sports a colonial helmet indicative of his past career as an agent of French imperialism and benefits from society's class, gender, and color hierarchy. The inherent social imbalances coupled with Julia's Christian principles render her acquiescent. That she must address both her husband and son as "Monsieur Pineau" illustrates the intransigence of patriarchy across generations. Her son Maréchal, Daisy's husband, in turn imposes his own system of control in the mid-twentieth century. While stationed in French Indochina, he creates another household that, after his tour ends, he moves into the apartment in the Hexagon with his legal family. Neither Daisy nor the unnamed Asian woman has a say in the arrangement; nor does Daisy's older sister Gisèle have the power or voice to object when her husband engages in adulterous relationships. Deemed property, Gisèle and Daisy suffer the indignities of their spouses' extramarital affairs; in Pineau's memoir, however, they are given an opportunity to break the cycle of silence through narration, and thereby reclaim their agency.

"There, Time Is Abolished": Official and Unofficial Histories

In the dark, confined space of the memory jail, timelessness reigns as memories flow: "La mémoire est une geôle. Là, les temps sont abolis. Là, les morts et les vivants sont ensemble" (7) [Memory is a jail. There, time is abolished. There, the dead and the living are together]. Sometimes the door opens, but no one leaves, as the principal activity—remembering—unfurls. Echoing Zora Neale Hurston's contention that: "Like the dead-seeming, cold rocks, I have memories within that came out of the material that went to make me. Time and place have had their say" (Hurston 1991), Gisèle Pineau's memoir offers an inventive take on memory as a repository, a space in which the living coexist with the dead. At times Daisy reunites with the other women who are deceased in the memory jail, while at other times she joins the author in telling their shared histories as living moments, always present, articulated, and available. Echoing Njelle Hamilton's reading of Marlon James' novel *A Brief History of Seven Killings*, Pineau frames her foremothers as "untouched by the ravages of human time and positions the narrator … outside of time, able to see past, present and future in sequence and out of order and as an enduring present instant [the text] constructs continued living as a revolt against the teleological imperative of death" (Hamilton 2018, 81). The unfolding of history is likened to memory—it is messy, repetitive, plotless, repressed, spectral yet, living and breathing. The writing process turns Pineau into a kind of archive; her embodied memories are facilitated by a memento that each character brings with her, that defines her, links her to the past, and opens the floodgates to memory: "trésors … [qui] gardent vivant le temps du dehors et ravivent les couleurs de la mémoire" (28) [treasures that keep time alive outside and revive the colors of memory]. Once again, troubling strict delineations between official or unofficial discourses in her memory-archive, Pineau includes and gives equal merit to organic and inorganic items, all derived from plants at various stages of processing:

Julia clings to a guava branch; Gisèle wears a straw hat; Daisy caresses a book; and Angélique folds and unfolds the yellowed page from a newspaper.

Julia's branch from a guava tree is the one she kept close to her body to combat her feelings of exile in Paris. This tropical tree is not only abundant in her native commune Goyave, after which it is named, but on the island in general. Known for its flavor and smell, the fruit also has nutritional and therapeutic properties. She chews on the branch "sans doute pour en tirer quelque sève au goût de son pays" (126) [undoubtedly, to extract a bit of sap with her country's taste], and smelling it makes her remember her son's childhood. At once a weapon ("armée de sa branche de goyavier" [59]) and a product of nature that she tries to replant in the new space, it symbolizes her garden and desire to carry her native land wherever she goes. To cope with homesickness in the memory prison, Julia also draws butterflies on the walls, reproducing the shape of the island, and calls upon her senses to transport her back to her village, which also was the site of a historical maroon camp.

The story stimulated by Julia's guava branch recounts the stages of her development in site-specific spaces. Despondent in France, she carefully prepared dishes from her homeland, leading Brinda Mehta to talk about her "cultural resistance through the dynamics of food in the urban ghetto" (Mehta 2009, 96). She consoled her young granddaughter Gisèle by telling her about her hometown and praying each night that they would return together to Guadeloupe. The language of these intimate moments is Creole, her mother tongue, as opposed to French, the language of her son's household. Creole, which Guadeloupean social scientist Dany Bébel-Gisler posits is the "archive matérielle et symbolique des peuples de la Caraïbe" (Bébel-Gisler 1989, 218) [material and symbolic archive of the Caribbean people], along with Guadeloupean cuisine, then, both embodied by Julia, resist French hegemony. The second step of Julia's evolution is reinvention. Upon her return to Routhiers in 1967, she renounces her previous isolation by joining a local church choir and, no longer fearing her husband Astrubal, a veteran "Démobilisé pour cause de blessure à la tête" (78) [demobilized because of a head wound], she forbids him from battering her ever again. Whereas Astrubal's brain, the site of reasoning and memory, was damaged to the extent that he was discharged from the armed forces, Julia's memories find refuge in her granddaughter's *geôle* and will serve as a resource to shape her own life for the better. Residing in Gisèle's memory jail, Julia: "s'invente une vie en Afrique" (155) [invented a life in Africa for herself]. Inspired by Daisy's and Angélique's stories about the Congo, she imagines herself growing up among monkeys and lions. While this problematic vision based on misinterpretations, misconceptions, and stereotypes constitutes a setback, the guava branch nevertheless has a twofold function: it prompts her memory and illustrates her desire to connect ties to her ancestral homeland.

While Julia longed to return to Guadeloupe, Daisy imagined a life far from her native (is)land. She spends her time in the memory jail rereading the romance novel she brought with her, identifying with its fictional characters, a tactic that has always helped her cope with adversity. As a young seamstress, she dreamed of a marriage that would take her to France, where "elle va construire sa vie de roman" (74) [she will construct a novel life]. To that end, she, a light-skinned daughter of a former plantation manager and successful small-business owner who went bankrupt, crossed class and color lines and quickly married dark-skinned Maréchal, because he was a French-speaking career military man, a World War II sergeant on leave. Migration to the Hexagon, however, didn't engender the fantasy life depicted in the books she borrowed from the library. Life was difficult; her husband terrorized the household. While he was stationed in Algeria, Daisy was confined in a sanitarium in France due to postpartum depression, while newborn Elie was temporarily placed in foster care and the other children stayed with her sister. Once the family was reunited, they relocated to independent Senegal and Congo, hardly the idyllic locales portrayed in romance novels she devoured. Frustrated as a wife, but fulfilled as a mother, Daisy willingly loses herself in her books: "La lecture lui donne le rêve, l'évasion, l'illusion. [...] Elle existe à travers ses personnages d'encre et de papier" (55–56) [reading gives her the space to dream, escape, an illusion. [...]. She exists through her characters on ink and paper]. Living vicariously—"Elle lit pour s'évader de son quotidien" (116) [she reads to escape from her daily life]—not only provides a brief respite, but "cette occupation lui est aussi nécessaire que le boire et le manger" (116) [this activity is as necessary as eating and drinking]. The book, then, is a tangible symbol of her vivid imagination, which allows her to escape to a mythological France construed as paradise, where romantic adventures end happily. The reader can assume that the protagonists in these novels are white, rendering her dreams unattainable due to her race. Unlike Julia who refuses assimilation, Daisy, a *bovaryste*, embraces and makes the Hexagon the center of her fantasy world, as well as that of her sister whom she turns into a heroine riding in a white car to the Eiffel Tower on her

5 A SITE OF MEMORY: REVISITING (IN) GISÈLE PINEAU'S *MES QUATRE...* 91

honeymoon with her second husband.[8] Furthermore, Daisy is an unwitting accomplice of her husband and father-in-law, who as military men are agents of French post-colonial policy and colonial expansion, respectively, the violence of which they bring into their homes. In the memory jail, however, her thinking evolves somewhat. Admitting to having distanced herself from her African heritage, she is moved to tears reading aloud the list of newly freed individuals in Angélique's newspaper. This is Daisy's pivotal moment of empathy and appreciation for Angélique's achievement and her realization that the distant past is connected to the present. Nevertheless, the historic and historical materiality of the colonial newspaper and its proclamation contrasts sharply with the frivolous nature of the romance novel that stimulates her memories in the "geôle."

Angélique brings into the memory jail her cherished page from the 1831 edition of the *Gazette officielle de la Guadeloupe* that reports the governor's granting freedom to her children, the oldest of whom is twenty-four and the youngest, eight.[9] Until that date, according to the *Code noir*, they were considered property. Just three years earlier her own status had changed to that of a free woman, and in 1837, she would finally persuade Jean-Féréol to marry her, on his deathbed. Her "involvement" with Jean-Féréol Pineau had begun as rape, when his parents, accompanied by her mother Rose, a cook and maid, left the plantation overnight to attend a burial in Grande-Terre. In a dispassionate tone, Angélique provides few details after he, twenty-eight, entered her room when she was fourteen years old: "il prend dans ses mains mes tétés. Et c'est ainsi que tout a commencé avec mon maître" (164) [he took my breasts in his hands. That's how it started with my master]. Listening to Angélique's story, Julia knows what would follow, for it is so similar to the one her grandmother used to tell as a cautionary tale about sexual exploitation during the slavery era: "Elle sait ce qu'il va advenir de la fillette de quatorze ans. Le grand méchant loup va la manger" [she knows what will happen to the young fourteen-year-old girl. The bad wolf is going to eat her]. Knowing the inevitability of rape of young, enslaved girls by white men in the household and her inability to protect her daughter, Rose, overcome with guilt and shame, refuses to speak to Angélique from then on. When Angélique becomes pregnant, Dame Véronique, Jean-Féréol's mother, banishes the couple to the family vacation home in Les Saintes. What renders this situation ironic and more complex is that Dame Véronique, the wife of the elderly plantation owner Jean-Baptiste Pineau, is a slaveholding free woman of color who seeks to maintain the entrenched race, class, and color hierarchies. Ashamed of her blackness, she "voulait que sa descendance blanchisse et fallait dire adieu aux alliances familiales projetées avec la mulâtraille ... Fallait dire adieu à tous les beaux rêves d'une progéniture au teint clair et aux cheveux pas grainés" (165) [wanted her descendants to be light-skinned and would have to give up hopes of family marriages with 'those mulattos' [pej] ... had to say goodbye to those beautiful dreams of light-skinned, straight-haired progeny]. Her unwavering objection to her white-identifying son—who has no problem exercising exploitative patriarchal authority—being involved with a black woman is rooted in her desire for her offspring to "pass" in white society in order to fully benefit from its privileges.

Bitter and aware of her powerlessness, Angélique raised her children with no illusions about her arrangement with Jean-Féréol:

> Je le voyais pas comme le père de mes enfants, seulement comme mon maî-tre. Un vieux maître de trente-cinq ans qui avait pris ma virginité et m'avait privée de ma mère pour contenter sa chair. [...] Obligée de rester couchée sous lui. Forcée par entraînement à pas lui résister, à ouvrir les cuisses et, sans joie, attendre qu'il en ait terminé (167-8) [I didn't see him as the father of my children, only as my master. An old, thirty-five-year-old master who had taken my virginity and deprived me of my mother in order to satisfy his flesh. [...] Forced to lie under him. Forced by training not to resist him, to open my thighs and, joylessly, wait until he had finished].

Her mantra "Toute ma vie j'ai dû me battre" (143–4) echoes Sofia's often-quoted line from the novel and film *The Color Purple*, "all my life I had to fight," rendered in the French translation as "Toute ma vie j'ai été forcée de me battre" (Walker 1992, 39; Meyjes 2007). Whereas Sofia asserts that she will not be a victim of Harpo's brutality, Angélique repeats the line several times to her listeners at the beginning of her stand-alone *récit*, accentuating her struggle against specific individuals who were an integral part of an oppressive and violent system. Although her request for marriage is not granted until a few days before Jean-Féréol's death, the newspaper, whose contents Angélique had memorized, refers to her as "Dame Angélique," the title she finally earned as a free person that encapsulates her achievement of subjectivity. This former enslaved woman, rape survivor, and "concubine" is reinvented further as she advances from Dame Angélique "négresse, libre de couleur" to Dame Angélique Pineau when she marries and quickly becomes a widow, inheriting her husband's estate—land, homes, shops, sugar cane fields, and enslaved persons. From her early years of sharing a bed with her mother for protection from the men in the household to sleeping in her former owner's bed is an extraordinary trajectory, as she inherits the property from the person who once owned her and her mother. That Angélique's memento is neither her freedom papers nor her marriage certificate is a strong indication that she treasures her children's emancipation, a fundamental legacy that will have a major impact on their and their descendants' lives.

Associated with Aunt Gisèle, the straw hat that she brings into the memory prison has a practical purpose and a psychological function: "la soustraire à la vue des autres et, dans le même temps, la préserver de la vision des laideurs du monde" (42–3). In other words, she wears the hat not only to avoid being the object of the gaze, but to protect her from seeing the ugliness around her. Life for Gisèle is a war and "face aux ennemis" [facing enemies] she needs a combat helmet (43), like the one her future brother-in-law and sister's father-in-law would wear. If theirs, however, could not provide them with adequate protection from physical harm in wartime, how could hers, which was made of straw? Having married for love and delighting in the status of a middle-class, stay-at-home "Madame" (29), Gisèle becomes horrified by the physical changes to her body after giving birth three times in four years and overwhelmed by her household responsibilities. Her unsympathetic husband claims ownership of her body, like Jean-Féréol and Astrubal/Le Bourreau deemed Angélique's and Julia's, respectively, their property.[10] That he insists on sleeping with her when she is unwilling would be considered spousal rape today. Silent, withdrawn, and more fragile after her husband is murdered, poisoned perhaps by a jealous husband, Gisèle falls into a deep depression, stops taking care of herself and her children, and dies at age twenty-seven, "emportée par le chagrin" [dead from grief]. Delicate like her never-used hand-painted porcelain dinnerware set for twelve and in no way "une guerrière, non plus une résistante" (46) [neither a warrior nor a resistor], she does not possess the tools to resist or reinvent herself like Angélique, Julia, and Daisy. In the memory jail, she depends on her seventy-five-year-old "younger" sister Daisy to braid her hair and help her reconstruct her own story. It is Daisy, for instance, who recounts Gisèle's wedding day on September 17, 1942, when she, at age ten, served as her bridesmaid.

Parole de nuit or Parole de la mémoire

The transgenerational gathering in the "geôle" imitates the traditional Caribbean *parole de nuit* in which people assemble at night to witness a storyteller perform tales that everyone knows. That outdoor space is an important site of memory, according to Glissant: "Un des lieux de la mémoire antillaise a bien été le cercle délimité autour du conteur par les ombres de nuit" (Glissant 1990, 51) [one of the sites of Antillean memory was the circle around the storyteller demarcated by the night shadows]. Pineau's narrators as well as audience in *Mes quatre femmes* are exclusively female, which upends the pervasive image reinforced by Raphaël Confiant's *Les Maîtres de la parole créole* (1995) in which all the twenty-six *conteurs* interviewed are male, thereby rendering their female counterparts silent and invisible. Pineau's *geôle* is a psychic space in which the women storytellers assume the narration one by one, passing the metaphorical baton to the next speaker. Angélique, steeped in the oral tradition and speaking most often in the first person, recognizes the structure and appreciates the content despite the shift to various contemporary settings; she "s'extasie sur ces contes du temps moderne" (103) [is ecstatic over these modern oral stories].

Pineau embraces Fabienne Kanor's declaration regarding her particular responsibility as a writer—"faire savoir, that is, to inform about the past" (Kanor 2016)—and her characters welcome the charge. To that end, Julia, for example, the most experienced *oralituraine*, goes as far as to tie together the threads of the others' stories. Espousing the ethics of Caribbean storytelling, she passes on knowledge, educating her granddaughter about her culture and heritage. Harryette Mullen's concept "resistant orality," which refers to enslaved African American women narrators who were excluded from other discourses (Fulton 2006, 22), is relevant to the characters in this text. Daisy is a gifted oral storyteller as well as an enthusiastic reader: "Daisy raconte si bien qu'Angélique tombe dans ses filets et se laisse prendre à l'histoire de sa vie" (115) [Daisy spoke so well that Angélique fell into her net and let herself be caught up by her life story]. Sharing her story has personal healing benefits in that it seems to lift a burden from her shoulders: "elle se sent légère [...] c'est comme si elle s'était lavée de ses années de mariage" (142). While Gisèle isn't as articulate as the others, she joins forces with Daisy to construct a story about their side of the family: "Daisy et Gisèle mettent en branle leurs souvenirs. Elles chicanent sur des détails, ajustent leurs récits et finissent par s'accorder sur une version consensuelle de l'histoire qu'elles livrent d'une même voix à Julia et à Angélique" (25) [Daisy and Gisèle set their memories in motion. They quibble about the details, adjust their stories, and end up by agreeing on a consensual version of the story that they deliver with the same voice to Julia and Angélique]. At one point, Daisy, who crossed the Atlantic Ocean in a ship with her mother-in-law, picks up her story where she left off: "Julia n'a plus envie de causer. Elle laisse la parole à Daisy qui raconte la vie à bord" (103) [Julia doesn't want to talk anymore. She let Daisy speak, who recounts her life on board]. Angélique, opening her *récit* with "Moi, aussi" (143) [me, too], identifies immediately with the others before sharing her personal experiences. Angélique juxtaposes her memories with excerpts from the *Code noir*, thereby blending *histoire* and *Histoire* and oral and written discourses. The last and the longest uninterrupted piece recounted in the present tense, her *récit* therefore resembles a traditional slave narrative, opening with birth information and closing with the achievement of freedom.

A repository of memories and history, the *geôle* in *Mes quatre femmes* is paradoxically a jail and a sanctuary, a site of trauma, of reflection, of regrets, of solace, of pain, and of healing through storytelling, all of which contribute to an alternative, family archive. A literal *lieu de mémoire* (Nora 1989), where time and space are reconceptualized, it is where lives are recounted, dreams recalled, and identities reconstructed. By placing four of her blood relatives in that confined space, Pineau retraces and merges their individual stories so that the reader can imagine, anticipate, and understand their impact on her own journey and chart the progress, sometimes limited, made by Guadeloupean women over time. Her admission about her childhood in *Folie, aller simple: Journée ordinaire d'une infirmière*, which chronicles her experiences as a psychiatric nurse, that "J'étais toujours plongée dans des livres, assise à côte de la vraie vie, fuyant de toute mon âme la réalité du quotidien" (Pineau 2010, 108) [I was always deep into books, seated next to real life, fleeing daily reality with all my soul] echoes Daisy's claim, suggesting that her penchant for reading had passed from mother to daughter and with the same objective of escaping the present in order to cope with adversity. With the exception of Aunt Gisèle, the narrators collectively are instrumental in descendant Gisèle's storytelling predisposition and literary endeavors.[11]

Toni Morrison's assessment about the relationship between ghosts, haunting, and writing is relevant to Pineau: "I think of ghosts and haunting as being alert. If you're really alert, then you see the life that exists

96   R. LARRIER

beyond the life that is on top" (Montagne 2004). Pineau is attentive: "Ce sont des femmes qui me hantent. C'est aussi pour cela que je les ai placées dans une geôle, qui est une sublimation de la mémoire" (Avignon 2007) [It's women who haunt me. It's also for that reason that I placed them in a jail, which is a sublimation of memory]. Their voices, rendering soothing, auditory images, serenade her as she writes: "J'écris encore avec le ronron de leurs voix et tous leurs ramages." The soft, purring voices ("ronron") and bird songs ("ramages") provide background music for her writing sessions (Pineau 2010, 171–2). Fittingly, "ramages" also denotes the leaf pattern of a tree branch, and thus metaphorically, the foundation of a genealogical tree, whose intricate, intertwining roots form a rhizome. She is comforted by these ghosts lodged in her memory,[12] where their ancestral encounters form an essential part of her being: "Celle-là a dessiné le pays. Celle-ci a légué le nom. La troisième a posé la langue. La quatrième a cédé le prénom" (12) [that one drew the country. This one left her name. The third one gave me language. The fourth one gave me her first name]. She incarnates these disembodied souls, grateful for their eternal presence and storytelling gifts. Inseparable and joined forever across space and time, this "living" legacy residing in her "geôle obscure de la mémoire" establishes a feminist genealogy of survival, agency, and creativity.

NOTES

1. All quotations from *Mes quatre femmes* are taken from this edition and page numbers will be cited in parentheses. All translations are mine.
2. Conventional representations of haunting in literature evoke an atmosphere of darkness and gloom, as seen in Gabriele Schwab's *Haunting Legacies: Violent Histories and Transgenerational Trauma* (2010), Maria del Pilar Blanco and Esther Peeren's edited volume *The Spectralities Reader: Ghosts and Haunting in Contemporary Cultural Theory* (2013), and Kathleen Brogan's *Cultural Hauntings: Ghosts and Ethnicity in Recent American Literature* (1998). Although Martin Munro compiled a broad range of representations for his anthology *The Haunted Tropics: Caribbean Ghost Stories* (2015), it won honorable mention in the Adult Horror category of Foreword INDIES Book of the Year Awards (Anonymous 2015).
3. Nevertheless, Tituba is figured as a frightening witch on the cover of the 1989 paperback edition of the novel.
4. For a discussion of "traditional" ghosts in other texts by Pineau, see Githire (2005) and Maisier (2012).

5 A SITE OF MEMORY: REVISITING (IN) GISÈLE PINEAU'S *MES QUATRE...* 97

5. There are streets named after her, statues erected in her honor in Guadeloupe and France, and UNESCO created a pedagogical unit—including a comic strip—for schools (https://unesdoc.unesco.org/ark:/48223/pf0000230936). In fiction, there are André Schwartz-Bart's *La Mulatresse Solitude* (1972a) and his and Simone Schwarz-Bart's *L'Ancêtre en Solitude* (2015), which follows three generations of her descendants.

6. On the possibility of trauma inherited from slavery, see Charles-Nicolas (2015), and Carey (2018). In late October 2016, the colloquium L'Esclavage: quel impact sur la psychologie de la population? was held in Guadeloupe: https://la1ere.francetvinfo.fr/martinique/esclavage-quel-impact-psychologie-populations-410159.html

7. Conversely, Gladys M. Francis analyzes the belly of Gina Bovoir in Pineau's *Cent vies et des poussières* as a symbolic site of powerlessness, alienation, and pain (Francis 2017, 17–19).

8. See Jean Price-Mars (2022) on "bovarysme collectif" in relation to Haitians in *La Vocation de l'élite*.

9. Pineau reveals that it was her father who came across the reference to Angélique (see Avignon 2007).

10. Gisèle's spouse proclaims repeatedly: "Tu es ma femme" but she hears: "Tu es mon esclave … Tu es ma propriété … Tu m'appartiens … Tu es ma jument" (42) [You are my wife; You are my slave … You are my property … You belong to me … You are my mare].

11. Gisèle also credits her father for fostering an atmosphere conducive to education by purchasing hard-covered collections of Balzac, Zola, LaFontaine, Racine, and Corneille, and ordering encyclopedias through the mail (Pineau 2007, 137).

12. "Je vis ici comme avec les fantômes, avec ceux qui ne sont plus là, mais je me sens bien." [I live here like with the ghosts, with those who are no longer with us, but I feel goodl] http://ile-en-ile.org/gisele-pineau-5-questions-pour-ile-en-ile/

References

Agnant, Marie-Célie. 2006. *The Book of Emma*. Trans. Zilpha Ellis. https://vdoc.pub/documents/the-book-of-emma-5mgq20c80sn0. Accessed 30 June 2022.

Anonymous. 2015. *Foreword Indies 2015 Winners Horror (Adult Fiction)*. https://www.forewordreviews.com/awards/winners/2015/horror/. Accessed 1 Dec 2019.

Avignon, Christine. 2007. *L'écriture est un combat: Entretien de Christine Avignon avec Gisèle Pineau. Africultures*. http://africultures.com/lecriture-est-un-combat-5946/. Accessed 1 Dec 2019.

98   R. LARRIER

Bébel-Gisler, Dany. 1989. *Le Défi culturel guadeloupéen: devenir ce que nous sommes.* Paris: Editions Caribéennes.

Blanco, Maria del Pilar, and Esther Peeren. 2013. *The Spectralities Reader: Ghosts and Haunting in Contemporary Cultural Theory.* London: Bloomsbury.

Brogan, Kathleen. 1998. *Cultural Hauntings: Ghosts and Ethnicity in Recent American Literature.* Charlottesville: University of Virginia Press.

Carey, Benedict. 2018. Can We Really Inherit Trauma? *New York Times,* December 10. https://www.nytimes.com/2018/12/10/health/mind-epigenetics-genes.html. Accessed 1 Dec 2019.

Charles-Nicolas, Aimé. 2015. Folie et psychiatrie dans la Martinique d'antan. Des questions pour le temps present. *Annales Médico-psychologiques revue psychiatrique* 173 (4). https://doi.org/10.1016/j.amp.2015.03.00.

Condé, Maryse. 1989. *Moi, Tituba, sorcière ... Noire de Salem.* Paris: Mercure de France.

Confiant, Raphaël. 1995. *Les Maîtres de la parole créole.* Paris: Gallimard.

Francis, Gladys M. 2017. *Odious Women and the Palpable Aesthetics of Transgression.* Lanham: Lexington Books.

Fulton, DoVeanna S. 2006. *Speaking Power: Black Feminist Orality in Women's Narratives of Slavery.* Albany: Suny Press.

Githire, Njeri. 2005. Horizons Adrift: Women in Exile, at Home, and Abroad in Gisèle Pineau's Works. *Research in African Literatures* 36 (1): 74–90.

Glissant, Edouard. 1990. *Poétique de la Relation.* Paris: Gallimard.

Glover, Kaiama L. 2021. *A Regarded Self: Caribbean Womanhood and the Ethics of Disorderly Being.* Durham: Duke University Press.

Halbwachs, Maurice. 1997 [1950]. *La mémoire collective.* Paris: Albin Michel.

Hamilton, Njelle. 2018. 'Jah Live': Messianic Time and Post-Traumatic Narrative Disorder in Marlon James's. *A Brief History of Seven Killings. Journal of West Indian Literature* 26 (2): 80–95.

Hurston, Zora Neale. 1991. *Dust Tracks on a Road.* New York: Harper Perennial.

Kanor, Fabienne. 2016. Là d'où je viens. *Contemporary French and Francophone Studies* 20 (3): 404–410. https://doi.org/10.1080/17409292.2016.1173851.

Maisier, Véronique. 2012. L'Ecriture au service de la parole dans les romans de Gisèle Pineau. *Nouvelles Etudes Francophones* 27 (2): 30–44.

Mehta, Brinda. 2009. *Notions of Identity, Diaspora, and Gender in Caribbean Women's Writing.* Palgrave Macmillan.

Meyjes, Menno. 2007. *The Color Purple. Screenplay.* DVD. Warner Brothers.

Montagne, Renee. 2004. *Interview: Toni Morrison's 'Good' Ghosts.* Morning Edition National Public Radio September 20. https://www.npr.org/transcripts/3912464?storyId=3912464?storyId=3912464.

Munro, Martin, ed. 2015. *The Haunted Tropics: Caribbean Ghost Stories.* Mona: University of the West Indies Press.

Nora, Pierre. 1989. Between Memory and History: Les Lieux de mémoire. *Representations* 26: 7–24.

Pineau, Gisèle. 1992. *Un papillon dans la cité.* Paris: Sepia.

———. 1996. *L'Exil selon Julia.* Paris: Stock.

Pineau, Pineau. 2002. L'Identité, la créolité et la francité. In *La Culture française vue d'ici et d'ailleurs,* ed. Thomas C. Spear, 219–224. Paris: Karthala.

Pineau, Gisèle. 2007. *Mes quatre femmes: récit.* Paris: Philippe Rey.

———. 2010. *Folie, aller simple: Journée ordinaire d'une infirmière.* Paris: Philippe Rey.

Pineau, Gisèle, and Marie Abraham. 1998. *Femmes des Antilles: traces et voix cent cinquante ans après l'abolition de l'esclavage.* Paris: Stock.

Price-Mars, Jean. *La Vocation de l'élite.* https://ekohaiti.com/wp-content/uploads/2021/01/La-vocation-de-le%CC%81lite.pdf. Accessed 1 July 2022.

Schwab, Gabrielle. 2010. *Haunting Legacies: Violent Histories and Transgenerational Trauma.* New York: Columbia University Press.

Schwarz-Bart, André. 1972a. *La Mulâtresse Solitude.* Paris: Seuil.

Schwarz-Bart, Simone. 1972b. *Pluie et vent sur Télumée Miracle.* Paris: Seuil.

Schwarz-Bart, Simone, and André Schwartz-Bart. 2015. *L'Ancêtre en Solitude.* Paris: Seuil.

Thomas, Bonnie. 2004. Reflections on the French Caribbean Woman: The Femme Matador in Fact and Fiction. *Kunapipi* 26.1. http://ro.uow.edu.au/kunapipi/vol26/iss1/11. Accessed 1 Dec 2019.

———. 2010. Transgenerational Trauma in Gisèle Pineau's *Chair piment* and *Mes quatre femmes. International Journal of Francophone Studies* 13 (1): 23–38.

Veldwachter, Nadège. 2004. An Interview with Gisèle Pineau. *Research in African Literatures* 351: 180–186.

Walker, Alice. 1992. *The Color Purple.* New York: Harcourt Brace Jovanovich.

Wilson, Elizabeth. 1990. 'Le voyage et l'espace clos'—Island and Journey as Metaphor: Aspects of Woman's Experience in the Works of Francophone Caribbean Women Novelists. In *Out of the Kumbla: Caribbean Women and Literature,* ed. Carole Boyce Davies and Elaine Savory Fido, 45–57. Trenton: Africa World Press.

Open Access This chapter is licensed under the terms of the Creative Commons Attribution 4.0 International License (http://creativecommons.org/licenses/by/4.0/), which permits use, sharing, adaptation, distribution and reproduction in any medium or format, as long as you give appropriate credit to the original author(s) and the source, provide a link to the Creative Commons licence and indicate if changes were made.

The images or other third party material in this chapter are included in the chapter's Creative Commons licence, unless indicated otherwise in a credit line to the material. If material is not included in the chapter's Creative Commons licence and your intended use is not permitted by statutory regulation or exceeds the permitted use, you will need to obtain permission directly from the copyright holder.

PART II

Radical Remapping

CHAPTER 6

Connecting Diasporas: Reading Erna Brodber's *Nothing's Mat* through African Fractal Theory

A. Marie Sairsingh

Erna Brodber's intervention in Caribbean literary and philosophical discourse, and specifically in the discourse of black ontology evinces a dual concern with engaging conventional history and transcending it via mythology and with evoking a gender inflection that expands these discussions considerably. Given that the emergence of an Afro-Caribbean subjectivity was impeded by damaging versions of colonial history foisted upon the region, and that female subjectivity was doubly marginalized within this matrix, Brodber's emphasis on gender seeks to denaturalize the androcentric assumption of the male as the principal (and only) subject of history. Like many other Caribbean women writers, she challenges the subordinated status of women in historical representation and in Caribbean philosophical thought and seeks to bring equitable balance to these discussions by foregrounding women, as seen in such works as *Jane and Louisa Will Soon Come Home* (1980), *Louisiana* (1994), and *Myal* (1988).

A. M. Sairsingh (✉)
University of the Bahamas, Nassau, Bahamas
e-mail: marie.sairsingh@ub.edu.bs

© The Author(s) 2023
O. Ferly, T. Zimmerman (eds.), *Chronotropics*,
https://doi.org/10.1007/978-3-031-32111-5_6

If, in the nationalist era of the 1960s, Caribbean thinkers' engagement with history "set the agenda of intellectual discourse," "influenced the [...] themes of creative expression" (James 1959) and added momentum to political and social transformation of the region, Brodber's investment in stories that foreground women in history contributes to post-nationalist discussions of freedom and to the reconceptualization of the category "human" in its broadest meaning. Foundational to Brodber's poetics is her investment in history and African cosmogonies, both of which establish the provenance of African worldviews in reshaping discourse on *being* and *existentiality* in the contemporary Caribbean and in the globalized world. Her oeuvre presents a broadened conceptualization, or a radical remapping of the contours of *the Caribbean self* and engenders a narrative scope that challenges masculinist constructs of Caribbean selfhood.

In her latest novel, *Nothing's Mat*, (2014), Brodber's theorization of black ontology takes in a wide swath of Afrodiasporic space, exploring a widening circle of personal, psychic, and philosophical journeying. In this novel she utilizes a fractal paradigm, based on African cosmogony and aesthetics, to probe the ways in which those explorations of ontology operate across space and time. Examining Afro-Caribbean existence within a larger framing of the African diaspora, through the construct of African fractal geometry, and focalizing "woman" narratives of history within a liberatory schematic, *Nothing's Mat* extends the continuing emancipatory project in literary representation. The frame of fractal tropology offers possibilities for understanding African and African diaspora cultural phenomena and identity, and, specifically, what it means to be woman, to be black, to be human. The novel returns us to Africa, as its fractal epistemology is more African than diasporic. Yet, while it is peopled with Black characters who reside variously in Britain, Jamaica, Panama, and the United States, their interconnected lives and heritage bring into focus the genealogy of the term "African diaspora."

Pan-Africanism stressed the commonalities among Africans globally and articulated political imperatives in the interest of global Black liberation. In the mid-1950s, the concept of "diaspora" became prevalent and, according to Brent Hayes Edwards (2003), signaled an important intervention in Pan-Africanist discourse that simultaneously acknowledged constitutive differences in "formations of black internationalism," and provided a "conceptual metaphor" for the analysis of these formations, while implicitly signaling a "linking or connecting across gaps" (11). Defining the African diaspora, Michael Gomez (2005)[1] focalizes "comparisons and relationships between communities of African descended people geographically separated or culturally distinct" (2). He identifies common elements such as an affinity with Africa as a place of origin, enslavement of ancestors, adaptation to a new environment, continued struggle against discrimination, the significance of Africa in the lives of African-descended peoples, and the reification of color and race (2). The concept of African diaspora functions, then, as an important and useful frame for mapping the black experience across historical, geographical, and cultural spaces and times and thus, for examining Erna Brodber's *Nothing's Mat* within a historical and cultural frame as well as within a literary tradition and genealogy characterized by diasporic intersections. The critical questions as to how we can extrapolate these historical, social, and cultural divergences and simultaneously recognize similarities of the Black experience within the different spaces and times are explored in *Nothing's Mat*. The African diaspora creates a space beyond the boundaries of nation and makes possible meaningful cross-cultural exploration of the existential realities of African-descended peoples residing in different locations and temporalities, as the characters in the novel reside in Britain, Jamaica, Panama, and the United States.

The divergences and synergies in the narratives show the interconnectedness, the intricately woven histories of family members whose presence is symbolically plaited into the structure of a mat, which itself stands as a metaphor for the potential unity of the African diaspora. I want to suggest Brodber's use of a mat, rather than the usual anthropological diagrammatic structure of a family tree, as an innovative and important trope that represents a radical remapping of the concept of 'family', and an epistemological shift in presenting a family history and the metaphorical genealogy for the diaspora. The mat and the process of weaving have important cultural and communal associations with African indigenous labor and cultural preservation, and as such, are intricately connected to a material history of continental Africans, and the associated historical narratives of Africans in the diaspora. Brodber's especial focus on African mat weaving highlights these functions within Africa and its diaspora. As well, she presents the woven mat as a counter-historical narrative to the written colonial records. In virtually all of Brodber's creative and intellectual work, history is a focal element.[2] Her philosophy of history functions centrally in the formation of an Afro-Caribbean/African diasporic consciousness. In *The Continent of Black Consciousness*, for example, Brodber (2003) elaborates on the crucial role of historical knowledge in a people's advancement toward self-consciousness, self-affirmation, and collective progress (xi). In *Nothing's Mat*, she similarly gives centrality to "rediscovery" and reweaving of Black history within the milieu of contemporary Jamaica, and to reaching back to ancestral foundations that underpin her fictional ontology.

Brodber transforms the genre of the historical novel by engaging particular fictional strategies that facilitate in-depth probing of Afro-Caribbean selfhood and prompt us to reformulate our understanding of historical time and the constituents of subjectivity. A significant element in this fictional ontology is that Brodber revises linear time, offering an alternative temporality marked by an expansion of "the living present." This process mediates time and perception, ultimately reconciling and bringing cohesion to the seemingly asymmetrical backwards and forwards movement within a plasticity of consciousness. Moreover, a significant element in Brodber's fractal poetics is that it provides a frame for overturning traditional concepts of linearity in the treatment of history. Fractal structure undoes the rectilinear concept of time, and thus broadens the scope of imaginative thought. This has implications for the novel's conceptions of historical time and of blood relations and diasporic unity.

Writers of the African diaspora frequently display thematic commonalities, often addressing forced migration, dislocation, racial slavery, and colonial domination, or the more contemporaneous experience of displacement, exile, and un-belonging. Indeed, Brodber examined some of these thematic elements in *Louisiana* (1994), exploring the meaning and reaches of diasporic spaces—material or metaphysical—to enact a transcendence of oppressive systems within postcolonial milieu. In *Nothing's Mat*, she extends these themes to articulate the power of resilience within Afro-diasporic communities and the diverse ways in which these communities reclaim a sense of belonging, located-ness, and historical significance. Moreover, the various narratives of the novel represent interconnected points within a fractal design/paradigm. The novel incorporates the post-slavery era, and moves through to the contemporary moment, charting the struggles of the formerly enslaved to achieve physical and psychic reconstitution. The narrative shifts from one locale to another: from the Black immigrant experience in Britain, represented by Herbert and Bridget, and their children Evan and Princess, all cousins to Nothing, to the rural experiences of Cousin Nothing in Jamaica, to the pioneering enterprise of Euphemia in Panama, to the black power enlistment of Joy (Nothing's cousin, once removed) in the United States. Yet, the historical, social, cultural, and geographical divergence of these experiences is superseded by the similarity of the existential concerns that these narratives reveal. I posit Brodber's employment of fractal structure as philosophical positioning and as textual architectonics. Fractals signify on several levels: those of her cultural, historiographical and imaginative work. Historiography, anthropology, and social science coalesce within Brodber's project yielding a broad set of principles that collapse disciplinary boundaries and provide alternative ways of reading literary and cultural experiences.

African Fractals and African Knowledge Systems

Fractal geometry is ubiquitous within African cultural practices and knowledge systems; it is seen in African divination systems, social organizations, textile design, and architectural design. The five essential components of fractal geometry are, according to Ron Eglash (1999), recursion, scaling, self-similarity, infinity, and fractional dimension. In his study of African fractals, Eglash traces the prevalence of these architectural designs in the spiritual, artistic, and everyday life and work across African communities and in the African diaspora, and asserts that, "traditional African settlements typically show this 'self-similar' characteristic: circles of circles of circular dwellings, rectangular walls enclosing ever-smaller rectangles and streets in which broad avenues branch down to tiny footpaths with striking geometric repetition" (4). Eglash's research shows fractal geometry as fundamental to African knowledge systems (3). These knowledge systems and wisdom traditions upon which Brodber draws render usable constructs for examining the realities of, and creative responses to, the cultural and socio-political milieus that form the setting of her novel.

The several narrative threads of this complex novel are contained across geographical space through the construct of the Caribbean family, which serves as a metonym for diaspora. The sisal mat at the center of the novel, which traces and articulates shared familial history, serves not only as the fabric of the Caribbean lineage that the protagonist, Princess, attempts to investigate, but also as the structural framework of the novel itself, which shifts recursively through time and space. The fractal configuration both of the mat and the novel reinforces the revolving structure of connectedness and diaspora, where an understanding of the past provides necessary context for reconciliation, relationships, self-affirmation, and growth within the contemporary space. In the novel, Cousin Nothing, or Conut as she is sometimes called, introduces the mat as the best means to respond to Princess's request to trace her personal history as part of her senior project on the Caribbean family. Princess, born in England of Jamaican parents, selects this project and travels to Jamaica to meet her cousin, whose name she finds mysterious and intriguing. Her investigations into her past provide contexts for self-knowledge that sustain her throughout her life; Princess continually returns to Jamaica throughout her intellectual studies, eventually settling in Jamaica and completing the mat and experiencing a deep connection with "ancestral spirits and energy" (Brodber 2014, 106). Her journeys between England and Jamaica recall the journeys of previous generations in her family, reflecting the recursive elements of the mat structure.

The making of the mat begins with strands of sisal harvested from a ping wing macca plant that Cousin Nothing identifies as one with a growth progression that "follows the natural path" (13). Referring to the structure of the leaves, she observes, "one leaf would emerge, then another, then two—the sum of one and one—then three—the sum of two and one, then five would emerge—the sum of two and three … the number of leaves continuing to determine the next number of leaves to infinity" (13). Connecting this to a "law of creativity laid down by the Supreme Being," Cousin Nothing asserts that "there was a natural process to growth, and it was that we should always double back to base before going forward" (13). This process becomes the means by which Princess not only creates the sisal mat but also theorizes the Caribbean family and establishes her journey to personal development. The mat is symbolically invoked early in the novel when Princess describes herself as existing "in a sea of nothingness" (4). As Princess nervously explores her feelings of nothingness, and the fact that her "parts are not talking to each other," she is relieved to note that her "frontal lobe is still intact," signaling that she is "still human" (3). This grounded-ness is fed by her revitalizing memories, which reassure her of her own humanity. In her state of loneliness, Princess broods about her sense of disconnection. "Nothing is happening," she laments. "Nothing. Not attached" (4). Her desire for rootedness, for connection, takes her back to Cousin Nothing and as she recalls her singing, "I have an anchor," she wonders about her own need of an anchor in that moment (5). References to strings, webs, anchors, and roots, as well as to memory and humanity, invoke connectivity. The structures themselves are fractal, representing a crisscrossing constellation of metaphors that move out to form a meta-constellation. Conceptually, they function as the medium through which one connects to combat the loneliness of exile and the un-belonging that often portrays the diasporic experience.

On Family History and Diaspora History

The novel shifts abruptly to Princess's young adulthood, when she is at the initial stage of selecting a topic for her senior project. Her mother suggests that a study of her father's "alternative" Caribbean family would necessitate a reformulation or revision of received European notions of family. Turning to Princess's father, she asks, "Where are you going to put Conut, your mother's sister who isn't your mother's sister?" (5). This question, proposed in jest, lies at the heart of *Nothing's Mat*, a novel in which family, and by extension the African diaspora, must be conceived in ways that challenge linear structures, whether of generations or of blood. In order to map her family using linear formulations, Princess's mother interjects, "they would have to be born again and in some order" (5). In fact, upon meeting Conut and arranging to stay with her to complete her family tree, Princess is faced with just such a challenge:

> "So you want to know your family line," Conut states.
> "Yes," I said and went for my diagram.
> She glanced at it, put it on the table, and said "Come."

Thus begins Princess's memory project that traverses the length of the novel and the greater part of her life as, together with Conut (Cousin Nothing), she weaves a mat encompassing the life stories of her forebears, not in a linear tree, but in a fractal formation, weaving backward and forward to integrate the past, the present, and the future, and the interstitial spaces that transcend fixed temporality. As Princess weaves the sisal mat and learns the stories of those that have come before her, she gains a greater sense of her own purpose, value, and significance, both within her family and within the community she is invited to join. Princess's growth, evinced in her expanding knowledge base and her pursuit of familial and romantic relationships, involves repeated returns to Jamaica from England. Her journeys back to Conut to complete the sisal mat enrich her knowledge of family and of self. The mat is intricately linked to identity reconstruction, and reflects a complex system in which circularity, replication, and self-similarity weave the narrative of Afrodiasporic cultural histories, the process of claiming and asserting Afrodiasporic cultural and personal histories, and the resilience to the atrocities that those histories contain.

Brodber's use of the West Indian family, in all its diversity, resonates with the discourses of diaspora and fractality, as generations of family members represent both variance and similarity, simultaneously. When Princess arrives in Cousin Nothing's village, she hears the villagers saying, "What a way she look like Conut. Same fine body" (6). Opting to stay in the village, she is pleasantly surprised to find a full wardrobe of Conut's clothes that fit her (6). This theme of the past continually returning in the present is prevalent throughout the text and undergirds the fractal concept of looping, with circular patterns extending out, then turning backward. This recursive nature of fractals reveals that, "no matter the number of fractalizations, the parts are interconnected into a whole which is self-similar to the parts" (Voicu 2014, 226). As a partial replication of Conut, Princess herself provides one of many examples of this self-similarity in the generations presented in *Nothing's Mat*. Conut, whose birth comes as a surprise to her mother and grandmother, as well as to her two possible fathers, is acknowledged by Mass Eustace as his child when "he look[s] in the baby's face [and sees] his mother" (Brodber 2014, 20). This opinion is shared by his twin sister, Euphemia, who finds "her mother's nose upon the child" (20). Mass Eustace and Euphemia both grow attached to Conut, and he finds himself looking forward to playing with "his miniature mother" (21). Even as Mass Eustace sees his mother in Conut, her mother, Clarise, sees her own paternal grandmother, "one of those who come from somewhere else" whom she encountered only once. Before Clarise's untimely death from tuberculosis, she shared with her daughter her one memory of this African woman who performs her spinning dance: "I see her spinning around, spinning around like dry leaf can spin by themselves when they catch up in spider's web and breeze is blowing. Just spinning with her hands spread out like wings to balance her so that she can't drop to the ground" (58–59). For Clarise, Conut is a loop back to this African grandmother, another symbolic anchor, whom she never got to know, but whose memory sustains her. Clarise laments that, 'I never see my grandmother again and nobody tell me anything, so I say to myself that she spin and spin and her feet lift up off the ground and she fly to the heaven in the sky" (59), and bestows this narrative to Conut, who continues the dance (59). "She look so much like my grandmother," Clarise muses; "funny, for when Mass Eustace see her he always saying how she have his mother face" (59).

This recursive generational pattern of births continues with the birth of Princess's daughter, Clarise the second, who is pet-named Polly, after Princess's aunt. Polly (the second) also performs Conut's spinning dance. Observing her, Princess marvels, "I had once been privileged to see Nothing in a pose which I felt was impossible, a skill that Nothing didn't want spoken about. I have never mentioned it to anyone, yet here was this child contorted like the bird into which I had seen Nothing turn herself, the bird into which Clarise's grandmother, the African, had perhaps turned herself to fly away home to wherever, and about which Clarise had told Nothing when she was just a baby" (102). This recursive nesting reinforces the relationships between the generations, linking the diasporic present to the ancestral past, superimposing upon linear constructions of generational time a fractal structure that allows, in a sense, for "infinity within a finite boundary" (Welch 2010, 99). Princess abandons the acyclic graph model for creating the "Family tree" in favor of the configuration of the sisal mat, with its concentric circular patterns to represent her family's history, honoring the maxim, "your end is your beginning" (Brodber 2014, 14). She and Conut comb the strings of the ping wing macca tree, and "twist the strings into strong cord" as Conut shares her knowledge of the family. At the start of the senior research project, Princess "tried to put the data into the grid [she] had brought" (14). She later chooses instead to "focus on the never-ending circles that [they] were making that seemed like a mat of family" (14). As evinced in the naming practices and resemblances of family members across generations in *Nothing's Mat*, this "self-similarity" in which patterns of the whole repeat within each of its parts represents microcosm and macrocosm. This relationship between the macrocosm and the microcosm resonates not only with the example of Princess's particular family, but also with the Caribbean family, and with the African Diaspora.

Princess's work on Conut's mat results in the successful completion of her senior project, which is very well received, and launches her career as a researcher. More importantly, her research garners commendation and her professor's observation that "the literature speaks of the Caribbean family as 'fractured' [but] you might be able to prove that it is fractal" (36). This intellectual pursuit becomes Princess's life's work as she continues working with Conut to expand the sisal mat and to complete her journey toward self-history and self-knowledge. Her relationship with her cousin named "Nothing," and the history Nothing bequeaths, enriches her life in ways she could not have predicted at seventeen, when she embarked on her first journey to Jamaica.

On 'Smadditization'

While Brodber's character "Nothing" represents history's repository, such a representation is paradoxical to the idea of "Nothing-ness" in Caribbean historiography and with various regional critics' "quarrel with history."[3] In his 1962 text, *The Middle Passage*, V.S. Naipaul, commenting on the lack of history in the West Indies, asserts, "The history of the islands can never be satisfactorily told. ... History is built around achievement and creation; and nothing was created in the West Indies" (2001, 20). This statement ignited the ire of many Caribbean intellectuals, poets, cultural theorists, social theorists alike, who variously responded to counteract this notion of *nothingness* that had become a specter in West Indian historical consciousness.

Nothing becomes the channel to recovery, in spite of her own inauspicious beginnings. Clarise, her mother, had been naïvely unaware of her own pregnancy, and it was not until the premature emergence of the baby at seven months that she attained full knowledge of her preceding condition. This newborn would have been thrown into the latrine were it not for the scream that drew the attention of Miss Maud, Clarise's "mother." The narrator tells us, "Miss Maud asked her what is wrong. Clarise said, "Nothing, mam." Miss Maud retrieves the child and indignantly asks, "So dis ya something wid two legs, ten toes and ten fingers, and a head is 'nothing'? Ah dat you baby name, Gal?" Miss Maud responds to neighbors' queries as to whether something is wrong with, "Nothing wrong." Although the child is named June, she is thereafter dubbed "Nothing."

For Brodber, the narratives of personal, national, regional, and global history are paramount to the completion of the project of emancipation for Caribbean peoples. *Nothing's Mat* offers redress to the rhetoric of history-less-ness and to the histories of dispossession, and foregrounds women in this regard. The presence of the title character, in spite of her name, negates the purported history-less-ness, since she is in fact history's repository. Nothing weaves the family history into the structure of the sisal mat, with the circular patterns, recursive maneuvers and reversions, which symbolize the history of the individual family, the West Indian family, and the wider African diaspora family, as it reclaims an ontological mooring for the reconstruction of the self. The title character and her history are made material and productive, providing the framework for connecting to the past and to the diaspora. They also reformulate the epistemologies that inform our understanding of history's form, function, and purpose. Princess's collection of Conut's history challenges and reconfigures the conceptions of the West Indian family in "the literature," that is, in traditional academic constructions; her continued research represents the reconfiguring of history that is now insisted upon by those, like Princess, (and, indeed, Brodber herself) who are inspired to collect and value the historical experiences and oral accounts rendered by latent repositories of history within the African diaspora. "My presentation did not use the straight lines and arrows that one normally sees in family trees," Princess remarks, "I used the circles as in Conut's mat" (36). She recalls her parents being worried about her teacher's response to the non-traditional structure of her research results. Her teacher's response, citing Conut's phrase, "in what odd places does wisdom reside" (36), speaks to the changing ideologies of historicism in the academy, and to the rejection of monumentalism as the only legitimate index of historical contributions.

This impulse to reclaim the elided Caribbean ontology is evident in the theorizations of many Caribbean writers and scholars; some commentators have asserted the need to reclaim a self, submerged within the wreck of colonial history. Rex Nettleford (2003) is credited with the neologism, "smadditization," derived from the Jamaican vernacular word, "smaddy," which in translation, means "somebody." Hence, smadditization refers to the process of *becoming* or being *acknowledged* as somebody. This implies that personhood had previously been denied or unrecognized. Using Nettleford's neologism, Charles Mills (2013) explains smadditization as "the struggle for the insistence on personhood … a kind of ontological self-engineering" (328). Mills's usage of the term entails "the valorization of oneself as an agent of moral and cognitive evaluation" (334). He submits that Caribbean achievement lies in "the re-creation of a self in an ontological construction more daring than any essayed in the world of European philosophy. The survival of the person and the reinvention of the self in the Caribbean experience in general and in the Black experience in particular, is one of the most remarkable feats of human history" (338).

This process, then, of coming into being, is a concern for Brodber as she renders the historical narrative of a person who, though known as "Nothing", is the guardian of history. Princess's research, and Brodber's work in *Nothing's Mat*, involve mapping and recording those remarkable achievements that are not to be found in the structures and monuments constituting European-derived epistemologies, but in the everyday lives, the struggles and resistances, as well as the folk ways and the self-sustaining practices of peoples of the diaspora, particularly those of women. Princess's growth as a scholar and ethnographer shifts the narrative of history and historiography. Extending her research to attain a terminal degree, she turns her energies to augmenting Conut's mat by including "the details that Cousin Nothing did not know about, [sticking] them around the circumference of the mat [to] give it closure" (40). In the text, Princess becomes "Dr. Something" (Brodber 2014, 40), achieving the status of Smaddy.

ON REDEFINING FAMILY/DESTABILIZING FILIATION

While Princess's growth is strongly symbolized in her intellectual journey, it is also portrayed in her relationships with her extended family and with the family she eventually raises herself. Just as the fractal formation of the sisal mat destabilizes linear constructions of historical time, it also demands a rejection of linear constructions of blood relations. Referring to her grandmother's siblings, who are seemingly not her siblings, Princess dismisses these distinctions in a meaningful aside, "[D]oes kinship terminology matter?" This begs the question as to why humans draw lines of demarcation between blood relations, and everyone else (23). These lines appear increasingly arbitrary in the example of Princess's family, just as they do in theories of diaspora. Indeed, the terms and expressions of kinship are stretched, doubled, and extended in the novel, rendering it difficult to distinguish who is related to whom, and through what means. Fosterings, adoptions, and connections of love frequently supersede traditional blood relationships.

Brodber provides us with earlier narratives of fosterings, adoptions, and connections of love in her rendering of the story of Maud, the matriarch of the story. Maud serves as the point of recursion in Princess's family history. It is significant that Brodber places a woman at the center not only of the history of Princess's family but also at the center of symbolic diasporic history. Maud's place in history is reified not only in the mat, but in her actions as mother and as a revolutionary figure, initiating the infamous burning of the courthouse in the Morant Bay rebellion of 1865, a signal moment in Jamaican history. Situating Maud as a pivotal contributor to the rebellion, Brodber reconfigures Jamaican history not only to include the contributions of women, but also to subvert masculinist constructions of black revolutionary politics and activism. She dislodges the conception of the absent female in showing Maud's militarism. The invisibility to

6 CONNECTING DIASPORAS: READING ERNA BRODBER'S *NOTHING'S MAT...* 115

which women had historically been consigned in discourse is vigorously questioned and corrected in *Nothing's Mat*. Michelle Rowley's observations regarding new historiographical approaches among Caribbean women are germane here:

> By questioning the absence of women from historical texts, Caribbean feminist historiographers opened a pathway to discuss the implications of archival silences and fissures. ... These historically produced ... rhetorical practices raise peculiar ontological questions for black women in that while we lay claims to the capacity to produce knowledge, we must first ... have figured out how to argue ... our way into being. (Rowley 2010, 10)

At sixteen, Maud flees Morant Bay with Clarise, the sister of her slain betrothed, and raises "Gal" as her own child, though she is merely nine years Clarise's senior (Brodber 2014, 48). Recovering from being gang raped by seven Maroons who sought revenge for her role in the Morant Bay rebellion, Maud travels on foot from Stony Gut to Kingston, and in that time, cares for the "Gal" she barely knows. Maternal impulses, what Maud refers to as feeling "mother things," develop in spite of her own personal agonies as the two travelers attempt to escape to safety from the turmoil of their home. She comes to understand that "her little sister would have to be her child, and [with that, simply put,] she was." Maud admits that, "De child vex but me can't take that on for as mi tell her mi is now her mother and she have to listen to what me say and obey. Then mi realize that me now have to behave certain way so that she can respect what me say and obey me" (49). Clarise is grudgingly thankful for the security provided by "this lady, who call herself my sister and sometimes my mother" (55); "I didn't really know her well, this woman who sey she is in charge of me, and I don't know if she knew me" (53). While recalling her brother Modibe's intentions to marry Maud and therefore make Maud and Clarise sisters, Clarise ponders, "How can someone be "going to be" your sister. Your sister is born your sister;" however, she accepts Maud as her sister-mother, stating, "This female who say she was in charge of me must be my sister" (53). This acceptance is based not on her biologically determined assumption but on the lived experience of nurture, protection, and love she receives. "Sometimes," she recalls, "when we were in the cave on the beach, she would put her hand around my shoulder. That feel good and I feel like I have a mother. Also, I know that she wasn't sleeping most of the time we were in the sea cave, but instead watching over me" (53–54).

116   A. M. SAIRSINGH

This destabilization of bloodlines begins at the outset of the narrative as Princess reflects on the function of titles and manners in Jamaican culture, and particularly on references that shift traditional significations of familial positioning. Terms such as "Uncle Brother," Princess suggests, may refer to an "adult male who might have been called 'Brother' as a pet name by his younger sibs" only to have a handle put to his name out of respect later in life, hence "Uncle Brother" (1). Names and titles, familial relations and linear bloodlines are undercut, most particularly by the introduction of Princess's cousin, Conut, or Cousin Nothing, who appears to be Princess's paternal grandmother's "sister who isn't' [her] sister" (5). Adoption, as well as traditional and nontraditional fosterings, recurs throughout the novel and amongst Princess's diasporic family. She learns that her own mother "had been left on a bridge" in the middle of the road to be crushed by traffic, but was, luckily, taken to safety, and adopted. In Jamaica, Princess encounters Keith, a young man likely poisoned by Mass Eustace in his efforts to ward off potential thieves trying to steal his dasheens and other crops. Most likely out of guilt, Eustace fosters the child, who was born malformed, and offers his mother "a square of land to work" and helps her to "build a little house in the bush" to raise her son (12). Conut assumes the care of Keith after Eustace dies, taking on the role of mother to the "dasheen boy" whom she reveals to Princess. Another example of adoption occurs when Mass Eustace's sister, Euphemia, an enterprising woman, travels to Panama to trade in yams and develops her own laundry business there, eventually inviting and adopting Pearl, one of her nieces, who is in fact Princess's grandmother.

After her failed first marriage to an American man with whom she has two children, Pearl returns to Jamaica and marries Neville, the other possible father to Conut (who, saved earlier from the responsibilities of fatherhood, has achieved higher education, as the pastor had earlier predicted). Neville helps raise Pearl's first two children, John and Sally, along with their subsequent two, Polly and Herbert, the latter being Princess's father. The four children grow up as siblings, not half-siblings. The two older ones are sent to America for schooling and are made American citizens by their father, who assumes responsibility for their later upbringing. They remain close as adults and Sally eventually names her own son John the second. Sally's son, John and her brother John's daughter, Joy grow up as siblings. It is the unfair arrest of Joy's "brother-cousin" John that spurs her black activism and makes her the "revolutionary sister-cousin" of the family (78). Clearly, navigating the relationships in *Nothing's Mat* requires a fractal frame of mind! At the heart of these intertwining relationships is recursivity. As Princess acknowledges, "she and [Joy] were just a repeat of Nothing and Pearl" (95). These reiterations of the previous generations strongly suggest that family relationships can be fostered regardless of blood, time, or geographic space. This idea is inherent in the underlying thesis of Princess's work, that the Caribbean family, and, by extension, the African diaspora, is fractal rather than fractured, and that history, memory, and connectivity can bridge distances of blood, time and region to engender a deep sense of belonging. Princess is optimistic about her own children's potential for growth, given the wealth of knowledge she has shared with them about their ancestors and their history through the sisal mat. She predicts that they will make their own mat when the time is right and asserts that "the experience will certainly connect them to another set of kin and another set of happy energy. They won't know the nothingness that set me to completing Nothing's mat, because they understand more about ancestral spirits and energy than I knew at thirty" (106). Brodber's novel posits history and self-knowledge as the bridge to happiness and spiritual connection. As a metaphor for the African diaspora, the mat reveals the ways in which the survivors of the Middle Passage constitute a family, separated by time, space and blood, but still evincing strong potential for unity.

On Liberation

Brodber's creative work operates within the sphere of asserting female presence, and provides productive framing concepts through which freedom can be imagined. For example, her imaginative account of the Morant Bay rebellion shows not only women's resilience in the face of abuse and violation, and their ability to ensure their own survival, but demonstrates also their participation in the fight for social justice. Brodber situates women firmly within the discourse of resistance. Her fiction, with its focus on female representation, furthers this discussion of self-definition, compels a wider discussion of gender, and invites an examination of the novelist's modes of intervening in the discourse of Caribbean feminism. While she sees her work as part of the Afro-Caribbean women's tradition that seeks to illuminate the multifarious expressions of women's existence, Brodber refuses the category of Afro-Caribbean *feminist* writer, specifically. If feminism is a modality that seeks to privilege the liberation of women over other dominated subjects, it is not a position with which she is aligned.

Rather, her emphasis is on the liberation of all oppressed groups and classes of persons in society, which, in her view, is a moral and political imperative and, as such, a necessary condition for the emancipation of women.

While Brodber eschews the label "feminist," her acute awareness of the liberatory imperative in her own ideological stance and in her work enables us to see how and why she foregrounds the struggle of women, and of Black women in particular, as part of the wider struggle of people for justice and equality. She sees race as the most contested of categories in the discourse of Caribbean freedom and in the global project of human liberation. In *Nothing's Mat*, placing the Black female as protagonist serves to foreground *her* narrative, which had been underserved within the intellectual and literary traditions largely informed by the masculine inflections of male forerunners who were the founding architects of early literary traditions. *Nothing's Mat* extends this work, as Cousin Nothing, arguably, can be read as symbolic of not only Caribbean history, but women's history, redeemed from nothingness. Brodber's gender politics is thus mediated through her overarching consciousness of race and concomitantly, of freedom, which in her view, takes precedence in the project of human liberation, even as she situates the Afro-Caribbean woman within the poetics of self-determination. As Rowley points out, colonialism, the Middle Passage, and the Kala Pani, as events within the long arc of history "hold specific ontological urgency for women in and of the African diaspora" (Rowley 2010, 3) since within these occurrences, women have arguably been the most systematically excluded and denigrated.

Nothing's Mat brings into sharp focus this project of recuperation, restoring the place of the Black woman and, by extension, all of humanity. Principal characters in Brodber's novels, mainly women, engage in existential quests and politics of the self in ways that are similar to characters of Caribbean liberatory novels that precede her, mostly written by men. Beyond a shift in sex, Brodber's narratives introduce gendered dynamics that bring greater scope to the Caribbean quest for selfhood and self-affirmation and, through incorporating female narrative voice, agency, and autonomy, enable the constructions and emergence of the feminine subject. Brodber's literary discourse on history and on identity, apprehended through the frame of fractal geometry and through a lens that illuminates the female role within these matrices, adds to several bodies of scholarship simultaneously: Caribbean women's literary tradition, Afrodiasporic studies, and Africana philosophy. Analyzing the fractal construct at work in *Nothing's Mat* reveals it as an inventive strategy for reading familial interconnectedness and resemblances, and for reinforcing a consciousness of diasporic relationalities. Brodber's innovative use of fractals to present Afro-Caribbean and diasporic history reveals how the intricacies of these histories evince self-similarity across space and time. Brodber presents interwoven narratives across geographical space through the construct of family, which serves as a metonym for diaspora. In this fictional ontology she revises linear time, offering an alternative temporality that is marked by an "expansion of the living present," and which mediates time and space, ultimately reconciling and bringing cohesion to the seemingly asymmetrical backward and forward movement within a plasticity of consciousness. The fractal construct, then, bears the potential for extending "family resemblances" outward, anchoring us within a metaphysics of relationality in ways that transcend spatial and temporal fixedness, and offers an equitable epistemological frame for envisioning a collective humanity.

NOTES

1. Gomez outlines these characteristics of African diasporic identity in his book, *Reversing Sail: A History of the African Diaspora* (Cambridge University Press), 2005.
2. Brodber's nonfiction (historical) texts include *The People of My Jamaican Village 1817–1948* (1999); *The Continent of Back Consciousness: On the History of the African Diaspora from Slavery to the Present Day* (2003); *Woodside: Pear Tree Grove P.O.* (2004); *The Second Generation of Freemen in Jamaica, 1907–1944* (2004); and *Moments of Cooperation and Incorporation: African American and African Jamaican Connections, 1782–1996* (2019).
3. Edward Baugh. "The West Indian Writer and His Quarrel with History." *Small Axe*, vol. 16, no. 2 (no. 38), 2012, pp. 60–74. This article was previously published in *Tapia*, 1977.

   Other writers of the region including Édouard Glissant, George Lamming, Wilson Harris, and Derek Walcott have similarly engaged the discourse of history in the Caribbean.

REFERENCES

Baugh, Edward. 2012 [1977]. The West Indian Writer and His Quarrel with History. *Small Axe* 16.2 (38): 60–74.

Brodber, Erna. 1994. *Louisiana*. London: New Beacon Press.

———. 1999. *Myal*. London: New Beacon Press.

———. 2003. *The Continent of Black Consciousness: On the History of the African Diaspora From Slavery to the Present Day*. London: New Beacon Press.

———. 2014. *Nothing's Mat*. Kingston: University of the West Indies Press.
Edwards, Brent Hayes. 2003. *The Practice of Diaspora: Literature, Translation, and the Rise of Black Internationalism*. Cambridge, MA: Harvard University Press.
Eglash, Ron. 1999. *African Fractals: Modern Computing and Indigenous Design*. New Brunswick, NJ: Rutgers University Press.
Gomez, Michael. 2005. *Reversing Sail: A History of the African Diaspora*. Cambridge: Cambridge University Press.
James, C.L.R. 1959. The Artist in the Caribbean. *Caribbean Quarterly* 54: 177–180.
Mills, Charles. 2013. Smaddditizin. In *Caribbean Political Thought: Theories of the Post-Colonial State*, ed. Aaron Kamugisha, 326–340. Kingston: Ian Randle Publishers.
Naipaul, V.S. 2001 [1962]. *The Middle Passage*. London: Picador Press.
Nettleford, Rex. 2003. Our Debt to History. In *Slavery, Freedom and Gender: The Dynamics of Caribbean Society*, ed. Brian L. Moore, W.W. Higman, Carl Campbell, and Patrick Bryan, 276–294. Kingston: University of the West Indies Press.
Rowley, Michelle V. 2010. Whose Time Is It?: Gender and Humanism in Contemporary Caribbean Feminist Advocacy. *Small Axe* 31 (14.1): 1–15.
Voicu, Christina-Georgiana. 2014. The Fractal Identity in Jean Rhys' Fiction. *Studia UBB Philologia* LIX.3: 225–232.
Welch, Kerri. 2010. *A Fractal Topology of Time: Implications for Consciousness and Cosmology*. Dissertation. California Institute of Integral Studies.

Open Access This chapter is licensed under the terms of the Creative Commons Attribution 4.0 International License (http://creativecommons.org/licenses/by/4.0/), which permits use, sharing, adaptation, distribution and reproduction in any medium or format, as long as you give appropriate credit to the original author(s) and the source, provide a link to the Creative Commons licence and indicate if changes were made.

The images or other third party material in this chapter are included in the chapter's Creative Commons licence, unless indicated otherwise in a credit line to the material. If material is not included in the chapter's Creative Commons licence and your intended use is not permitted by statutory regulation or exceeds the permitted use, you will need to obtain permission directly from the copyright holder.

CHAPTER 7

Writing "In Transit": Literary Constructions of Sovereignty in Julia Alvarez's *Afterlife*

Megan Jeanette Myers

> *Wouldn't it make a great book? ... Short chapters about the people who keep our world going? Invisible people we don't even know about?*
> —Julia Alvarez, Afterlife

Antonia, the protagonist of Julia Alvarez's *Afterlife* (2020), incessantly ponders not the meaning of life, but instead of *afterlife*. Afterlife for the recently widowed protagonist necessitates an understanding that prioritizes affection and empathy as opposed to action. Yet, in its own way, the novel represents a call to action, with a keen focus on current events and an open commentary on political and social realities both on the island of Hispaniola and in the United States. Further, Alvarez's recent novel centers and decenters global sites of sovereignty and offers various interpretations of Dominican American women—Antonia and her sisters—and Mexican migrant workers—Mario and Estela—as "in transit." While this chapter touches on how an understanding of in transit in *Afterlife*

M. J. Myers (✉)
Iowa State University, Ames, IA, USA
e-mail: mjmyers@iastate.edu

© The Author(s) 2023
O. Ferly, T. Zimmerman (eds.), *Chronotropics*,
https://doi.org/10.1007/978-3-031-32111-5_7

121

connects to the same term that serves as the crux to the 2013 Tribunal Court sentence in the Dominican Republic (also known as TC-0168 or *la sentencia*), the pages to follow also suggest that one can read the novel as a diasporic reflection on global, recurring themes of citizenship and statelessness. In this way, *Afterlife* offers readers a subtle commentary on how characters appear or are positioned as not always physically in motion or in transit, but as displaced—be it physically or metaphorically—or trying to place themselves. These disjointed relations to space allow a nuanced understanding of belonging, of sovereignty, and of what it means to be in transit.

This chapter asks how contemporary writers like Alvarez—on both sides of the island and from Hispaniola's diasporic reaches—harness diverse genres of literature to offer calls to action and declarations of solidarity, thus offering new ways to both understand and complicate global notions of sovereignty. I consider *Afterlife* to explore how writers from Hispaniola's diasporic communities can engage with an intra-island dialogue with respect to guiding concepts such as Sandra Pouchet Paquet's notion of nomadic subjectivity and Katherine Zien's articulation of acts of sovereignty within a Caribbean context. In transit narrative frames a recent interest in a transnational Hispaniola literary tradition—to quote the "intellectual project" as categorized by Kiran C. Jayaram's and April J. Mayes' anthology *Transnational Hispaniola* (2018, 2)—and connects this interest to the *desnacionalización* or denationalization of Haitians and Dominicans of Haitian descent. Antonia daydreams about writing a novel centered on the "invisible people we don't even know about" (Alvarez 2020, 33)—the same people that nonetheless keep our world going—and Alvarez's *Afterlife*, via its questioning of sovereignty on a global scale, suggests that "in transit" individuals are often those most rendered invisible. This chapter positions *Afterlife* as a novel that allows for a radical remapping of the term "in transit" as I do not only understand it from a Dominican national context, but also a literary one.

I label literary texts as in transit to accentuate how they move through time, and, relatedly, to highlight an emphasis on space and nation. My interest in the term in transit stems from its purposeful use in the 2013 Tribunal Court ruling, but the contextualization of in transit as understood in *Afterlife* interprets the term more broadly. My attempt is to approach in transit in various ways to contextualize its presence in literature.[1] Reconoci.do's campaign of *vidas suspendidas* is one example that can be understood alongside a definition of in transit; the campaign surfaced as an initial response to the Effects of Resolution 12 on Dominicans of Haitian descent,[2] an earlier 2007 decision of the Dominican Republic's Central Electoral Board to restrict Dominicans' access to official, governmental forms of identification. As Mayes (2018) notes, the campaign focuses on the Dominican *cédula* or identification card and how its politicized use often restricts access to education, marriage, banking, and other social services to Dominicans of Haitian descent (213). In many ways, the idea of a life being "suspended" resonates with a spatiotemporal understanding of the fluidity of in transit. The three elements of in transit narrative, as introduced herein, include: (1) a complex approach to space and geography and a scope that leans toward the transnational or intranational; (2) a reflection, albeit subtle, on politics and, oftentimes, a consciousness with regard to the nomenclature of in transit (or, similarly, *apátrida, desnacionalizado/a*, etc.); and, (3) the presence of themes relating to (im)migration. Each of the three identified categories builds on the aforementioned work of scholars Pouchet Paquet (2010) and Zien (2017), largely for the ways they both offer conceptualizations of Caribbean space and time.

DOMINICAN (AMERICAN) LITERATURE BEYOND "LA SOMBRA DE TRUJILLO"

Afterlife, marking Alvarez's first adult novel in over a decade, weaves together three plotlines that each center on a unique crisis—be it personal, familial, or societal. The novel's protagonist, Antonia Vega, is a retired English professor who just lost her husband, but her own introverted ways of dealing with the sudden death and loss of her partner are challenged when her sister disappears and, concurrently, a pregnant and undocumented teen arrives to rural Vermont in need of assistance. As a Dominican immigrant, Antonia confronted and challenged notions of belonging as an "Other" in a small, rural town in Vermont—in which she had given up "trying to explain the colonial intricacies of her ethnicity" (Alvarez 2020, 13)—long before she began navigating her new status as widow. My analysis of the novel approaches both belonging and nationalism from the perspective of this female protagonist and outlines a classification for literary texts deemed "in transit narratives."

In addition to a close reading of the novel, Alvarez's activism—both inside and outside of the literary realm—proves helpful to consider. In 2013, shortly after enforcement of TC-0168 began, Alvarez penned a

124   M. J. MYERS

letter to the Editor of the *New York Times* alongside Junot Díaz, Edwidge Danticat, and Mark Kurlansky. In the brief letter the writers classify the ruling as institutionalized racism and proclaim: "For any who thought that there was a new Dominican Republic, a modern state leaving behind the abuse and racism of the past, the highest court in the country has taken a huge step backward with Ruling 0168-13" (Kurlansky et al. 2013, n.p.). Beyond uniting her voice with other writers of Hispaniola's diaspora to denounce TC-0168, Alvarez is also a founding member of Border of Lights, a volunteer collective committed to remembering victims of the 1937 Massacre while also highlighting the solidarity that exists among Haitian and Dominican border communities.[3] While critics highlight how Alvarez's narratives incessantly return to her *patria*—one of many Caribbean diasporic writers considered "dialoguers with the reality and memory of their homelands" (Oboler 1996, 308)—it is also true that her perspective is often female-centered. Tegan Zimmerman confirms that Alvarez's "quest" in *In the Time of the Butterflies* (1994), for example, is to "provide a feminist polyphonic alternative to the patriarchal master narrative of the nation and recuperate the lives of the Mirabal sisters" (Zimmerman 2020, 96).

Further, Alvarez's historically rooted novels, including *In the Time of the Butterflies* and *In the Name of Salomé,* often fall in line with the multitudinous twentieth-century Dominican and Dominican American texts that speak to "la sombra" or the shadow of Trujillo, an image that Neil Larsen (1988) notes "refuses to disappear" (123, all translations mine). Given the masculine pulse of the Trujillo regime—a pattern analyzed by Maja Horn in *Masculinity After Trujillo*—these female-centered texts that offer counter-narratives of twentieth-century Hispaniola are critical to arriving at a more complex and nuanced understanding of the 1937 Massacre and the Trujillo Regime. Horn highlights the "centrality of gender notions in structuring Dominican political, public, and private imaginaries" and contextualizes such gendered discourses in the literary realm (Horn 2014, 9). Other recent Dominican American novels—of Angie Cruz, Elizabeth Acevedo, and Nelly Rosario, for example—also center the female diasporic experience, a pattern that *Afterlife* follows. Does Alvarez's recent novel, then, mark a new type of novel for the author? Does an exploration of afterlife render a new reckoning with post-life or with a spatiotemporal reality that is disjointed from the earthbound experience? With regards to notions of time in particular, a discussion of afterlife urges readers to confront unknown futures and unmapped realities; the title alone frames the novel's compartmentalization of the passing of time.

Considering the ways in which Alvarez's *In the Time of the Butterflies* in some ways decenters Haitian–Dominican relations or predates the current trend in Transnational Hispaniola Studies to reexamine interisland relations, *Afterlife* not only acutely tackles themes related to anti-Haitianism, but goes a step further to confront social and political injustices on a global scale. Alvarez, for example, addresses the criticism of her bestseller *In the Time of the Butterflies* and defends her historical ex/in-clusions: "I've been taken to task sometimes because the novel did not address the massacre and the Mirabal sisters were alive then. 'Why didn't you say more about the Haitian Massacre?' It's important to remember that I was writing from the point of view of particular characters. None of my research into their lives yielded an awareness or response to what happened. I can't colonize my characters and plant in their heads and sensibilities what isn't there—especially for historical characters" (Myers 2021, 450). *In the Name of Salomé*, another example of Alvarez's historical fiction, comments on Dominican poet and educator Salomé Ureña's heritage. The novel includes "several moments when the fictional Ureña experiences her non-whiteness vis-à-vis the white-presenting elite that surround her" (Ramírez 2015, 53). As related to the massacre in particular, these two historical narratives differ from Haitian American Edwidge Danticat's *The Farming of Bones* or René Philoctète's *Massacre River*, that both detail the 1937 Massacre and Dominican–Haitian relations during the Trujillo Era.[4]

On the whole, when compared to *trujillista* narratives, literature related to the 2013 Tribunal Court ruling in the Dominican Republic is much less developed. Unlike the vast analyses that explore what has been deemed by some scholars "Trujillo narrative," literature that responds in both overt and subtle ways to the 2013 sentence is diverse and interdisciplinary, but not as recognized or critically acclaimed as the vast body of Dominican texts that examines what scholar Rita De Maeseneer (2006) refers to as "la brega con el pasado" (23).[5] Furthermore, the works that are in dialogue with the 2013 sentence and respond to the ongoing institutionalized racism and oppression against Haitians and Dominicans of Haitian descent in the Dominican Republic represent a variety of genres and media forms. Examples include the collection of testimonies *Nos Cambió la Vida*[6] and two recent documentaries *Hasta la Raíz* (*Down to the Root*, 2017) and *Apátrida* (*Stateless*, 2019). While these three examples center on Dominicans of Haitian descent living in the Dominican Republic, much of the public outcry and outward criticism in the wake of the sentence stemmed from the US diaspora, led by campaigns such as We Are All Dominican or the solidarity-building organization In Cultured Company.[7] How do consciousness-raising, community-building initiatives, then, resonate in literature from Hispaniola's diaspora? Building on Pouchet Paquet's nomadic subjectivity and reflecting on (im)migration and nationalism understood via Rigney's acts of sovereignty, the remainder of this essay critically examines a model of in transit narrative. Further, this chapter reads Alvarez's *Afterlife* as reflective of such themes and as a new way to conceptualize interpretations of and conscious reconciliations with the meaning of in transit in literature.

TC-0168 of the Dominican Republic's Constitutional Court uses this exact term, in transit, to deny Dominican nationality to Haitian migrants and their Dominican-born descendants. The ruling states, with regard to "in transit foreigners," that such individuals are "not considered to be in an unlawful situation, but instead lack the right to a Dominican nationality" (Sentencia 2013). To clarify the use of this term, the 2013 ruling reverts back to—and reinterprets—the 1929 constitution that established the right of *jus soli*, or birthright citizenship. *La sentencia* considers Haitian workers as nonimmigrants who were granted only "temporary admission" into the country and thus classifies them as in transit. How, then, can we read "temporary admission" in Alvarez's *Afterlife*? What other meaning can a term like in transit engender when moving beyond the term's political classification? Or rather, how do the characters in Alvarez's novel experience and move through space and time and understand the contested notion of belonging?

AFTERLIFE AS IN TRANSIT NARRATIVE

The first classification of in transit narrative, related to an interest in geography and intranational spaces, builds on Pouchet Paquet's understanding of Gilles Deleuze's "nomadic subjectivity" (1973, 82) as well as on Edouard Glissant's errantry as defined in *Poetics of Relation* to address and problematize how Caribbean diasporic writers might appear (im)mobilized within mobilized and constantly shifting spaces. My interest in a nomadic subjectivity of characters in narratives such as *Afterlife* considers the wanderlust of nomadic thought as a repeated element of Caribbean literature for the ways "that it highlights the networks of negotiation and association that characterize Caribbean consciousness as an ongoing and contradictory process" (Pouchet Paquet 2010, 68). The second category of in transit narrative is the most straightforward in the sense that it reflects a tangible interest on the authors' part to infuse the often-cited political nomenclature surrounding *la sentencia* or similar examples of denationalization into their works. Zien articulates sovereignty by discussing the multiple players in the enactment of a sovereign act, building on the idea that sovereignty "functions as a norm of political life that, like any norm, requires continuous affirmation through rituals and theatricality in order to sustain its prescriptive force" (Zien 2017, 5). This definition is a useful jumping point as it helps to formulate, albeit from a Panamanian perspective, how individuals become in transit, stateless, or denationalized.

There are sometimes conflicting terms employed as synonyms of in transit and, relatedly, to describe TC-0168. Haitian Canadian novelist and scholar Myriam J.A. Chancy comments on "the variety of ways that language has done us a disservice in explicating the gravity of the situation" with regard to *la sentencia* and she confirms that:

> Some reports have placed the accent on the fact that the ruling appears to designate all progeny of undocumented/"in transit" people, of various nationalities, when it is clear that the targeted population are primarily of Haitian descent. As the Dominican government touts its project of "naturalization" for those affected, eligibility criteria is, at best, murky. It isn't just a question of whether or not a Dominican citizen is an offspring of undocumented or "in transit" Haitian laborers ("in transit" meaning that they may have legal working papers but not legal residency), it is also a question of whether or not the individual is seen as a *desirable* citizen of the State. The hallmark of desirability is thus to be measured in terms of middle-class status via education and occupation. The working poor need not apply. (2014, n.p.)

Thus, the Dominican government controls which individuals—based on race, economic status, occupation, and other factors—are "desirable" citizens. Alvarez, in *Afterlife,* offers her own perspective on desire and what or who is desirable—for a life goal, for a life partner, etc.—but, like desire in the way that Chancy uses it here to describe the underpinnings of *la sentencia,* the idea of desire in the novel also delves into a commentary on politics and undocumented workers in rural Vermont, the setting of *Afterlife.* The question that the protagonist, Antonia, herself an immigrant, repeats throughout the novel centers on *who* or *what* is most important; while she at first caves to the pleading recommendations of friends and family who stress the essentiality of self-care, her answer is that she is the most important one. Yet, the family tribulations involving her three sisters and a budding relationship with two young Mexican migrant workers shift her perspective toward the novel's end. While *Afterlife* postulates that for *some* individuals in states like Vermont migrant workers are "undesirables," for Alvarez these two young secondary characters become some of the people who matter most—a relationship that launches the novel not only into themes of migration and internal reflections of a Latina woman in a predominantly white small town, but also on geography and the complexities of place and politics in the United States.

Finally, the third distinction within the in transit narrative classification denotes themes of migration or immigration. In *Afterlife*, many of the primary characters are in transit, as understood in political-temporal terms or otherwise. Notably, in transit narratives do not necessarily reflect Haitian–Dominican dynamics or relationships (political, social, cultural, or otherwise), and Alvarez's novel addresses migration from both the perspective of Antonia and that of the undocumented population in Vermont.

A Complex Approach to Geography and Space in *Afterlife*

The aforementioned compilation, *Nos Cambió la Vida*—organized by Reconoci.do and funded by Centro Bonó—begins with an introduction by Farah Hallal that outlines the ruling and contextualizes a multi-perspective approach to geography: "¿Qué hace que tu patria sea tu patria? Estas memorias dan descripciones exactas, no solo de una ubicación geográfica: también la geografía de la pobreza y de la violencia queda muy bien descrita" (Hallah 2018, 11). [What makes your homeland your homeland? These memories give precise descriptions, not only of a geographic location, but the geography of poverty and violence are also well-described herein]. These words introduce the testimonies of Dominicans of Haitian descent included in the collection and the portrayal of geography as connected to poverty, violence, and other social status markers, highlighting the complexity of diasporic space in narratives like *Afterlife*. Pouchet Paquet's understanding of nomadic subjectivity in postcolonial discourse offers a concrete concept to better decipher the "implied open-endedness" of nomadic thought (Pouchet Paquet 2010, 66). Most helpful to the analysis herein is the scholar's exploration of spatial mobility as key

7 WRITING "IN TRANSIT": LITERARY CONSTRUCTIONS OF SOVEREIGNTY... 129

to nomadic thought, noting that nomadism "highlights the networks of negotiation and association that characterize Caribbean consciousness as an ongoing and contradictory process" and confirming that it necessitates and "inhabits multiple dimensions of time and space" (68).

Alvarez's *Afterlife* is a negotiation of space on multiple levels; what first appears as the story of a widowed, Vermont-based English professor quickly shifts to a plot much more global in scope. This international focus does not solely resonate from Antonia's musings about growing up in the Dominican Republic—noting, for example, that in primary school for her and her sisters "the only geography they were taught as children was of their half island" (Alvarez 2020, 85)—but it also appears as a sense of (immigrant) characters feeling immobilized within moving and changing spaces. The work is a constant reflection on modern society and politics— and how to come to terms with a world, or a country (whether one's *patria* or not), that seems to be in an incessant state of suffering and vio- lence. At one time Antonia asks, "The default for most of the world is not happiness. Why then do we feel aggrieved when suffering strikes us?" (171).

Coupled with Antonia's inner thoughts, the protagonist's three sisters serve to amplify calls for diversity and inclusion on a (inter)national scale. One sister, Izzy, once shared with her sisters her plans for a Latino arts center in Massachusetts and classified the project as "a way of importing diversity into that part of the state, a model to be copied throughout other white-bread areas of the country. Instead of migrant workers on a farm, a cultural takeover: migrant poets, dancers, and artists" (49–50). While Izzy and her sisters, who immigrated to the United States from the Dominican Republic, are not in transit in a political sense, such inclusions offer a clear depiction in *Afterlife* of "the shifting figurations embedded in exile, migra- tion, travel, journey, flight, quest, itinerancy ... and so on" (Pouchet Paquet 2010, 69). My insistence on utilizing Pouchet Paquet's under- standing of nomadism to discuss characters' relation to geography in in transit narratives also builds on the notion of Deleuze that "The nomad is not necessarily one who moves" (Deleuze 1973, 149). While Deleuze offers a philosophical interpretation on nomad thought and what he later refers to as "Nomadology," his understanding of the concept offers an alternative to an emphasis on set boundaries and he confirms that there is "a completely other distribution, which must be called nomadic, a nomad nomos, without property, enclosure or measure" that does not involve "a division of that which is distributed but rather a division among those who distribute themselves in an open space—a space which is unlimited, or at least without precise limits" (Deleuze 1968, 36). *Afterlife* functions without set boundaries and the characters challenge political understandings of borders. Estela questions why she won't have the same rights as her son, born in the United States, and the novel continually questions and challenges the simple freedoms of movement through geographical spaces that are allotted to some, but not to others. Antonia meditates over the fact that she has freedoms Estela does not. For the protagonist, "[t]he cage door is open—Antonia could just fly away" (Alvarez 2020, 157).

POLITICAL CONSCIOUSNESS AND IM(MIGRATION) IN *AFTERLIFE*

While a flexible definition of nomadism bolsters my delineation of the first element of in transit narratives, the second and third categories gesture toward a more politicized understanding of what it means to be in transit, stateless, denationalized, etc. While there is no concrete mention of TC-0168 or the large-scale, discriminatory consequences of *la sentencia* in *Afterlife*, there is a clear consciousness throughout the novel directed toward the complexity and waywardness of law enforcement in the United States and a repeated call for immigration reform. One useful way to understand the political underpinnings that might tie *Afterlife* to the subtle commentary on *la sentencia* stems from an understanding of sovereignty. Barbadian writer George Lamming, in an interview with David Scott, discusses nomadic consciousness and confirms: "[W]hatever location you have, the one thing I want to hold on to, is that acre of ground because you don't decide that. That acre of ground is that Caribbean wherever I encounter it; it does not matter how I end myself in Asia, in Africa, or wherever." Lamming stresses the importance of holding onto that space—a sense of permanency and (Caribbean) rootedness regardless of location—by stating: "[N]o limitation of sovereignty in the political sense can alter that, because that acre is also itself a component of the imagination" (Scott 2002, 162; qtd. in Pouchet Paquet 2010). Lamming's conceptualization of sovereignty—and its possible limitations—offers an entrance into Zien's delineation of sovereignty.

While Zien begins by framing what she refers to as "sovereign acts" within the backdrop of the representations of sovereignty in the Canal Zone during the US Occupation, a complexity of the systems of belonging in this context becomes apparent: "The Canal Zone's vexed sovereignty status influenced which bodies were allowed into, and excluded from, the Zone, and how residents and employees created identities and social networks" (Zien 2017, 5). What pertains most to the analysis at hand is the fact that Zien confirms that the Canal Zone "performed" various styles of sovereignty (6), thus defining sovereignty as freedom from external control or autonomy. This framework can be applied to the plight of Dominicans of Haitian descent in the Dominican Republic and, moreover, an understanding of in transit narrative. Given Zien's emphasis on the lack of clear frameworks of sovereignty and citizenship in the Panama Canal Zone[8]; this flexibility of the notion(s) of sovereignty emphasizes, in Zien's words, how "Sovereignty's mise-en-scène disparately enfolds spectators into the viewing practices of the (non)citizen subject and that which I am calling the subjunct—a status between citizen and noncitizen. The subjunct, a syntactical term, constitutes an interstitial zone between inclusion and exclusion" (16).[9] Hispaniola is an island with dual sovereignty, and it is also an island for which global actors—in particular the US-based Haitian and Dominican diasporas—play an important role. In addition to these off-island communities, global entities like the United Nations and the Inter-American Court of Human Rights also have a role in dictating matters related to social justice and human rights, notwithstanding an individual's nationality. Eugenio Matibag and Teresa Downing-Matibag (2011) note that in the Dominican Republic "Also among the global actors are the leaders of sender nations"—like Haiti—"who might question how a receiving country enacts its sovereignty when they perceive its leaders and people disrespecting the rights of its citizens-in-transit" (95). The Dominican Republic's claims to sovereignty are not inclusive, instead the rights of those individuals deemed in transit are nebulous and fluctuating. As Matibag and Downing-Matibag proclaim, "the Dominican government has performed its sovereignty in a manner as unwieldy as a horse held by the reins of multiple masters (97).

In the case of political entities such as in the Dominican Republic, the underlying concept of legitimate sovereignty is open to contestation not only by citizens but also by these global actors who have an interest in intra-island relations. I argue, then, that in transit narratives written from the diaspora, like Alvarez's *Afterlife*, serve as a contestation of sovereignty. They ask: Who is the ultimate authority? The police and local sheriff, for example, play a central role in *Afterlife* and Antonia is thrust into the job of alerting local migrant workers to the pending arrival of *la migra* (Alvarez 2020, 18, 49). The two parallel plot lines—one of Antonia's missing sister and the other of young Mexican migrants Mario and Estela—both face encounters with law enforcement. While a local sheriff and, later, private detectives work to locate Antonia's sister Izzy, the what-ifs with regard to Mario and Estela related to governmental authorities differ. If pregnant Estela were to arrive at the hospital without an accompaniment to deliver her baby, the hospital would be required to notify the Department of Children and Families (DCF) who would then "notify ICE about an underage undocumented minor, and the likelihood is Estela will be deported before another brown US citizen can be born" (165). The citizenship status of her child, to be born on American soil, is not lost on the seemingly innocent Estela, though. She asks Antonia: "Doñita, why can't I live here, too? If my child is born here, he will have the right, and I, his mother, won't?" (188).

Then, at the novel's end, Antonia is en route to the airport in Boston with Estela, Mario, and their newborn when they get stopped by a sheriff on Route 7 in Vermont who asks for their documents. In this scene—as Estela whispers hail Mary's from the backseat—there is a clear recognition of laws that need to be changed, a push toward reform. Antonia references Lula, a local Mexican migrant who operates a food truck and serves as a reference point for many migrants in the area, when she offers: "What she wants is the laws changed, Sheriff. She wants to keep cooking her enchiladas and selling them so she can build a house that will not tumble when the next hurricane hits Mexico" (250). The tropes of empowerment and belonging permeate *Afterlife* and citizenship becomes a constant meditation of the protagonist; as Zien affirms, "Citizenship, after all, is tenuous and gauzy even when legally conferred, capable of being overridden by distinctions like 'terrorist,' 'criminal,' 'ex-convict,' and 'enemy combatant.' The permeability of citizenship, and its potential for rupture by a sovereign decision, force us to acknowledge not only the fluidity of the borders between citizen and noncitizen, but also the existence of other statuses beside and within citizenship" (Zien 2017, 16).

Further, it is important to reach a broad conceptualization in *Afterlife* of how the characters themselves can be understood as in transit and the different ways that this nomenclature can be interpreted within in transit narratives. Antonia and her three sisters—and not just Estela and Mario—are clearly depicted as immigrants. Antonia's "broken English" (Alvarez 2020, 11), constant code-switching, and struggles with identifying as Dominican American in the United States—often mistaken in Vermont for Mexican or Spanish (13, 176)—permeate the novel in its entirety.[10]

One of the reasons *Afterlife* serves as an interesting model of in transit diasporic narrative is because in transit can relate to more than just Alvarez's conscious decision to include a plot detailing undocumented migrant workers. In transit can also be viewed in *Afterlife* from a multi-generational perspective, as a possible framework to harness an understanding of life stages that would not have been perceptible for narrators of Alvarez's earlier novels such as *How the García Girls Lost Their Accents* or *¡Yo!*. Antonia, retired and recently widowed—who still feels the hyphenation of immigration—grieves her old life and the company of her partner; Antonia materializes as a character in transit given that she attempts to find herself while seeking to find her voice. In a similar sense, to reference the Reconoci.do campaign *vidas suspendidas*, if an individual's life is suspended or halted due to discriminatory, race-based national policies, what, then, becomes of your "afterlife?" Can an afterlife, in this case, be interpreted as the phase *after* this transitory status? As proof that she also meditates on the meaning of an afterlife, Antonia offers her own response: "What, if anything, does it mean? An afterlife? All she has come up with is that the only way not to let the people she loves die forever is to embody what she loved about them" (Alvarez 2020, 115).

From the Diaspora, with Love: Centering Global Sites of Sovereignty

Afterlife classifies as a female-led narrative in which Alvarez writes *women* in transit and models gendered constructions of nation and citizenship in Hispaniola and its growing diaspora. Harnessing the focus on gendered constructions of mobility and nationalism offers an in-depth consideration of the Caribbean tropes of femininity that travel to and in diasporic spaces; Alvarez gives space to female voices to enable or inhibit "sovereign acts" and offers a unique and diverse female-led depiction of Hispaniola's female in transit subjects. To return to Zien's sovereign act, it is worthwhile to note that an "act" in itself denotes a conscious decision to react or perform. Does Alvarez do the same? In writing *Afterlife* with conscious nods to themes of belonging, nationalism, and geography, Alvarez *acts* upon her own *reaction to* TC-0168 and ushers in a new era of transnational Hispaniola literature in which authors from both sides of the border write about similar themes from an activist-centered, politicized perspective. *Afterlife* moves from the past trend in Dominican literature dominated by historical narrative and *la sombra* of Trujillo to instead place transnational works, activist and anti-racist movements, and calls for solidarity in conversation with one another. Alvarez's understanding of in transit in the novel speaks not only to individuals displaced in a political sense, but also to an understanding of the stages-of-life and how individuals move through time. The novel complicates a modern notion of one's lifespan by confirming that lived experiences can alter the passing of time and an individual's reflection on life and death. Caught in her own web of negotiations with and against time—longing for the past while rebuilding her future—Antonia finds her immigrant-self through her interactions with Mario and Estela and she reconciles her place among her Dominican sisters, too. The delineation of in transit narratives offered herein proffers a different model to think through authors' responses to contemporary politics/realities—on- or off-island—and a new perspective on Hispaniola (and diaspora)-based literature that responds to TC-0168 (and its aftermath) in subtle ways, offering a radical remapping of the concept of "in transit."

NOTES

1. My decision to represent "in transit" without a hyphen, regardless of the grammatical need when using the expression as a qualifier to a substantive, stems from the use of the term as written in Spanish—"en tránsito"—and also for purposes of consistency with regards to "in transit narrative."
2. Report can be found here: http://catunescopucmm.org/unesco_files/pdf/Vidas_Suspendidas.pdf
3. See borderoflights.org and The Border of Lights Reader: Bearing Witness to Genocide in the Dominican Republic (2021) for more information.
4. Danticat's Everything Inside (2019) similarly explores (im)migration as a repeating trope in the collection of eight short stories and the Caribbean and its diaspora serve as the backdrop for the myriad of characters to whom readers are introduced. The stories, in particular "Seven Stories" and "Dosas," offer various interpretations of Haitian and Haitian American women and relate to gendered constructions of nation and citizenship in Hispaniola and its growing diaspora.
5. For more on Trujillo narrative, see the work of Neil Larsen and Ana Gallego Cuiñas. Gallego Cuiñas (2006), offers multiple terms to identify the literary subgenre that falls within historical narrative responding to the Trujillo Era. She offers the following classifications: novela del trujillato, narrativa de Trujillo, narrativa trujillista, and narrativa trujilloniana (16).

7 WRITING "IN TRANSIT": LITERARY CONSTRUCTIONS OF SOVEREIGNTY... 135

6. For more on these testimonial essays and documentaries, see Mapping Hispaniola. Nos cambió la vida "shares the consequences of the denationalization of Dominicans of Haitian descent brought about by the Tribunal Court's 2013 ruling. The various authors—from different geographic areas such as El Seibo, San Pedro de Macorís, Barahona, and Santo Domingo—not only reveal their personal experiences with race-based discrimination both before and after TC-0168, but also divulge histories of gender violence and bullying. This collection of testimonies is a traceable model of 'in transit' narrative given its clear focus on the political status— or lack thereof—of the Dominican-born Haitian youth" (Myers 2019, 121).

7. Find more information on both of these collectives at their respective websites https://weshomedominicannyc.wordpress.com/ and https://www.inculturedco.org/

8. Zien clarifies: "The subjunctive sovereignty set forth by the Panama Canal Treaty destabilized the treaty as a legal document and a performative utterance and marked the terrain of the Panama Canal Zone for decades to come. In lieu of clear frameworks of sovereignty and citizenship, performances materialized the Canal Zone as a shifting mise-en-scène, opening the Zone's discursive and physical terrain to competing interpretations and claims by US and Panamanian governments, as well as assertions of belonging by local residents and labor migrants" (2017, 5).

9. See political theorist Wendy Brown's definition of sovereignty in *Walled States.* (2010)

10. There is also constant code-switching in *Afterlife.* Words in Spanish appear un-italicized unlike in previous works of Alvarez. Here, she seamlessly switches between languages without translations: "No hay mal que por bien no venga, Mami would say" (2020, 77). Antonia also insists on her lack of confidence with her English: "The minute they touched ground in DR, a more self-assured self took over. But in English, even after years of education and employment, the worm of self-doubt still eats away at the core of her certainties" (2020, 109). Such characterizations are similar to how Alvarez depicts herself as the "gringa-dominicana" in *In the Time of the Butterflies* when referencing her limited Spanish skills in opening pages.

References

Alvarez, Julia. 2020. *Afterlife.* Chapel Hill: Algonquin Books.
———. 1994. *In the Time of the Butterflies.* Chapel Hill: Algonquin Books.
Brown, Wendy. 2010. *Walled States, Waning Sovereignty.* Brooklyn: Zone Books.
Chancy, Myriam. 2014. New Year's Resolution: Love Thy Neighbour. *Myriam J.A. Chancy* (blog), January 24. http://myriamchancy.com/2014/01/01/new-years-resolution-love-thy-neighbor/, Accessed 5 June 2020.

136 M. J. MYERS

Danticat, Edwidge. 2019. *Everything Inside*. New York: Knopf.
De Maeseneer, Rita. 2006. *Encuentro con la narrativa dominicana contemporánea*. Madrid: Iberoamericana.
Deleuze, Gilles. [1968] 1994. *Difference and Repetition*. Trans. Paul Patton. New York: Columbia University Press.
———. [1973] 1990. Nomad Thought. In *The New Nietzsche*, ed. David B. Allison, 142–149. Cambridge: MIT Press.
Gallego Cuiñas, Ana. 2006. *Trujillo, el fantasma y sus escritores: Historia de la novela del trujillato*. Paris: Mare & Martin.
Hallah, Farah. 2018. Introducción. In *Nos cambió la vida*. Santo Domingo: Centro Bonó.
Horn, Maja. 2014. *Masculinity After Trujillo: The Politics of Gender in Dominican Literature*. Gainesville: University Press of Florida.
Kurlansky, Mark, Junot Díaz, Edwidge Danticat and Julia Alvarez. 2013. Two Versions of a Dominican Tale: To the Editor. *The New York Times*, October 29.
Larsen, Neil. 1988. ¿Cómo narrar el trujillato? *Revista Iberoamericana* 54 (1–2): 89–98.
Matibag, Eugenio, and Teresa Downing-Matibag. 2011. Sovereignty and Social Justice: The 'Haitian Problem' in the Dominican Republic. *Caribbean Quarterly* 57 (2): 92–117.
Mayes, April J. 2018. Ties That Bind: *La Sentencia* and Citizenship in Contemporary Hispaniola. In *Transnational Hispaniola: New Directions in Haitian and Dominican Studies*, ed. April J. Mayes and Kiran C. Jayaram, 201–217. Gainesville: University Press of Florida.
Mayes, April J., and Kiran C. Jayaram, eds. 2018. *Transnational Hispaniola: New Directions in Haitian and Dominican Studies*. Gainesville: University Press of Florida.
Myers, Megan Jeanette. 2019. *Mapping Hispaniola: Third Space in Dominican and Haitian Literature*. Charlottesville: University of Virginia Press.
———. 2021. Spreading Change and Sparking Light: A Conversation with Julia Alvarez and Bill Eichner. In *The Border of Lights Reader: Bearing Witness to Genocide in the Dominican Republic*, eds. Megan Jeanette Myers and Edward Paulino, 438–456. Amherst: Amherst College Press.
Myers, Megan Jeanette, and Edward Paulino, eds. 2021. *The Border of Lights Reader: Bearing Witness to Genocide in the Dominican Republic*. Amherst: Amherst College Press.
Oboler, Suzanne. 1996. Narratives of National (Be)longing: Citizenship, Race, and the Creation of Latinas' Ethnicities in Exile in the United States. *Social Politics* 3 (2–3): 291–315.
Pouchet Paquet, Sandra. 2010. The Caribbean Writer as Nomadic Subject or Spatial Mobility and the Dynamics of Critical Thought. *Journal of West Indian Literature* 18 (2): 65–94.

Ramírez, Dixa. 2015. Salomé Ureña's Blurred Edges. *The Black Scholar* 45 (2): 45–56.
Scott, David. 2002. The Sovereignty of the Imagination: Interview with George Lamming. *Small Axe* 12: 72–200.
Sentencia TC/0168/13. 2013. *Constitutional Court*, http://tribunalconstitucional.gob.do/sites/default/files/documentos/Sentencia%20TC%20 0168-13%20-%20C.pdf. Accessed 25 May 2020.
Zien, Katherine A. 2017. *Sovereign Acts: Performing Race, Space, and Belonging in Panama and the Canal Zone.* New Brunswick: Rutgers University Press.
Zimmerman, Tegan. 2020. Unauthorized Storytelling: Reevaluating Racial Politics in Julia Alvarez's *In the Time of the Butterflies*. *MELUS* 45 (1): 95–116.

Open Access This chapter is licensed under the terms of the Creative Commons Attribution 4.0 International License (http://creativecommons.org/licenses/by/4.0/), which permits use, sharing, adaptation, distribution and reproduction in any medium or format, as long as you give appropriate credit to the original author(s) and the source, provide a link to the Creative Commons licence and indicate if changes were made.

The images or other third party material in this chapter are included in the chapter's Creative Commons licence, unless indicated otherwise in a credit line to the material. If material is not included in the chapter's Creative Commons licence and your intended use is not permitted by statutory regulation or exceeds the permitted use, you will need to obtain permission directly from the copyright holder.

CHAPTER 8

When the Tout-Monde Is Not One: Maryse Condé's Problematic 'World-in-Motion' in *Les belles ténébreuses* (2008) and *Le fabuleux et triste destin d'Ivan et Ivana* (2017)

Valérie K. Orlando

Maryse Condé's *Les belles ténébreuses* (2008) and *Le fabuleux et triste destin d'Ivan et Ivana* (2017) evoke our current "world-in-motion"[1] as a space and time that offer very little to those who are marginalized. She challenges us to think about Martinican philosopher Édouard Glissant's aspirational "Tout-Monde"—"un monde qui fait bouger choses et gens" (1995, 35) [a world that makes things and people move]—and whether or not it could ever be a reality on a planet that is increasingly hostile to ideas about global shared citizenship, despite the relational environments in which we live. As we read her novels written in the last few decades, we are

---

V. K. Orlando (✉)
University of Maryland, College Park, MD, USA
e-mail: vorlando@umd.edu

© The Author(s) 2023
O. Ferly, T. Zimmerman (eds.), *Chronotropics*,
https://doi.org/10.1007/978-3-031-32111-5_8

140   V. K. ORLANDO

reminded of what Marc Augé notes in *Pour une anthropologie de la mobilité* (2009):

> In the 'surmodern', 'overmodern' world, subject to the triple acceleration of knowledge, technology and the market, the gap is growing every day between the representation of a borderless globality that would allow goods, people, images and messages to circulate unrestrictedly and the reality of a divided, fragmented planet, where the divisions denied by the ideology of the system find themselves at the very heart of this system. (14)[2]

In general, Condé's novels studied here entreat us to think about the following questions: What exactly are the global, nefarious winds (and from where do they come) that blow characters across the four corners of the world? Why can't her multicultural and diverse protagonists build meaningful relationships and enjoy a positive *being-in-the-world*[3] in a Tout-Monde of exchange and "relation" as Glissant defines it? How do young Caribbean and African peoples' choices and the environments in which they must operate, determine their identities, agency and ultimately their selfhood? Can these choices radically remap the world of relation?

This chapter thus analyzes how Condé's novels reveal skepticism with respect to Glissantian ideals about Relation in the Tout-Monde of exchange. The fundamental questions she asks demonstrate a concern that positive mobility, transnationalism, human contact and exchange are, in the angst of our current era, illusions for many Africans and Caribbeans who experience increasing global tensions. Islamic radicalization, gender inequality, economic exploitation and environmental disasters in Condé's *Les belles ténébreuses* and *Le fabuleux et triste destin d'Ivan et Ivana* thus express a chaotic world-in-motion fraught with socioeconomic and political disjunctures that counter the Glissantian aspirational Tout-Monde.

EDOUARD GLISSANT'S ASPIRATIONAL TOUT-MONDE OF RELATION

As early as 1981 in *Le discours antillais*, Édouard Glissant proposed to the francophone literary world his "relational philosophy," which was useful in describing the importance of movement and discovery in novels by authors of French expression. Particularly, his philosophy of Relation in *Le discours anitllais*, and as expressed later in *Poétique de la Relation* (1990), *Tout-monde* (1995), *Traité du Tout-Monde* (1997) and *Philosophie de la*

Relation (2009), offered an aspirational theoretical framework of how to think about the Caribbean as it reflected "the refusal ... to distinguish among poetry and ideology or politics" (Hachad 2013, 126). At the dawn of the twenty-first century, writers from the francophone world made us all *voyageurs* through narratives touting the positivity of mobility and movement in a Tout-Monde where all relations were possible and borders were fluid. In *Eloge de la créolité* (1989), Jean Bernabé, Patrick Chamoiseau and Raphaël Confiant further celebrated Glissant's mapping of the multiple, *creolized* diverse world that presented to Caribbean people a way of looking at their history through multiple spaciotemporal lenses: "Our History is a braid of stories. We have tasted all languages, all dialects. ... We are at the same time, Europe, Africa, nourished by Asian, Levantine, Indian, and we also recognize the legacies of pre-Columbian America. Creolity is '*the diffracted but recomposed world*,' a maelstrom of signified in a single signifier: a Totality" (26–27, translation M. B. Taleb-Khyar).

Glissant's relational Tout-Monde philosophy contributes to a theoretical framework for thinking about remapping a world and a body of literature made in, and emerging from, motion, encounters and the *créolisation* that results from movement and mixing. Such a world exemplifies the importance of free-circulation and exchanges not threatened by neoliberal capitalist "disjunctures," which Arjun Appadurai explains are evident in "the complexity of the ... global economy." Socioeconomic and political disjunctures are the results of "increasing inequality with respect to land, money, and security" (1996, 3). These static challenges make up our chaotic "world-in-motion," as Appadurai defines it, and have "produce[d] fundamental problems of livelihood, equity, suffering, justice and governance" (Appadurai 2000, 5). The chaotic world-in-motion presents barriers to individuals' rights to enjoy a phenomenologically understood *being-in-the-world*; a position of the self that in Glissant's framework is positive, cosmopolitan and autonomous, yet operating also in harmony with others and the environment (Meyers 2008, 79). The Tout-Monde promotes a *créolization* that allows for mixing and the "connecting many cultures ... resulting in something new" (Glissant 1997, 37). This creolization is recognized in works by Glissant, as well as in the later writings of Jean Bernabé, Patrick Chamoiseau, and Raphaël Confiant (1990), as having emerged in part from the brutality of colonialism. Therefore, they recognize that créolization is inherently a double-edged sword—one side promotes the positivity of multiculturality, the other the past of violence and brutality.

142   V. K. ORLANDO

The relational world of the Tout-Monde has often offered a roadmap for understanding the themes of authors of French expression from the Caribbean who search for the answers to contemporary questions of immigration, migration, locality and positionality in the twenty-first-century world. Inspired by Gilles Deleuze and Félix Guattari's *Mille Plateaux, capitalisme et schizophrénie* (1980), Glissant's Tout-Monde places importance on intersectionality, positionality and *rhizomatic*, nomadic wanderings: "La notion de rhizome ... récuse l'idée d'une racine totalitaire" (2009, 23) [The notion of the rhizome ... rejects the idea of a totalitarian root, my translation]. Glissant affirms the importance of rhizomatic thinking in *Philosophy of Relation*, noting that "what I call a poetics of Relation" means that "all identity extends in relation to the Other" (23).[4]

However, Glissant's conception of the rhizome and the fruitful wanderings it ensures in a relational Tout-Monde of exchange is not without tension. Jarrod Hayes points out in *Queer Roots for the Diaspora: Ghosts in the Family Tree* the challenges to Glissant's conception with respect to Caribbean identity and sense of place:

> In spite of the fact that Glissant's notion of the rhizomatic was inspired by Deleuze and Guattari, his version not only is attached to a specific geocultural context—the Caribbean—but also allows for an identity rooted in that place. Like Deleuze and Guattari, Glissant rejects the root; unlike them, he keeps rootedness. (12–13)

It is within this tension between movement and rootedness as affecting identity, place and a sense of being-in-the-world that I situate Condé's *Les belles ténébreuses* and *Le Fabuleux et triste destin d'Ivan et Ivana*. Her version of a Tout-Monde lacks the positivity of Glissant's and moves beyond his and the major Creolist theorists of the 1990s Chamoiseau, Bernarbé, Confiant's conceptions of it in order to engage with twenty-first-century challenges, such as increasing violence against women that are unprecedented in their severity.

As many of Condé's characters reveal, the need to be rooted in a country/nationality/ethnicity in order to form identity and to enjoy the freedom of discovery as the subject travels the world is fraught with complication. Her novels disclose that in our current time, free-circulation, mobility and rhizomatic exchange in a world of relation have become increasingly problematic ideals and physical impossibilities as we face

8 WHEN THE TOUT-MONDE IS NOT ONE: MARYSE CONDÉ'S PROBLEMATIC... 143

progressively global, isolationist political climates in the West that are fueled by ever-growing hyper misogyny, xenophobia, racism, fear and, at the writing of this chapter, the scourge of the COVID-19 pandemic. The tension between the Glissantian aspirational Tout-Monde and the chaotic world-in-motion fraught with socioeconomic and political disjunctures as described by Appadurai is a constant theme in Condé's narratives. For Condé, being a *sujet global* [global subject], benefiting from the positive relations one can make through goods and exchanges in a Western-hyper-capitalist-cosmopolitan model, is a reality only for the very few. Condé's protagonists are severely hampered, profiting little from free-circulation and relations with Others as they become bound in scenarios that lead them down paths where choosing to do good is often stymied. Condé's protagonists struggle to forge their identities and find their place in the world. This identity challenge is particularly burdensome for young men and women of color—Kassem in *Les belles ténébreuses* and Ivan and Ivana in *Le fabuleux et triste destin d'Ivan et Ivana*—as both novels demonstrate. Their rhizomatic wanderings in the twenty-first century do not lead to identities that link abundantly with others but rather to a present, as notes a character in Condé's *Le fabuleux et triste destin d'Ivan et Ivana*, where "nous vivons dans une telle époque que personne ne sait où donner de la tête" (251) [we live in an era where no one knows which way is up].

Les Belles Ténébreuses

Maryse Condé's 2008 *Les belles ténébreuses* focuses on two men, Ramzi and, the younger, Kassem. Kassem is a bi-racial Frenchman, son of a Guadeloupean father and a Romanian mother while in the opening pages, Ramzi is described as "30-something ... mixed of a thousand bloods" (27). He is charismatic, smoking cigars from Havana especially made for him, as he wears a black dinner jacket like that of "Keanu Reeves in *The Matrix*" (115). Ramzi, also mixed ethnically and nationally, is an entrepreneur who dabbles in illegal spheres and invents a perfume called "Nefrititi" with a reprehensible Italian partner named Aldo Moravia. Ramzi's more sinister persona involves working as an embalmer known for rendering the dead, particularly young women, more beautiful than in life with special "face powders and creams" (100). Kassem eventually comes to believe that Ramzi is, in fact, a serial killer who laces his perfume and lipstick products with deadly poisons that kill hundreds of young women who eventually wind up on his embalming table. This killing enterprise takes on global

144 V. K. ORLANDO

proportions as Ramzi moves his operation from an unnamed African country to France and then to the United States. Although Kassem realizes that Ramzi is "a *serial killer* … [t]he most dangerous in humanity's history," he cannot prove it (239).[5] Ramzi's global cosmopolitan image (as a man who speaks multiple languages and is culturally astute) gleans him invitations as a guest in the homes of powerful men across the world. He becomes a "Supreme Leader" of "the Revolution" (first Muslim and then later for an undefined, loosely religious cause) which he claims "will help" humanity (113). Kassem, who is diminished by his own precarious existence, thus cannot challenge Ramzi's international reputation, making repeatedly evident Condé's message that only the most strong and cunning capitalists survive. Her title's meaning constantly haunts the narrative as "les Fleurs des ténèbres" become darker for Kassem as the story progresses (72).

Kassem slowly realizes in his dealings with Ramzi that darkness and beauty, and good and evil, are intertwined. Another lesson the young man learns is that only the powerful gain money and fame, allowing them ultimately to come out ahead. This power is always won at the expense of those who are weak and without means to challenge the might of strong capitalist networks as notes Ramzi to Kassem in the closing pages of the novel: "Personne n'est indifférent à l'argent. C'est l'argent qui mène le monde. Mais attention à toi! Ce sont les individus comme toi qu'on coffre" (281) [No one is indifferent to money. Money rules the world. Watch yourself! It's individuals like you who they lock up]. Here, Ramzi is referring to Kassem's visible bi-racial identity that from the beginning of the narrative has made his life difficult. Although Condé's novel pleads for the right of each individual to self-define, or as Glissant would affirm, forge relations by not claiming a national identity, a race or a genealogy, Kassem as an example proves this to be impossible. Nations and nationalities can be fraught with positives and negatives as Kassem is regularly reminded. *Métissé*, half Guadeloupean, half Romanian, born in France, but always feeling like he has been relegated to the margins, the young man's sense of identity is constantly conflicted.

LE FABULEUX ET TRISTE DESTIN D'IVAN ET IVANA

Condé's most recent novel is a narrative reflecting our current times, depicting the inordinate challenges many are facing on a daily basis as they try to navigate the socioeconomic and political "disjunctures" of the twenty-first century that Appadurai defines. *Le fabuleux et triste destin d'Ivan et Ivana* many say will probably be Condé's last work since at eighty-three her health is failing. The author had to dictate her narrative because of a degenerative illness that prevents her from using her hands. The oral quality of the novel is woven into the fabric of the prose, and is evident in many instances as the denouement of the story of twins Ivan and Ivana unfurls. The narrator directly interjects her voice, reminding readers that this story is, indeed, one that must be *told*. It is destined to be passed down as a lesson for generations to come. The twins' "triste destin" is "une illustration frappante de cette mondialisation qui souffle sur nous comme un mauvais vent" (346) [a shocking illustration of this globalization that blows on us like a bad wind].

While they are nonidentical twins, "Ivan et Ivana avaient d'abord été un seul œuf. Puis une mutation s'était produite" (347) [Ivan and Ivana were first one single egg. Then a mutation happened]. Being "the same but different" haunts their existence, from the time that they are "divided into two" (374). Ivana is seemingly destined to do good and succeed; Ivan is the opposite, as his destiny is determined by violence, crime and one bad experience after another, experiences over which he seems to have little control. Condé is perhaps evoking the ancient concept of *marassas*, the divine twins as in Vodou. Ironically, these are mythical children born as embodying love, truth and justice, yet with respect to Condé's twins, their trajectories are anything but these qualities. They also represent links between earth and heaven as well as personifying astrological knowledge. Marassas twins can be mythical lovers tied into the same soul.[6] Indeed, Ivan and Ivana's incestuous relationship is one of the central themes of Condé's plot and integral to the denouement of moral choices each makes. The mythological (and sexualized) twins' trope facilitates Condé's wish to present readers with a series of hypotheses on how one's being-in-the-world is determined by fate, destiny and/or luck.

Growing up in poverty in Guadeloupe, raised by their mother Simone and grandmother Maeva who considers them as "deux maudits" (two damned) (94), Ivan and Ivana are from the outset forced onto different paths. As their lives unfold, Condé presents readers with an age-old question, is one born evil or good, or does environment play a role in the individual's proclivity for doing/being one or the other? Where Ivana excels at school, Ivan is consumed by jealousy and rage. Although given multiple opportunities to exceed, like Kassem, Ivan is constantly pulled into relationships with others that lead to his manipulation, unfulfilled identity quest and ultimate self-destruction. His mother, Simone, thinking that perhaps their estranged father (a Malian musician named Lansana with whom she spent one night only) could set Ivan on the right path, sends both children to Mali. Condé's commentary on gender here comes into play.

In her descriptions of the gender dynamics to which Simone, her daughter and grandmother are subjected, Condé also exposes a weakness in Glissant's notion of the Tout-Monde.[7] Gender inequality is a given and very much determines the outcomes of women's lives that are more often than not oppressed by violent realities. Simone's deference to her male partner and her daughter Ivana's lack of agency in the face of masculine domination demonstrate women's incapacity to go against the grain of patriarchal forces in society, particularly in the Caribbean and Africa. Although doing well and making her way in the world, despite poverty on the island, Ivana is compelled to bend to the rules of the father, which force her to accompany her brother to Africa. Her dreams of either becoming a nurse or police officer in order to help people are dashed by her brother Ivan's constant cycle of mishaps and bad choices. Early in the novel, in a rage of jealousy, Ivan goes to prison for murdering Ivana's high school sweetheart. When he is released, Simone decides to send both children to Mali. In Mali, Ivana succeeds again to make the best of a situation in a war-torn country where Islamic jihadists threaten the local community, particularly women, every day. She volunteers at a local orphanage and dedicates herself to singing and studying the traditions of her father's village.

Condé's lesson about the influence of environments on individuals' lives and outcomes is encapsulated in Ivan's constant insistence that "Je suis ce que je suis" (224) [I am what I am]. He is constantly manipulated and consumed by the will of others. In Mali, his father's heavy hand and unwillingness to get to know him also push him first to join the local militia, then to become caught up in radical jihadism, murder and a life that spins out of control. From the chaos of Mali, the twins travel to France where Ivana follows her dream to be a policewoman, enrolling in the police academy in Paris. Contrastingly, Ivan, after failing at an internship and a series of odd jobs, is engulfed again in drug dealing and, eventually, consumed by a terrorist group operating in the *banlieues* of Paris. Bending to the will of the group, he is convinced to carry out an ultimate act of violence: an armed attack on a retirement home for police veterans where

8 WHEN THE TOUT-MONDE IS NOT ONE: MARYSE CONDÉ'S PROBLEMATIC... 147

Ivana happens to be working as a volunteer. In a blaze of gunfire, he accidentally kills her.

FATE, DESTINY AND LUCK IN THE TRAGIC DISJUNCTURES OF GLOBALIZATION

In Condé's narratives, the *prise de conscience* necessary for her young people to achieve a positive and fulfilled being-in-the-world never takes place. The lessons they do learn are fourfold: first, physical and metaphorical geographies of relation, which could facilitate multiple crossings of boundaries and the creolization so celebrated in Glissant's Tout-Monde, do not lead them to a better understanding of how to navigate the complicated and debilitating socioeconomic and political disjunctures of globalization. Second, ignorance about the world and their past lead characters to being duped, and worse still, death. They often become victims at the hands of powerful people and forces around them. Condé emphasizes that because of ignorance and their general lack of knowledge about their pasts, as well as their naiveté in navigating the world's challenges in the present, her young characters are destined to be disempowered. Third, if not powerful enough to make their own paths, individuals will become the identities made for them by others. Environments shape characters' representations of themselves. Kassem becomes what Ramzi sees him as being: a lackey. Ivan becomes a terrorist, manipulated constantly by radicals with a cause. Fourth, patriarchal systems lead to women experiencing increased violence, even death at the hands of men consumed by their desire for power. Although Ivana exceeds in her desire to follow a path that she has chosen, she becomes a victim to the patriarchal systems in which she is bound. Her mother, Simone, also is a victim of the powerful, which are usually men relying on strict systems of patriarchy. Both women end up martyrs for their people.

GEOGRAPHIES OF RELATION THAT LEAD NOWHERE

On a certain level, the physical spaces, geographies, topologies and temporalities of Condé's novels exemplify Glissant's theories of relation as characters operate in a multicultural Tout-Monde; they follow their "traces,"[8] as Glissant notes: "We all know that the line is what put us all, no matter from where we come, in Relation" (1997, 18). Kassem in *Les belles ténébreuses*, with his French passport in hand, travels to an unnamed francophone African country to work in a hotel-park called Dream Land (in English in the text). Once there, he encounters many of the same inequalities and unjust practices that play out in society along the lines of color, class and access (or not) to power as he experienced at home. The hotel is frequented by "Swedes, Danish, Fins, Germans and Americans" who he notes are "the pure natives of nationalities with hard-currency and weak sun" (22). Kassem emphasizes "this is the rule" for global subjects positively networked and with economic means. The white, the privileged, those with passports from first-world countries, enjoy the power of making relations freely and without fetters, allowing them to "'profit from the poor'" (22). Rich, cosmopolitan, global subjects circulate in a world in relation and are able to avoid being victims exploited by capitalism. For the despotic government ruling the African country, maintaining order and protecting the international reputation of the Club Med-like park is achieved by betraying the indigenous people who live there. Just after a terrorist bomb goes off killing everyone in the hotel, the country's dictator Jean-Benoit Cinque's (known as Big Boss) police force profits from the attack to round up the "jobless, the homeless, whores, Senegalese, and carpet sellers" in order to demonstrate to Westerners that the more undesirable populations of the country are being kept in check (23). Kassem is saved by luck simply because the hotel's head chef sent him out to pick tomatoes. Condé's views on luck and how the randomness of events can affect individuals' lives are the lessons we draw from Kassem's survival. He is constantly put into positions where the reader is forced to ask, is he compromised because of, or despite, his actions.

The world-in-motion described in *Les belles ténébreuses* opens in the unnamed African country's capital Porto Ferraille (an interesting name evoking French/Spanish/Portuguese references as well as trash and garbage heaps). Characters go see Tom Cruise in *Collateral* or *La Guerre des mondes* by filmmaker Luc Besson. Kassem and Ramzi forge relationships with many others from the world's historic past and present. Either these people (primarily famous male figures and creatives) are depicted in his immediate reality, or in the histories they learn as wandering migrant subjects with no roots: Marco Polo, Malcom X, Hilarion Hilarius,[9] Fidel Castro, Jesus, Hitler, as well as the famous French soccer player, Zinedine Zidane, and the cyclist Lance Armstrong all cross the protagonists' path (Modenesi 2011, 218). Further weaving the threads of their cosmopolitan existence, both Kassem and Ramzi draw on a multitude of literary works they attribute to shaping their identities: from Rimbaud's *Ophélie*, Baudelaire's *Les Fleurs du mal*, to Léopold S. Senghor's *Femme noire* and Césaire's *Cahier d'un retour au pays natal*. The protagonists also engage with the music of Vivaldi, Antonin Dvorak's *Requiem* and François Couperin's *Leçons des ténébres*, which echoes Condé's title. Once the protagonists arrive in the United States at their final destination in New York, they flock to Harlem where they are surrounded by the music of Marvin Gaye and Billie Holiday (190).

Despite a multitude of connections, including Afrocentric texts and music, people and places, Kassem's reality cannot escape the lurking darkness of the post-9/11 climate. The first decades of the twenty-first century have produced traumas of terrorism, Islamophobia, and radicalization, overwhelmingly presenting outcomes that are more adverse for people of color. Condé's narrative is full of a generation of lost souls, displaced by socioeconomic hardships, wars, famine and natural catastrophes that leave the have-nots with less and less. Her novel reveals that even in a world of free-circulation, young people, particularly men who take out their frustrations on the bodies of women, are constantly pushed to the margins and find themselves at the mercy of manipulators, neocolonial neoliberalism, and vapid and morally corrupt revolutions. Kassem, and so many young people like him, is left in merciless freefall. He, like Ivan in *Le fabuleux et triste destin d'Ivan et Ivana*, is a nomad following paths that lead to no sense of purpose. His journey, completely organized by Ramzi who needs him to help carry out his nefarious deeds, allows no enlightenment and strength for a "retour" to one's "pays natal," as Aimé Césaire describes in *Cahier d'un retour au pays natal* (1939); a work, ironically, that is quoted by Kassem in *Les belles ténébreuses* and Ivan in *Le fabuleux et triste destin d'Ivan et Ivana*. Being able to return to a homeland for Kassem and Ivan no longer is a possibility since they have been so far removed from their sense of place due to the violent lives that have cut them off from family ties, friends and community belonging.

The geographical spaces of nations and continents in *Le fabuleux et triste destin* are as conflicted as the protagonists that inhabit them. Condé takes readers through a geographical map that connects the ethnic details of the twins' lives from their time in utero to their brief adulthoods living and traversing countries and continents. Like many of her novels, the author traces an Atlantic triangle that spans from the Americas (Guadeloupe) to Africa (Mali) to Europe (France). We begin "In utero: ou Bounded in a Nutshell" (in English in the original, a quote from

W. Shakespeare's *Hamlet*). We then travel through "Ex Utero" in Guadeloupe to "In Africa" (Mali) and then "Out of Africa," to France, ending with "Affaires d'Utérus: On n'en sort pas" and a final "Epilogue." Often nations and borders impede Ivana and Ivan from realizing their dreams, hopes and aspirations; yet, on the other hand, local communities provide them with meaningful work and instruction for how to understand the world. Ivana works in an orphanage in Mali and Ivan, for a short time, finds joy in tutoring children at a mosque in Paris. As her characters interact with local communities in Guadeloupe, Africa, and then France, Condé highlights the "glocal" tensions that arise in our era. A term that emerged in the 1990s, glocal describes how global sociocultural and economic networks influence local political policies, moral codes, and social interaction. It is a term "related [to] notions of hybridity, fusion, creolization, and mixture" and often evokes ideas of insecurity in individuals and communities that arise from a sense of loss (of identity, tradition, language, etc.) in their local lives (Roudometof 2015, 776). Loss of these social attributes cause communities to feel that they are at the mercy of outside forces over which they have no control. In *Le fabuleux et triste destin*, the author intertwines her protagonists' personal stories with larger ones that reveal how the tension between local and global forces have influenced the Caribbean. She explains how "the Antilles for centuries" have depended on France for their livelihood causing immense "irreversible traumas" for inhabitants (Condé 2017, 67). These traumas are enmeshed in "capitalism and slavery" (a direct reference to the book by Eric Williams originally published in the 1960s)[10] and have since contributed to the "suspicion of globalization" (65).

Knowledge Is Power and Ignorance Can Never Bring Bliss

In the new millennium, Condé's male migrants embark on journeys without clear set goals that lead them often to failure and even death. One of her underlying messages is that young people pay with failure because they are ignorant about their pasts and origins. Not *knowing* the origins of one's identity hinders moving forward in the future. In *Les belles ténébreuses*, although seemingly a cosmopolitan millennial, Kassem is made from the negative affirmations that define him. Searching for his identity, he is "embarrassed by his ignorance" about the world (186). He professes

8 WHEN THE TOUT-MONDE IS NOT ONE: MARYSE CONDÉ'S PROBLEMATIC... 151

knowing the great authors of the French canon, Rimbaud, Baudelaire, Molière and La Fontaine, but, nevertheless, is ultimately swayed by Ramzi's misinterpretations of only one book, the *Qur'an*. Eventually, Kassem discovers that he cannot live in perpetual movement without a place to call home. *Les belles ténébreuses* describes a planet that is beautiful in its potential yet, as Ramzi tells him, without power, money and knowledge, Kassem will never be allowed to "tie his star to a wagon" (293). He has made the wrong choices that leave him stuck. Lamenting the fact that he didn't pursue a university education after high school, but instead chose to chase money, leads him to remark that the path he has followed has led him to mediocrity: "Pressé de mener une vie mediocre!" (277) [In a hurry to live a mediocre life].

In *Le fabuleux et triste destin*, Ivan and Ivana are categorized as "[t]hese adolescents who never have been to the countries of their ancestors. They do not know them ... they lived in happy self-satisfied ignorance" (278). Both Ivan and Ivana "didn't know the origins of the people of Guadeloupe. They all were ignorant about the fact that all Caribbean people had been brought from Africa in slave ships" (107). The twins, like Kassem, pay for their ignorance; for Ivan this ignorance poses particular hurdles that ultimately condemn him to a future full of evil acts. As philosopher Georges Bataille (1990) remarks, "Good is based on common interest which entails consideration of the future" (15). Not knowing his past means that Ivan cannot plan his future and perhaps the good that he could do for himself and others. Ultimately, Ivan embodies the name given to him by his father: "Celui qui marche sans savoir où il pose ses pieds" (121) [he who walks without knowing where to place his feet] (121). Ivana, on the other hand, recognizes her ignorance more often and then tries to remedy it in order to make a future for herself. She excels in school, takes up volunteer work in an orphanage once she realizes she must live for a while in Mali and, eventually, dedicates herself in France to advancing in her studies to be a policewoman. In Mali, she is known for "son amour pour tout ce qui l'entourait" (117) [her love for all that surrounds her]. However, for all her love for others, and what she learns along the way in her travels, she cannot save her brother or herself.

152   V. K. ORLANDO

ONE IS NOT BORN WITH AN IDENTITY, ONE IS DEFINED BY OTHERS

Simone de Beauvoir's famous phrase, "one is not born a woman, one becomes one,"[11] looms large not only for the women in Condé's novels, but also for others in different contexts. The driving questions Condé asks pertaining to identity formation, which also involves gender, class and race politics, focus on encouraging readers to think about spaces—physical, psychological, and political—and how these shape both young men and women. A question that surfaces repeatedly in both novels is: How does one evolve into an identity?

From the beginning pages of *Les belles ténébreuses*, Kassem's bi-racial heritage makes his life difficult. This compromised sense of self also contributes to his uncertainty about his sexual orientation. He finds that he is attracted to women as well as to the charismatic Ramzi, who infantilizes and manipulates him as he shapes him with his power. When he is mistakenly identified by police as a Muslim terrorist because of his darker skin color and "Arabic-sounding name," Kassem's life spins out of control; he is thrown in jail and accused of the terrorist bombing (21). While incarcerated, he innocently explains to his jailors that his "Muslim" sounding name is thanks to his "father, an authentic Guadeloupean Frenchman" who gave all his children first names "beginning with K" (21). But in the post-9/11 era, where the world is policed by hypervigilant, antiterrorism forces of security, explaining one's identity as simply multiculturally undefined, is virtually impossible. Once liberated from jail, without work and possibilities in the African country, labeled by his dark skin and Arab sounding name, Kassem's only means of help is the association of Muslims headed up by Ramzi An-Nawawi. Immediately upon his arrival in Ramzi's institute for wayward men seeking a cause, the young Guadeloupean is fit into his new identity as a Muslim although he hasn't converted. This new identity is literally fabricated from the outset by the very clothes that Ramzi gives him to wear: a silk caftan and a pair of sandals. Kassem notes that he "felt like an identity usurper," yet is not strong enough to stand up to what has been imposed on him (33).

In *Le fabuleux et triste destin d'Ivan et Ivana*, while Condé's story emerges with the birth of the twins, the author focuses particularly on Ivan and how he is bound to the evil that ultimately defines his identity and eventually takes his life. The author concentrates on examining whether it is the environment or the innate qualities of people that lead them to do acts of evil. Condé maps out Ivan's downfall focusing on how evil reveals itself predominately through personal trauma. This trauma experienced on the individual level echoes in Condé's larger project of exposing the past trauma of slavery as contributing to present-day instability among populations of color. The trauma encountered in these environments sets Ivan on a specific track from which he cannot extrapolate himself. The author leaves us wondering whether consciously or unconsciously Ivan, whose choices never bring positive ends, wills a cyclic trauma on himself, described by Jacques Lacan as "a particular destiny" that "demands insistently that [a] debt be paid ... desire keeps coming back, keeps returning and situates us once again in a given track, the track of something that is specifically our business" (Lacan cited in Ruti 2009, 1115).

Condé articulates well how terror, betrayal and disaster contribute to shaping environments that only bring pain for her characters. Ivan's gravitation to terror, betrayal and disaster, force him on a destiny-path that generates "a tapestry of pain" (Ruti 2009, 1114). The environments he encounters either cause him trauma or force him to commit his own acts of evil. The incessant repetition of trauma ultimately affects his mental state, his judgment, and eventually annihilates Ivan's existence. The accumulation of encounters with forceful manipulators leads to Ivan's radicalization. Condé makes a point about twenty-first-century, global networks that feed terrorism and how these affiliations hold power over individuals, leaving little possibility of escape. In an interview, remarking on radicalism in the Caribbean, she asserts: "Terrorism is not usually associated with the Caribbean ... there are young people in Guadeloupe who are being seduced by terrorists. They are so desperate ... Terror is a possibility for survival. I didn't make this up; it exists. Therefore, my Ivan can become a terrorist" (Jordens n.p.). Ivan's path to radicalization traces a path from Africa to France where his participation in networks of drug dealers and jihadists pursue the young protagonist, ultimately generating the violence that kills him and his sister. What he views as Ivana's betrayal of his love (when she begins seeing other men), also contributes to his ultimate downfall. Condé suggests that evil acts emerge from the unfulfilled love the twins can never share. In an interview with Peter Jordans, the author elaborates on the questions of morality and separation that are evident in her novel. She asks her readers to consider the possibility of unfulfilled sibling love as a catalyst for evil which, in turn, engenders violence and terrorism: "And the children don't understand why they have to leave the warm and peaceful space where they have stayed for so long, lying against one another, seeing nothing, while occasionally recognizing the soft and singing voice of the person who carried them, their mother Simone. No longer are they allowed to be together, truly one. They have to accept the separation" (Jordens 2019, n.p.).

154 V. K. ORLANDO

Corrupted sexuality for Ivan and Kassem is a significant component in Condé's narratives. With respect to Ivan, because of his sexual attraction to his sister, is it easier to condemn him? This is a question that dangles in the last few pages of Condé's narrative as Ivan dies from the wounds endured in the terrorist attacks. Evil arises out of the failed fulfillment of desire; the lack Ivan feels in his life because he cannot (should not) sexually have his sister. He has been "robbed of something unfathomably precious" that cannot be countered (Ruti 2009, 1117). Disaster is the result. The good in Ivana is not enough to take care of the evil in the world that causes Ivan's downfall.

Condé's novels are at once personal and universal. She entreats us to reflect on the human condition in our "world-in-motion" and the tensions among time, space and gender that frame the actions of young people who must live in it. Condé's writing describes the challenging spaces of young people living in the margins, suffering the socioeconomic and political disjunctures of global capitalism. As a commentary on our current era, her works give us pause about the viability of a positive Tout-Monde. Her pessimistic assessment of this world compels us to reconsider the parameters of Glissant's conception of Relation as offering the possibility to radically remap what has been engrained in the status quo of history determined by the victorious. Glissant himself recognized in *Philosophie de la relation* that relation is not always able to counter "les sublimations, qui ornent volontiers les dominations contre lesquelles nous résistons" (2009, 38) [the sublimations, which willingly adorn the dominations against which we resist]. He raises the possibility that a universal Tout-Monde, creolized and equal, may remain forever elusive (1997, 37–38). Yet, Glissant also suggests that writers like Maryse Condé will help us navigate and perhaps better understand this very problematic, unequal world. It is to them that we must listen: "Écoutons le cri du monde. Passons outre les obligations et les petitesses de chaque jour, faisons cortège à ces écrivains et à ces artistes dérivés loin de chez eux, consentons qu'ils nous apportent beaucoup, nous aidant à tisser ce réseau ... dans le Tout-Monde" (1997, 251). [Let's listen to the cry of the world. Let us go beyond the obligations and smallness of each day, let us give procession to these writers and artists pushed far from home, let us consent that they bring us a lot, helping us to weave this network ... in the Tout-Monde].

NOTES

1. This is a term developed by Arjun Appadurai in *Modernity at Large*.
2. All translations in this essay are mine, unless otherwise indicated.

8 WHEN THE TOUT-MONDE IS NOT ONE: MARYSE CONDÉ'S PROBLEMATIC... 155

3. As explained in Being and Time (NY: Harper-Collins, 1962) by Martin Heidegger as well as in the phenomenological philosophy and writings of Maurice Merleau-Ponty and Jean-Paul Sartre.
4. Glissant bases his rhizomatic philosophy on the work of Gilles Deleuze and Félix Guattari's philosophical work Mille Plateaux: Capitalisme et schizophrénie (Editions de Minuit, 1980) wherein they explain the importance of not being rooted, but rather traveling along multiple paths and trajectories. Glissant began exploring Deleuze and Guattari's concept in Caribbean Discourse (1981) and then expanded on its theme in Poetics of Relation (1990). See also Jarrod Hayes, Queer Roots for the Diaspora: Ghosts in the Family Tree (2016).
5. Italicized words in English in the original.
6. See: Livret de pratique Vaudou marassa jumeaux: mini guide de pratique vaudou by Magali Tranchant, alias Mambo Marie Laveau (2019).
7. In his overall conception of the Tout-Monde and Relational philosophy, Glissant is faulted for having paid little attention to gender.
8. Glissant is drawing on Deleuze and Guattari's concept of "lines of flight" as described in Mille Plateaux: Capitalisme et schizophrénie.
9. The character from Compère Général Soleil (General Sun, My Brother, 1955) by the famous Haitian author Jacques-Stephen Alexis. The story follows a young man of peasant origin named Hilarius Hilarion, who is thrown into prison after an attempted robbery, where he is influenced and politicized by communist organizer Pierre Roumel. Condé's character, Kassem, closely resembles Hilarion's trajectory.
10. Eric Williams, Capitalism and Slavery ([1944] 1994).
11. As she writes in Le deuxième sexe (1949).

REFERENCES

Appadurai, Arjun. 2000. Grassroots Globalization and the Research Imagination. *Public Culture* 12 (1): 1–19.
———. 1996. *Modernity at Large: Cultural Dimensions of Globalization.* Minneapolis: UMN Press.
Augé, Marc. 2009. *Pour une anthropologie de la mobilité.* Paris: Payot.
Bataille, Georges. 1990. *La littérature et le Mal.* Paris: Folio.
Beauvoir, Simone de. 1949. *Le deuxième sexe.* Paris: Gallimard.
Bernabé, Jean, Patrick Chamoiseau, Raphael Confiant. 1990. *Eloge de la créolité/ In Praise of Creoleness.* Trans. M. B. Taleb-Khyar. Baltimore: The John Hopkins Press.
Condé, Maryse. 2008. *Les belles ténébreuses.* Paris: Mercure de France.
———. 2017. *Le fabuleux et triste destin d'Ivan et Ivana: Roman.* Paris: JC Lattès.
Glissant, Edouard. 1981. *Le Discours antillais.* Paris: Gallimard.

———. 1990. *Poétique de la Relation: Poétique III*. Paris: Gallimard.
———. 1995. *Tout-Monde*. Paris: Gallimard.
———. 1997. *Traité du Tout-Monde: Poétique IV*. Paris: Gallimard.
———. 2009. *Philosophie de la relation: poésie en étendue*. Paris: Gallimard.
Hachad, Naïma. 2013. Paroles de l'abîme d'Edouard Glissant et d'Abdelkebir Khatibi. *Revue des sciences humaines* 309: 125–140.
Hayes, Jarrod. 2016. *Queer Roots for the Diaspora: Ghosts in the Family Tree*. Ann Arbor: University of Michigan Press.
Jordens, Peter. 2019. Interview with Maryse Condé about *Le fabuleux et triste destin d'Ivan et Ivana*. Repeating Islands: News and commentary on Caribbean culture, literature, and the arts. https://repeatingislands.com/2019/06/04/interview-with-maryse-conde-about-le-fabuleux-et-triste-destin-divan-et-divana/. Accessed 20 June 2022.
Meyers, Mark. 2008. Liminality and the Problem of Being-in-the-World, Reflections on Sartre and Merleau-Ponty. *Sartre Studies International* 14 (1): 78–105.
Modenesi, Marco. 2011. 'Je ne sais pas qui je suis' parcours d'identités multiples dans *Les belles ténébreuses*. *Francofonia* 61: 207–220.
Roudometof, Victor. 2015. The Glocal and Global Studies. *Globalizations* 12 (5): 774–787.
Ruti, Mari. 2009. The Singularity of Being: Lacan and the Immortal Within. *Japa* 58 (6): 1113–1138.
Tranchant, Magali (Mambo Marie Laveau). 2019. *Livret de pratique marassa jumeaux: mini guide de pratique vaudou*. e-voodoo.net. Kindle edition September 17.
Williams, Eric. [1944] 1994. *Capitalism and Slavery*. University of North Carolina Press.

Open Access This chapter is licensed under the terms of the Creative Commons Attribution 4.0 International License (http://creativecommons.org/licenses/by/4.0/), which permits use, sharing, adaptation, distribution and reproduction in any medium or format, as long as you give appropriate credit to the original author(s) and the source, provide a link to the Creative Commons licence and indicate if changes were made.

The images or other third party material in this chapter are included in the chapter's Creative Commons licence, unless indicated otherwise in a credit line to the material. If material is not included in the chapter's Creative Commons licence and your intended use is not permitted by statutory regulation or exceeds the permitted use, you will need to obtain permission directly from the copyright holder.

CHAPTER 9

Re-mapping the Caribbean Gothic in Nalo Hopkinson's *Sister Mine* and Shani Mootoo's *He Drown She in the Sea*

Vivian Nun Halloran

At the turn of the twenty-first century, Caribbean literature scholar Judith Misrahi-Barak heralded the arrival of a new generation of Caribbean Canadian writers who were "creating a future in which part of the Caribbean tradition is contained and yet it is a world apart. Caribbean-Canadian writers have attempted to create a new tradition while integrating the old one" (1999, 96). Jamaican-born Nalo Hopkinson and the cosmopolitan Dublin-born, Trinidadian raised, Canadian immigrant Shani Mootoo are two of the writers Misrahi-Barak identified as part of this group; their later works continue to dramatize the uneasy coexistence of traditional Caribbean and modern Canadian values within their protagonists' lives. As Caribbean Canadian immigrants and novelists, Nalo Hopkinson and Shani Mootoo frequently construct narrative circumstances that bring together Caribbean, diasporic, and Canadian-born characters. Hopkinson's *Sister Mine* (2013) is a supernatural fantasy caper,

V. N. Halloran (✉)
Indiana University, Bloomington, IN, USA
e-mail: vhallora@iu.edu

© The Author(s) 2023
O. Ferly, T. Zimmerman (eds.), *Chronotropics*,
https://doi.org/10.1007/978-3-031-32111-5_9

whereas Mootoo's *He Drown She in the Sea* (2005) tells a postcolonial, neo-Gothic love story. Both novels use water imagery to convey the diasporic connections linking Caribbean and Canadian life by discussing Canadian lakes as well as the Caribbean Sea or the Atlantic Ocean. In so doing, they challenge the prevailing concept of tidalectics, a term coined by (Edward) Kamau Brathwaite (1974) to describe the shared experience of oceanic connections linking various parts of the world together. Hopkinson's and Mootoo's preference for a more regionally specific idea of how water connects people to local landscapes recalls Maryse Condé's skepticism about the universalism of Édouard Glissant's Tout-Monde, something which Valérie K. Orlando discusses in her chapter in this collection.

The novels triangulate their central love stories through a connection to the Canadian landscape (the lake) that sparks the recognition of desire for a space in which the Canadian Caribbean character can dwell with her beloved. Through this mechanism each text questions the strict cultural hierarchies that forbid relationships between people of unequal social standing in patriarchal Caribbean culture. In *Sister Mine* and *He Drown She in the Sea*, Canadian lakes appear to be imbued with quasi-magical properties that resonate with the supernatural elements usually associated with Caribbean landscapes; Mootoo and Hopkinson imagine their respective lakes as entities with the power to root secondary characters to their new homeland's landscape. In contrast, the Caribbean Sea or Atlantic Ocean present only the possibility of an alternate (escapist) reality within the worlds of these novels. Together with each text's references to those who perished during the Middle Passage and Kala Pani journeys, respectively, *Sister Mine* and *He Drown She in the Sea* embrace narrative elements of the Canadian Caribbean Gothic through which Caribbean colonial history, along with threats from supernatural haints and nightmares about out-of-control tidal waves, haunt these love affairs and postpone the ultimate fulfillment of each protagonist's desire beyond the timespan of the novel.

The references to the Caribbean region in Hopkinson's and Mootoo's novels lack geographic specificity by design. This strategic vagueness contrasts with the references to actual Canadian and Latin American locales in both texts as sites where desire is located and fantasies of domestic bliss can be imagined in keeping with Paul Rodaway's concept of "sensuous geography." Rodaway (2002) outlines three central elements that render place into a sensuous geography and the most applicable to my reading of how *Sister Mine* and *He Drown She in the Sea* do so is "*the rediscovery of the sensuous (and the body)* as a potent part of social, political, historical and geographical experience" (7, emphasis original). In what follows, I argue that Nalo Hopkinson's *Sister Mine* and Shani Mootoo's *He Drown She in the Sea* offer a shared vision of Canada as the alternative "sensuous geography" where female protagonists claim the embodied self-determination that their Caribbean heritage denies them. This analysis of how tropes of femininity travel and differ between island and diasporic spaces parallels Megan Jeanette Myers' reading of Julia Alvarez's depiction of female "in transit" subjects in the novel *Afterlife* in her contribution to this collection.

CARIBBEAN GOTHIC

Though all the action of *Sister Mine* takes place in Toronto, the plot involves elements of various Afro-Caribbean religious traditions writ large without specifically naming a particular geographical tradition. These supernatural plot points constitute the novel's most explicit Gothic plot elements. The lovers in *Sister Mine* met as adults of different orders of existence: Cora was a human woman who fell in love with an Afro-Caribbean Celestial demigod, Boysie, whose power (mojo) is the ability to control the vegetation around him. This couple's love leads to the birth of a set of conjoined twins, the titular siblings Makeda and Abby, whose health deteriorates after being separated. The Celestial matriarch, Grandmother Ocean, punishes Cora for this initial transgression by turning her into a marine monster trapped in Lake Ontario. Grandmother Ocean's punishment parallels the twins' surgery since both interventions tear asunder the family unit. However, these events constitute the backstory to the action in *Sister Mine*. What Makeda wants most in the world is to be reunited with Cora, thereby mapping female desire in the novel vertically rather than horizontally, as longing for the maternal. To bring about this reunion, Makeda fantasizes about traveling to Puerto Rico, a US territory in the Caribbean, to gather materials she hopes would reinstate Cora to her human form. Since she is the twin who inherited none of her father's mojo, Makeda's unrealized fantasy stands in stark contrast to the magic the rest of her family members perform within the world of the novel. Her desire for a domestic reunion also has problematic overtones that recall Canada's investment in extractive industries at home and overseas, as I will discuss in the next section.

Much in the same way that Hopkinson refuses to identify a specific Caribbean island as the homeland from which her Canadian Caribbean characters migrated, Shani Mootoo also splits the setting of *He Drowns She in the Sea* between a fictional Caribbean island, Guanagaspar, and a specific Canadian city, Vancouver. Mootoo's preference for a fictionalized version of Caribbean islands was also evident in her first novel, *Cereus Blooms at Night*, which takes place in Lantanacamara. The dual setting strategy emphasizes how something as simple as the physical act of leaving one's island of origin allows the female protagonist, Rose, to break free from the sociocultural strictures within which she had been raised. The star-crossed middle-aged couple in *He Drown She in the Sea* are both Indo-Caribbean, but they belong to different social classes. Harry St. George's mother was a servant in Rose Sangha's family compound, and the two were childhood friends. Rose later married a rich and politically connected man and adopted his surname, Bihar. Only when she and Harry meet again as adults in Vancouver can they admit their mutual attraction and love. Both Rose and Harry fear the social reprisals that their rekindled relationship would bring in either Canada or Guanagaspar and so Rose fakes her own drowning and reunites with Harry as they sail off in search of a new land to call their own.

Much like Makeda in *Sister Mine*, Harry imagines himself saving his mother from an impending natural disaster—a tidal wave—that they never experienced in real life but is the central conceit of his nightmares. *He Drown She in the Sea* opens with the third person narrator emphasizing the geographic divide between the dream's Caribbean setting and Harry's physical location in Canada: "Almost a decade after he left Guanagaspar, a dream he used to have recurs. Though he lives by the sea now, the sea in his dream is invariably the other one, that of his earliest childhood" (1). The Caribbean Sea haunts Harry's memory even from the relatively safe distance of his Canadian life. As the text that frames Harry's and Rose's love story in *He Drown She in the Sea*, the nightmare does two kinds of work: First, it portrays the sea as Harry's proxy because it decimates those who humiliated and taunted him while he lived on the island. The sheer scale of the structural damage and the huge body count marks this nightmare as a Gothic text. The narrator describes in minute detail the stages of the sea retreating and then returning in full force as the wave crashes against the land, taking everything and everyone with it. However, despite the devastation Harry witnesses in the dreamworld, his family survives the onslaught unscathed. The second type of work the nightmare does is to

9 RE-MAPPING THE CARIBBEAN GOTHIC IN NALO HOPKINSON'S *SISTER...* 161

vindicate Harry's own judgment and good sense, for within the dreamscape he succeeds in saving his mother, and later Rose, from the menacing waters. By writing a recurring nightmare with a happy ending while leaving the lovers' actual fates a mystery, Mootoo suggests that Rose and Harry's shared rejection of the strict caste and class rules that kept them apart in Guanagaspar constitutes a victory regardless of whether they ever reach Honduras.

Together, the tidal wave nightmares in *He Drown She in the Sea* and the haints and supernatural family members in *Sister Mine* hearken back to another Caribbean narrative modality, the Caribbean Gothic. Discussing a wide array of multilingual literary texts set in the Caribbean, including those penned by Caribbean authors themselves, Lizabeth Paravisini-Gebert contends that the European textual inscription of the archipelago as a Gothic landscape full of magic and monsters led the area's inhabitants to highlight the strangeness and uncanniness of their own surroundings in their fictive works. This Caribbean Gothic style of writing, she argues, could be read as a critical meditation upon "the very nature of colonialism itself" (Paravisini-Gebert 2006, 233). Following this logic, Sandra Casanova-Vizcaíno seizes on the trope of time travel within Caribbean Gothic science fiction as a tool through which to analyze colonialism's lingering impact: "[T]ime travel—a device common in science fiction narratives—allows for the exploration of a past characterized by the monstrous and the uncanny. However, much like the Gothic mode, this past constantly returns in the present and projects itself into the future" (2018, 110). *Sister Mine* and *He Drown She in the Sea* bend narrative time through references to fantasies and nightmares, thereby partaking of the Caribbean Gothic mode even though neither text could be classified as science fiction. Kertsin Oloff's analysis of the Gothic elements of Haitian Marie Vieux Chauvet's novel, *Amour*, provides a framework through which to understand the physical violence Cora endures at her mother-in-law's hands in *Sister Mine* and the emotional abuse Rose endures from her husband in *He Drown She in the Sea*. Oloff argues that "it is through Chauvet's insistent focus on the ecology of the racialized monstrous-feminine that she exaggerates, and ultimately rejects, the social atomization and structural marginalization of women epitomized by female zombie tales" (2018, 122–23). Cora's and Rose's subject positions within their narratives resemble those of female zombies since each is forcibly alienated from the axis of power in their respective society. Their association with bodies of water—the lake and the sea—help Cora and Rose transform from a suffering victim into the object of desire for their respective partners: Makeda and Harry.

TIDALECTICS

Water imagery features prominently throughout both *Sister Mine* and *He Drown She in the Sea* as central plot points but these narratives complicate its original Caribbean connotation by shifting the emphasis from seas or oceans to Canadian lakes. Kamau Brathwaite elaborates the concept of "tidalectics" across his body of literary and poetic work. In *Contradictory Omens* (1974), for example, Brathwaite claims that "the unity is submarine" (64). For him water, especially the Atlantic Ocean, ties together not only the peoples of the Caribbean but also the past and present histories of capitalist exploitation of the peoples and resources of the islands and inhabitants of the Caribbean, Africa, and the Americas in an unending cycle that is even more pressing with the undeniable effects of climate change. In an interview she conducted with Brathwaite in 2005, Joyelle McSweeney asks him to respond to her summary of his theory of "tidalectics":

> A way that you have conceived of tide and tidalectics and almost taken that ocean of the Middle Passage and turned it into a cognitive space, a space in which perhaps Caribbean peoples can think outside the Western mode of the dialectic. A kind of tide which touches things. And as I was having this thought, I was really struck by this amazing tide in New Orleans. It does seem connected. (McSweeney)

McSweeney here encapsulates Brathwaite's previous references to water during their conversation in order to get him to expand on his views of the Greater Caribbean. And, although his response is tinged with a sense of foreboding due to the recent experience of Hurricane Katrina, it nonetheless also captures something of his view of the supernatural as another factor that links together these territories: "I always say that the one factor you can never take out, is the human one. And what human beings can do in New Orleans, now, we have no idea, but I get a sense that they are going to miracle-ize that place all over again" (McSweeney 2005). With this example, Brathwaite applies the logic of tidalectics to a place overcome by water from a large salt lake rather than the sea itself. By suggesting that miracles are the purview of humans, Brathwaite articulates a fluid continuity linking the physical (the weather, the flood) and the metaphysical dimensions of a major metropolis in much the same way that McSweeney claims Brathwaite turned the actual Atlantic Ocean into a theoretical space for the free play of ideas.

While Brathwaite's concept allows for the flexibility to think through the commonalities linking Caribbean nations to one another, rather than pausing on the differences that distinguish their daily realities, extending the notion of "tidalectics" beyond the Caribbean basin comes at a price. In her influential article, "Tidalectics: Charting the Space/Time of Caribbean Waters," Elizabeth DeLoughrey (1998) argues against the loss of specificity that such an expansion entails:

> The concern with remapping, or imaginatively occupying, Caribbean seascapes differ from other theories of "reterritorialization" because tidalectics are concerned with the fluidity of water as a shifting site of history and document the peoples who navigated, or were coerced into, transoceanic migrations. (1998, 19)

The references to two Hispanophone lands, Honduras and Puerto Rico, in *He Drown She in the Sea* and *Sister Mine* serve as examples of what DeLoughrey (1998) calls an impulse to "remap" or imaginatively occupy seascapes within the Caribbean Basin, but with the added twists of having the journeys being triangulated through Canadian urban centers and involving air travel as well as sea. There is no "emplacement" in these sites since neither Rose nor Harry in *He Drown She in the Sea*, nor Makeda in *Sister Mine* ever arrive at these destinations within the story arcs of their respective texts. *Sister Mine* and *He Drown She in the Sea* invoke the Caribbean region writ large through their strategic inclusion of the shared and overlapping histories of coerced migrations to the Caribbean basin, thereby introducing the idea that colonial history haunts both the mother-daughter's and the lovers' desires for a physical reunion.

DeLoughrey's criticism of tidalectics in the context of both Caribbean and Pacific Islands literature influenced Elvira Pulitano's (2008) analysis of the significance of river imagery in Edwidge Danticat's novels and short fiction. Pulitano explains that references to the sea are "used to glorify fluidity and unmarked territories in Caribbean discourses of identity," and warns against trying to universalize water metaphors as a key component of colonial histories writ large:

164 V. N. HALLORAN

> If on the one hand, the discourse of deterritorialization, as advanced by Gilles Deleuze and Felix Guattari, might work to account for the complex identity politics in the Caribbean, I agree that the same kind of discourse applied indiscriminately to all colonized peoples runs the risk of becoming a mere form of aquatic nomadologic model, one in which the political and socio-economic realities of the individual islands are consistently obliterated. (2008, 3)

While the vagueness or fictitious nature of the Caribbean settings of both *He Drown She in the Sea* and *Sister Mine* do intentionally obliterate, "the political and socio-economic realities of the individual islands" they reference, I would argue that they do so in the service of a larger goal: critiquing the patriarchal elements of Indo- and Afro-Caribbean cultures across the archipelago. Both novels deploy seafaring imagery to reject the misogynistic traditions that require a woman's complicity in her own disempowerment, such as remaining in a loveless marriage (Rose) or acquiescing to an overbearing mother-in-law's unreasonable demands (Cora).

CANADIAN CARIBBEAN GOTHIC

In *Sister Mine* and *He Drown She in the Sea*, Hopkinson and Mootoo infuse their shared traditions of Caribbean and Canadian Gothic with a political engagement with feminism and self-determination that breaks with the stranglehold that Indo- and Afro-Caribbean family traditions can place on their female family members to arrive at a new Caribbean Canadian Gothic. Their shared emphasis on the Canadian landscape via the discussion of the lake as a site of potential bewitchment or imprisonment reveals Hopkinson's and Mootoo's awareness of the white, settler-colonial literary tradition of Canadian Gothic as imagined by Margaret Atwood or Anne Hebert. Analyzing the prevalence of what she calls the "wilderness Gothic" in Atwood's literary works, Faye Hammill mentions two key concepts related to it: "[t]hese explicitly Gothic conceptions of the forested and frozen North" and "her haunted wilderness settings [which] are sites for the negotiation of identity and power politics" (2003, 48). Arnold E. Davidson (1981) also mentions the enduring role that the wilderness plays in the Gothic imagination of twentieth-century novelists like Anne Herbert. He contends that "[t]he questions originally prompted by the wilderness persist for Canadians, even if the wilderness does not, and they continue to be embedded in novels that are essentially gothic"

(246). As an example, he provides a close reading of Herbert's *Kamouraska*, which features a body of water (river, rather than lake) through which the lovers travel to kill the woman's husband. Thus, Hopkinson's and Mootoo's portrayal of the Canadian landscape as uncanny, when combined with an evocation of the historical horrors of slavery and indentured servitude, create their own Caribbean Canadian Gothic that reflects not only more diverse histories and cultures but specifically the interconnectedness of the diaspora situation that maintains footholds in more than one country simultaneously.

The novels' respective references to the established histories of the tragic toll that the triangular trade took on Africans enslaved and transported to the Caribbean during the Middle Passage and later, on indentured Indian workers during the Kala Pani in *Sister Mine* and *He Drown She in the Sea* suggest that Caribbean colonial history continues to haunt the diasporic experience abroad. *Sister Mine* refers to this obliquely, through a discussion of Makeda's room decor:

> The blue of the ceiling was the same colour as the porch ceiling of our—of Abby's house. Dad had done that for me ages ago. Ghosts can't cross water without help. Plus they're stupid. Get the right shade of blue, paint your floor or ceiling with it—doesn't matter which, 'cause ghosts don't have a right way up—and they'll mistake it for the glint of light on water and be unable to pass. Paint your porch ceiling that colour, and your door and your window frames, and you have a haint-proof house. (3)

This tradition is most closely associated with the Gullah people of the Sea Islands off the coast of South Carolina and Georgia in the United States. However, critics like Robert L. Broad (1994) have noted the association between haints/ghosts and the Middle Passage in novels like Toni Morrison's *Beloved*, which simultaneously invokes the cruelty and death that took place on board the vessels transporting enslaved Africans and bringing them to Caribbean and American shores and also reinforce the belief that ghosts/haints are unable to cross water.

Like *Beloved*, Hopkinson's *Sister Mine* literalizes the metaphor of the ghost/haint and Makeda spends the majority of the novel trying to stay safe from, and then learn to counter, the attacks of the various supernatural haints who pursue her and her family:

My haint was upon me. Its small, heavy body scrambled, quarrelling, up my side. Hideously contorted baby face, brown as my own, its hair an angry, knotted snarl of black. Now it had those large hands at my throat. It punched small knobkerries of knees against my rig cage, all but knocking the breath out of me. I staggered. Managed not to fall. One of the haint's searching thumbs pushed brutally past my teeth into my mouth. It tasted of dirt, and of nastily salty skin. (57)

This haint attacks Makeda when she is outside by the shore of Lake Ontario. Thus, the blueness of her new apartment's ceiling provides a brief respite from such chases and the novel differentiates between the mindless haints, who cannot tell the difference between aquatic and paint-based barriers, and Cora, whose punishment bars her from emerging out of the waters of Lake Ontario.

Grandma Ocean had seen to Mom. Grandma's province is the waters of the world, salt and sweet both. She tossed Mom over her shoulder into one of them, and didn't even look back to see which one she'd landed in. She didn't deprive my mother of life, but of the beautiful form with which, Granma convinced herself, Mom had bewitched her sons. Loch Ness has Nessie, its monster of fame and fable. Okanagan Lake has Naitaka a.k.a. Ogopogo, a snake demon. As with them, no one has ever found proof that the monster that people began sighting in Lake Ontario just under thirty years ago really exists. She does have a name, though, and it's Cora. I call her Mom, or I would, if I ever met her. (95)

According to the metaphysical calculus at play within the futuristic world of *Sister Mine*, Cora is an anti-haint, a still-living being imprisoned within a watery jail by her vengeful Caribbean goddess/mother-in-law. Because Lake Ontario is the location of Cora's confinement, her fate does not inherently recall the thousands who died during the Middle Passage journey.

He Drown She in the Sea recalls the history of a different transatlantic journey that is the origin story for the Indian diaspora in the Caribbean and beyond. The name, Kala Pani (meaning "dark water"), refers to the journey through which Indian workers were transported to the Caribbean plantations where they served out their indenture contracts. Dolly, Harry's mother, reminds her son that though Guanagaspar's Indo-Caribbean population is divided into the economic elites and those who work in the service economy, their ancestors share a common history of displacement and mistreatment:

> She and Mrs. Sangha were Indians and Indians alike. Their circumstances were different, it was true, but their ancestors had all landed up in Guanagaspar the same way, by boat from India and as indentured servants. Mrs. Sangha's family came as indentured servants, and it was only chance that had led them down different paths. Mrs. Sangha was a madam and Dolly was a servant, and the boy would have to learn that difference, too. (123)

Though her intentions are good, Dolly breaks Harry's heart when she explains class prejudice to her young son in simple terms: Rose's family can be friendly toward the St. Georges but cannot consider them either peers or actual friends. This new knowledge emotionally scars the boy as the tidal wave nightmare sequences that open and close the novel demonstrate.

By toying with the trope of sea imagery as a hallmark of Caribbean storytelling, and then rejecting it in favor of a celebration of the freeing possibilities offered through the considerably larger urban and rural Canadian landscapes, both novels suggest that interaction and exchange between and across diasporic populations enrich each subject's sense of self within a specific nation-space. Instead, the novels propose a third-space as a possible alternative to the cultural and geographic deterritorialization that their protagonists experience from their home countries. Because of her experience in Vancouver, Rose not only reconnects with her childhood flame, Harry, but she also draws inspiration from her daughter's freedom and independence and used it to fake her own death after returning to Guanagaspar. Through this subterfuge, Rose sets a trail for Harry to follow and they successfully reunite at their friends' Uncle Mako and Tante Eugenie's house. The narrator recounts that "Rose, before she 'drowned,' had made contact with a man who fixed up documents to help people leave the island and enter a foreign country without the intervention of Immigration" (317). Learning about Rose's newfound determination and ingenuity shocks Harry. In a grand display of her hard-won independence, Rose plans to navigate, and three days later the pair will rendezvous with another vessel that will smuggle them to shore. Rose and Harry's sea voyage maintains some of the echoes of the Kala Pani journey as described earlier because the lovers will face the "same-same"

168   V. N. HALLORAN

future together. Through the artifice of her drowning, Rose Bihar abandons her husband thereby "leaving something unsavory behind" while Harry St. George is once more "looking for a fresh start" (178) with his beloved in yet another foreign land.

CANADIAN LAKES AND LATIN AMERICAN LOCALES

In *He Drown She in the Sea,* Canadian lakes are simultaneously attractive and repellent, offering the possibility of inclusion at the cost of Harry's complete assimilation to dominant, white, Canadian social norms. Before Harry and Rose rekindle their childhood love for one another, he had considered pursuing a relationship with a Canadian woman, Kay. Though intrigued by the possibility, Harry fears that such a relationship would entail the complete loss of his Caribbean identity since Kay represents "the Canada of postcards, and tourism posters" (39). When he thinks about a possible future with her, Kay's thorough embodiment of the ideal of an outdoorsy Canadian woman appeals to Harry. Interacting with her makes him want to feel accepted as a citizen of his adopted country: "Yes, it would be very Canadian of him to be able to say that he used to get up early on mornings, drive to a lake high up, awfully high up, in the mountains, and go canoeing" (40). However, as alluring as Harry finds Kay, the thought of being together with her also frightens him. He even goes as far as to imagine some solidarity as a fellow immigrant with Kay's Iranian ex-husband, who abandoned her and their family: "Harry wondered if she had taken Ali out on a lake in an attempt to Canadianize him" (44). This is a transformation both Ali and Harry ultimately refuse. The lakes Harry sees in his mind's eye function as metaphors for a large baptismal font, bestowing upon immigrant bathers absolution from the original sin of having been born elsewhere and baptizing them in the name of the Dominion of Canada.

If the Canadian mountain lakes in *He Drown She in the Sea* have outward, sacramental connotations, Lake Ontario in *Sister Mine* is evocative of amniotic fluid since Makeda's mother Cora became imprisoned there days after delivering her twins by cesarean section. Makeda fantasizes about collecting a sufficiently large amount of drift glass in her mother Cora's favorite color, blue, to succeed in "hoodooing her back into a woman from the sea monster shape they'd told me she'd been forced into" (62). And, Makeda decides that the only likely locale where she could find such a prize would be in Puerto Rico:

Apparently Puerto Rico used to use a lot of cobalt glass in olden times, and much of it made its way into trash heaps there and, eventually, into the water. I'd never been to the Caribbean. Ever since I read about the Puerto Rican driftglass as a kid, I'd had this fantasy image of myself down there, surrounded by an ankle-height circle made up of hundreds of perfectly rounded, frosted pieces of deep-blue driftglass, each one found by me personally. My mother's favourite colour. Of me standing in the middle of the circle, spreading my arms wide, throwing my head back and summoning my mother forth from the depths of the waters. Of hoodooing her back into a woman from the sea monster shape they'd told me she'd been forced into. (62)

In this brief internal monologue, Makeda demonstrates her knowledge of arcane geographical information about this US territory in the Caribbean. This passage conflates the historical reality of cobalt mining in Puerto Rico, which the US Department of the Interior chronicled in a 1959 report that makes no reference to glass of any kind, *Nickel-Cobalt-Iron Bearing Deposits in Puerto Rico* (Heidenreich & Reynolds, 1959), with an embedded allusion to Samuel R. Delany's 1971 short story collection, *Driftglass*. Thus, in this formulation, Makeda's imagined power to reverse her mother's curse depends as much on the plentiful availability of cobalt, a Puerto Rican natural resource, as it does on the postmodern allusion to pioneering fantasy writer Delany, who occupies the space of another of her Afro-diasporic "ancestors."

Makeda's fantasy constitutes a female imaginary that negates or seeks to subvert the male-identified matriarchy that has separated the mother from her children in this family. It also posits a new and embodied vision of sustainability wherein discarded goods, drift glass, can be repurposed to simultaneously clean the island's waterways and reunite mother and daughter. The latter accords with a pattern Gina Wisker (2007) pointed out in Hopkinson's short story, "A Habit of Waste," in which: "Hopkinson's female protagonist regains and re-establishes self-worth and body image in the face of that which would deny her. In this sense, the tale enacts a transformation as the protagonist moves beyond cultural and historical constraints" (120). In *Sister Mine*'s imagined scene in a Puerto Rican beach, the treasure trove of drift glass only has affective, rather than monetary, value.

Though Makeda does not actually free Cora within the novel, she rescues her twin sister from the haints and helps her father, whose dementia threatened Toronto with overgrown kudzu, regain control over his powers. Through imaginative exercises like fantasizing about the Puerto Rican sea glass and standing on the shore of Lake Ontario, hoping to catch a glimpse of her mother Makeda becomes self-assured and overcomes her deep-seated jealousy of her sibling and resentment of her father. Focusing on what these landscapes have in common, the water, rather than what separates them allows Makeda to mother herself into being as an independent woman who can afford to care for others, including her unsuspecting fellow Torontonians and keep them safe from attack by supernatural forces.

He Drown She in the Sea engages in some neocolonial fantasizing of its own when the novel introduces the idea of Honduras as a destination where Rose and Harry can live out their lives together unfettered by the fear of social reprisals. In a transaction that both resonates with contemporary discussions of human smuggling and also recalls the traumatic Kala Pani journey through which both Harry's and Rose's ancestors arrived in the Caribbean, Rose has secured new identity documents, learned how to navigate using a compass, maps, and the stars, and acquired a boat in which to set sail for Honduras (317). Despite having rekindled their childhood attraction for one another in Vancouver, neither can imagine beginning a new chapter of their lives together there. Thus, the idea of Honduras functions as a bit of a deus ex machina within the narrative: it is only mentioned in the last few pages of the novel and neither Rose nor Harry has any personal connections to it, thereby suggesting that their quest has imperial overtones of discovery and conquest. The novel's open ending makes it unclear whether the couple survives the pirogue sea journey and, thus, the future of this domestic idyll is as much wish-fulfillment in *He Drown She in the Sea* as in *Sister Mine*.

Unlike Canada, which is a former British colony with English as one of its two official languages, the two Hispanophone national territories of Honduras and Puerto Rico play a purely symbolic role within the territorial imaginaries of *He Drown She in the Sea* and *Sister Mine*. Neither Rose and Harry nor Makeda spend any time wondering about the practicalities of making themselves understood in these spaces, for their value is primarily as escapist fantasies providing an alternative between oppressively strict Caribbean culture and seemingly open Canadian landscapes which nonetheless try to seduce immigrants into assimilating into the ways of the Great White North. By interacting with other characters from circumstances entirely unlike their own in Canada, Rose Bihar and Makeda finally reckon with their past and realize how much the relationships of their youth mean to them. Shani Mootoo explicitly situates *He Drown She in the Sea* within a spectrum of possible iterations of Indianness and indigeneity, from Indo-Caribbean protagonists, to diasporic Indian Canadians, and tourists from India, all against a backdrop of forests, lakes, and landscapes indigenous to North America. For her part, Nalo Hopkinson's explicit allusions to Christina Rossetti's "Goblin Market" and Samuel R. Delany's *Driftglass*, along with the many layers of popular culture references from hoodoo trees to Jimi Hendrix, anchor her narrative firmly to both a Gothic sensibility and North American Afrodiasporic cultural networks. However, Hopkinson's Toronto is far from a haven of multicultural harmony. One of the first things Makeda does when negotiating the rent with her new landlord is challenge his profiling of her as a potential drug dealer based on the color of her skin, thereby demonstrating that redlining is still a facet of the local real estate market. In conclusion, neither *Sister Mine* nor *He Drown She in the Sea* absolve Toronto or Vancouver from any of the actual problems that afflict such urban centers. In their evocation of Canadian freshwater landscapes, both texts find the freedom to imagine woman-led futures that treat their desires for romantic love or familial connections seriously and worthy of having a space in which to live them out.

REFERENCES

Brathwaite, Edward. 1974. *Contradictory Omens: Cultural Diversity and Integration in the Caribbean*. Mona: Savacou Publications.

Broad, Robert L. 1994. Giving Blood to the Scraps: Haints, History, and Hosea in *Beloved*. *African American Review* 28: 189–196.

Casanova-Vizcaíno, Sandra. 2018. 'I'll Be Back': The United States' Occupation of Puerto Rico and the Gothic. In *Latin American Gothic in Literature and Culture*, ed. Sandra Casanova-Vizcaíno and Inés Ordiz, 109–121. New York: Routledge.

Davidson, Arnold E. 1981. Canadian Gothic and Anne Herbert's *Kamouraska*. *Modern Fiction Studies* 27: 243–254.

DeLoughrey, Elizabeth. 1998. Tidalectics: Charting the Space/Time of Caribbean Waters. *SPAN* 47: 18–38.

Hammill, Faye. 2003. 'Death by Nature': Margaret Atwood and Wilderness Gothic. *Gothic Studies* 5: 47–63.

Heidenreich, W. L., and Burton Mark Reynolds. 1959. *Nickel-Cobalt-Iron Bearing Deposits in Puerto Rico. No. 5532*. US Department of the Interior, Bureau of Mines.

Hopkinson, Nalo. 2013. *Sister Mine*. New York: Grand Central Publishing.
McSweeney, Joyelle. 2005. Poetics, Revelations, and Catastrophes: An Interview with Kamau Brathwaite. Rain Taxi.
Misrahi-Barak, Judith. 1999. Beginner's Luck Among Caribbean-Canadian Writers: Nalo Hopkinson, André Alexis and Shani Mootoo. *Commonwealth (Dijon)* 22: 89–96.
Mootoo, Shani. 2005. *He Drown She in the Sea*. New York: Grove Press.
Oloff, Kerstin. 2018. Commodity Frontiers, 'Cheap Natures' and the Monstrous-Feminine. In *Latin American Gothic in Literature and Culture*, ed. Sandra Casanova-Vizcaíno and Inés Ordiz, 122–137. New York: Routledge.
Paravisini-Gebert, Lizabeth. 2006. Colonial and Postcolonial Gothic: The Caribbean. In *The Cambridge Companion to Gothic Fiction*, ed. Jerrold E. Hoggle, 22 19–57. Cambridge: Cambridge University Press.
Pulitano, Elvira. 2008. Landscape, Memory and Survival in the Fiction of Edwidge Danticat. *Anthurium: A Caribbean Studies Journal* 6.
Rodaway, Paul. 2002. *Sensuous Geographies: Body, Sense and Place*. New York: Routledge.
Wisker, Gina. 2007. Moving Beyond Waste to Celebration: The Postcolonial/Postfeminist Gothic of Nalo Hopkinson's 'A Habit of Waste'. In *Postfeminist Gothic: Critical Interventions in Contemporary Culture*, ed. Benjamin A. Brabon and Stéphanie Genz, 114–125. London: Palgrave Macmillan.

Open Access This chapter is licensed under the terms of the Creative Commons Attribution 4.0 International License (http://creativecommons.org/licenses/by/4.0/), which permits use, sharing, adaptation, distribution and reproduction in any medium or format, as long as you give appropriate credit to the original author(s) and the source, provide a link to the Creative Commons licence and indicate if changes were made.

The images or other third party material in this chapter are included in the chapter's Creative Commons licence, unless indicated otherwise in a credit line to the material. If material is not included in the chapter's Creative Commons licence and your intended use is not permitted by statutory regulation or exceeds the permitted use, you will need to obtain permission directly from the copyright holder.

CHAPTER 10

Imagining Beyond Division, an Environmental Future: Pauline Melville's *The Ventriloquist's Tale* and Elizabeth Nunez's *Prospero's Daughter.*

Elaine Savory

Donna Haraway, an important scholar of the history and significance of science and of feminism, offers us a new way to understand the world, to radically remap it, so to speak. She says we "exist by permission of a vast and complex web of life and the resources which support it," biodiversity providing opportunity for productive exchanging of resources, in which the human and nonhuman "compose and decompose each other" (2017, M45). Haraway offers the term "sym-poesis," adapting from the biological term symbiosis. This she explains means "complex, dynamic, responsive, situated, historical systems. It is a word for worlding" (2017, M45). She adds "we are compost, not post-human; we inhabit the humusties, not the humanities" (2017, M45). One form of life needs another, to facilitate survival and evolution. But she warns this is in grave danger of

---

E. Savory (✉)
The New School, New York, NY, USA
e-mail: savorye@newschool.edu

© The Author(s) 2023
O. Ferly, T. Zimmerman (eds.), *Chronotropics*,
https://doi.org/10.1007/978-3-031-32111-5_10

being destabilized in our time, though we have a great deal of collective knowledge that should have enabled our clever species to foresee and avert disaster. Such thinking asks how we can imagine complex interactions between one form of life and another, when there is reciprocal need and such interactions ensure survival. This goes beyond culture, beyond species, to enter a consciousness that is planetary, not to ignore the damaging divisions that human society endures but to offer a way to embrace the glorious diversity of both human and nonhuman, intended to live in productive interaction.

The Caribbean is a very complex region, diverse in every respect, but it has to battle divisive, siloed thinking imposed by colonial race, gender and class hierarchies. Among its people (and of course among them, its writers), there are alternative and often hidden ways of being and imagining. Learning to live with imposed structures and hegemonic acceptance of them does not necessarily erase resistance and understanding of other ways of imagining the world, often inherited from the long past.

Pauline Melville's *The Ventriloquist's Tale* (1997) and Elizabeth Nunez's *Prospero's Daughter* (2006) each tell stories about environmental consciousness as an ally in dissolving race, gender and class division and prejudice. A healthy environment thrives on diversity, inclusion and inventiveness, on symbiotic interdependence that shifts according to need, so do human cultures and literatures. Given that within Caribbean space and time, it is possible to hold two contradictory ideas simultaneously, both of these novels ask important questions as to how to bring together seemingly insurmountable divisions resulting from a painful past and a complicated present, and try to answer them in environmental, sympoetic terms.

At the Crossroads of Colonial and Caribbean Thought

In a postcolonial Caribbean world, survivals from ancient cultures (Amerindian, African, Asian) exist alongside a colonially induced set of hard divisions (race, class, gender). In trying to imagine ourselves more toward the old ways, we have sought for models and what we have found has been helpful as part of the journey. The crossroads is an example of which I once thought was helpful, imaging a central intersection where the separate pathways of race, gender, class, nation could be in conversation but from which it is possible to understand the separate sources of identity and the choices made about them, as paths leading away (1990, 30–31). Henry Louis Gates in *The Signifying Monkey* (1988) showed the significance of the crossroad in Yoruba culture and in the diaspora, wherever the trickster god Esu is understood and honored. The crossroad has associations with misunderstandings that might turn into productive transformations with other kinds of exchanges and transitions. As Lydia Cabrera shows, in Haitian Vodoun, the crossroad is a place that absorbs dangerous energy and infection, and is deeply associated with healing: "The patient is cleansed three times with a rooster that is passed over the entire body. The rooster dies because it has absorbed the illness and is taken to a crossroad (2001, 37). The crossroad thus has an important ongoing place in Caribbean and in West African collective memory as Brathwaite's work shows us.[1]

Kamau Brathwaite's poetic vision of the cosmos *MR* (2002) is a crossroad with MAN at the center encircled by NAM, the spirit, a reversal and an opening in West African tradition.[2] But this map of the cosmos has a strong connection to a West African understanding of the crossroad and explicitly permits transitions of time and space as in Vodoun ceremonies. Brathwaite's concept of space/time comes from many places (Africa, Asia, Europe in the person of Einstein) (251). He combines them into the idea that the cosmos is both a "clock" of Time and a "series of thresholds/ mirrors/corridors" that is Space. Time is both ancient and disturbingly modern; space both the old infinite world and the new imprisoned one of colonially shaped modernity. Time and space are not necessarily understood in Einstein's kinetic relation. Beryl Gilroy, describing her own novel, *Boy Sandwich*, identified space as a "psychological and physical construct" and time as "organic and linear memory" (n.d., 1). Their interrelation opens up infinite possibilities, but as two separate identities in implicit dialogue in her text.

The crossroads also implicitly acknowledges separations. Sylvia Wynter's metonym "Man," echoed in Brathwaite's use of the crossroads, is also reminiscent of James Baldwin's similar term for white racist maleness in America [see his collection of stories *Going to Meet the Man* (1967)]: Man is what has failed us, and she asks us to adopt "Human" instead as a fully inclusive concept for our species. As Aaron Kamugisha (2006) says, Wynter's thinking reimagines "our very understanding of what is the nature of being human" (142). Caribbean thinking has demonstrated over and over again strong moves to undo the hegemony of Western separatisms, in defiance of persistent neocolonial continuities of them.

Environmental awareness requires us to embrace interconnection, an interaction across difference, a move against the divisiveness of the colonial, neocolonial and capitalist enterprise. As early as Wynter's "Afterword" to *Kumbla*, she asked us to see our "human self-interest" in the frame of its increasing degradation "in our planetary environment" (1990, 366). In her conversations with Katherine McKittrick (beginning 2007), Wynter notes that whereas the Industrial Revolution laid down the path to our present climate crisis, liberation from formal colonization in the mid-twentieth century continued an impassioned persuasion of the formerly colonized into thinking they had the problem of third-worldness or underdevelopment and that to escape this they needed to imitate the colonial centers in their pillage and burn habits with fossil fuels and other forms of capitalist exploitation of natural resources. Kathryn Yusoff (2018) reminds us that Wynter represents a vital moment in slave resistance as also an environment pact, so the kissing of the earth before slave rebellions was "an oath-act that maintained a social contract with the earth often to the point of death" (37). Yusoff, a geologist, explains there is a "White Geology," which is "a category and a praxis of dispossession" (68). She goes on:

> It has determined the geographies and genealogies of colonial extraction in a double sense, first, in terms of settler colonialism and the thirst for land and minerals, and second, as the category of the inhuman that transformed persons into things. (68)

Cultivation of the plantation by the enslaved, even whilst ordered and supervised by planters, as well as the cultivation of provision grounds, had to be also resistance to that attempt to reduce people to exploitable resources. Wynter argues that people of African descent fashioned a new environmental language, as they could, what Yusoff names, following Wynter, "the praxis of the human through a relation to the earth" (2018, 39), a relation, not separation. By the time of the conversations with McKittrick (2015), Wynter had come to think that our species now has to confront "the overall negative costs" on a planetary level, of pursuing "neoliberal consumer-driven cum politically liberal democratic" goals and strategies (2015, 43). What has brought us to this dire place in terms of threat to long-term human survival is thinking of the world and all we do divisively.

A Transformative Sympoesis

Scholarly work often traps the writer in terminology that reinforces divisions even when the writer, like Melville or Nunez, tries to avoid them. When Wynter tries to write beyond separatisms in academic work she is sometimes hobbled by language itself employing hyphenated pairs of terms such as "nature-culture" or "bios-logos". Similarly, Ladelle McWhorter lists separate elements by which we codify identity, "racial, ethnic, religious, and other forms of diversity" (2010, 75), reinforcing them as separate categories even as she argues for a collective social change embracing everyone.[3]

Post-structuralism enabled us to see how language so often works by defining what is in terms of what is not (red is not blue, rich is not poor). But creative uses of language can layer and juxtapose meaning and bypass the literal. It is important to remember that Wynter began as a creative writer, a novelist (*The Hills of Hebron*, 1962). Her academic style is convoluted and sometimes circular in argument, perhaps moving toward creative assimilation of disparate modes of expression, importantly avoiding straight lines of limited argument. Carole Boyce Davies (*Black Women, Writing and Identity*, 1994 and *Caribbean Spaces*, 2013) has experimented with combining scholarship, theory, criticism and memoir in one work as a way of encompassing her Caribbean experience and knowledge, raising important questions about how we might integrate different formal modes of approaching a topic, weaving them together.[4] For writers concerned with social justice like Melville and Nunez postcolonial perception can planetary and species-wide thinking without enabling globalizing power. The novels discussed here go beyond the crossroads and Wynter's concept of Man to speak to an ecological spacetime that proposes symbiosis between peoples and their places, between humans and other species.

Melville has Guyanese ancestry (mixed British and Amerindian) and knows her cultural inheritance from Guyana though she resides in the UK. Nunez is Trinidadian and has long worked in New York. Both Guyana and Trinidad and Tobago have diverse populations, and while tensions have at times divided the population (African/East Indian), both cultures embrace the idea of mixing. Indeed, Kit Candlin (2012) argues that Grenada, Trinidad and mainland Demerara (now part of Guyana)

178   E. SAVORY

constituted a group of frontier societies difficult for colonial administrations to manage, "a place of competing empires and confusing racial mixes in barely developed colonies" (175), where, nevertheless, enslaved people labored on plantations in appalling conditions. Contradiction and plurality of existence have particularly marked these societies. In these stories, colonially determined racial and class binaries are both supported and resisted and mixing is commonplace, destabilizing those very same colonial racial and gender hierarchies, what Greg Thomas calls "the sexual politics of empire" (2007, 11).

Prospero's Daughter represents a battle between old "purities" and separations and new amalgamations of cultural difference that oppose racial hierarchy. In this sometimes too programmed retelling of Shakespeare's *The Tempest* (1611), Dr. Gardner is another version of the worst of Wynter's white supremacist "Man." He is a reincarnation of Prospero, not a magician now but a British doctor who has betrayed his profession at home and fled to escape a malpractice accusation. His name is an ironic echo of "gardener," but he has no instinct to nurture anything, only to control it as in forcing interconnection in plants by making hybrids, an echo of actual planter attempts at eugenics with regard to their slaves' procreation. Cultivated and wild plants as well as health and disease are two major threads in the novel by which Nunez explores colonial and decolonial odes of existence, both deeply engaged with the environment.

In Shakespeare's play, Prospero exerts power over Caliban because he is afraid of a union between him and his daughter, a union even Caliban does not imagine as more than sexual. The island on which Prospero and his daughter are shipwrecked is a magical place. Nunez's story is set on the real island of Chacachacare, off the main island of Trinidad. The novel references people suffering long-term leprosy and the actual island really did hold a leprosarium (1920–50). Patients were isolated because of lack of an effective cure, when leprosy was sufficiently widespread to seem like a sort of plague.[5]

Leprosy is not centrally a part of the novel, but rather an important context for it. In this time of COVID-19, we especially understand that health in the human body is also a matter of delicate balance, of exchange between elements both within the body and in its environment. A body is a delicate ecology, and if it becomes seriously unbalanced, there is disease (which we can understand as dis/ease, lack of ease). People vulnerable in a society made unhealthy by racism, sexism and class division might develop an illness because their body cannot defend against it.

10 IMAGINING BEYOND DIVISION, AN ENVIRONMENTAL FUTURE... 179

Janarden Subedi and Eugene B. Gallagher (1996) open the introduction to a collection of essays on society, health and disease by saying "(i)t is accepted today that health and disease are related to, and often stem from, the structure of a society" (xv).[6] Colonial Caribbean governments began to consider establishing public health legislation and a bureaucracy to administer it only after severe crisis (De Barros and Stitwell 2003, 2).[7] In the past, they had felt that the "inexhaustible supply of labour made health expenditures seem unnecessary" (De Barros and Stitwell 2003, 3). So, Gardner's behavior carries on this attitude toward health and wellness in the disadvantaged.

Dr. Peter Gardner is infected by an arrogance that does not value either the people or the island he comes to know. He is only on the island to evade the consequences of medical malpractice. He amuses himself by grafting one plant onto another, a bizarre and unnatural version of mixing. He has no interest in the few people left on the island with leprosy and represents a corrupted form of Western medicine (coming out of a culture dominated by mercantilism). This betrays its oath to do no harm. When Lucinda, who raised Carlos, the Caliban figure, is dying of terminal cancer, it is the remaining lepers on the island who help her and her household (133). Her illness just makes her vulnerable to Dr. Gardner, offering him opportunity to appropriate the house that should have belonged to Carlos.

Marguerite Fernandez Olmos and Lizabeth Paravisini-Gebert (2001) point out metaphors of healing as a "counterargument to the metaphor of illness has become perhaps the most frequent and effectively deployed weapon against colonial discourse." (xx). They also argue:

> With a reevaluation of traditional curative practices taking place worldwide, we would appeal for a reconsideration of the healing methods used by peoples accustomed to adaptation and reinvention; alternative and integrative strategies have been the tools of survival in these creative Caribbean societies. (2001, xix)

But Gardner's scientific training is alien to the island and turns plants into objects for experimentation.

When John Mumsford, inspector of police, arrives on the island to investigate a complaint of rape, he is struck by the odd vehemence of green at Dr. Gardner's house:[8]

180   E. SAVORY

Plastic, artificially, brilliantly green ... he saw that the flowers, too, were brilliantly colorful, artificially colorful. But what made him suck in his breath was not the brilliance ... but the variety ... of the colors on a single plant ... bougainvillea ... their petals splashed with polka dots, blue upon pink, violet on orange, yellow on red, the petals on some opened out flat like lilies. (Nunez 2006, 47)

Flowers are the sexual part of plants, so there is an important suggestion here that Gardner has a desire to pervert nature. British colonialism, as Richard Drayton's important study (2000) demonstrates, was obsessed with moving plants from one part of the Empire to another and "improving" them along the way, often by means of a sojourn at Kew Gardens in London, so they could be grafted and domesticated—changed from their original botanical nature to suit a new environment. Gardner (or any colonialist) corrupts knowledge for self-interest and mastery over not only other humans but also the environment.

His botanical experiments are not the only violence he visits upon the world, human and nonhuman alike. He wants to cut down trees. In this he repeats Prospero's desire to claim the island as his own. The trees he fells were planted by Carlos's father. First the chennette, then the coconut, breadfruit, chataigne, avocado, plum, orange, grapefruit, sapodilla, soursop and two mangos (Nunez 2006, 128–9). Gardner gets rid of other plants (ixora, wild poinsettia, a vine called chain of love, buttercups). He could not be more different than Carlos's father, who taught him to respect the nonhuman (iguana, snake, nightjar, butterfly, keskidee, mockingbird, parrot). Not only does Gardner want to have control over plants, he orders all fruit to be cooked (and he bans tropical fruits altogether). He thinks nature threatens to destroy him in the tropics.

Jill Casid (2005) makes the persuasive argument that European landscape gardening contained the seeds of its own undoing, through "transplantation and intermixing," which "release the garden's uncanniness," so that it might become an "unsettlingly queer place of overwhelming and excessive beauty and stench" (xxi). Gardner is terrified by natural ebullient growth, even though he grows plants boisterous in their manufactured monstrosity. His own desire is turned into an extension of material possessiveness and power-seeking. He abuses his daughter sexually whilst protecting her virginity (even her name, a bit too obviously, underlines this obsession), equating that with her marriage market value.

Gregg Thomas points out that "the rule of Europe has assumed a notably erotic form" (2007, 23). Gardner lets slip that Virginia's mother was too pure for sex and she died in childbirth. Carlos also thinks the man Gardner has in mind to marry Virginia was more impressed with an orchid Gardner bred than with her. Gardner too has a vicious hostility toward the evident attraction between his daughter and Carlos. His sense of nature is as sick as his warped understanding of science. Though he loves to graft plants onto each other, he resents the mixing of races. He is clearly unfit to be a father, but he wants to interfere with the potential for other men to have families. Greg Thomas's essay, "The 'S' Word" (2006) engages with Wynter's discussion of the ways the plantation displaced enslaved men from their own family life. The plantation exploited land and people together, distorting the sexual and emotional lives of those working on it whenever possible.

Virginia and Carlos express a very different attitude to the natural world when they come together. They reach toward the nonhuman in fellowship, in mutual resistance to Gardner. It is in saving a wild bird from his fury, respecting its right to be, that Carlos and Virginia begin their friendship (161–3). They are both sensitive to the natural world. On a walk with Gardner, when still young, Carlos describes a place where razor grass and trees grow freely, and there are colorful orange berries and pink, yellow, red and lavender flowers. When Carlos tries to warn Gardner about the poison in the manchineel fruit, the doctor yells "everything on this island is diseased" (Nunez 2006, 191).

Carlos and Virginia, in their union, represent a healthy response to nature, but their mixing provokes strong responses from those who fear it. She is white. He has blue eyes and freckles and "the skin color of a colored man" (Nunez 2006, 64). Gardner, trying to dismiss Carlos, says his mother was a "blue-eyed hag" and his father was Black (reflecting Prospero's description of Caliban's mother in *The Tempest* (54)). Mumford repeats a Trinidadian story that mixing Black and white blood produces "black and brown dots on the white" (55). Carlos explains that his mother was born in Algeria to English parents, who disliked living in Algiers but did so to make money. Her African nanny, a Black woman, taught her Arabic. Her first love was a Black man, though her parents forbid it. Her second love was also Black, Carlos's father. Carlos represents a healthy mixing of the races, and he is also keen on Gardner's daughter. It is significant that he and Virginia find themselves alone as two potential lovers in a paradisiacal spacetime "untouched, unchanged by human hands," an "organic," "pure" place (Nunez 2006, 209), where they are building a relationship within nature, trying to evade the gender, class and race tensions of the cultures in which they were raised.

By the end of the novel, they keep flowers grown by her father as an act of healing the past. They watch fruit trees flourish which replace those he cut down (332) and establish an alternative way of living, healthy, simple, calm, as they expect their first child, whom they will raise as an islander. Their relationship transcends race and embraces nature just as it is, without a desire to shape or curb it. Virginia, however, is not as fully rounded a character as Carlos, and her love of nature as well as her sexuality seem tepid. She knows the botanical (scientific) names of plants because she learned them from her father, but she is not entirely shaped by him or she could not be Carlos's partner.

As she rides in a small boat to confront her father, along with Carlos and Inspector Mumsford, almost at the end of the story, Virginia becomes absorbed in watching tiny fish:

> [B]lue, purple with blue; red, yellow with red; green, orange with green, all the dazzling colors of the rainbow-dating through the emerald-green reeds of sea-plants shimmering above the speckled white sand ... I was not thinking of my father when I saw those fish, when I saw those green reeds, when my eyes traveled further across the silken blue water. I was thinking: *This is my sea, my place in the world. This is where I belong.* (Nunez 2006, 302)

This is not an escapist adoration of nature as compensation for something being lost (as pastoral was a coping mechanism for European elites separated from the country). It expresses a claim to belong to what is not human, to a world that appears to have some sort of balance and equity. But to her credit Virginia makes no attempt to name the fish or the reeds formally, a kind of possession.

Derek Walcott (2005) reminds us that this impulse to name is at the core of colonial appropriation: "Here is an unknown plant. Take the arrogance of an Old World botanist naming this plant then, this one on the grass verge of the beach that I do not even have a name for, and I now believe that my ignorance is more correct than his knowledge" (56). At the end of the novel, Virginia tells Carlos that her father violated her, emphasizing a strong link between colonialism and incest in regard to the region. Sexual predation in the past threatens the happiness of the present. Virginia is afraid, for she carries Carlos's child, but he just takes her hand supportively. Carlos's embrace of all nature, including plants cultivated by Gardner, is one with his acceptance of Virginia. The novel has an evident polemic, which reduces character complexity, and so maybe the ending is not as convincing as it might have been if Nunez had set her story free from the controlling project of rewriting *The Tempest*.[9] But if we think of it as an extended parable that critiques European colonialism as destructive to both humans and flora and fauna, it works well.

Meanwhile, *The Ventriloquist's Tale*, published nine years earlier than Nunez's novel, portrays forbidden love in different generations of Guyanese society through complicated characters who at the same time protect and reinvent traditions. In this story, the environment is also a powerful player and mixing is a kind of dialogue not just between people but between people and their places. The McKinnon family has as patriarch Scotsman Alexander McKinnon. He has mixed race children with his two Wapisiana wives, who are also sisters. His cultural practice has changed through his experience of living with the nomadic Atorad people in the rain forest of Guiana and through learning Wapisiana and accepting Wapisiana custom. He knows the land and the plants he grows, and his thinking reflects Amerindian cultural norms toward European attempts at forcible farming: "[T]he land seemed set against it" (1997, 98). In Georgetown, the capital, gossip says he is more Indian than European (100). This raises some important questions about what we mean by mixing. Intrusion of outsiders who seek to impose alien ideas and practices that violate balance and equity is conquest: But when the outsider changes, going toward local norms, then they come to belong to a multiracial culture.

Melville's story is centered in Amerindian apprehensions of modernity, which combine traditional knowledge and awareness of the outside world that has brought change. Her novel's narrator is Brazilian novelist Mário de Andrade's eponymous character Macunaíma, as the amusing opening makes clear (other narrator avatars are Chico and Sonny). Albert Braz (2007) points out that Andrade's character can be seen both as the symbol of South American cultural and racial hybridity, and also its opposite, cultural resistance to mixing. He argues that Melville's novel can be read as suggesting that "cultural and biological mingling poses a major danger to the people of the savannah" (19). But it is surely more complicated than that: it is not miscegenation itself which is the problem, but the retention of hierarchies from alien cultures which prevent openness to change and learning. Traditional cultures are not static, even when isolated from

184   E. SAVORY

outside influences. Further, the novel suggests that when cultures remain primarily endogamic, they become unsustainable.

Take for instance that Danny's father is Alexander McKinnon, so he is mixed race. Danny identifies with the Wapisiana. He is accepted by his Wapisiana grandmother because he is "reddish-brown" and speaks her language, ignoring his mixed ancestry. She tells him a creation story of the Macunaima. Her story describes the sun as "still a person like us" looking for a wife. He tries to seize a woman bathing, who to get away promises to send him a wife. She sends a white woman who crumbles into white earth, then a black woman who melts as wax. Finally, a "reddy-bronze colour" woman becomes the sun's mate, with whom he has several children, who become the Macunaima (105). This fable suggests preference for separate identifying characteristics, sitting alongside the many elements in the story that identify mixing, for good or ill.

Quite early in the novel Rosa Mendelson, in Guyana to do research in an aspect of colonial literary history, explains to anthropologist Michael Wormoal that she believes in "a mixture of the races" (78). But he thinks this idea is against the tide: meaning, presumably, the Eurocentric intellectual tide. Everyone, he says, is retreating "into their own homogenous group" (78). Rosa's assertion was provoked by Wormoal worrying about "how rapidly Indian culture is disintegrating these days–contaminated mainly by contact with other races" (78). The European scholar defines Indigenous spacetime as unchanging and static in relation and in opposition to a European sense of spacetime as progress and continual movement. He teases Rosa that as a Jew she must stick together with other Jews in Israel, to which she responds that she often supports the Palestinians. She brings Wormoal to admit that his work is itself risking "contaminating the Indians" through his presence, and that in the end it will only enrich European and American cultures, not the people he studies (79). Thinking of interaction as contamination argues for separation. But if it is done the right way, Rosa has faith in its importance. This is affirmed by her attraction to Chofy McKinnon, mixed himself.

The narrator, voice of Amerindian belief in a contemporary moment, explains that: "[T]he sort of death you die determines your afterlife, not the sort of life you lived ... We progress through life towards the perfect state of being an animal. ... Animals that behave badly—a jaguar, for instances, that hesitates before the kill—would slide down the scale to become human" (355). This is a striking refutation of the usual view of "developed" people that animals are below humans. The narrator says,

"In my language, hunting means making love with the animals. The hunt is courtship, a sexual act. ... You have to understand the desires of your prey" (7). Danny repeats a folk belief, "Animals are people in disguise" (122). The traditional healer, Koko Lupi, cured her measles infection when she was very young, by summoning the spirit of the jaguar. This is another example of an embrace of the other which challenges the primacy of human experience.

There is a tension between old mores (Amerindian traditions) and new, imported ones. For Danny and Beatrice, brother and sister, incest is a phase in their growing up. Tanya Shields (2014) reads this as an important part of Amerindian tradition and cultural identity. But its moorings seem uncertain as the novel proceeds. Perhaps Melville is suggesting that in this shifting social situation, sexuality, like everything else, has to be evaluated from multiple directions. Tradition unmoored from its full meaning is confused but beliefs that are certain, like the Christian Father Napier's, are likely to do damage.

Sexuality is a prime avenue for undermining social rules. Ballantyne and Burton, (2009) introducing a book on gender and intimacy in global empire, ask "not just how intimacy was constructed but also how it was *embodied* across the restless world of empires" (7). Imperial regimes "were invested in governing the 'unruly and unfulfilled passions' of their subjects, both European and native" (Ballantyne and Burton 2009, 8). Beatrice and Danny refuse to curb their youthful desires, resisting the intrusion of Father Napier's alien and strict moral codes. Beatrice's sexual desire is deeply connected to her experience of plants, as when "the vivid electric blue of jacaranda petals started her nipples tingling in the same way. Certain blossoms with a particularly vibrating wavelength of color affected her sexually like that" (Melville 1997, 129).

But nature does not always stay in balance. The rains can be a disaster, inundating the land and bringing ill-health to the cattle and people through invasive insects and parasites (136). Weather, the manifestation of the nonhuman, can be treacherous, as much subject to imbalance at times as the human world. It is something with the power to change lives in an instant.

> The red earth blows in the wind, coats drinking water, and filled the creases of clothing, clogged the feathers of the bows and arrows, blocked up the barrels of guns, covered the saddles and harnesses hanging on the walls, choked the plants and made everyone's skin thirsty, like a red plague (91).

186   E. SAVORY

Some humans live close enough to nature to identify with its changes and rhythms.

This is true of the boy who is said to have his existence "tied into the landscape and the seasons, rainy or dry" (14). Chofy carves turtle-shell patterns onto flat stones (18), linking the animate and inanimate. The Wapisiana tell of a time long ago "when we could all speak the language of plants and animals," until a man made a bow and arrow and killed a deer. After that, they lost their immortality: they were separated from nature (122–3). Descriptions of the city, by contrast, in the novel are dominated by the human.

The narrator tells us he discovered a word at the bottom of a muddy lake, which turned into many words and then into many "ramshackle bones" (5). This language, while associated with loss of Amerindian people and culture, is not gone, but capable of informing the world in its own way and on its own terms. Alexander Weheliye, in a discussion of race and the body, cites Zora Neale Hurston's striking statement "the white man thinks in written language and the Negro thinks in hieroglyphics" (2014, 51). Sweeping generalization as this is, such a bold claim reverberates not only with the "hieroglyphics" Melville's narrator finds on the first stone from the lake, which are language, but also with Kamau Brathwaite's employment of hieroglyphs in his later work (e.g., *Golokwati* 2000; *Born to Slow Horses* 2005). In both, postcolonial metropolitan language and the ghost of prior language, represented by hieroglyphics, are creatively in dialogue. Melville's narrator speaks of many skeletons coming back from the dead bringing their words with them, words the narrator understands: Rosa, too, is interested in ways the past informs the present: the two are braided and many-stranded.

Father Napier turns into Wynter's figure of the "Man," working as an agent of Eurocentric power, specifically Catholicism. In trying to remake relationships and attachments, he triggers a coalition of enemies, led by Beatrice. She obtains poisonous beans that are hidden in his food by a female ally, who is afraid of Napier's attempt to limit men to one wife. The poison severely harms Napier and kills his young companion. The boundaries between food and poison are understood well in a place in which ancient knowledge has long known a whole range of plants and their properties: it becomes an ally in a cultural war.

Lizabeth Paravisini-Gebert calls the clearing of forest for sugarcane farming "ecological trauma" (2011, 183). As forests disappeared, so did much of the knowledge of plants in those forests. But in Guyana and

Trinidad and Tobago, forests still survive, and with them, to some extent, the ancient practices of traditional healing that drew on plants that grew there. That Beatrice uses a plant-derived poison to try to murder someone in the twentieth century demonstrates the extent to which the intrusion of colonialism causes a reactive violence, quite against the nurture brought by old communal values.

The Ventriloquist's Tale, like *Prospero's Daughter*, links divisive thinking with illness. The narrator tells us:

> It was while I was in Europe that I nearly became infected by the epidemic of separatism that was raging there. The virus transmutes. Sometimes it appears as nationalism, sometimes as racism, sometimes as religious ortho-doxy. My experience in the rain forests of South America provided me with no immunity to it (355).

This connection of sickness and separatism is important: health comes from integration, plural identity and complex cultural experience, drawing on both present and past (Time) and on infinite and finite space.

Though the anglophone novel, like much of colonially inherited cultural forms, had its birth in a British culture increasingly turning toward hierarchy based on class, race, gender and nation, Caribbean writers have often tried to reinvent it to tell stories that express resistance to such reductive strategies. Nunez and Melville tell stories that encourage us to embrace the realization of universal interconnection in a world still mired in division, a *worlding* that we so badly need in our moment where greed and power have so damaged the fecundity and balance of our earth. This is a radical remapping, not only of places but of the people who inhabit them who have forgotten from whence they came.

NOTES

1. Interestingly, Richard Drayton (2000) ends his book on British colonial plant predations and movements with the idea of the crossroads connected to Caribbean *Vodun*, a "space in which people secure the needs of the present and the future through negotiation with each other, and with their memories of the dead" (274).
2. Brathwaite also sees the power of the crossroad as a place where journeys begin that make profound changes in the traveler (2001, 257). This special place may be represented as watergate, sea/water/river, wood, stone, metals, rains, fire—all elemental aspects of our earth, coming together.

3. McWhorter (2010) reminds us that evolution works by genes adapting, (mutating), to respond to environmental changes. Genetic variation is the key to survival of a species. Of course, the term "species" itself was co-opted by racism, as nineteenth-century racists sought to establish people of color as separate from whites. In the same way, prejudice against queer people has sought to justify itself by arguments about what is good for the species human.

4. Davies's (2013) intention is to reach those who have not had advanced education while also speaking to academic readers. She has even included, in her second book "deliberate reflective breaks." This bridge between academic and public education, academic and "creative" writing is interesting in the context of this discussion of how to represent the complexities of Caribbean identity and culture.

5. There is an intriguing moment when Virginia meets a young girl on the island. Her first inkling of her presence is a branch moving, though there is no breeze. Then a small bunch of wildflowers is left propped against a tree trunk, and some days later, a single hibiscus. Now the girl is visible. Virginia is relieved to see her skin is a "silky flow of brown chocolate," flawless, not afflicted by leprosy (Nunez 2006). The girl comes back only briefly, and then Virginia sees the tell-tale marks of leprosy on her face. Was this the beginning of more than friendship, until the disease manifested, a disease that has become a part of the ecology of the island?

6. Subedi and Gallaghar (1996) go on to talk about the "social production of health and disease." In the present COVID -19 crisis, we are seeing much evidence that this is true.

7. De Barros and Stitwell also point out that the whole tropical colonial world was high rates of mortality and morbidity, especially among Europeans. But they also point out that colonial medicine, in its focus on origins of disease in African practices and cultures helped to create a particular "African identity" that sustained the idea of difference- convenient for colonial aims and practices (2003, 5).

8. The ironic references to Jean Rhys's *Wide Sargasso Sea* (1966) (such as the Ariel figure of Shakespeare's play fusing with Rhys's character Amélie) work well to set up a delicate intertextual connection between the two novels. For example, the husband in both Rhys's novel and her short story "The Imperial Road" recoils from vivid green foliage in the tropics, but Gardner outdoes the brightness with his own lurid "plastic" green plants around his house. Garden also sexually violates Lucinda's racialized daughter, Ariana (the Ariel figure).

9. The title of Nunez's novel reverberated very much with me, since the last lines of my poem "miranda: the first voicing" (1998) are as follows: "it is for me to turn & / confront that prison: / *prospero's daughter.* It is clear that Shakespeare's representation of the father–daughter bond is deeply interesting to women writers now. But although Nunez chose to title the novel this way, we do not greatly enter into Virginia's sense of self.

REFERENCES

Baldwin, James. [1948] 1967. *Going to Meet the Man*. London: Corgi.

Ballantyne, Tony, and Antoinette Burton. 2009. *Moving Subjects: Gender, Mobility, and Intimacy in an Age of Global Empire*. Urbana: University of Illinois Press.

Brathwaite, Kamau. 2005. *Born to Slow Horses*. Middletown, CT: Wesleyan University Press.

———. 2002. *Golokwati 2000*. New York: Savacou North.

———. 2001/2. *MR*. New York: Savacou North.

Braz, Albert. 2007. Mutilated Selves: Pauline Melville, Mario de Andrade and the Troubling Hybrid. *Mosaic: An Interdisciplinary Critical Journal* 40(4) (December): 17–33.

Cabrera, Lydia. 2001. Black Arts: African Folk Wisdom and Popular Medicine in Cuba. Trans. Margarite Fernandez Olmos. In *Healing Cultures: Art and Religion as Curative Practices in Caribbean and Its Diaspora*, ed. by Margarite Fernandez Olmos and Lizabeth Paravisini-Gebert. New York: Palgrave. 29–42.

Candlin, Kit. 2012. *The Last Caribbean Frontier, 1795–1815*. New York: Palgrave Macmillan.

Casid, Jill H. 2005. *Sowing Empire and Colonization*. Minneapolis: University of Minneapolis.

Davies, Carole Boyce. 2013. *Caribbean Spaces: Escapes from Twilight Zones*. Urbana: University of Chicago Press.

———. 1994. *Black Women, Writing and Identity: Migrations of the Subject*. New York: Routledge.

De Barros, Juanita and Sean Stitwell. 2003. Introduction: Public Health and the Imperial Project. Eds. Juanita De Barros and Sean Stilwell. *Caribbean Quarterly* 494 (December): 1–11.

Drayton, Richard. 2000. *Nature's Government: Science, Imperial Britain, and the "Improvement" of the World*. New Haven: Yale University Press.

Gates, Henry Louis, Jr. 1988. *The Signifying Monkey: A Theory of African-America Literary Criticism*. Oxford: Oxford University Press.

Gilroy, Beryl. n.d. *Space Time and History in Boy Sandwich*. Typescript, Given to Elaine Savory by Beryl Gilroy.

Haraway, Donna. 2017. Symbiogenesis, Sympoiesis, and Art Science Activisms for Staying with the Trouble. In *Arts of Living on a Damaged Planet*, ed. Anna

190 E. SAVORY

Tsing, Heather Swanson, Elaine Gan, and Nils Bubandt, M25–M50. Minneapolis: University of Minnesota Press.

Kamugisha, Aaron K. 2006. Reading Said and Wynter on Liberation. In *After Man: Towards the Human: Critical Essays on Sylvia Wynter*, ed. Anthony Bogues, 131–156. Ian Randle: Kingston.

McKittrick, Katherine. 2015. *Sylvia Wynter: On Being Human as Praxis*. Durham: Duke University Press.

McWhorter, Ladelle. 2010. Enemy of the Species. In *Queer Ecologies: Sex, Nature, Politics and Desire*, ed. Catriona Mortimer-Sandilands and Bruce Erikson, 73–101. Bloomington: University of Indiana Press.

Melville, Pauline. 1997. *The Ventriloquist's Tale*. New York: Bloomsbury.

Nunez, Elizabeth. 2006. *Prospero's Daughter*. New York: Ballantine.

Olmos, Margarite Fernandez, and Lizabeth Paravisini-Gebert. 2001. *Healing Cultures: Art and Religion as Curative Practices in the Caribbean and Its Diaspora*. New York: Palgrave.

Paravisini-Gebert, Lizabeth. 2011. Deforestation and the Yearning for Lost Landscapes in Caribbean Literatures. In *Postcolonial Ecologies: Literatures Of the Environment*, ed. Elizabeth Deloughrey and George Handley, 99–116. Oxford: Oxford University Press.

Rhys, Jean. 1966. *Wide Sargasso Sea*. New York: Norton.

Savory Fido, Elaine. 1990. Textures of Third World Reality in the Poetry of Four African-Caribbean Women. In *Out of the Kumbla: Caribbean Women and Literature* ed. by Carole Boyce Davies and Elaine Savory Fido, 29–44.

Savory, Elaine. 1998. Miranda: The First Voicing. *The Caribbean Writer* 12: 63–72.

Shakespeare, William. [1611] 2004. *The Tempest*. New York: Norton.

Shields, Tanya. 2014. *Bodies and Bones: Feminist Rehearsal and Imagining Caribbean Belonging*. Charlottesville: University of Virginia Press.

Subedi, Janardan and Eugene B. Gallagher. 1996. Introduction. *Society, Health, and Disease Transcultural Perspectives*. Upper Saddle River, NJ: Prentice Hall, xv–xviii.

Thomas, Greg. 2007. *The Sexual Demon of Colonial Power: Pan-African Embodiment and Erotic Schemes of Empire*. Bloomington: University of Indiana.

———. 2006. The "S" word: Sex, Empire and Black Radical Tradition. In *Caribbean Reasonings, After Man, Towards the Human: Critical Essays on Sylvia Wynter*, ed. Anthony Bogues, 76–99. Ian Randle: Kingston.

Walcott, Derek. 2005. Isla Incognita. In *Caribbean Literature and the Environment: Between Nature and Culture*, ed. Elizabeth M. Deloughrey, Renée K. Gosson, and George Handley, 51–57. Charlottesville: University of Virginia Press.

Weheliye, Alexander G. 2014. *Habeas Viscus: Racializing Assemblages, Biopolitics and Black Feminist Theories of the Human*. Durham: Duke University Press.

Wynter, Sylvia. 1990. Afterword. In *Out of the Kumbla: Caribbean Women and Literature*, ed. by Carole Boyce Davies and Elaine Savory Fido, 355–366.

———. 1962. *The Hills of Hebron*. London: J. Cape.

Yusoff, Kathryn. 2018. *A Billion Anthropocenes or None*. Minneapolis: University of Minnesota Press.

10 IMAGINING BEYOND DIVISION, AN ENVIRONMENTAL FUTURE... 191

Open Access This chapter is licensed under the terms of the Creative Commons Attribution 4.0 International License (http://creativecommons.org/licenses/by/4.0/), which permits use, sharing, adaptation, distribution and reproduction in any medium or format, as long as you give appropriate credit to the original author(s) and the source, provide a link to the Creative Commons licence and indicate if changes were made.

The images or other third party material in this chapter are included in the chapter's Creative Commons licence, unless indicated otherwise in a credit line to the material. If material is not included in the chapter's Creative Commons licence and your intended use is not permitted by statutory regulation or exceeds the permitted use, you will need to obtain permission directly from the copyright holder.

PART III

Epistemic Marronnage

CHAPTER 11

Spiritual Crossings: Olokun and Caribbean Futures Past in *La Mucama de Omicunlé* by Rita Indiana

Joshua R. Deckman

Rita Indiana represents a growing number of contemporary women authors and public intellectuals that address questions of Caribbean space and time in historically informed and complex ways. From her work in periodicals to her musical productions with her band Los misterios, Indiana is often considered as one of "the most creative and critical voices of her generation" (Horn 2018, 255). Most prominently, she has been an outspoken critic of Dominican racial relations, as well as Dominican views on Haitians and the politics that underwrite geopolitical boundaries since her debut novel *La Estrategia de Chochueca* (1999).[1] Additionally, in her songs, performance pieces, and short stories, Indiana critically explores the temporal and spatial textures of the Dominican Republic, with a palpable interest in the spiritual inhabitance of multiple temporalities that work on and affect change in the present—while paving the way for possible future worlds. This is seen best in Indiana's critically acclaimed novel, *La Mucama de Omicunlé* (2015).

J. R. Deckman (✉)
Stetson University, DeLand, FL, USA

© The Author(s) 2023
O. Ferly, T. Zimmerman (eds.), *Chronotropics*,
https://doi.org/10.1007/978-3-031-32111-5_11

195

196   J. R. DECKMAN

Though others have previously touched upon Indiana's interaction with Caribbean spirit worlds in her works (García-Peña 2016; Ramírez 2018), very little scholarship highlights the ways in which we might reconceptualize island spatial politics and temporalities through the lens of Afro-diasporic spiritual practices, specifically patakis of the Yoruban tradition. I argue that the novel serves as a point of departure for conceptualizing spatio-temporal crossroads, while uncovering painful histories of betrayal in order to conjure visions of social change, resistance, and alternative modes of being.[2]

In the first section of this chapter, I briefly review the theories paving the way for a spiritual understanding of the text in question. In the second section, I discuss the ways in which Olokun, Yoruba god/dess of the sea, is invoked in the novel, and how this figure is intimately tied to the fate of the protagonist. In the third section, I discuss the pataki story of Iroso as it relates to the function of the text. The last section outlines the fate of Acilde, the betrayal of their mission, and the return to a cycle of violence. This final section also demonstrates how failure to carry through the attempt to repair the present is especially instructive, that is, it demonstrates how the novel itself engages in the pedagogical discourse of the Yoruban pataki to propose an alternative approach to island politics.

Paths of Spirit Conjured

Throughout the novel, Indiana engages with Black Atlantic spiritual systems, particularly as they represent complex systems of *patakis*, or fables that are meant to aid in the healing process of individuals, communities, as well as the natural world. While other scholars have analyzed the "espiritismo," "spiritual," and "yoruba" systems that undergird Indiana's novel, none have directly addressed the text in terms of a divine pataki. I argue that reading this novel in relation to a pataki tethers the text to a longer history of spiritual liberation. By following in the footsteps of Olokun, the novel engages in the pedagogical teachings of the divine—thus offering an alternative direction and political project that might perhaps work to address and "undo" violent processes of colonization and imperial rule.

This push toward an engagement of religious figures, practices of the African Diaspora, and ghostly presences as a decolonial methodology has been questioned and revised in various ways in the past decade. Recently, Maha Marouan (2013) has laid a fundamental groundwork to think geopolitical space and temporalities from a spiritual locus of enunciation—the ways in which women and other marginalized sectors of society work from a space of spiritual imagination and ancestral connection to make sense of colonial legacy and to articulate a vision of futures untethered from this legacy. For Marouan (2013), African diaspora religious beliefs and practices are used in texts throughout the Americas to preserve historical and cultural links to the past. Specifically, she writes that certain women authors and cultural producers "map African diaspora religions as sites of liberation," arguing that "the openness offered to women in African diaspora religious systems can be traced to the West and Central African cultures that do not exclude women from the domain of priesthood and spiritual authority" (2013, 12). For this reason, spiritual practices or elements of African-derived religions permeate narratives that call for a radical historical pedagogy in the move toward social change, in which Black women's bodies are at the center. This becomes especially important when we remember that historically these religious practices were often deemed illegal, particularly in the context of the Atlantic world. Women who had knowledge of healing, herbs, and other non-Western practices were often deemed dangerous, witches, or worshippers of Satan, who could potentially "contaminate" the Hispanic and Catholic project of nation-building with their poisonous beliefs. Thus, the suppression of Black women and the illegality/marginality imposed upon their traditional systems of belief is often at the center of the modernizing project.

Consequently, African diaspora women religious figures and nonmaterial entities are often rearticulated as radical agents of decolonial knowledge. For example, Solimar Otero's *Archives of Conjure: Stories of the Dead in Afro-Latinx Cultures* (2020) builds upon this emerging scholarship to consider the voices of the departed, the spirits, and the ancestors as active participants in the creation of ephemeral and textual archives that may perhaps speak back to historical power hierarchies. Otero argues that stories about the spirits and divine beings are made more complex by the specters of history that dwell between their lines. In this sense, we are presented with the idea of a "crossing" associated with spiritual space— from "unfinished stories," the voices of the spirit realm recall and remap the present in a journey through the ebb and flow of palimpsestic history, often to teach a lesson or proclaim a warning. These stories, songs, and other related teachings of African diaspora religious systems thus serve as a rigorous and necessary theoretical and temporal approximation with immediate and urgent political, social, and cultural knowledge that may, perhaps, be used to create a new and more hospitable future. In this sense, they pertain to the concept of the chronotropics invoked in the Introduction to this volume.

My chapter follows these divergent crossroads of spirit to center the figure of Olokun as described by Cuban ethnologist Lydia Cabrera. I engage with Cabrera throughout as an ancestor herself, weaving the patakis of Yemaya-Olokun through time and space in order to communicate their revolutionary insight into Caribbean women's subjectivity. A woman of the border and crossroad, Cabrera was a "daughter of Yemaya herself [not unlike our protagonist] whose ties to the ocean make her an ambivalent sojourner who never felt entirely at home in one place" (Otero 2020, 5). Her own experience with sexual exile (sexile) as well as her recurrence to "secrecy, coding, and layering" in her scholarly work demonstrate the many ways that she has wielded her power to subvert patriarchal systems of knowing in order to communicate other knowledges that bleed through and beyond the borders of Cuba—gesturing toward a spiritual understanding of Caribbean spacetime that is not bound to any one nation. Here, Cabrera will act as a *santera* who will wade with us in the waters of time and guide our understanding of the novel.

While the story addresses the space of the Dominican Republic, due to the diasporic nature of the religious ritual invoked throughout, the text urges the reader to consider a pan-Caribbean approach. As Indiana demonstrates (through intra-Caribbean travel and engagement with Cuban *santería* outside of Cuba), the urgency to engage in a decolonial methodology is one that is not bound to national borders. Upon opening the pages of *La Mucama*, one enters into a mystical space in which a new type of consciousness emerges—a sacred space imbued by the memories of the Atlantic and marked by the rituals of the oppressed. As the reader follows the pataki and the teachings of the archive of spiritual voices conjured in Acilde's path through time, they are also on a quest of transformation. Olokun shares their secrets in this space through her transcorporeality of being, that is, the ways in which her spirit becomes multiple, a receptacle that is filled with urgent messages of death and rebirth.

An Invocation of Spirit

The first chapter presents a dystopian landscape. The island is broken, driven apart by a virus found in the Blackness of the "other side." The eastern side is quarantined, and futuristic guard-towers hurl noxious gas at those dark invaders who try to escape west of the border. Once identified and exterminated, Haitian bodies are taken away and "disintegrated" by protectors of the Republic to rid the Western side of potential contamination (Indiana 2015, 12). This futuristic scene conjures an image of the 1937 Parsley Massacre, a time when those bodies caught between the borders of both island nations were actively exterminated in Rafael Leónidas Trujillo's attempt to consolidate a "Dominican" identity (Derby 2009, 25). Acilde, the protagonist, watches the scene unfold with disinterest, looking away to continue with the mundane task of cleaning her employer's windows. PriceSpy, an application embedded in the protagonist's eye, informs the reader that the Caribbean is facing destruction. It is not surprising, then, that amid the ecological/political chaos in which the protagonist finds herself, the reader is immediately immersed in a world where the spiritual practices and mystical healing rituals of the African diaspora take center stage.

The tales of Yemaya-Olokun are rooted in a fluid metaphysical crossing of multiple boundaries, sexual, temporal, and geophysical. That is, Olokun's secrets flow deep and the epistemic currents that they traverse carry multiple meanings and messages. Perhaps submerging oneself into these waters sheds a new (or very old) light on the ways that we understand the borders of certain spatio-temporal boundaries, the limits of the present, and the shaping of history itself. In her *Yemaya y Ochun*, Cabrera details the stories of Yemaya-Olokun, *la hija de las dos aguas*, as a powerful but also compassionate deity, who lives in the depths of the sea: "En el más profundo nació Olokun, el oceano. Olokun, la yemaya más vieja—yemaya masculino, raiz" (1996, 21) [Olokun, the ocean, was born in the most profound depths. Olokun, the ancient Yemaya—masculine Yemaya, root]. This androgynous being is the root from which all other life emerges, the origin of the rhizomatic nature of diasporic complexity forged in the violent crossing of the Middle Passage. However, the deity instills fear and respect in those who know her and the many *caminos* that she travels: "Bamboche [an interlocutor of Cabrera] me confesaba que a él le inspiraba el mar un temor inmenso, y era de parecer que de Olokun, abismo insondable y soledad infinita, debía de hablarse lo menos posible" (1996, 25) [Bamboche confessed to me that the sea inspired in him a great fear, and it seemed like Olokun, that unfathomable abyss and infinite solitude, should be spoken about as little as possible]. Thus, Olokun rarely possesses her children, for fear that they would not resist her power. Instead, she makes herself known through her stories, encrypted and shrouded in mystery.

200   J. R. DECKMAN

Most teachings from/by Olokun represent tales of destruction, of warning, and of transformational healing. These stories, meant to instruct and impart knowledge as well as the power for change, take the form of *patakis:*

> The etymology of the term pataki comes from the standard yoruba word pataki, meaning important. In Cuba, patakis are the stories of the orichas told in formal ritual circumstances and in informal conversation. At the heart of the meaning of the term pataki is the importance of creating a pedagogy for living in complex and shifting circumstances through story. The tales conjure the deities into our imaginations and invoke instruction and reflection that is both communal and deeply personal. (Otero 2020, 104)

This quote is triply significant. First, it outlines the gravity of the stories (both oral and written) that come from or are inspired by the oricha in *regla, espiritismo, palo,* and similar traditions. By conflating the formal ritual conjurings of these stories as well as "informal conversations," Otero also underscores the importance and sacredness of these tellings—where their power can transform the mundane and quotidian, high and low cultural productions, into sacred spaces of knowledge detached from Westernized understandings of reality. Second, the quote underscores the function of the pataki as pedagogy. Here, I understand pedagogy as the radical relationship between imagination, language, and personal/collective engagement in the wider community (Freire 1970; Alexander 2006). The complex relationship between the oricha, the storyteller, and the receptor creates a network of knowledge production and divine epistemic interventions that seeks to uncover a hidden truth in order to effect action in the present—a learning that, to borrow from Gloria Anzaldúa, takes place in the crossings of spirit and story, in the *travesia* of time and space.[3] Walter Mignolo, among others, comments on this temporal rupture— drawing from Chicana feminist and queer theorist, Anzaldúa: "Modernity is a fiction that carries in it the seed of Western pretense to universality ... decolonial thinkers are interested in uncovering hidden connections and relations between events, processes, and entities in the colonial matrix of power" (Mignolo 2012, 113–114). This network, brought together by divine story, must work[4] to understand how the past has given shape to the present and how they may use this knowledge to heal past transgressions and conjure new futures—not seeking salvation, as in the Judeo-Christian tradition, but actively working toward self-empowerment and communal benefit. Third, the reference to a political praxis that lies within these stories that is both "communal and deeply personal" reflects the multiple levels at which these patakis communicate their knowledge. It is at once a story about personal growth, which may perhaps also be interpreted as a story of historical/cultural growth, a story that heals the community, the island, as well as the self.

Commenting on this pedagogical/healing aspect of the pataki, Alai Reyes-Santos (forthcoming), in a forthcoming chapter,[5] specifically addresses the patakis of Olokun:

> her stories illuminate a path of justice and kinship as we travel with Olokun through time and space to decipher the mysteries she is now letting come up to the surface, the mysteries of how we easily betray ourselves, our own, and those who seem to be another kind of being...[they] reveal the wounds our betrayals have left for us to heal as we build necessary kinship. (2)

Here, Reyes-Santos connects the pedagogy of the pataki and the urgency of healing to the building of (forgotten) kinship relations in terms of fragmented community. It is through divine storytelling that "we" might be brought together in solidarity to fight for the present, but also brought closer to those that have come before us—the line of ancestors whose knowledge lights the path forward. The stories connect us to both the past and the present, and offer multiple visions of the future as they circulate and are shared among the community of receptors.

This circular/relational space is a type of radical space of "crossing" that allows us to consider disparate moments of the past, present, and future without flattening them into sameness, a chronological tease. Both Alexandra Perisic and M. Jacqui Alexander comment on the idea of non-linear crossings that are opened through the practice of stories, narratives, and beliefs. Perisic (2019) addresses the need to explore connections (in her case, global connections of precarious lives) without conflating them into "yet another false universal model" (175), while Alexander (2006) details historical processes of oppression across time and space to argue that intergenerational memory and spiritual knowledge is a central element to countering colonial and imperial narratives for women of color—maps of crossings that offer a glimpse into alternative histories and new knowledge from which to give form to alternative lives. These crossings in

202   J. R. DECKMAN

the spiritual stories of the oricha give voice to the epistemologies of the colonized in order to rechart an-*other* understanding of history.

The book's opening pages serve as a type of mystical incantation to the sea itself, celebrating its sensual, healing, and transformative qualities: "En la colección de la vieja predominan los motivos marinos, peces, barcos, sirenas y caracoles, regalos de los clientes, ahijados y enfermos terminales" (13) [In the collection of the old woman, there was a sea motif that took over, fish, boats, mermaids, and shells, all gifts from clients and the terminally ill]. The collection of materials is ritualistically prepared—altar-like—and kept by Acilde in her housework, creating a visual and tactile link to the ocean that also includes mythological references to the many paths of Yemaya. Each object connects Acilde to fish, mermaids, and the secretive powers of the cowrie. The residual connection vested in the otherwise mundane duties of Acilde as housekeeper tempts the reader to weave an interlaced mythological network—that is, to conjure up connections between the sea, healing, transformation, and the oricha herself. After this invocation, the reader learns how Acilde has broken one of the figures, a pastel-colored pirate. Esther responds: "algo malo se fue por ahí" (13) [something bad moved there]. Later in the novel, Acilde will take as an avatar the pirate Roque while working toward securing herself a comfortable place in the past—an eventual "betrayal" that shows this "something bad" has never fully left the stage. These references open a space to consider how the traditional stories of Yemaya influence the novel and guide our understanding of Acilde's narrative.

"Olokun, la Yemaya Más Vieja"

One of the most recounted patakis of Olokun is that of *Iroso*. This particular pataki illustrates Yemaya-Olokun's power and mercy, through a story of betrayal. Iroso, as Cabrera lays out, was the youngest of a powerful king's three boys: "estos lo envidiaban porque el rey lo prefería, y llenos de odio, decidieron perderlo" (1996, 50) [these envied him because he was the king's favorite, and filled with hate they decided to make him disappear]. The brother, betrayed by his own kin, was tricked into a large wooden box and thrown into the sea. However, Yemaya-Olokun observes their actions and takes mercy on the boy. Instead of sinking, the box floats to a kingdom where Yemaya-Olokun has arranged for him to inherit the throne. In the multiple tellings of this pataki, there always exists an element of betrayal and of unknowing. The story warns the receptor to open their eyes and look more closely into the world surrounding them. There exists a danger to heed the teachings of Olokun, as those who receive the sign of Iroso may lose their way, get lost, and live too much in the past—which blinds them to the urgencies of the present and the transformations of the future. In the same way, they may take too much pride in themselves and fail to consider the needs of their community, becoming lost in lies and deception. These dangers do not only pose a personal threat, but the inability to recognize one's duty to community may lead to cycles of violence and the perpetuation of colonial patterns.

The pataki and sign of Iroso plays a central role as the novel begins. We learn that Esther Escudero, *ewo* of Yemaya herself, was initiated into the Palo tradition in Cuba. Esther had fallen in love with her *jefa* (boss), whose husband grew suspicious: "Al parecer, el tipo pagó para que me hicieran un trabajo, brujería mala, y la menstruación no se me quitaba. Yo pensaba que me iba a morir" (22) [It seems like the man paid for them to curse me, dark magic, and the menstrual blood would not stop. I thought I would die]. In an effort to save Esther's life, the two women escape to Cuba where, in Matanzas, she meets Belarminio Brito, or Omidina, a babalawo and child of Yemaya who eventually saves her. After initiation, Esther is given the name Omicunlé and told that she and her children will be protectors of Yemaya's house. Here, Omicunlé refers to the starry mantle worn by Yemaya, which covers the sea and protects its inhabitants—it is a symbol of motherly care, healing, and power. The scene effectively foreshadows Esther's divine connection to Acilde, as Acilde is said to be the true daughter of Olokun.

As Esther tells Acilde about her introduction to the world of the Oricha, she performs a diloggun divination, interpreting16 cowrie shells to read the energies surrounding the protagonist. As the shells scatter around the women, Esther observes "Iroso," the number four, emerge from the shells: "nadie sabe lo que hay en el fondo del mar" (25) [No one knows what lies at the bottom of the sea]. Esther's utterance seems filled with foreboding, but hopeful that she has found the daughter of Olokun. After hearing her fate, Acilde is adorned by Esther with an ileke, a chain of blue glass beads dedicated to Yemaya-Olokun: "Llévalo siempre porque aunque no creas te protegerá. Un día vas a heredar mi casa. Esto ahora no entiendes, pero con el tiempo lo verás" (28) [Wear it always because it will protect you. One day you will inherit my house. You do not understand this yet, but with time you shall see]. Here, Acilde is marked by Yemaya's presence, as these ileke are used as in the path toward initiation: "Los *ileke* son para quienes los reciben 'un paso adelante en el camino que lleva el Santo'—a la iniciación—un reconocimiento de su nexo con la divinidad" (Cabrera 1996, 121) [The ileke are for those who receive them "a step forward in the path that leads them to their saint"—to initiation—a recognition of their connection to the divine]. As Cabrera notes, Acilde's fate is now interwoven with the divinity, and, without knowing, has been set on the path toward spiritual initiation.

Furthermore, Acilde, in her sexual transactions on the periphery of her city, yearns to exert her power and control through corporeal ambiguity, one that also places her on the periphery of her society and make her vulnerable to her family's violent prejudices: "A Acilde le daban golpes por gusto, por marimacho ... Tenía manos de hombre y no se conformaba: quería todo lo demás ... hasta las viejas aborrecían sus aires masculinos" (18–19) [They beat Acilde for pleasure, for being a tomboy ... she had the hands of a man and she would not conform: she wanted everything ... even the old women hated her masculine traits]. She is abused by those who consider her an abomination as "marimacho," a display of female masculinity that seems to threaten the order of family life. Acilde attempts to use this ambiguity to her economic advantage, often feigning manhood to gain sexual clients: "Antes de trabajar en casa de Esther, Acilde mamaba güevos en el Mirador, sin quitarse la ropa, bajo la que su cuerpo—de diminutos pechos y caderas estrechas—pasaba por el de un chico de quince años. Tenía clientela fija, en su mayoría hombres casados, sesentones cuyas vergas solo venían a linda en la boca de un niño bonito" (14) [Before working in Esther's house, Acilde sucked men off in Mirador, without taking off her clothes, under which her body—of small chest and skinny hips—passed for that of a fifteen-year-old boy. She had steady clients, mostly older married men, sixty-year-olds whose dicks only came in the mouth of a pretty boy]. She poses as a 15-year-old boy to take advantage of society's perversions, seducing old men who seek the sexual services of underaged boys. Acilde inhabits these sexual crossroads in an effort to gain control of her life and wield her body on her own terms. This defiance of gender and sexual norms is also an economic endeavor that helps her to save toward a sex change through the expensive injection, RainbowBright.

Similarly, Cabrera, more than once, reminds us of those times when Yemaya is also gender fluid: She writes: "A Yemaya le gustaba cazar, chapear, manejar el machete. En este camino es marimacho y viste de

11 SPIRITUAL CROSSINGS: OLOKUN AND CARIBBEAN FUTURES... 205

hombre ... Yemaya es a veces varonil, hasta volverse hombre" (1996, 45–46) [Yemaya loved to hunt, ride, and wield the machete. In this path, she is masculine and dresses like a man ... Yemaya is manly, until she becomes a man]. Yemaya as a rebellious and defiant deity is made clear in Cabrera's documentation. In similar ways, both Acilde in her desire for control and Yemaya-Olokun in Cabrera's pataki display a range of "female masculinities," putting into question our understanding of traditional corporal boundaries. Thus, in presenting herself with both masculine and feminine traits, Olokun/Acilde ritualistically opens a space of metaphysical crossings in order to reorganize the energies of the universe and conjure the forces necessary to pave a new road of possibilities—for it is in the connections forged through her sex work that she ends up working for Esther Escudero, that "vieja santera," and stumbling into possession of Olokun's secrets—a fate that may perhaps transform her physically and spiritually, while opening the reader's eyes to what lies hidden in the murky waters of the present.

Acilde's embodiment of Olokun is cemented in a ritualistic scene of initiation, in which she is symbolically crowned as a daughter of Yemaya-Olokun. There are several markers of this ceremony that are easily missed if one is not attuned to the "hidden" messages that are transmitted as Acilde dons the thorny crown of the anemone, thus claimed by the deity. The ritual begins when Acilde is made to cleanse her body, shaving herself from head to toe. Her companion Eric places a bowl of raw rice under her bed as an offering and constructs a rudimentary "tent" made of white linen over her body. The body is prepared to be reborn into its new form and altered reality. While readying the ritual, Eric is metaphorically transformed into a symbolic Osain. Described as a type of *médico*, knowledgeable about herbs and healing, he becomes the one that prepares the body, offers the sacrifice, and cleanses the ritual space. Osain is often essential in the consecration of new initiates into the Palo tradition as they are chosen by their Oricha, preparing the *ewe* (herbs) and *haciendo Osain* in order to receive their spirit: "Se hace Osain para componer el *Omiero*, 'agua sagrada' que purifica, regenera y cura, pues en ella se concentran ... las influencias de los Orichas que les infunden sus energías" (Cabrera 1996, 156) [Osain is made to ready the Omiero, holy water that purifies, regenerates, and cures ... In this, the influences of the Oricha are concentrated and give their energy]. As Eric positions the body and uses his "medicinal knowledge" to administer the RainbowBright,[6] and thus the proper dosage to transform the body, we witness the ritual that opens space and time to the will of the divine. This ritual provides us with insight into the past and future, at the crossroads of spiritual space, for Olokun is given passage to "infuse her energies" into the narrative.

To close the ritual, Eric crowns Acilde with the tentacles of the anemone. Many have commented on the symbolic act of crowning in establishing alternative sovereign imaginaries and in elevating the marginal body to the level of mythic royalty, specifically in terms of Black diasporic bodies as they wield an alternative sovereign agency (Negrón-Muntaner, Ramirez, Jaime). However, here I argue that the scene of crowning represents a breach in the temporal fabric of Caribbean imaginaries, the gift of a new set of "eyes" with which we might freely travel to disparate moments in time, connected by the sacred presence of the oricha. This kari-ocha, coronation of the oricha, alters reality. After coming to her senses, the newly initiated truly awaken from another world: "tiene la sensación de llegar de muy lejos … le zumban los oídos, todo es extraño y nuevo para ella, diríase que regresa de otro mundo" (Cabrera 1996, 165) [she seems as if she is arriving from far away … her ears buzz, everything is strange and new for her, it could be said that she is returning from another world]. As Acilde begins her transformation, her mind retreats and divine intervention bends the biological framework of the world. The Babalosha completes his duties; Eric chants to Olokun, marks the space surrounding the confused Acilde, newly awoken in a male body, and finally crowns him with the mysteries of Yemaya-Olokun.

From this moment, Acilde is crowned as *ewo* of Olokun. Time is fractured in the text and the reader is transported to forgotten moments of history, all marked by the same self-serving "betrayals" as we enter Iroso. The body is transported into the past and is found by a fisherman amongst the coral in *yola*. In a type of oceanic womb, the body is pulled from the sea and hidden away to be examined: "Te estábamos esperando, viniste de muy lejos a salvarnos, lucero del agua" (107) [we were waiting for you, you came to save us from afar, shining star of the sea]. Once Acilde, now a man, removes the *escamas* from his eyes, the reader is simultaneously gifted a new vision capable of inhabiting the scars that a history and present of coloniality have left to fester. He is also able to heal those moments through a recognition of the sacred mysteries and life-giving force of the sea that has woken inside of him.

Into the Pluriverse

Through the spiritual archive of Olokun, then, the reader is offered a view from the margins of time, subverting colonial-linear notions of past, present, and future in a fiction that reveals the true nature of historically engineered disaster. Olokun teases open this "colonial matrix of power" to question the ways in which the universe is organized, proposing a type of relational pluriverse. Here, the new "sight" provided by the Oricha begs the question of how "we" can create another mode of knowing the world which presupposes a process of relation between body, space, and time; and where "we" might perhaps unveil how the violence of the past exists in an unbroken cycle, affecting the structures of the present while propelling the archipelago toward a broken future of crisis—that has, in many cases, already arrived.[7]

After entering the new spatio-temporal alignment allowed by Olokun, Acilde weaves together (1) a dystopian future, (2) a "past" that is eerily similar to this reader's own timeline, and (3) an even more remote past filled with a group of seventeenth-century pirates. Acilde inhabits a new avatar in each of these timelines as herself, Giorgio Menicucci, and Roque (Acilde-Giorgio-Roque). Each of these visions *relate* a history of plunder and disaster that befalls the island space over and over again. Acilde quickly uses their newly acquired "powers" of sight and other-worldly knowledge to further their own status in the new time frames, where they take on the aliases of Roque, the pirate, and Giorgio, the wealthy benefactor of the Sosúa Project (an art collective that strives to save the Dominican coastline) set in the 2000s. They are also quick to use a new acquaintance, Argenis—the misogynist Dominican artist, accidentally stung by the same anemone in the 2000s—to amass wealth and secure a space for themself. Not a true child of Olokun, Argenis cannot control his visions, becoming stuck between the seventeenth century and his own life. In Argenis' timeline (early 2000s), Acilde surrounds themself with a group of international, self-serving artists and intellectuals who "sell" their "artivism" while profiting from the very land they claim to save. As the sign of Iroso has warned, Acilde has ignored her calling, and thus the "misterios del fondo del mar" that Esther had foretold—betraying the desires of Olokun. In her transformation, she has not become the protector/healer that her nation and community needed. It is worth noting that Olokun does not continue to manifest itself through her child, once the passage/crossing has been completed, the child must learn from it. It is up to Olokun's

208   J. R. DECKMAN

child to take the lesson and pursue change, something that Acilde has failed to do.

In this way, her avatar in the 2000s is not unlike those pirates that are quick to disavow the rules of the crown in their colonizing missions of "discovery" to claim their own riches and fame. As Roque, she seeks to hide a treasure in the past so that she may uncover it as Giorgio, securing her wealth. Interestingly, Yolanda Martínez-San Miguel comments on the narrative of pirates, buccaneers, and *filibusteros* in seventeenth-, eighteenth-, and nineteenth-century Caribbean networks, as they offer "other" visions of colonial expansion that exist beyond official "national" and "imperial" archives. In this sense, pirates are also a people of the crossroads—defiant figures who do not follow the rules laid out for them, or rather figures who conjure ways to forge their own paths outside of official judicial/imperial order:

> They are protagonists that falter in the context of epic and imperial narratives, yet they flourish in the fascination with uncontrolled richness and freedom... Their narratives become foundational fictions for the coloniality of diasporas in the Caribbean... [they] represent protagonists who lose themselves in the process of trying to achieve a leading role in protonationalist narratives. (Martínez-San Miguel 2014, 36–71)

We can thus see how Acilde, just like the repeated history of pirates, buccaneers, and imperial landgrabs, begins to "lose herself" in her own "leading role" in an emerging narrative of healing. Just as Roque betrays his mission to the king, so does Giorgio betray his mission to save the reef, and Acilde her mission to Esther/Olokun. Each character becomes fragmented, giving into a desire to dominate and work from a space of self-importance and self-preservation. While this may at first seem like a bold and radical move for Acilde, who personally seeks liberation and self-actualization, her path ultimately leads her to self-destruction—and toward the same dystopian future that she set out to deter. For, it is in betraying her community for her own benefit that she denies her new complex reality and condemns the world, yet again.

After using her/his wealth, influence, and power to get close enough to the politicians that initiated the Caribbean's decay, her/his plan falls through. With gun in hand and intentions of exterminating the president culpable for the economic/ecological disasters of the future, thus "cleansing the waters," Acilde/Giorgio falters and fails to act. In a moment of self-defence she/he chooses her new life over the salvation of her region: "Podía sacrificarlo todo menos esta vida, la vida de Giorgio Menicucci, la compañía de su mujer, la galería, el laboratorio ... En poco tiempo se olvidará de Acilde, de Roque, incluso de lo que vive en un hueco allá abajo en el arrecife" (180–181) [She/he could sacrifice everything except this life, Giorgio Menicucci's life, the company of his woman, the gallery, the lab ... soon, she/he will forget about Acilde, Roque, even about what lives in the depths of the sea]. Acilde effectively decides to end her life and her life as Roque, choosing to fully inhabit Giorgio's reality. By giving up her "complex truth" of crossing and diaspora, her identity as a Black transman of the Dominican Republic, she chooses to forget the teachings of Olokun in favor of her new life as the Italian Giorgio, his laboratory in Sosúa, his wealth, and his wife. As a fragmented whole, Giorgio cannot face himself and gives up his history (future), breaking the bonds of community that tied them together. He cannot love or accept his past and therefore cuts it away, knowing that in doing so he risks the same ecologic/economic collapse that she/he had set out to prevent: the ecological disaster, the virus, and the rampant racial disparity that marked her past/future. In fully "becoming man," Acilde is quick to replicate the patriarchal order of the world.

"Nadie Sabe Lo Que Hay en El Fondo Del Mar"

Reyes-Santos writes: "Olokun keeps beckoning us to face how we betray ourselves and each other; to face water crossings as moments of deep pain, deep loss, and deep transformation; to find out who we can be on the other side, what kind of futures we create, if we just dare to live our complex truths" (27). While Acilde may not have literally and metaphorically "pulled the trigger," in failing to act the future is thrust back into uncertainty. As Iroso tells, we must be careful to not "lose sight," to squander the knowledge bestowed by the Oricha, or the way forward is lost and we betray ourselves, our community, and the direction of the world.

Here, we see how Olokun has become a channel through which we are shown several possible worlds that have fallen due to various forms of betrayal. When our protagonist finds herself in the salty womb of the sea for the first time, we are in the presence of a pataki of rebirth and caution. This pataki is meant to motivate the reader to break the cycle of violence that emerges from the past and act upon the present in order to move ahead in solidarity. We must learn from the mistakes of

210   J. R. DECKMAN

Acilde-Giorgio-Roque, learn from their search for salvation that it is not possible nor profitable to make the same mistakes again and again. The pataki that Olokun weaves reminds "us" that in order to "heal" Haiti and the Dominican Republic from certain disaster, we must understand the ways in which a history of economic mismanagement and racial exclusion is always present and acting upon current realities. Once recognized, we may perhaps make the courageous decision that Acilde cannot: the decision to sacrifice what is comfortable to move against a colonial patriarchal system that turns bodies/geographies into exploited and dying spaces of historical amnesia.

NOTES

1. However, her activism is not solely anchored to Quisqueya. Indiana has also been a vocal advocate for the LGBTQIA+ communities throughout the Caribbean and beyond, speaking out against the Código Civil in Puerto Rico. In a 2020 tweet that appears in a variety of popular and academic news articles, she attacks the Puerto Rican senate for pushing the bill through in the midst of a global health crisis: "Mientras estamos encerrados el senado de #Puerto Rico aprueba un código civil que pone en peligro todos los logros de la comunidad #LGBTQ en la isla. No me casé por romanticismo, si no para que la ley protegiese a mi familia como a cualquier otra. #WandaMisDerechos #CodigoCivil" (May 12, 2020).
2. This line of research follows recent publications on *La mucama* ..., including Rosana Herrero-Martín's "Olokun or the Caribbean Quantum Mind: An Analysis of Transcultured Metaphysical Elements within Rita Indiana's Novel *Tentacle*." In this article, Herrero-Martín (2019) relates Caribbean fractality and the spiritual spacetime of the orisha to the top quantum theories and notions of universal interconnectivity.
3. This dialogue is not unlike the creative process of border knowledge as Anzaldúa lays out in her work, something that I will touch upon toward the end of this chapter.
4. I use the term "work" as Joseph M. Murphy has outlined in his text *Working the Spirit*, which underscores the communal solidarity of worship, as well as the physical, intellectual, and psychological growth that must take place to "conjure" the deities in question.
5. Forthcoming in the collection *Oxala*, edited by Alline Torres, Victor Miguel Castillo de Macedo, and Joshua Deckman.
6. Here, it is important to mention that RainbowBright is reminiscent of *Rainbow Brite*, an animated series introduced by Hallmark and Mattel in the early 1980s. The show featured a host of characters who inhabit a desolate world devoid of color. It is their mission to combat the forces of evil

and return their reality to its "bright" and happy existence, filled with a spectrum of lucid colors. Recalling this connection adds another understanding to the importance of this "miracle drug," as yet an additional reference to the opening of a portal to heal a desolate world, unveiling what has been lost and yet to be recovered.

7. I write this chapter from quarantine during the Covid-19 pandemic. One only has to take a brief look at the Listín Diario and other news outlets to see how a global pandemic is exacerbated by the colonial/imperial baggage of the island. While Haiti has closed its border for fear of disease, many Haitians are also forced to the streets to continue protesting and fighting for social dignity in the shadow of contagion. Perhaps Olokun will send someone to "cleanse our waters."

REFERENCES

Alexander, M. Jacqui. 2006. *Pedagogies of Crossing: Meditations on Feminism, Sexual Politics, Memory, and the Sacred*. Durham: Duke University Press, Combined Academic.

Cabrera, Lydia. 1996. *Yemaya y Ochun*. Miami: Ediciones Universal.

Derby, Lauren. 2009. *The Dictator's Seduction: Politics and the Popular Imaginatio in the Era of Trujillo*. Durham: Duke University Press.

Freire, Paulo. 1970. *Pedagogy of the Oppressed*. Sacramento: Continuum Press.

García-Peña, Lorgia. 2016. *The Borders of Dominicanidad Race, Nation, and Archives of Contradiction*. Durham: Duke University Press.

Herrero-Martín, Rosana. 2019. Olokun or the Caribbean Quantum Mind: An Analysis of Transculturated Metaphysical Elements within Rita Indiana's Novel *Tentacle. Journal of West Indian Literature* 27 (2): 52–67.

Horn, Maja. 2018. A Sweet Sweet Tale of Terror: Rita Indiana Hernandez Writes the Dominican Republic into the Global South Atlantic. In *The Global South Atlantic*, ed. Kerry Bystrom and Joseph R. Slaughter, 102–122. Fordham University Press.

Indiana, Rita. 2015. *La Mucama De Omicunle*. Editorial Periferica.

Marouan, Maha. 2013. *Witches, Goddesses, and Angry Spirits: the Politics of Spiritual Liberation in African Diaspora Women's Fiction*. Columbus: Ohio State University Press.

Martínez-San Miguel, Yolanda. 2014. *Coloniality of Diasporas: Rethinking Intra-Colonial Migrations in a Pan-Caribbean Context*. New York: Palgrave Macmillan.

Mignolo, Walter D. 2012. *Local Histories/Global Designs: Coloniality, Subaltern Knowledges, and Border Thinking*. Princeton: Princeton University Press.

Otero, Solimar. 2020. *Archives of Conjure: Stories of the Dead in Afrolatinx Cultures*. New York: Columbia University Press.

Perisic, Alexandra. 2019. *Precarious Crossings: Immigration, Neoliberalism, and the Atlantic*. Columbus: The Ohio State University Press.

Ramírez, Dixa. 2018. *Colonial Phantoms: Belonging and Refusal in the Dominican Americas, from the 19th Century to the Present*. New York: NYU Press.

Reyes-Santos, Alaí. Unpublished. Iroso: Afro-Latinx Sacred Stories of Betrayal and Kinship in Diaspora. In *Oxala: Afro-Latinx Futures, Imaginings, and Engagements*, ed. Joshua Deckman et al. New York: SUNY University Press.

Open Access This chapter is licensed under the terms of the Creative Commons Attribution 4.0 International License (http://creativecommons.org/licenses/by/4.0/), which permits use, sharing, adaptation, distribution and reproduction in any medium or format, as long as you give appropriate credit to the original author(s) and the source, provide a link to the Creative Commons licence and indicate if changes were made.

The images or other third party material in this chapter are included in the chapter's Creative Commons licence, unless indicated otherwise in a credit line to the material. If material is not included in the chapter's Creative Commons licence and your intended use is not permitted by statutory regulation or exceeds the permitted use, you will need to obtain permission directly from the copyright holder.

CHAPTER 12

Creolizing Science in Mayra Montero's *Palm of Darkness*

Carine M. Mardorossian and Angela Veronica Wong

Two decades into the twenty-first century, and on the cusp of irreparable human damage to multiple ecosystems and our environment, political inaction on climate change has calcified into a seemingly immutable drive to extinction. It is even more disheartening, then, to revisit novels and scientific knowledge from the 1990s that already recognized and detailed climate change. Published in 1995, Mayra Montero's *In the Palm of Darkness* follows a US herpetologist, Victor S. Grigg, as he sets out on a quest for an elusive endangered amphibian in the mountains of Haiti.[1] Weaving in Grigg's search with the life story of his Haitian guide Thierry Adrien, Montero also includes details on the disappearances of multiple frog species since the 1970s across the globe. This accelerated disappearance in time of species from different spaces across the world evokes a four-dimensional spacetime that recognizes the union of time and space first proposed by mathematician Hermann Minkowsdki (1908). It also evokes through a triangulation between femininity, patriarchy, and

---

C. M. Mardorossian (✉) • A. V. Wong
University at Buffalo, SUNY, Buffalo, NY, USA
e-mail: cmardoro@buffalo.edu; angelawo@buffalo.edu

© The Author(s) 2023
O. Ferly, T. Zimmerman (eds.), *Chronotropics*,
https://doi.org/10.1007/978-3-031-32111-5_12

213

imperialism the ways in which women become associated with the Haitian environment, in ways that are in turn oppressive and resistant, conciliatory, and revolutionary.

That Victor Grigg and Thierry Adrien's intersecting stories seem at first to provide the novel's main narrative thrust is remarkable for a woman author who has described herself as a "frustrated biologist" (Prieto 2000, 90). Why, we may ask, would a female writer whose yearnings overlap with the vocation of her two protagonists not have women play these main part(s) in the novel? Why have instead a recurring homosocial bonding between two men whose relationship seemingly reproduces the same mutually reinforcing masculinities present in her previous work? Indeed, Montero's first novel *La trenza de la hermosa luna* [*The Braid of the Lovely Moon* (1987)] was also about the friendship between two men, a "houngan" or Vodou priest and a humble sailor, who, after many years, meet in Port-au-Prince during the days of the fall of Jean-Claude Duvalier.

What is more, insofar as these male characters' own relationships with feminine or nonhuman forms of otherness seems at best peripheral and at worst instrumental in the novel, one cannot help but think of the form of male homosociality which Eve Sedgwick (1985) defines in *Between Men: English Literature and Male Homosocial Desire*. Building on Gayle Rubin, Sedgwick (1985, 26) analyzes male bonding and male relationships through the schema of a triangle, where "man uses a woman as a 'conduit of a relationship' in which the true *partner* is a man." Similarly, in *In the Palm of Darkness*, the representation of sexual otherness, alongside that of nonhuman alterity, not only brings the two male protagonists together but mainly plays backdrop to their personalized human tragedies in the book.

Yet the novel also suggests an alternative dynamic, one in which the environmental disaster, a spatial consideration, combines with the temporality of frog disappearances, to stand as the main narrative. And despite the protagonists' desperate attempts to overpower the otherness of the world around them, it is this spacetime dimension that ultimately drives the human adventures and pursuits that constitute the plot. In fact, in *In the Palm of Darkness*, the two male protagonists' instrumentalizing relationship with nonhuman and sexual otherness is neither naturalized through time nor obscured in space; it is rather made visible and exposed through their very attempts at normalizing their hierarchical ways of relating to what they see as destabilizing sites of uncontrollable difference in need of containment. The novel reveals femininity in particular as the embodiment of the othering processes and projections through which an anxious masculinity repeatedly and vainly seeks to assert its domineering foothold in an unstable world. It is important, in this respect, that two women characters in the novel are scientists.

Like the femininity with which they are associated, frogs in the novel function as a natural symbol of change and liminality: they live between water and land (space), in their different physical embodiments of life stages (time)—from tadpole to frog, and with the crucial role they play in multiple ecosystems as both predator and prey. In addition to their importance as barometers of biological conditions, they have also, however, long held a place of fascination in mythology and religion, often as symbols of fertility and promiscuity. Frogs therefore truly embody the novel's creolizing impulses regarding the compatibility of a scientific and Afro-Caribbean cosmology insofar as they stand for the physical and material landscape on the one hand and for metaphorical and spiritualized considerations on the other.[2] Montero thus joins a long line of Caribbean women writers whose fiction literally stages a juncture where a transnational, queer feminist and creolized ecology can develop which, as under threat as it is, is specific to the Caribbean.[3] Ecocritics, in particular, have been particularly attentive to the workings of desire in relation to the environment and other-than-human species, in a way that epitomizes the entanglement spacetime represents.

Feminist and queer reformulations by Greta Gaard (1997), Catriona Mortimer-Sandilands and Bruce Erickson (2010), and Nicole Seymour (2013), for instance, have provided a systematic exploration of the potential intersections of ecofeminist and queer theories. Our analysis follows these important theorists' lead, albeit with a variation, namely that our queer reading is not anchored in any material or recognizable queer identity so much as in a queer reading that reveals the "unnatural" processes through which the norm constructs or reinstates itself as authoritative.

Victor opens the third chapter in the book by stating, "I began taping my conversations with Thierry when I realized that between stories, he was inserting important information about the frog" (Montero 1997, 18). The relationship between the two men which seemingly constitutes the main framing device in Montero's novel is neither an equal one nor the main gist of the narrative: the American herpetologist dichotomizes Thierry's tales and "information," and Victor's use of the term "stories" reflects his dismissal of Thierry's way of knowing and telling in favor of what the scientist sees as "information" embedded in the latter's life anecdotes and shared culture. The punctuated mode of delivery this revelation highlights is reflected in the structure of the novel itself, which interlaces objective (as defined by Western scientists) segments on global frog species' disappearances with the hyperlocal human and subjective experiences that are infused with Haitian mythology and landscape. While seemingly incongruous, these dry scientific inclusions do, however, pull the story about the doomed adventures of a scientist in Haiti into a global, existential, and interspecies problem to establish a more geographically expansive scale, one that stands at multiple crossroads: between races, genders, and epistemologies. In this context, the kind of masculinist and triangulating homosociality that Sedgwick identified in *Between Men* (1985) is exposed as unequipped to deal with global phenomena the male protagonists can neither address nor comprehend. In other words, the novel does not place the environmental consciousness it evokes in the background of its human characters' storyline, but rather foregrounds the eerie, unexplained mass frog disappearances through the natural world's disenchantment with—and resistance to—human intrusion, one it also associates with a beleaguered femininity.

The bringing together of scientific facts about amphibians with the polyvocal narratives of the characters' lived experiences also allows us to examine the implications of a Caribbean (that is to say, of a creolized) perspective for our understanding of scientific discourse in the novel, whose mode of inquiry has historically been associated with a masculinist and colonizing ethos. *In the Palm of Darkness* evokes science's masculinist and colonizing history by repeatedly juxtaposing Western science and Haitian cosmology, self and other, male and female scientists, with the objective and subjective dimensions of the human experience. In fact, the traditional dichotomy between Western science/rationalism versus Caribbean/Haitian magic/Vodou gives way to a mutual entanglement through Victor and Thierry's very gendered search for what could be the last specimen of an endangered species of frog in Haiti.

In so doing, Montero's novel provides a powerful counterpoint to the more widely known but sensationalizing representation of the science/Vodou encounter in Wade Davis's bestselling *The Serpent and the Rainbow* (1985). Vodou, Haiti's African diasporic religion that emerged between the sixteenth and nineteenth centuries, developed out of a process of syncretism that brought together the traditional religions of West Africa and Roman Catholicism. It is what Montero referred to as "the most beautiful and sublime aspect, of our 'mestization.'" She further explained:

> [p]eople often ask me if I practice these religions and I tell them that I respect them profoundly and have a great aesthetic, even philosophic affinity, with these magicoreligious systems. That is why I have an altar in my house, a syncretic altar within a syncretic system; because on that altar, voodoo [*sic*] gods cohabit with gods from Santería and Madonnas, and Catholic saints. This wonderful mixture is what we are, what gives us depth and spirituality as a people. (Prieto 2000, 89)

Montero's altar reveals how one side in the science/Vodou binary represented by the two men's approaches to the natural world in *In the Palm of Darkness* is more open and welcoming of difference than the other. Indeed, perhaps in Montero's understanding, Vodou is not only open to difference, but its syncretism invites an interchange between belief and knowledge systems.

Montero lays the foundation for exploring and defining what happens at the juncture between science and alternative knowledges even as she also exposes the grounds for our failure to find intercultural and indeed interdisciplinary connections to support any conservationist goal. The sinking of the boat at the end of her narrative (and with it, the deaths of the two men and "their" endangered frog) is evidence of this doomed encounter. This representation therefore echoes not the unceasing quality of the creolization process that is allowed to proceed unfettered in culture but rather a "halted" one, as described by the Barbadian poet Edward Kamau Brathwaite (1974) in his pioneering observations about cultural and social creolization.

In *The Development of Creole Society in Jamaica*, Brathwaite (1971) defined creolization as "a way of seeing the society, not in terms of white and black, master and slave, in separate nuclear units, but as contributory parts of a whole" (Brathwaite 1971, 307). For Brathwaite, "the friction created by this confrontation [slavery]" was not only "cruel" but also "creative."[4] He would later (1974) expand on his theoretical framework by highlighting the process of victorious "acculturation" that distinguished the assimilatory policy of the European Creoles from the halted "interculturation" that defined the post-slavery Creole identities involved in a process of resistant intercultural exchange. This "interculturation," Brathwaite claimed, was stopped in its tracks because the Creoles failed to

218   C. M. MARDOROSSIAN AND A. V. WONG

take "the culture of this black ex-African majority as the paradigm and norm for the entire society" (Brathwaite 1974, emphasis ours, 30).

Similarly, in *Introduction à une Poétique du Divers*, Édouard Glissant's (1996) concept of creolization evokes Brathwaite's (1971) as he too claims that when the cultural elements that are intermixing are not equivalent, that is, when the African element is demeaned and considered inferior as in the case of slavery, creolization "does not really take place. It takes place in a bastardizing and unjust manner ... it does take place but leaves a bitter, uncontrollable residue" (Glissant 1996, 17–18). Glissant even compares the form of creolization that occurs in the plantation world to a bird that only flaps one wing (18).

These theorizations of a failed creolization are echoed in *In the Palm of Darkness*, in its fictional staging of an encounter between two dichotomous realities, Western science and Afro-Caribbean cosmologies. Their ultimate incompatibility in the novel strongly evokes Brathwaite's (1974) process of "halted interculturation" (30) or Glissant's (1996) "bitter, uncontrollable residue" (18), since the failure clearly resides in the Western character's inability to heed the signifying processes and wisdom of alternative Haitian knowledges (represented by the two Haitian characters Thierry Adrien and Boukaka). At the same time, in having the US and Haitian characters share space and time in incurring the same fate, the novel's staged intersection also suggests an alternative to the binary, one that we will invite the reader to consider at the end of our discussion. Propelled by the questions raised in Montero's text, we are driven to explore what is potentially creolizable if not creolized in the Western scientific approach. We see as emerging a possible common denominator between traditions and forms of knowledge that could instill a cooperative humility in lieu of the colonizing hubris with which scientists like Victor Grigg conduct their business in non-Western cultural or environmental landscapes whose association with femininity is far from incidental.[5] As such, it is important to take seriously the challenge posed by the text's recurring association of scientific conclusions with the notion of an unsolvable "mystery." This is a mystery with which both the environment and the female characters that inhabit it are consistently associated in the novel, in keeping with the triangulating structure we identified at the onset of our analysis.

The novel opens with a fictionalized representation of an easily identifiable process of scientific discovery and collection. American herpetologist Victor Grigg and his Haitian guide Thierry Adrien are lying in the Haitian underbrush on the Mont des Enfants Perdus, having just recorded the voice of the elusive *Eleutherodactylus sanguineus*, a tiny but real, that is, not fictional, endangered frog Victor was hired to find. The fieldtrip leads the latter to reminisce about his wife Martha, "a woman of science" (Montero 1997, 7), a marine biologist and "meticulous collaborator" (7) as well as about the circumstances that led his eminent colleague, the famed Australian herpetologist Vaughan Patterson, to hire him to locate a specimen of the elusive frog. Interspersed between the narrative chapters (which are told in Victor's and Thierry's respective voices and relate their subjective experiences and relationships), we are also given sections that detail various frog species' extinctions in the detached and objective language of science. And ironically, these sections conclude with a sense of puzzlement and mystery rather than scientific answer or elucidation.

Throughout the novel, we are repeatedly reminded of how scientific processes of data collection, analysis, and "conclusions" fail to fully explain the frog die-off, whether it is spatially or temporally. Ecological processes are instead represented as interactions of multidimensional and multifactorial influences that are not amenable to a reductionist approach to understanding. Pollution may be deemed the most significant factor and still not fully explain the loss of a frog species in what is indeed, as science itself recognizes, a complex phenomenon. This is why scientists talk of "contributing" factors.[6] There are often emergent properties within natural systems where relational processes between various organisms continue to affect the life forms in question. A statistical correlation between pollution and the disappearance of frogs therefore does not preclude other factors at play that have yet to be examined. This is also, then, how "mystery" remains part of the scientific approach to any life form's development, and why the novel's representation of the compatibility of science with a belief system like voodoo is not as far-fetched as may first appear. Afro-Caribbean spiritual practices, based on openness and adaptation, touch on and inform every facet of human life, and therefore step in to provide a metaphorical and embodied language for the mysteries that motivate scientific research.

What is more, the novel creates a distinction between the scientific process itself and its practitioners, suggesting an ironic intersection or "contact zone" between the humility that grounds science's approach to "the mystery" of multifactorial, natural phenomena and the self-possession with which the novel's Haitian guides appeal to alternative knowledges to explain the same ("the Law of the Water"). At the same time, in staging an encounter between Western science (via Victor's collection of specimens) and Afro-Caribbean cosmologies (via Thierry's alertness and ability to "read" his surroundings), *In the Palm of Darkness* exposes the profound ways in which the convergence and confluence of these two worldviews is only truly recognized by the Haitian cosmology that resides in the "palm of darkness." By contrast, the Western scientist Victor remains resistant to the alternative realities and knowledges his guide tries to share with him.

Victor Grigg is determined, for instance, to see his research hover above the tragic and deadly realities that constitute the daily lives of the Haitian people and of women in particular, a perspective that is emblematic of the problem with his scientific worldview. Montero's novel describes a 1980s Haiti where violence is a permanent presence, at times peripheral but too often central to day-to-day Haitian experiences. This violence compromises Grigg's and other Western scientists' determined searches for disappearing flora and fauna, which is the only self-interested reason for which they object to its ubiquity. Driven by the promise of his own research and success (in exchange for finding the frog, Patterson promises Victor funding for two years to travel anywhere and research anything), Victor embarks upon the mission to extricate the last "specimen" of *grenouille du sang* from the very environment in which the endangered animal would be most likely to reproduce, insisting that his knowledge should evolve independently of the people or environments at the expense of whom it acquires its authority. Unwilling to fully confront the human dangers, the scientists in the novel simply move forward with their searches, claiming these to be above the unpredictable but omnipresent violence that shapes human relationships in the book.

This compartmentalizing view is challenged by the mirroring Montero stages between the global frog disappearances and the human disappearances and oppression at the hands of the TonTon Macoutes, a reference that helps situate the time frame of the story in the 1980s. The novel rarely provides reasons for the Macoutes's violence; it simply presents the fact of a person's death, often through the reappearance of their lifeless, and appendage-less, body. Yet, unlike the scientific puzzlement over the frog disappearances, Haitians understand the violent deaths, and violence, as a transaction and the result of interaction between people. On Haiti's Mont des Enfants Perdus, a mountain of lost children, Thierry and Victor discover buried human bones and remains. Thierry immediately alerts Victor to the danger around them but the latter refuses to believe Thierry, expecting them to stay on the mountain. When Thierry states that they will need

12 CREOLIZING SCIENCE IN MAYRA MONTERO'S *PALM OF DARKNESS* 221

to leave the mountain as they are not wanted there, Victor first pretends not to hear, and then recalls, "[Thierry] seemed sincere and yet I felt obliged to doubt, to deny the absurd danger that threatened to interfere with my work, to forget everything except the one thing that brought me to the mountain: Nothing very serious can happen to a man when all he looks for, all he wants, is a harmless little frog" (41).

Victor convinces himself of the inconsequential nature of his search and presence on the island, even the inconsequential nature of the frog itself in relation to Haiti's sociopolitical reality, but from the outset Thierry has known of the importance and value of the frog. Within the novel, the frog portends the doomed outcome of the search. Describing his rejection of Thierry's expertise and knowledge as an "obligation," Victor ascribes his doubt to his training as a scientist. Yet, the frog proves throughout the search process not to be harmless at all, since the detached, scientific prose dividing the chapters demonstrates precisely how harmful the scientific competitiveness over the frogs can be, including to science itself. After all, the mysteries of the frog disappearances highlight what the science does not know or cannot declare understood.

Throughout the novel, Victor Grigg makes quite a number of offhand comments that reveal his ingrained dismissive attitude toward Thierry's knowledge of Haiti. Victor animalizes his guide by seeing him as a rare species that should be recorded before "it" disappears too. When Victor is in the hospital, after being attacked as a warning that he should leave the mountain where he was conducting the search, he has no interest in the spiritual laws that Thierry offers to share: "I can teach you the Law of Water" (65). The gulf that separates the two men's ways of relating with each other and their environment is enhanced by the reader's awareness that Victor had tried to replace Thierry, claiming "some people just don't have the right chemistry and Thierry and I hadn't taken to each other" (61). This was shortly before Thierry spent the first night in the hospital tending to his boss's wounds and comforting him; Grigg recalls, "Neither of us really slept that night" (63). Despite this selfless devotion, Victor again conveys the idea that Thierry is not to be trusted: "He walked out of the room, not making a sound, and I was reminded of Bengali servants in the movies, the ones who always end up stabbing their masters" (66). The resonance with slavery and its association of racial difference with savagery is striking. One may also remember the unnamed male narrator's objectifying view of the Caribbean environment and its people in Jean Rhys's *Wide Sargasso Sea* (1966). Evidently, Victor struggles to identify with his guide and what he represents. Nor does he respect or register the latter's knowledge and expertise.

In a chapter tellingly entitled "Barbara," Thierry's words (in direct speech) are interrupted by Victor's disconnected and interspersed thoughts (in indirect discourse), in what become competing perspectives that embody—via the narration—both the Haitian's desire to engage and the Westerner's inability to listen. Thierry's attempts at sharing the Haitian spiritual laws he solemnly refers to as "the Law of Water" are consistently interrupted by Victor's inner stream of consciousness about his wife Martha, who has left him for the "Barbara" of the chapter's title. Again, the men's unequal relationship is triangulated through Victor's reference to gender and sexuality. The structure of alternating direct and indirect male speech in the later chapter echoes the narration of the first one, when we first encountered the two men in the Haitian underbrush and saw Victor's thoughts similarly stray to his failing conjugal relationship. In both cases, however, the focus is less on his unrequited love and loss of a longtime partner than on his wounded ego. As evidenced by the title of the later chapter, he is more concerned about Barbara, his rival, than the loss of his better half's relationship. It is his sense of masculinity that is at stake: "the fact that Martha ate ostrich with [Barbara] and not with me ... a subtle blow" (138). At the beginning of the book, he introduced his wife as "*what you might call* a woman of science" (emphasis ours, 7) with a "very suspicious mind" (6) and a "perverse delight in trivial details that went beyond simple scientific curiosity" (7). The latter statement is particularly ironic in light of his own inability to remain focused on the professional task or professional relationship at hand without getting lost in thoughts about his domestic affairs. Tellingly, he refers to Martha crossing herself before going to bed as a "childish habit" (75), which shows that his disdain for spiritual matters is not only racialized but also gendered.

It is again and again through a triangulation between femininity, patriarchy, and imperialism that women become associated with the Haitian environment, which is in turn perceived by the protagonists as a mere backdrop to their homosocial tribulations. Victor's paradoxically dismissive obsession, built on his unspoken feelings of emasculation, with his wife Martha's lesbian relationship overlaps with his disregard for Thierry's perspective and collection of the last specimen of an endangered frog. It reveals a condescending attitude toward women that somewhat veils his dismissal of Haitian alterity, an attitude which seems to reproduce a similar process of gendering. The novel, then, stages a rejection of a white phallogocentric science and society in favor of subordinated people and contexts that do not objectify the environment and humans, but it does so by making visible the gendered and racialized processes of othering through which any discourse will seek to normalize its self-proclaimed authority and superiority.

Accordingly, Montero parallels the Haitian environment's resistance to Western and human intrusion with the gendered violence experienced by women. The violence enacted on, inscribed upon, and demonstrated through women's bodies is racialized, though never explicitly so. Thierry surmises that Haiti causes white women to go crazy, as the women find themselves drawn to the dangerous mountains. The first story Thierry tells Victor about the last time he saw the *grenouille du sang*, which is also the first story in the book, associates the frog with a white woman who had apparently taken refuge in the mountains: "I was looking for a woman, sir" (20). Hired by a German man to recover his missing wife, Thierry sets out alone and overnight to Castaches Hill, where they believe the woman to be. Thierry tells Victor,

> You can't imagine how many women go out of their minds as soon as they set foot in Haiti, decent women who come for a little sun and end up on the burros with twisted hooves that go up to the Citadelle. [...] after that, I don't know why, they come back deranged, their clothes all dirty and their eyes popping out of their heads (5).

Thierry continues,

> If they brought a husband with them, the husband drags them back to the ship or plane they came on. If they're alone, and some of them are, the police pick them up and put them in insane asylum. Then the doctors get word to their families and before you know it, a brother, a father, a son shows up, it's always a man who comes for them, and they're handed to that man (26).

The novel never identifies these women as white, but the implication is that Haiti drives white women to insanity.[7] This "madness" rejects white European knowledge (which is masculinized in the novel), as well as the proclaimed superiority of scientific rationalism. What is more, the white women who go up the mountain, like the mountain itself, also cause fear in Haitians.

224   C. M. MARDOROSSIAN AND A. V. WONG

In the Palm of Darkness evokes, then, to borrow the Caribbean novelist Tiphanie Yanique's words, the

> long, unfortunate tradition in literature set in the Caribbean, written by Americans or Europeans, of crazy women. Either women from the Caribbean are crazy, or women go to the Caribbean and end up crazy. During the Victorian Era, the idea was that if the slave master goes down to check on his plantation in the Caribbean and he takes his wife, he is taking a risk because she might lose her mind. That was a real thing that people thought— white women were going to go crazy… But probably when you think about what was really happening, the women couldn't stand the violence of slavery (Yanique 2014).

Yanique's prescription of white women's madness as a psychological rejection of slavery places white women, at least some of them, against the institution of slavery. Yet there might also be another way to consider white women's "madness," where they are not merely manifesting the conscience of the European colonizers, but rather confronting their complicity within the system as well. We may read Martha's "competition" with Victor as a scientist herself along the same lines, when she does not accompany Victor on his trips, or when she ultimately rejects their heterosexual relationship.

Throughout the novel, women of color's bodies are violated, albeit in a more sexualized way than their white counterparts'. In keeping with the slavery-derived stereotypes of black female sexuality as available, men's sexual aggression or violation of nonwhite women is consistently recast as consent or agency. For example, prior to meeting Victor, Thierry helped another scientist, called Papa Crapaud (the French word for toad), search for frogs. One day, Papa Crapaud returned from a trip to Guadeloupe with frog specimens and a new woman, "the catch he had brought" (68)—Ganesha—who turned out to be an unfaithful, potentially murderous wife, likely of a South Asian background, which is suggested through her appearance ("she … wore a little ring in her nose and a blood mark on her forehead" (69)) and of course her name, which she shares with the elephant-headed, many-armed Hindu deity.

In highlighting Ganesha's alleged dirtiness, which made the house smell like cow piss and cow dung, Thierry associates her racial and gender difference with a debased sexuality directly related to her spiritual belief system (69). In this, Thierry's view of Ganesha rejects Montero's altar of syncretism, which is open, and establishes the masculinist limitations of his alternative knowledge system. Papa Crapaud explains that "Ganesha wasn't like other women, and the *loas* that came down to her table were the *loas* of other lands who liked cow piss and cow dung, cow dung and rice milk" (70). Ganesha's cultural difference and her different spirits and gods seem to imbue her, however, with an intoxicating sexuality to men, who would line up outside her door and whom she would invite in when Papa Crapaud was out hunting frogs.

Despite his friendship with Papa Crapaud or maybe precisely because of it, as Sedgwick might argue, Thierry succumbs to his attraction to Ganesha, describing their sexual encounter as a moment of hunt and capture: "I came up behind Ganesha and put my hands around her. She twisted and tried to run away, I caught her at the door" (71) but eventually "instead of hitting me or running away she went down on all fours and offered her rump like a dog" (72). Where white women are driven mad in Haiti and rendered dangerously useless, women of color are identified with a sexual agency that, the male narrator asserts, they deliberately subordinate to white or black men's will. Thierry claims that Ganesha's sexuality ("She knew what each man needed" (72)) overpowers Haitian men, thereby absolving the latter of responsibility for their sexual aggression (72). The novel's treatment of Ganesha, who is also framed as a vector of venereal disease, thus implies an antagonism between alternative knowledges through an engendering of racial and sexual difference that goes beyond any black–white binary. The troubling view among black men of South Asian women as submissive in the extreme can certainly be traced back to colonial attitudes, but it also exposes the very real divisions, prejudices, and antagonisms between Afro- and Indo-Caribbean communities.

Despite being subjected to processes of othering by Victor, Thierry reproduces these himself in relation to femininity, as seen in his animalization of Ganesha (a particular type of othering that happens, in the novel, in relation to South Asia) as well as the many revelations of men's sexual dominance of women throughout the novel. Thierry is unable to recognize his own complicity with the forces that subjugate Haitian women and the Haitian environment, and whose triangulating dynamics cast women in the role of the "conduits" through which men's homosocial bonds are enacted (Sedgewick 1985, 26). Also significant in this regard is Thierry's sleeping with Froufrou, his father's "wife," in a seeming reenactment of the Oedipus complex. Thierry's sexual relationship with FrouFrou functions very much as yet another form of the triangulation we have been discussing.

Such triangular structures are also true of the ways in which Western knowledges repeatedly reinstate their disciplinary and epistemological superiority, sometimes at a second remove. When faced with the herpetologist Emile Boukaka's expertise and impressive data gathering, Victor reframes it as nonscientific by comparing it to music and art; he condescendingly dismisses the Haitian's knowledge, which is based on the local fishermen's or farmers' observations:

> I made an effort to handle *with some grace* the enormous quantity of data provided by Boukaka. I was amazed by his capacity for detail, his precision, *I can even say* his erudition. When we said good-bye he shook my hand; I was about to tell him that he reminded me of a famous musician, ... Thelonious Monk ... I remembered a composition of Monk's that wasn't played too often: 'See you later, beautiful frog.' (Emphasis ours, 96–7)

From Victor's perspective, such association with music is, as with Thierry's association with opacity, ultimately delegitimizing and belittling.[8]

While we are made aware of the many discourses contending for attention across time and space, and tradition and modernity in the novel (from Vodou to anthropological and scientific practices), racial and/or sexual difference clearly function as "metaphorical hinge[s] between scientific and anthropological discourses" (according to critic Ángel Rivera (2001)) on the one hand, and a nonscientific, religious world on the other. For instance, Thierry and Boukaka's status as in-between is evident insofar as they both appeal to Haitian cosmologies at the same time as they are also referred to as "herpetologists" from the outset, a term that makes no sense outside of a Western scientific context. Thierry is both the local guide who facilitates Victor's scientific data collection and recordings and a believer in the syncretic practices of Vodou. He insists on turning off the recorder to describe "the Law of Water" since: "The law [Thierry] was about to teach me could exist only in the mind and on the tongue of men" (74). Similarly, Emile Boukaka shares scientists' "capacity for detail," "precision," and "erudition" (97) and gathers "enormous quantity of data" (97) while being critical of the limitations of Western scientific thought: "You people invent excuses: acid rain, herbicides, deforestation. But the frogs are disappearing from places where none of that has happened" (96). Neither man expresses the need or desire to choose between the various discourses that intersect in their lives, thereby suggesting the possibility of a creolized science that would benefit from alternative knowledges rather than stand in opposition to them. Boukaka states, for instance, that "[w]hat I've learned, I learned in books ... But what I know, everything I know, I took from fire and water, from water and flame" (97). Boukaka's division of "learning" from "knowing" creates another dualistic framework, joining Thierry's "knowledge from experience" against Victor Grigg's "knowledge from science."

Similarly, despite his determination to compartmentalize life into disciplines and categories as well as genders and races, Victor is unconsciously susceptible to what he would (dis)regard as superstitious. As much of a scientist as he is, Victor's revelation of his selection of science as a career is reminiscent of Thierry's storytelling approach to reality. Indeed, the reader learns that Victor's mother gave him a painting of a midwife toad (Alytes obstetricians), so named because the male frogs carry the fertilized eggs on their back and protect them until they hatch; she had begun painting it "when she learned she was pregnant and finished it on the day I was born," a fact that convinced her that his life would be somehow intertwined with frogs—and it was (21). This is the kind of "old wives' tale" or "midwife's tale" we associate not with science but with a much historically maligned oral history. Paradoxically, the foundations of scientific practice for Victor lie in the same realms he would dismiss in the name of science. At the same time, the very mother who claimed to set his future trajectory in motion through her superstitious prediction also instilled in him the desire to become a scientist through an endorsement of science as we know it: "My mother always said you had to look at life as if it were the suspicious start of a crime: tying up loose ends, finding clues, following the trail coldly, as if it didn't even concern you" (20–1). As with other women represented in the text, she is able to transcend dichotomies to espouse a more inclusive, syncretic view of the world.

The novel repeatedly challenges what Caribbean novelist Wilson Harris identified as "the break which occurred between science and art, science and an imaginative psychological, even magical apprehension of the universe, [which] entailed a cultural fragmentation that impoverished the European tradition and was to culminate in the Enlightenment and a constricted rationalism" (Maes-Jelinek 1998, 41), and it is maybe in the violent subjugation of women that it articulates the costs of such a break (which is itself a fraught representation). This being said, while rationalism as the sole way of knowing is certainly questioned, it is also not outrightly condemned as a way of knowing. Indeed, the text also seems to suggest that scientific rationalism and magical apprehension, in Harris's words, do coexist—maybe that the one can be found in the other, even if it does not actually provide an alternative path forward from this "break," except partly through the Haitian people's storytelling, or women's worldviews, which reveal an uncanny ability to reconcile the two.

Montero's novel shows the limitations of "science" by undermining the Western habit of polarizing worldviews and epistemologies while she celebrates Vodou and Haiti's openness to different ways of seeing. As the quote that gave the novel its original title—*Tú, la oscuridad*—puts it, "You, darkness, enfolding the spirit of those who ignore your glory" (181). In other words, Thierry and the alternative Afro-Caribbean cosmology he represents "enfold" other realities and knowledges that Victor's Western and hierarchical worldview is more likely to dismiss, yet both are taken to task for the triangulating structures through which they may seek to project their own authority. Both are shown capable of a violent erasure of femininity in their anxious attempts at making sense of an unstable world. Maybe, then, the form of "creolizing science" the novel schematizes would best be seen as one that recognizes usually opposed dimensions of human existence as compatible, creolized forms of knowledge that do not melt difference so much as "enfold the spirit of those who ignore your glory" (181).

Notes

1. Mayra Montero is a Cuban-Puerto Rican writer who was born in Cuba in 1952 and has lived in Puerto Rico since the mid-1960s. In Puerto Rico, Montero has had a successful journalistic career, which, she has claimed, provides "excellent training for anyone who wants to become a writer" (Prieto 2000, 89). Tú, la oscuridad (1995, In the Palm of Darkness) is a precursor in twenty-first-century ecocriticism and sets the stage for the biological theme that runs through her creative and journalistic writings.
2. The coquí, a species of frog endemic to Puerto Rico and belonging to the family Eleutherodactylidae, is the national symbol for the island, which Montero has made her home since the 1960s.
3. Other Caribbean women writers who have similarly fictionalized the imbrication of gender, ecology, and postcoloniality in their work include Edwidge Danticat (2013), whose Claire of the Sea Light also portrays the frog as a hybrid symbol that represents the environment as well as its transcendence (Mardorossian and Wong 2020).

4. As Chris Bongie (1998, 55) noted, however, this statement could be somewhat self-contradictory, since Brathwaite's argument presupposes the existence of two separate identities in conflict with each other.
5. This is not to say that the intermixing of cultures, languages, and races embodied by "creolization" can just be transposed onto the nonhuman, environmental, or scientific world. We are not implying that the data-driven systematicity of science is amenable to mixing with alternative sources of knowledge such as religion or Vodou. By "creolizing science," we do not mean to challenge either its processes or the novel's condemnation of its imperializing applications.
6. Since the novel's publication, it has been determined, for instance, that the chytrid fungus (Batrachochytrium dendrobatidis) was a contributing factor in the global decline of amphibians. It was not previously something that was in the scientists' frame of study because it required swabs followed by molecular and DNA tests to discover the fungal pathogen (Manke 2019). The emergence of another piece of the puzzle neither delegitimizes previous studies per se nor constitutes a failure of science, however. Neither does its discovery explain the cause of the fungus's predominance at that moment in time. This example reminds us that scientific knowledge too is an unceasing process but no less meaningful and legitimate for being so.
7. Again, the trope of the mad Creole woman here may be an intertextual reference to Wide Sargasso Sea, Rhys's twentieth-century response to Charlotte Brontë's nineteenth-century British classic, Jane Eyre.
8. As Rivera notes, Monk's jazz style is characterized both by silence as a central compositional element and by a strange angular quality that is not easily assimilated. The strangeness is due to long periods of silence punctuated by his bebop jazz compositions: "*In the Palm of Darkness* is constructed on one of Monk's key musical elements (i.e., silence) ... The reader ... will be able to read silence from a new point of view" (Rivera, 2001).

REFERENCES

Bongie, Chris. 1998. *Islands ad Exiles: The Creole Identities of Post/Colonial Literature.* Stanford: Stanford UP.

Brathwaite, Kamau. 1974. *Contradictory Omens: Cultural Diversity and Integration in the Caribbean.* Kingston: Savacou.

———. 1971. *The Development of Creole Society in Jamaica.* Oxford: Clarendon.

Danticat, Edwidge. 2013. *Claire of the Sea Light.* New York: Vintage.

Davis, Wade. 1985. *The Serpent and the Rainbow: A Harvard Scientist's Astonishing Journey into the Secret Societies of Haitian Voodoo, Zombies, and Magic.* New York: Simon and Schuster.

Gaard, Greta. 1997. Toward a Queer Ecofeminism. *Hypatia* 12 (1): 114–137.

Glissant, Edouard. 1996. *Introduction à une poétique du divers.* Paris: Éditions Gallimard.

Maes-Jelinek, Hena. 1998. 'Latent Cross-Culturalities': Wilson Harris's and Wole Soyinka's Creative Alternative to Theory. *European Journal of English Studies* 2 (1): 37–48.

Mardorossian, Carine, and Angela Veronica Wong. 2020. Magical Terrestrealism in Edwidge Danticat's *Claire of the Sea Light.* In *The Palgrave Book of Magical Realism in the Twenty-First Century,* ed. Victoria Chevalier and Richard Price, 197–211. New York: Palgrave Macmillan.

Manke, Kara. 2019. Scientists Track Frog-Killing Fungus to Help Curb Its Spread. *Science Daily* September 23. https://www.sciencedaily.com/releases/2019/09/190923155128.htm. Accessed 16 July 2022.

Montero, Mayra. 1987. *La trenza de la hermosa luna.* Mexico City: Anagrama.

———. 1995. *Tú, la oscuridad.* Barcelona: Tusquets.

———. 1997. *In the Palm of Darkness.* Trans. Edith Grossman. New York: HarperCollins.

Mortimer-Sandilands, Catriona, and Bruce Erickson, eds. 2010. *Queer Ecologies: Sex, Nature, Politics, Desire.* Bloomington, IN: Indiana University Press.

Prieto, Jose Manuel. 2000. Trans. Marina Harss. Interview: Mayra Montero. *Bomb* (Winter): 86–90. https://bombmagazine.org/articles/mayra-montero/. Accessed 16 July 2022.

Rhys, Jean. [1966] 2011. *Wide Sargasso Sea.* London: Penguin.

Rivera, Ángel. 2001. Silence, Voodoo, and Haiti in Mayra Montero's *In the Palm of Darkness. Ciberletras* 4. http://www.lehman.cuny.edu/ciberletras/v04/Rivera.html. Accessed 16 July 2022.

Sedgwick, Eve Kosofsky. 1985. *Between Men: English Literature and Male Homosocial Desire.* New York: Columbia University Press.

Seymour, Nicole. 2013. *Strange Natures: Futurity, Empathy, and the Queer Ecological Imagination.* Urbana: University of Illinois Press.

Yanique, Tiphanie. 2014. Why Is There a Crazy Caribbean Woman in the Attic?: Tiphanie Yanique on *Land of Love and Drowning.* Brooke Obie Interviews Tiphanie Yanique. *LARB: Los Angeles Review of Books* July 23. https://lareviewofbooks.org/article/crazy-caribbean-woman-attic-tiphanie-yanique-land-love-drowning/. Accessed 16 July 2022.

Open Access This chapter is licensed under the terms of the Creative Commons Attribution 4.0 International License (http://creativecommons.org/licenses/by/4.0/), which permits use, sharing, adaptation, distribution and reproduction in any medium or format, as long as you give appropriate credit to the original author(s) and the source, provide a link to the Creative Commons licence and indicate if changes were made.

The images or other third party material in this chapter are included in the chapter's Creative Commons licence, unless indicated otherwise in a credit line to the material. If material is not included in the chapter's Creative Commons licence and your intended use is not permitted by statutory regulation or exceeds the permitted use, you will need to obtain permission directly from the copyright holder.

CHAPTER 13

Monstrous Genealogies: Indo-Caribbean Feminist Reckonings with the Violent Past

Lisa Outar

Caribbean writing has long been preoccupied with themes of haunting by the violent past, specifically the ways in which experiences of trauma and loss borne from slavery, indentureship, colonialism, and the gendered exploitations of the plantation echo from one generation to another, refusing conventional boundaries of space and time. In various ways, Caribbean writers must confront that which is inherently irreparable, unspeakable, and unescapable about the past, while relying on cultural forms and the power of the imagination to evoke decolonial futures that make life bearable to the generations that inherit plantation legacies and navigate their contours. Of particular interest in this chapter are the ways in which Indo-Caribbean women writers seize examples of the haunting past and renarrate them through literary forms that engage and revise mythologies of the feminine and folklore. I highlight the trenchant critiques of both cultural and national norms regarding gender posed by such interventions and the innovative reimaginings of time, space, agency, and corporeality that are deployed. As I will show, writers Vashti Bowlah, Krystal M. Ramroop, and Ingrid Persaud depict the ways in which

L. Outar (✉)
Independent Scholar, Rome, Italy

© The Author(s) 2023
O. Ferly, T. Zimmerman (eds.), *Chronotropics*,
https://doi.org/10.1007/978-3-031-32111-5_13

233

personal and collective trauma and its repression pierce the lives of Caribbean women in nonlinear, noncontainable ways, requiring them to live trapped by violent pasts but also equipped with potentially radical tools with which to shape new presents and futures. In redirecting images of monstrous femininity contained both within patriarchal understandings of gender and within folklore, these Indo-Caribbean women writers challenge conventional understandings of the relation between past and present, the human and the nonhuman, the monstrous and the maternal in order to offer feminist visions of revenge for the injustices of the past and the specter of more empowered futures. We see in particular a seizing upon a theme of the return of the repressed: what is bottled up about traumatic pasts by the characters themselves and by the Caribbean societies they inhabit roars back to powerful life in vibrant new forms. We also see violence seized upon as a reparative tool, one that can be used to mete out justice to those who harm women as well as a means of clearing space and accessing agency by figures who are deemed abject by society and even by those who love them.

I start with an examination of two recent short stories: Vashti Bowlah's "The Churile of Sugarcane Valley" (2015) and Krystal M. Ramroop's "Midnight's Mischievous Mistress" (2020). I draw upon scholarship on the gendered invocations of folkloric figures in Caribbean culture to explore more fully what Indo-Caribbean representations of figures such as the churile, the diablesse, and the soucouyant suggest about new possibilities for negotiating simultaneously vulnerable and powerful spaces of femininity as well as traditional modes for representing trauma and history. Bowlah and Ramroop turn to figures from Caribbean folklore to depict the prevalence of gender-based violence in our communities, to name the specificities of Indian women's experiences in the region and to force potentially liberatory inversions in their decolonizing quests. In the second half of the chapter, I assess Ingrid Persaud's 2020 novel *Love After Love* for its rejection of heteropatriarchal notions of what is considered natural in Caribbean kinship systems and its poignant exploration of how charges of monstrosity and unnaturalness are both imposed upon and redeployed by Caribbean women. The idea of vengeance, of a reckoning with what is repressed and glossed over in community narratives about women's suffering, echoes in all the texts I examine. While Persaud engages with themes of cleansing violence and with alternate models of powerful femininity to be found in Caribbean Indian religious traditions,

Bowlah and Ramroop turn to figures from Caribbean folklore to imagine new worlds where justice is attainable for women.

FOLKLORE AND FEMINISM

Scholars of Caribbean folklore have pointed to its complex place in Caribbean letters and cultural imagination. Gerard Besson (2012) notes the devaluation of local traditions of folklore in the push to self-definition after colonialism. Giselle Liza Anatol (2015) acknowledges the deleterious effects of colonial identity on local folklore traditions, but more optimistically sees a burgeoning of interest in such local forms in the postcolonial era even while she carefully unpacks the misogynistic and harmful messages about women contained therein. What is clear is that spectral figures limned by folklore drawn from various cultural genealogies of the region are a key part of a Caribbean literary landscape, and they challenge teleological understandings of history and time. Candace Ward argues that duppies, for instance, occupy the "liminal and disturbed space in the region's literature, a fluid interspace between the material and immaterial worlds where the fraught relationship between history and historiography is played out" (2012, 217). Little scholarly work has been done on specifically Indo-Caribbean folklore. Kumar Mahabir's 2010 *Indian Caribbean Folklore Spirits*, which primarily traces appearances of the figures of the raakhas, the churile, the saapin, Dee Baba, and the jinn Sheik Sadiq in oral testimonies with Indo-Trinidadians, is one such attempt, but much remains to be done to assess their importance for colonial-era and postcolonial expressions of identity and agency.

The two short stories that I examine here challenge the reinscription of "traditional gender, class and race messages" (74) that Anatol warns can arrive with folklore and that she sees as part of the conditioning of girls and women to accept roles of docility (a critque echoed in the indictment of conservative religious communities that we see in Persaud's novel). These works show how that which is denigrated about womanhood emerges in folkloric figures and in the real lives of the region's women, whether living at home or in the diaspora. Folklore here serves as an archive of women's suffering.

Vashti Bowlah employs the churile in such a manner in her short story "The Churile of Sugarcane Valley" and further uses the fearsome figure from Indo-Caribbean folklore to put forward a vision of feminist retribution. A description of the standard understanding of the churile as a woman who has died in childbirth is included within the story itself:

> Her long jet-black hair; unbound and disheveled, streams over her face as she wails sorrowfully, while her child cries for milk like a kitten's meow. Ever since she died during childbirth she has been seen dressed in a white gown covering her ankles as she seeks revenge on those who wronged her. Not that anyone believed in such things anymore, but a few elders in the village swore that they have seen her; sometimes standing at the side of the road, or under a tree. "A *churile* always gets revenge on those who hurt her," everyone agreed.

The main character of Neela is implied rather than explicitly named as the churile. With its structure in which Neela herself is never given voice, the story highlights how those who fall outside of the conventions of patriarchal societal ordering become the subject of suspicion and gossip and do not get to control their own stories. Upon her appearance in the village, Neela is immediately suspect because of her unmarried status: "At the ripe old age of thirty-three, she was the subject of old-maid jokes wherever she went. She was also the topic of choice when housewives met at the vegetable stalls or while they waited near the gate to collect their children after school." Filling at least one expectation of gendered labor by being caregiver to her grandmother does not dispel the gossip. The story in one way seems to confirm the community's perception of the older, unmarried woman as being a threat to societal order when Neela falls pregnant by the lothario, Raj, and subsequently dies in childbirth. Importantly, however, Bowlah does not end on the idea of the threat being thus removed and of social order being restored but rather suggests Neela's transformation into the feared churile and her rumored vengeful aspect. After Neela dies, "It wasn't long before Raj's body was pulled out of the rice lagoon by a farmer. It was rumored that the last thing he did was scream out Miss Neela's name in the dead of the night under the huge mango tree. The *churile* was never sighted again." Bowlah unerringly conveys the ways in which such myths, with all of their latent fears about uncontrollable women, were imposed upon some of the most vulnerable members of Caribbean society. Despite evidence of her unfair treatment, in life and death, Neela becomes a figure to be simultaneously scorned and feared for her disruption of a patriarchal order that attempts to hold female sexuality in firm check.

The nonpresence in the story of Neela, of the grandmother, and indeed of the illicit child itself means that their "real" temporality in the story is also rendered ghostly, itself an indictment by Bowlah of the erasure of women's complex personhood by the narratives forced upon them. Their identities remain at the level of community gossip with all of its superstitiousness and unconfirmed rumors. I would also argue however that Bowlah's story offers a reading of the churile as not just to be feared but onto whom can be displaced the sublimated desires of other women trapped within a patriarchal order that does not deliver justice for those devoured by it. While the story is in part an indictment of the gossiping, judgmental community of women who fail to protect one of their own by not warning her about Raj, Neela also becomes an agent for the comeuppance the women themselves desire for exploitative men: "'Well, I still feel sorry for she, for letting a good-for-nothing man like Raj fool she up like that,' added the third woman. 'If she did only ask somebody they woulda tell she about the other girls he fool up and then drop them like ah old shoe.'" No tears appear to be shed for the dead Raj and the detail that the churile is never seen again after his death is emphasized, implying that her rage is not directed at others in the community. Pity, fear, dread, and admiration are thus comingled in the perception of the churile and her potential to upend the hierarchical ordering of marital status and maternal identity as being the ultimate containers of female sexuality and self-definition.

Of the texts I examine in this chapter, Krystal Ramroop's story, "Midnight's Mischievous Mistress," offers the most powerful fantasy of what it would be like if individual women and children had some recourse for the harm that is done to them or if there was a powerful feminine figure who could stand up for those who are not able to effect justice for themselves. Patricia Mohammed (2009) describes the Caribbean folkloric figure of the diablesse as "one of the most popular of the archetypes [of gender in the region], [she] is the quintessential woman as devil, the temptress who leads the unwitting men astray into the forests at night, the cloven hoof character who disguises her animal instincts with a pretty dress" (75). Angelo Bissessarsingh (2013) highlights the cross-regional nature of this figure arguing that in Trinidad "the devil woman herself almost always makes an appearance clothed in the style which has become synonymous with the French Antilles." Maica Gugolati's (2018) work usefully traces appearances of the figure in both Martinique and Trinidad concluding, "Based on interviews on both islands, it emerged that La

Djablesse teases men and the concept of masculinity, while challenging ideas of domination and the perceived gender boundaries in the public as well as the private domain. This legendary female figure challenges the stereotypes of the gender system constructed during the colonial and postindependence period" (152).

Following the archetype, Ramroop's diablesse, Marie, is a chimera, taking the form of a beautiful woman, aligned with the underworld, who possesses a cloven hoof. In her choice of name, Ramroop evokes "Ti-Marie"—the local Trinidadian name for the mimosa plant known variously as "shame bush," "Mary," "Mary shut your door," and "Touch Me Not!" elsewhere in the region, which withdraws onto itself when touched aggressively—as well as the various biblical Marys who run the gamut from virginal to prostitute. The name "Marie" thus signals both violated innocence and the possibility of powerful, protective femininity. Ramroop's story is also notable for her gender-confounding naming of a "Monsieur Diablesse" who, though recognizable as the archetypal ruler of the Underworld, also appears to be a force for gender justice, for wreaking vengeance against those responsible for the violence done to women in Trinidad. The story is thereby also a potent reversal of the Ti-Marie folktale tradition of the lesser Antilles, where the devil is the one who lies in wait for the young Ti-Marie, wanting to literally consume her.[1] The devils, the true face of evil in the world of Ramroop's story, appear to be the human men who harm the women they claim to love. The underworld depicted in the story is filled with their victims:

> At every hour of the day in the vibrant Caribbean country, domestic violence cases against women—accompanied by public and private footage for the Underworld records—poured into their department left, right, and center ... Marie had only met Monsieur Diablesse last year and after selling her soul to him for a small fee of revenge on the man who left her for dead (literally), he employed her full-time in the Underworld. She'd also seen and heard about the magic that her colleagues—though the women on Earth despised them—worked that left drunken men enchanted and disoriented and tonight, on her first death anniversary, Marie was keen on proving her competency to Monsieur Diablesse and earning her rank amongst the best.

The dreaded diablesse figure is thus herself identified as a victim of domestic violence, as both prey and predator, who seeks to punish the perpetrators of gendered violence. Ramroop does not shrink from including details of the nature of the horrific crimes committed against women—describing, for instance, Marie's childhood friend, Josephine, as present in the underworld because her husband doused her in gasoline and burned her alive—thereby preparing ground for the story's terrain of proposing that violence needs to be met with violence.

Marie proves her competence as a deliverer of just punishment on her first mission by strangling her prey, Steven, after he is seduced by her beauty and tries to pick her up: "She was glad he couldn't see her roll her eyes ... She was, however, ready to give him what he deserved." Here, we find a literal rejection of the archetype of "the angel in the house" for a powerful female devil, emerging from the underworld, upending divisions of life/death, human/animal and offering alternate imaginaries to the very real statistics of gendered violence in Trinidad and elsewhere in the Caribbean. In the absence of effective legal systems for punishing domestic violence and supporting its victims, writers turn to the realm of folklore and the fantastic, creating what Jana Evans Braziel calls "alterrains" within which "the devil (or author) is a source of rebellion, knowledge, and creation" (2001, 83).

One of the other compelling features of this story is the subtle but telling way in which Ramroop critiques the misogynistic underpinnings of certain Caribbean folklore traditions such as the figure of the soucouyant. The description of the unfaithful Steven as an abuser who would "leave black and blue marks on his wife, Nikita,—as if a soucouyant had sucked the blood from her skin—whenever she'd accuse him of infidelity" reads as a deliberate rejection of the trope that Anatol (2015) and others note of the othering and ascribing of malevolent powers to marginalized and vulnerable female members of a society, wherein, for example, older women who live alone are accused of being soucouyants. Ramroop initiates a key inversion here where male violence is given as the more likely reason for bruised women and children in the morning. She highlights in this description of Steven's abuse the very real possibility of the soucouyant being used as a convenient excuse to hide domestic violence. Existing as Gugolati describes "between invisibility and visibility, between silence and speech, between the sacred and the profane, and between the dreamy imaginary and reality" (2018, 174); the diablesse/jablesse thus becomes a vehicle for reconsidering the conservative applications of folklore to women's lives as well as the agent of a potent revenge fantasy, one of the many iterations of Caribbean feminist imagination. Mohammed (2009) notes the ways in which such folkloric figures are continually reconfigured within Caribbean feminist traditions:

The persona of La Diablesse has never been static in the evolving femininity of this terrain. She is constantly transforming herself, shedding layers of clothing and dispensing with the cloven hoof, as the much sought-after jammette of Port of Spain carnival in the 19th century, the ambiguous Jean and Dinah heroines of American occupation of the nineteen fifties, and in the Bacchanal woman celebrated by David Rudder. (80)

Braziel (2001) identifies Caribbean authors such as Jamaica Kincaid as themselves a jablesse who dispels "annihilating silence" (84) and "acts divinely: creating and destroying" (82). Here, Ramroop offers the diablesse as a Caribbean woman who maintains an ethical responsibility to her sistren even from beyond the grave. She deploys a "politics of alterity" (Braziel 2001, 86) in which the diablesse, rather than being "diabolical" as understood within a binary model of good/evil, is a figure who protects other women and offers visions of more just worlds.

Bowlah and Ramroop are part of an ongoing movement by contemporary Caribbean writers to take up this evolving culture of folklore and bring it to dazzling new life.[2] Both are pushing back against what Anatol (2015) calls "the inherently coercive social nature of folk-tales" (47). The "subversive power relationship" of these folkloric figures noted by Andre Bagoo in his conversation with Nicholas Laughlin (2013) about douens is part of what renders them so irresistible to this new generation of Caribbean writers as they challenge linear understandings of the effects of the violent past and flesh out new models for decolonizing and anti-patriarchal progress. As Mohammed reminds us, "The monsters of the Caribbean are not those which the Old World carried around in its head" (2009, 81). The meting out of justice these transgressive figures allow emerges as part of a distinctively Caribbean project of decolonization. Mohammed's allusion to the carnivalesque is apt: "This band of characters ... are the opening act in the jour'overt of our own origin stories, with characters that are neither European nor African, with roots and branches in many cosmologies and offering a free space for our imagination" (2009, 81).

Cleansing Violence, Creolized Religious Practices, and the Erotic

Ingrid Persaud's 2020 novel *Love After Love* also draws upon the uniquely creolized cosmologies of the Caribbean in its repudiation of heteropatriarchal violence and constraining models of femininity. As with her first novel,

If I Never Went Home (2013), in *Love After Love* the tentacles of traumatic pasts continue to haunt Caribbean peoples and their descendants. For example, the main character of Betty feels the ghostly traces of her abusive deceased husband: "Thing is, worse than the pain in my arm is Sunil's spirit in the house. The man in the walls, on the stairs, in the rooms. Before he passed he must have put he bad eye on me for truth" (Persaud 2020, 17). The violent past thus haunts Betty physically and spiritually. She feels real and phantom pain from her past injuries at the hands of her husband whom she killed in an act of self-defense and protectiveness toward her son. Despite his death, Betty continues to experience a vague sense of lingering malevolence as evidenced by the quote above.

As with Bowlah and Ramroop's stories, death is not presented as a permanent boundary. Instead, we find an embrace of local cosmologies where past and present, natural and supernatural, are entwined. Betty slowly loses her hope that respectable faith leaders can help her to free herself from the ways in which past suffering continually ruptures her current timeline: "Truth is I believe Sunil's spirit, his nasty bad eye, ain't ever leaving me no matter how much jharay I get" (20). In this way, Persaud establishes the non-teleological passage of time for those harmed by domestic abuse, the well-established patterns laid out by trauma theory of entrapment in past wounds.

Within this terrain, Persaud offers a powerful portrait of a nonheteronormative family. The novel lays out the rocky path of recovery for Betty and her son, Solo, after the abuse Betty suffered in her marriage, and their entwined journey with the memorable Mr. Chetan, who struggles with openly expressing his sexual identity in a Trinidad where he fears that public displays of same-sex love risk incurring violence. We find Persaud, as with Alison Donnell in *Creolized Sexualities* (2022), balancing not ignoring homophobia in the Caribbean while also seeing the region as a place where heteronormativity is "undone." *Love After Love* is a site where both homophobia and radical nonheteronormative possibilities are invoked simultaneously. The violence that Betty had already experienced at the hands of her husband and the perceived threat of violence that hovers over Mr. Chetan should he live his full self openly unites the characters and establishes a trust and solidarity built not upon revelation and public declarations of identity, but on mutual vulnerability, tenderness, and quiet acceptance. Betty is able to provide a loving substitute father figure for Solo in the form of Mr. Chetan: "He's not a father but he's a natural at fathering" (15). Persaud troubles ideas around what is "natural" for

242   L. OUTAR

definitions of family, kinship, manhood, sexuality, and parenting. She reimagines the possibilities for family in the Caribbean, for what are healing relationships that can sustain women, men, and children alike.

One critique I offer of the novel is the way in which the resolution of the conflict between mother and son is dependent on the Christ-like sacrifice of Mr. Chetan's gentle, nurturing body to the maws of homophobic violence. Solo's mourning the disappearance of this paternal figure and Betty's anger and pain at the loss of their deep, mostly platonic friendship finally brings mother and son together again, leaving the novel vulnerable to the trope Rosamond S. King identifies in *Island Bodies* (2014), where queer figures are instrumentalized in Caribbean literature, employed to deliver others to better versions of themselves though perhaps Persaud's novel is not fully "the backhanded gesture" that King describes.

Persaud's treatment of the son, Solo, is perhaps the best illustration of this author's embrace of the erotic as a site of healing and reparative justice. The character of Solo is a complex one in the novel, as he is both the integral third member of the nonheteronormative, tender family unit that Persaud portrays as well as a potent means of dispelling the ever present and virulent stereotype of gay male identity as being coterminous with child sexual abuse. The young Solo benefits from a particularly supportive and nurturing adoptive father-son relationship with Mr. Chetan. Despite the loving household that Betty is able to assemble in the wake of her marriage however, Solo's psyche and body reflect the unprocessed trauma of the past. Much of the novel depicts his struggle to reconcile Betty's role as a mother with her status as a woman capable of killing. The self-cutting that Solo engages in is one manifestation of his inability to deal with the upheaval of a conventionally understood social order where a mother can rise up to kill the husband who abuses her and threatens her child and who can embrace her sexuality in the aftermath of her marriage. In the novel, Solo, along with the suggestively named Mr. England (who is looking to make Betty his girlfriend/caregiver) and other figures of religious authority, propagates a debilitating binary between the maternal and the monstrous, the feminine and the frightening.

Solo's inability to reconcile the happy life he knew with the monstrous vision of an "unnatural" mother renders him incapable of accepting her maternal love even while it engenders self-loathing. Self-harm becomes a way of managing his unresolved trauma and strong emotions that cannot be directed at their sources: "I quickly learned to hide the marks. I wish I could explain how it made life easier. Licks shouldn't make you feel peaceful inside but, for me, that's how it was...I've come to accept pain as a second skin covering my whole body" (149, 167). This powerful image of pain creating a new person, a new identity is echoed in Persaud's invocation of the "splitting" deployed by Solo as by many victims of trauma, of separation from the self as a means of survival: "Ever since I started this cutting I avoid mirrors. I don't want to see Solo Ramdin, aka Habib Khan. I hate him" (152).

Unlike in the short stories, where Bowlah and Ramroop depict the direction of violence outward toward abusers, Persaud presents the *erotic* application of physical pain as a way of managing unresolved suffering. Ironically then, violence becomes part of the self-reparative work that is necessary to manage the wounds of the past. In describing his relationship with an immigrant from St. Lucia turned Brooklyn dominatrix, Solo states: "When it's bad the pain inside coils the barbwire tight right through my body. Loretta knows exactly how to cut me loose. The belt swipes my bare bamsee and the noise in my head dies down. ... Each welt on my body has cut the barbwire" (265–6). Loretta's role in this loving application of punishment is part of the novel's distinct landscape of inversion of concepts of love and pain necessary for negotiating the complexities of Trinidadian and Trinidadian diasporic contemporary life. Loretta's role as a substitute mother figure is clear in the text, and her playing it illustrates the multiple temporal spaces which the wounded characters occupy at any one time. Solo's arrival to her apartment is always accompanied by a ritual of a presentation of a birthday cake with precisely five candles—"Can't forget the candles" (263)—to Loretta who pretends to be surprised to receive it and then sings happy birthday to Solo: "I can hear Mammy saying, make a wish" (264). The five candles of course offer a signal of Solo's reversion to a moment in his childhood when he felt safe and loved, but also when he was prematurely burdened by his father's poisonous image of masculinity. The memory of his mother inviting him to make a wish is immediately followed by these lines: "Apparently Daddy used to tell me, Solo boy, you go get married, drink rum, have children, and then dead" (264).

Loretta's erotic use of the belt to beat Solo and to "cut him loose" from such tortured and irresolvable memories is paired with her indulgent manner with him and his desired role-playing. As an alternative mother figure and a mirror for Betty, Loretta balances the safety associated with the maternal role with its sharp-edged nature, potential for danger, and its psychosexual dimensions for the child. Solo's understandings of masculinity are very much tied up with the sexually charged physicality of his encounters with Loretta, the memories of his Janus-faced mother, and the ghostly presence of his father as is evident in this suggestive passage: "I wanted her to see me as a real man, with a little swagger, cool as this fall evening. Instead I opened my mouth and all kind of gibberish fell out. The mirror reflects a skinny Indian, eyes big, big like he's just seen a jumbie" (263). The text does not place heavy emphasis on stereotypes of Indo-Caribbean men as not as "manly" as compared to Afro-Caribbean and white men, but the way in which such narratives permeate a Caribbean landscape and shape the self-perception of young men is clear in this statement. The combination of Loretta's cooing "what a good boy" as Solo enacts the birthday ritual and her subsequent taunting of him with "Take it like a real man" as she whips him before intercourse all suggest the complex temporal positioning that these diasporic Caribbean characters must deploy as they attempt to confront the damage wrought both by personal history and the colonial past. Of vital importance for this imaginary is that the application of violence brings pain to the surface rather than allowing it to be repressed and passed on.[3]

Persaud's text also challenges theologies which can condone and help to support systems of colonial, racial, and gendered exploitation in the region's past and present. Betty recalls the failure of her religious community to acknowledge the suffering she underwent during the period of her marriage: "one time a woman in the church had the nerve to look me straight in my eye and tell me that if your husband doesn't put two good lash on you every now and then, how will you know he loves you" (121)? In addition to its suggestive relationship to the eponymous Derek Walcott poem about self-acceptance, the title, *Love After Love*, can be read in terms of the need to survive the landscape created by such expectations of heterosexual relationships. Persaud also uses the tender relationship that emerges between Betty and Mr. Chetan—first as roommates, then as friends and co-parents—to highlight the other failures of conservative church communities to serve the stigmatized. Mr. Chetan's experience of religion was one where "the leaders of the main churches—Catholics, Muslims, Hindus—were warning the government not to give the LGBTQ population protection under the Equal Opportunity Act ... When Miss Betty asks me why I'm always hiding myself I will remind her that apparently, I am not a child of any god" (258, 259).

While there are examples of creolized religion throughout the text, Persaud presents kali mai worship, its transgression of certain parameters of feminine respectability, and its practitioners' occupation of multiple states of reality at once when "trancing" as the pathway to true healing and self-acceptance for Betty. While scholars such as Stephanie Lou Jackson (2016) have pointed out the limitations of celebratory discourses when it comes to kali mai puja since, in practice, it often includes prescriptions for how women are permitted to participate, in *Love After Love* kali mai is offered as a woman-centered practice that enables Betty to embrace that which is marginalized, to break bonds of respectability, and to allow her wounded body and spirit to travel between past, present, and future in order to approach healing and full self-acceptance. Persaud explicitly ties the imagery of these practices to a kind of rebirth—a reconfiguration of the expectations of the maternal body (deemed unnatural and monstrous by her son) to the needs of self-preservation and surviving a painful past— "They scream and then stop, scream and stop. It didn't sound like pain— more like pushing something out from inside your body" (268).

Betty is at first cautious and surreptitious in her approach to this new form of embodied spiritual practice, aware of the judgments that will ensue from both middle-class Christian communities and conventional Hindu ones: "I could make the Presbyterian church my whole life and nobody would make an objection because that is correct devotion. This other thing's real different, too wild. Nobody must find out if I go to Kali temple" (270). Here, as with the depiction of Solo's journey, imagery of violence is seized and reconfigured as a feature of the essential reparative work that Betty must undergo: "Vibrations from the tassa drums were making my flesh shake. It was like a hammer breaking up all of the loneliness I was carrying" (155).

Betty's exploration of kali mai is synonymous with an acceptance of the powerful, terrifying aspects of womanhood as expressed in Hindu and Indo-Caribbean cosmologies and also an embrace of syncretic religious practices that work against the neat preservation of borders and hierarchies of community identity and respectability. In this way, the text pushes back against the Sita ideal of the faithful, submissive, chaste, long-suffering wife and mother that Sherry-Ann Singh (2012) argues wielded powerful influence on early Indo-Caribbean communities and that affects even non-Hindu Indo-Caribbean women. Drawing upon Singh's work, Aliyah Khan (2020) argues, "Humility and deference to her husband are her ultimate virtues … The Sita ideal of Indo-Caribbean women persisted until at least the 1970s, and it is never entirely absent from discussions of Indo-Caribbean women's public and private behavior that continue to frame the community's self-perceptions at home and abroad" (75). In her embrace of kali mai, Betty literally rejects ever-faithful Sita for celebration of the more terrifying goddess Kali, who has deep roots in Indian tribal folklore and who is usually depicted holding a severed male head in one of her hands, a sword in another, and is known to destroy the evil to protect the innocent. Persaud's novel thereby contains a potent critique of which versions of docile femininity are urged by conventional religious communities and which are bracketed as dangerous and marginalized. Unlike with the diablesse who Gugolati notes is marked by "the complete absence of maternity" (2018, 167), Kali, with a name that in Sanskrit invokes time, doomsday, and death, is associated with the possibility of violent liberation, sexuality, *and* motherly love. We can see Persaud's work as continuing then in the rich tradition that Ivette Romero-Cesareo notes of "Caribbean women writers whose works portray images of both destructive and constructive women/goddesses" (1997, 263).

Betty's embrace and celebration of kali mai involves a foregrounding of the frightening and the unruly aspects of womanhood, of the anti-patriarchal, the fiercely maternal—a harnessing of the monstrous for the purposes of women's liberation:

> Tanty and I made offerings to Mudder—a candle and cherries from my tree. It wasn't so long ago that I was frightened to even look at this murti with her tongue hanging out, all them skulls and blood dripping down. Now I understand that, yes, she is terrifying but that is on purpose. Mudder is the destroyer of evil. She's also a mother and woman. Her foot is on Shiva for women like me to know that we don't have to take shit from no man. At least that is how I understand it. One man in particular is trying to put his foot on me. We go see about that. (271)

The embodied "vibrating" and "trancing" which is part of kali mai worship [the policing of which when practiced by women is laid out in Jackson's work (2016)] is pushed from its latent sexual connotations to explicit articulation in Persaud's literary imaginary:

> I wanted to vibrate, to dance away all the worries I was holding. In that crowded, loud, smoky temple I suddenly felt strong. I let the drumbeat rock me until the energy, the Shakti, was flowing through my veins, warming me from inside, and when it reached my navel it exploded and I jumped up. I closed my eyes. Whatever was going to happen would happen. I surrender. My long hair is loose and the breeze is blowing through it. The white horse

I am riding is going too fast but I hold on. When I swing my cutlass is not just one tree falling. The whole forest just drop down. At the top of the mountain I climb on a man and we fuck until I scream. Mudder lifts me up as if I don't weigh an ounce and in the middle of the sky her bloody tongue licks me and I want to wrap myself around her leg. I pick up the baby and put him inside my dress. A hurricane is coming. (272)

In this potent scene where Betty is imagined as Kali herself, swinging her cleansing weapon, and also as the recipient of the care of a powerful mother figure, we see the transformative power of the storm Betty undergoes and that she herself will become in the social order around her.

Mr. England, who has returned from the diaspora to look for a good Trini woman to care for him in his declining years, is frightened when he comes upon Betty in the grips of this ecstatic worship and self-healing:

Bhadra Kali Kapalini Durga. Betty, you're frightening me. Stop this non-sense now. Stop it. This is black magic. I felt him grab me but Mudder told me to stop being afraid. With him or without him I'm just as alone and lonely. I don't need this blasted man. I bit his arm. What the fuck? You bit me. Why did you do that? I can't believe this is happening. Later, when the spirit had left, I looked around. Mr. England was gone. I don't think he will be back. (280)

As signaled by Persaud not demarcating Mr. England's dialogue from Betty's thoughts, "vibrating" thus operates in the text as a fugue state within which Betty can enact her violent rejection of patriarchal control. Much like Solo's sessions with the dominatrix, Loretta, a new temporal, spatial and bodily reality is entered in order to grapple with that which is too overwhelming in day-to-day life to confront head-on.

The combination of Mr. Chetan's sacrificial death and the embrace of woman-centered kali mai worship results in an opening up of even more widespread challenges to gender norms in the society. The end of the novel sees Betty insisting on carrying Mr. Chetan's coffin to its final resting place and her girlfriends stand with her: "Later they told me how proud they felt because in all the funerals they've been to, up and down Trinidad, this was the first time ever they'd seen two women carrying a coffin" (325). It is important to note that Persaud ends the novel on a note of vengeance, a moment tied up both with a rejection of patriarchal religious authority (who would dictate that only men get to carry a coffin, for example) and narratives of passive acceptance. The character Tanty, who helps Betty along her path to embracing the transgressive and liberatory possibilities of a spiritual life in kali mai, offers a narrative of divine feminine retribution to close the text: "Mr. Chetan suffered so much he's not going to suffer in the next life. And I have no doubt Mudder will punish the demons who did this" (325). Betty herself defiantly opposes the Christian pastor who, at Mr. Chetan's wake, urges forgiveness and attention to Jesus as an example of how to live in the wake of harm at the hand of others: "Man of the cloth or not I threw Reverend's ass out of my house...Fuck forgiveness" (297–8). The text thus reorients away from both Hindu Sita-like and Christian models of passivity and forbearance that aim to preserve respectability within an unjust system that demands the silent acceptance of abuse to an imaginary where women seize upon unsanctioned feminist traditions to reject violently bodily, spiritual, and cultural restraints.

The time- and space-inverting movements and innovations that Bowlah and Ramroop employ in their use of Caribbean folklore, and Persaud in her embrace of the erotic, challenges to heteronormativity, and redeployment of marginalized Indo-Caribbean spiritual practices, emerge as part of a culturally specific Caribbean project of feminist decolonization and mythmaking rich with both the legacies of indentureship and the broader terrain of Caribbean belonging. The work that these authors do to offer liberatory visions of the Caribbean present, ones where optimistically there can be a reckoning with the past, where some kinds of reparative justice or rebirths and renegotiations of gender norms is possible, is part of why the region continues to look to its writers for hope and inspiration even while still in the grip of the haunting tentacles of our painful past.

NOTES

1. For an example of this folktale, please see "Petit Jean et Petite Marie" https://www.potomitan.info/atelier/contes/conte_creole152.php
2. Jane Bryce (2014) argues that the turn to the fantastical has long been a feature of Caribbean writing, although "such writing tended to be less valued in canonical terms than more conventionally realist novels" (8).
3. Persaud shows repression operating in multiple registers in the text. We see repression of cultural knowledge, of more complex facets of motherhood and womanhood, of nonheteronormativity, and of public acknowledgment of women's abuse.

REFERENCES

Anatol, Giselle Liza. 2015. *The Things That Fly in the Night: Female Vampires in Literature of the Circum-Caribbean and African Diaspora*. New Brunswick: Rutgers University Press.

Besson, Gerard. 2012. Mermaids, Imps & Goddesses: The Folklore of Trinidad and Tobago. *First Magazine*: 52–56. https://issuu.com/pariapub/docs/gerard_besson_folklore.

Bissessarsingh, Angelo. 2013. Legend of the La Diablesse. *Trinidad and Tobago Guardian*, October 26. http://www.guardian.co.tt/lifestyle/2013-10-26/legend-la-diablesse

Bowlah, Vashti. 2015. The Churile of Sugarcane Valley. New York: Akashic Books. www.akashicbooks.com/the-churile-of-sugarcane-valley-by-vashti-bowlah/.

Braziel, Jana Evans. 2001. Jamaica Kincaid's 'In the Night': Jablesse, Obeah, and Diasporic Alterrains in *At the Bottom of the River*. *Journal X* 6 (1): 79–104.

Bryce, Jane. 2014. Adventures in Form: 'Outsider' Fiction in the Caribbean. *Journal of West Indian Literature* 22(2) (November): 7–25.

Donnell, Alison. 2022. *Creolized Sexualities: Undoing Heteronormativity in the Literary Imagination of the Anglo-Caribbean*. New Brunswick: Rutgers University Press.

Gugolati, Maica. 2018. *La Djablesse*: Between Martinique, Trinidad (and Tobago), and Its Pan-Caribbean Dimension. *Women, Gender, and Families of Color* 6(2) (October): 151–249.

Jackson, Stephanie Lou. 2016. From Stigma to Shakti: The Politics of Indo-Guyanese Women's Trance and the Transformative Potentials of Ecstatic Goddess Worship in New York City. In *Indo-Caribbean Feminist Thought: Genealogies, Theories, Enactments*, ed. Gabrielle Hosein and Lisa Outar, 301–319. New York: Palgrave Macmillan.

Khan, Aliyah. 2020. *Far from Mecca: Globalizing the Muslim Caribbean*. New Brunswick: Rutgers University Press.

King, Rosamond S. 2014. *Island Bodies: Transgressive Sexualities in the Caribbean Imagination*. Gainesville: University Press of Florida.

Laughlin, Nicholas. 2013. Douen Islands and the Art of Collaboration. *Caribbean Review of Books*. caribbeanreviewofbooks.com/2013/11/04/douen-islands-and-the-art-of collaboration/

Mahabir, Kumar. 2010. *Indian Caribbean Folklore Spirits*. San Juan: Chakra Publishing.

Mohammed, Patricia. 2009. Morality and the Imagination - Mythopoetics of Gender and Culture in the Caribbean: The Trilogy. *Journal of South Asian Diaspora* 1: 63–84.

Persaud, Ingrid. 2020. *Love After Love*. New York: Penguin Random House.

"Petit Jean et Petite Marie." https://www.potomitan.info/atelier/contes/conte_creole152.php

Ramroop, Krystal M. 2020. Midnight's Mischievous Mistress. Brown Geeks. the-browngeeks.com/midnights-mischievous-mistress-a-short-horror-story/. Accessed 25 July 2022.

Romero-Cesareo, Ivette. 1997. Sorcerers, She-Devils, Shipwrecked Women: Writing Religion in French-Caribbean Literature. In *Sacred Possessions: Vodou, Santeria, Obeah, and the Caribbean*, ed. Margarite Fernandez Olmos and Lizabeth Paravisini-Gebert, 248–266. New Brunswick, NJ: Rutgers University Press.

Singh, Sherry-Ann. 2012. *The Ramayana Tradition and Socio-Religious Change in Trinidad, 1917–1990*. Kingston: Ian Randle Publishers.

Ward, Candace. 2012. 'Duppy Know Who Fi Frighten': Laying Ghosts in Jamaican Fiction. In *Transnational Gothic: Literary and Social Exchanges in the Long Nineteenth Century*, ed. Monika Elbert and Bridget M. Marshall, 217–236. Farnham: Ashgate.

Open Access This chapter is licensed under the terms of the Creative Commons Attribution 4.0 International License (http://creativecommons.org/licenses/by/4.0/), which permits use, sharing, adaptation, distribution and reproduction in any medium or format, as long as you give appropriate credit to the original author(s) and the source, provide a link to the Creative Commons licence and indicate if changes were made.

The images or other third party material in this chapter are included in the chapter's Creative Commons licence, unless indicated otherwise in a credit line to the material. If material is not included in the chapter's Creative Commons licence and your intended use is not permitted by statutory regulation or exceeds the permitted use, you will need to obtain permission directly from the copyright holder.

CHAPTER 14

At the Crossroads of History: The Cohabitation of Past and Present in Kettly Mars's *L'Ange du patriarche*

Robert Sapp

In his essay "White Man's Guilt," James Baldwin (1985) asserts that the past is an actively lived experience continually informing our present (410). For Baldwin, confronting this history is particularly difficult for white Americans since, "What they see is a disastrous, continuing, present condition which menaces them, and for which they bear an inescapable responsibility" (409). The ease with which some would slough off a responsibility to the past heightens the danger of such a gesture since the simplicity of the act may have deleterious, though unintended, consequences. While Baldwin's essay addresses the history of racism and white supremacy in the United States, Haitian writer Kettly Mars (2018a) echoes the idea that history lives in the present as an inescapable responsibility in her novel *L'Ange du Patriarche*. As the novel explains: "Le présent n'est que la continuation des actes posés dans un autrefois qui revient frapper à nos portes souvent avec violence" (94) [The present is merely the

---

R. Sapp (✉)
College of Charleston, Charleston, SC, USA
e-mail: sappra@cofc.edu

© The Author(s) 2023
O. Ferly, T. Zimmerman (eds.), *Chronotropics*,
https://doi.org/10.1007/978-3-031-32111-5_14

251

continuation of acts from another time that return to knock on our door, often violently]. For authors like Baldwin and Mars, living in the present means facing up to and being responsible for the past. Exposing the past's empire over the daily lives of contemporary Haitians, Mars's text underlines the potentially tyrannical power of history and the danger of allowing history to serve as a single source of identity. In the novel, Mars turns to face an event in Haiti's past that has taken on mythical proportions: the Bois-Caïman ceremony. This founding event has served both those who vilify and those who glorify the Haitian Revolution. Understanding this event, for Mars, requires an openness to history, a spirit of cohabitation that she elaborates through the development of her protagonist, Emmanuela, as she comes to terms with the actual ghosts of her family's past.

Working within the framework of the Caribbean author's presumed quarrel with history, I propose a reading of *L'Ange du patriarche* in which Mars develops a notion of cohabitation through the figure of Emmanuela as a means of transcending the lost dialectic between inhabitants of the Caribbean and their past. As opposed to other characters, Emmanuela epitomizes a willingness to stand at the crossroads of the empirical and the mythical, the material and the ideal, to be cohabited by seemingly incongruous ideas. Emmanuela seeks to understand the tumultuous impact of a past event, an unfulfilled pact made with an evil spirit by her great-grandfather, on her present life. Her efforts to own up to a responsibility to the past precipitate a burgeoning openness toward what she sees as the contradictory positions of Christianity and Vodou. Depicting Emmanuela as cohabitated by seemingly conflicting ideas allows Mars to explore and transcend the presumed binaries of past and present. Ultimately, the attitude toward history embodied by Emmanuela is one in which the present is imbued with but not dominated by the past.

WRITING NONHISTORY

Edward Baugh's essay "The Western Indian Writer and His Quarrel with History" ([1977] 2012) traces Nobel laureate Derek Walcott's varying engagements with history to understand what Walcott means when he says, "In the Caribbean history is irrelevant" (Walcott cited in Baugh 37). For Baugh, "It is really not history with which he quarrels so much as the way in which men (and in this context West Indians more particularly) have tended to use or abuse history" (73). Walcott (1998) affirms the confluence of past and present on the Caribbean writer: "It is not," he says, "the pressure of the past which torments great poets, but the weight of the present" (40). In response to Baugh's text, Edouard Glissant (1989) describes the sense of "nonhistory" that occurs in the Caribbean. Like Walcott and Baldwin, Glissant understands the importance of the past as an experience lived in the present. He says, "The past, to which we were subjected, which has not yet emerged as history for us, is, however, obsessively present" (63). Yet, despite this obsession, the connection to history remains elusive. According to Glissant, a collective consciousness cannot be formed due to a severed connection between nature and culture: "The French Caribbean people did not relate even a mythical chronology of this land to their knowledge of this country, and so nature and culture have not formed a dialectical whole that informs a people's consciousness" (63). For Glissant, this ruptured dialectic might be restored through fiction: "the writer must contribute to reconstituting its tormented chronology: that is, to reveal the creative energy of a dialectic reestablished between nature and culture in the Caribbean" (65). In *L'Ange du patriarche*, Mars evokes a past that is actively lived in the present in an effort to reestablish the lost dialectic that Glissant observes. In Mars's text, the dialectic takes on many polarities: rich/poor, dream/reality, man/woman, angel/devil, fact/fiction. In this way, the text foregrounds openness to ambivalence. Furthermore, one might read Glissant's polarities as space (the world which one comes into and precedes being) and time (culture: the world in which one takes part). Through the description of Emmanuela's transformation, discussed further below, Mars contracts spacetime to push the discourse beyond binary restrictions of past and present.

Perhaps, Glissant's long-held view of an inaccessible Caribbean history does not apply to Haiti. Martin Munro (2006) suggests that unlike other Caribbean authors, and contrary to the view that the Caribbean is a "historyless" place, Haitian authors reveal a historical consciousness within the Haitian imagination that expresses an abundance of history (23). For Munro, it is the Haitian Revolution that sets Haiti outside of a Glissantian conception of the past and that has exorcised the void left by the Middle Passage (24). Munro explains, "however much modern Haitian fiction tries to exorcize the ghosts of history, it remains 'haunted,' it cannot 'conjure up' a new ontology" (28). In *L'Ange du patriarche*, Mars brings the ghosts of history to the fore.

While both Glissant and Baugh elaborate a pan-Caribbean struggle with the past, Myriam J. A. Chancy's early work brings into focus the engagement with Haitian history by Haitian women. In *Framing Silence: Revolutionary Novels by Haitian Women* (1997), Chancy posits that, rather than depend on the official, hegemonic understanding of Haitian culture to write their narratives, Haitian women writers redefine the writing of history. According to Chancy, these women offer a feminized version of Haitian history where fiction serves as a conduit for historical discourse that either silences women or refuses to tell their story. As she explains, "What Haitian women writers demonstrate is that the project of recovering Haitian women's lives must begin with the re-composition of history and nationality" (13). Indeed, consciously or otherwise, many Haitian women writers have taken up Chancy's call to write against androcentric national histories and uncover the feminine voice in Haiti's past.

And while Mars herself affirms that *L'Ange du patriarche* and the vision of female solidarity it depicts is, among other things, a feminist novel,[1] her approach seems less concerned with uncovering the lost female voices of history[2] or challenging androcentric versions of the past through the redefining of the writing of history that Chancy sees at work in other texts. Instead, as with previous novels (*L'heure hybride*, *Fado* and *Aux frontières de la soif*), in *L'Ange du patriarche*, Mars frames broader questions, in this case the incessant resurgence of the past in the present and the reconciliation of the ancestral in the modern, within the context of struggles and triumphs of daily life in contemporary Port-au-Prince.

Family History

Mars's intrigue offers a reading of contemporary Haitians' lived encounter with history through the lens of the present. The impetus of the narrative is the relentless menace of an evil spirit, L'Ange Yvo, who reclaims an unpaid debt from Emmanuela's family. Horacius Melfort, Emmanuela's great-grandfather and the eponymous patriarch, agrees to sacrifice a child of his own line to L'Ange Yvo in exchange for wealth and political power. Though Horacius does kill a child, it is not from his family; the pact is broken. Consequently, the spirit seeks vengeance on Melfort's family to atone for the blood that was not shed. The story Emmanuela hears about her family from her cousin Paula, affectionately known as Couz, the demon chaser, and the haunting that ensues directly disrupt the order of her life (paintings found askew in her house, the noise of the back gate opening when no one is there, a presence that she can sense).

Initially, Emmanuela does not disregard the story as pure fantasy. Rather, she expresses the frustration of its impact on her life emphasizing the fact that it had nothing to do with her and that she had no hand in the decision. She underscores the distance, not so much the temporal span but the economic gap, that separates her from her great-grandfather saying, "Il a été très riche et très puissant en effet. Mais aujourd'hui il n'en reste plus rien […] Et je devrais payer pour une fortune dont je n'ai pas profité, un pouvoir que je n'ai pas choisi, une décision que je n'ai pas prise?" (Mars 2018a, 52–53) [He had been rich and powerful but today there is nothing left […] And yet I should have to pay for a legacy from which I never gained a penny, a power I did not choose, and a decision I did not make?]. When she asks why she is being punished for a decision that was not her own and why she must atone for the sins of the (great-grand) father, Emmanuela's frustration with this story is understandable since she had no previous knowledge of it and no personal involvement with it. Yet, through the optic of historical materialism, a reading emerges that suggests that even though Emmanuela claims to experience no direct benefit from Melfort's pact with this evil spirit, the wealth acquired by her ancestor is passed from generation to generation and ultimately establishes the material basis for her economic position.[3] The text confirms this both in how the impoverished citizens of Port-au-Prince perceive Emmanuela and how she sees them. Emmanuela's socio-economic status, while far from affluent, sets her beyond the misery of Port-au-Prince. She works as a manager in a branch of Secobank in the Bon Repos neighborhood of Port-au-Prince, owns her own house in a middle-class neighborhood and drives a car to work. In a scene that describes her morning commute, the reader gets a sense of her class status as she attempts to pass through the barricade of burning tires set up by protesters: "Elle avait été flagellée d'injures, traitée de sale putain de bourgeoise, ménacée d'être flambée avec sa sale voiture de sale putain de bourgeoise achetée avec l'argent du peuple" (42) [She had been insulted, called a dirty bourgeois whore, threatened to be burned alive in her bourgeois whore car bought with the people's money]. While driving through the barricade, Emmanuela looks down with pity on the disenfranchised of Port-au-Prince whom she calls: "Ces pauvres gens, ces éternels résignés n'avaient que ces moments d'effervescence politique et la folie du carnaval pour se défouler […] depuis deux siècles qu'on les faisait jouer aux petits soldats des mêmes guerres"(42) [The poor, these eternally resigned who only have these effervescent moments of political turmoil and the madness of the carnival to unwind [...] for two centuries they have been made to play as cannon fodder in the same wars]. Here, in a scene that reflects the frequent protests of present-day Haiti, Emmanuela evokes an oppressive cycle of history that binds these *pauvres gens* to their social class.

Interestingly, though the number is vague (two centuries), Mars makes a point in the previous citation to tie the present misery of the majority of Haitians, not to the slave trade, nor to enslavement, but to the span of time including and following the Haitian revolution. Here and throughout the novel, Mars links the present to Haitian history, to a moment that would come to define Haiti, the first Black Republic, as it was becoming a reality. In this way, she offers an engagement with history that might, as Glissant understands, restore the dialectic between nature and culture. The citation suggests that both Emmanuela and *ces pauvres gens* are bound by the same yoke of history, that indeed the past is "obsessively present" and is lived as a burden.

The family history of a deal with the devil parallels a moment in Haitian history that has taken on mythical status both for those who seek to trace Haiti's current misery to an inauspicious origin and for those whom it is a predominant source of identity: the Bois-Caïman ceremony. Though details of the event itself are hard to corroborate as fact, it is widely held that many enslaved people of St. Domingue met in August of 1791, just before the insurrection, at a plantation between Gallifet and Le Cap for a religious ceremony (Dubois 2004, 30). During this religious ceremony, officiated by Boukman, an early leader of the insurrection, and a woman,[4] a proclamation is made, distinguishing the god of the colonists from the god of the enslaved. Afterward, those in attendance swore an oath of secrecy and vengeance, a pact that was sealed by drinking the blood of a sacrificed black pig.

For scholars like Laurent Dubois (2004) and Colin Dayan (1995), this event underscores the significance of religion in the Haitian Revolution and marks the moment in which Haitian Vodou enters the historical record. As Dayan explains in her seminal study on Vodou in Haitian culture *Haiti, History, and the Gods*, "Vodou enters written history as a weird set piece: the ceremony of Bois-Caïman. The story is retold by nearly every historian, especially those outsiders who enjoyed linking the first successful slave revolt to a gothic scene of blood drinking and abandon" (1995, 29). For example, in the earliest written account of Bois-Caïman (published in 1814), Antoine Dalmas, a former surgeon at the Gallifet plantation who survived and fled to the United States, says: "it was natural for such an ignorant and stupid class to take part in the superstitious rituals of an absurd and bloody religion before taking part in the most horrible of assassinations" (Dalmas in Dubois 2004, 30). So, while for some Bois-Caïman is a source of national pride and religious identity, it has, from the first accounts, served "outsiders" as a source of criticism of the insurgents' cruelty and savagery offering, for some, a justification for enslavement and critique of the revolution. Dayan underscores the underlying contradiction of this event as a source of identity: "what matters is how necessary the story remains to Haitians who continue to construct their identity not only by turning to the revolution of 1791 but by seeking its origins in a service quite possibly imagined by those who disdain it" (29).

It is not haphazard that *L'Ange du patriarche* should be driven by a broken deal with an evil spirit. Emmanuela's own struggle with history parallels the ambivalent rapport with the Bois-Caïman ceremony that Dayan understands. The oblique reference to Bois-Caïman in the pact that her great-grandfather made is further corroborated by the fact that L'Ange Yvo enlists the help of a *lwa* named Marinette *pye chèch*. This particular *lwa* is believed to be the woman who officiated the ceremony with Boukman; it was she who slit the black pig's throat. She is ruthless and unpredictable, a force of both vengeance and liberation. Indeed, twice in the novel female characters, under the power of Marinette, kill someone by slitting the victim's throat. Though Dayan does not directly equate this *lwa* with the woman who sacrificed the black pig, she does underline the ferocity of her feminine force and offers more insight into the revolutionary strength of this *lwa*:

> The feared Marinète-bwa-chèche (Marinète-dry-bones, dry-wood, brittle or skinny arms) said to *mange moun* (eat people) is also called Marinèt-limen-difé (light-the-fire). Served with kerosene, pimiento, and fire, she is the *lwa* who put the fire to the cannons used by Dessalines against the French. Marinèt, with the possible subtext of the French Marianne, as a national image of revolution and republican fervor, also reconstitutes legends of ferocity distinctly associated with black women. (1995, 35)

In the novel, Mars taps into a force that is both liberating and vengeful but insists that it was Marinette who assisted in the Bois-Caïman ceremony. When Couz explains to Emmanuela that Marinette sacrificed the black pig at Bois-Caïman, she also identifies this moment as both the beginning of the Haitian Revolution and, according to the West, the origin of Haiti's misfortunes (Mars 2018a, 97). Couz evokes the ambivalence of this event and, as with Dayan before, the danger of the outsiders' narrative. It is the moment that would set off the revolution and, to some, the source of Haiti's present economic struggles.

Like Couz, two other characters in the novel evoke the danger of drawing identity from a history elaborated by an outsider. Both Patricia (Emmanuela's friend and a vodouisante from Nouailles, an area outside of Port-au-Prince) and Serge (Emmanuela's lover) pick up on the reference to Bois-Caïman upon hearing what afflicts Emmanuela's family, and both, despite their oppositional beliefs, rebuff the claims that Bois-Caïman had anything to do with a spiritual pact.

Though Patricia serves the *lwa* and helps Emmanuela to understand the nature of the spirits afflicting her, she balks at the narrative that depicts that Bois-Caïman as a deal with the devil that ceaselessly condemns Haiti. She says, "Oh, please, Emmanuela! … Je ne crois pas en cette théorie de pacte avec le diable qu'on nous réchauffe à chaque fois qu'un malheur frappe Haïti. Et le pire est que nous aussi nous avons fini par l'intérioriser, cette théorie" (102) [Oh, please, Emmanuela!... I don't believe in this pact with the devil theory that they cook up each time a catastrophe hits Haiti. Worse still, we have internalized this theory]. Here, Patricia highlights the fact that Bois-Caïman is frequently evoked as a source for Haiti's woes and that many Haitians have come to believe this theory. Furthermore, Patricia laments the fact that people are more inclined to believe that the enslaved of St. Domingue were helped to freedom by celestial powers rather than through their own force and a determination of the human spirit. "Beaucoup disent que des esprits démoniaques ont aidé les esclaves à gagner la guerre. Évidemment, c'est plus facile de dire que les démons nous ont aidés que de reconnaître que des femmes et des hommes noirs en esclavage ont gagné cette guerre sauvage" (101 ellipses in original) [Many say that these demonic spirits helped the Enslaved to win the war. Evidently, it is easier to say that demons helped us rather than to recognize that enslaved women and men won this savage war]. Patricia's comment reveals a further misuse of the Bois-Caïman ceremony: not only does it attempt to explain Haiti's current struggle, but it also serves as a denial of the humanity of the enslaved who fought for and won their freedom since it would have been, in the words of Michel-Rolph Trouillot (1990), "unthinkable" that they might be able to conceptualize the notion of freedom let alone to win it without the help of dark celestial powers. Again, that racist vision of Antoine Dalmas, who gives the first written account of Bois-Caïman, comes back as an echo from the past.

The second character to identify and rebuff the Bois-Caïman narrative in Emmanuela's family history is her lover, the stern and severe Serge Destin.[5] Serge counters Emmanuela's story of spirits with a rational, materialist view of history. In fact, in describing their initial meeting, the text emphasizes Serge's interest in Haitian history. She comes to his office as a representative of the bank hoping to interest him, a successful entrepreneur, in new services. While there, she notices volumes by Thomas Madiou, Anténor Firmin, and Placide David on his shelf. These, as opposed to the outsiders like Dalmas, are Haitians writing the history of Haiti. Of particular interest is Firmin, who strongly advocated for the validity of Vodou as a source of Haitian identity, writing against the notion, held by the Haitian elite, that Vodou, and its source in African religions, propagated a negative view of Haiti.

Serge approaches history from a fact-based, rational explanation, citing economic, political, and environmental factors to understand what circumstances contributed to the enslaved people's victory. Knowing this, Emmanuela has put off telling him that a vengeful angel haunts her family due to her great-grandfather's pact. Instinctively, Serge reads the deal with the devil narrative as a joke and offers his own explanation of the circumstances which contributed to the success of the insurrection (112). He cites the rivalry between France, the United States, and England as a big advantage to the enslaved people and their revolt. He also mentions the impact of Yellow Fever on the troops sent by Napoleon to reconquer and re-enslave the Haitians. As he explains, "Ce sont les circonstances qui mènent l'histoire, mon amour. Les circonstances que l'on subit, celles que l'on crée et celles dont on profite. Alors, il vaut mieux les créer et en profiter" (113) [Circumstances make history, my love. The circumstances which one must suffer, those that are created and those from which one profits. Better to create circumstances and gain from them]. Though more feasible than the support of a demonic horde, these circumstances cited by Serge, in their own way, lessen the great sacrifice and determination of the enslaved people's insurrection. In all his examples, he emphasizes outside influences rather than focusing on the internal forces of the Haitian Revolution.

His appreciation for the circumstances of history has allowed Serge to exploit the present. As he says, it is better to create circumstances and

260   R. SAPP

profit from them. His use of the term *subir* in the above citation reveals how these circumstances, while giving an edge to some, disadvantage others. This close reading of Serge's language might seem contrite if the reader were not aware of his penchant for sadomasochism and bondage.

SERGE AND SUBMISSION

Though reserved and austere in public, in the bedroom Serge introduces Emmanuela to sadomasochistic games of submission. Emmanuela's role as a submissive partner, in the bedroom but also at Serge's disposition whenever his schedule allows (she is "the other woman"), reveals an unequal partnership in which the power lies with Serge. Consequently, in explaining to Serge that spirits are influencing her life, Emmanuela asserts her independence. She knows what his reaction will be, yet she does it anyway. Furthermore, she explains that they cannot have intimate relations because she has just completed a *lavé tèt* (vodou spiritual cleansing) and must remain abstinent for the next few days. That she would use Vodou to deny him is the ultimate insult to Serge's rationalism and, for Serge, creates an irreparable schism between the two. Still, in the moment when she asserts her independence, he aggressively tries to regain dominance through a sexual act. Responding to "un impérieux désir de la voir agenouillée devant lui [...] livrée à sa volonté," Serge orders her, "Tu vas te mettre à genoux ... et maintenant" (113–114) [an imperious desire to see her on knees before him [...] subject to his will, Serge orders her, 'You will kneel...right now']. Emmanuela, uncharacteristically, refuses. Discussed in more detail below, this refusal marks a crucial transition in Emmanuela, allowing herself to be cohabitated, to sit at the crossroads of two contradictory ideas.

The text invites a reading of Serge as the incarnation of certain oppressive powers of historical facts or as he might say, circumstances. In submitting to Serge's sexual games, Emmanuela submits to an exclusive vision of history based on recordable, archived facts. This not only limits one's view of history but also reveals the manipulative force of whoever is dominating the narrative.

Reflecting on their relationship, Emmanuela affirms that, while Serge provided material needs, something intangible was lacking (119). Similarly, returning to the Caribbean writers' quarrel with history, Baugh cites Mexican writer Octavio Paz, who suggests that there may be more at play than the circumstances of history. According to Paz, "A historical event is not the sum of its component factors but an indissoluble reality. Historical circumstances explain our character to the extent that our character explains those circumstances. Both are the same. Thus, any purely historical explanation is insufficient...which is not to say it is false" (cited in Baugh 2012, 65). Likewise, Serge and the circumstances of history that he espouses are experienced as rigid, oppressive, and insufficient in the novel. While Serge offers a rational discourse, presumably backed by Haitian historians, the text seems to subvert such an adherence to the facts of history.

Emmanuela's break with Serge marks a crucial moment in her development. Early in the text she is dubious of Couz's claims of a spirit haunting her family. Speaking of Emmanuela, the text says that the irrational unsettles her (Mars 2018a, 94). Confessing her belief in the story, allowing herself to undergo the *lavé tèt* (cleansing), and refusing to submit to Serge, Emmanuela displays an openness to multiple histories, a cohabitation of ambivalence.

Cohabitation: Restoring the Dialectic

What I am calling cohabitation is, simply put, the ability to embrace multiple, conflicting beliefs at once, to embrace ambivalence. Dayan explains how our notion of contradiction expands within the Vodou tradition:

> The history told by these traditions defies our notions of *identity* and *contradiction*. A person or thing can be two or more things simultaneously. A word can be double, two-sided, and duplicitous. In this broadening and multiplying of a word's meaning, repeated in rituals of devotion and vengeance, we begin to see that what becomes more and more vague also becomes more distinct: it may mean *this*, but *that* too (1995, 33)

The novel contains several such instances of cohabitation. For example, Couz believes that the Archangel Michael will save her from the spirits attacking her. Yet, in the moment she knows she is under attack by the spirits, she reaches for a vial of nitroglycerine to save her life since she also knows that she has already undergone three bypass surgeries. If, as Dayan insists, we must set aside our notion of contradiction, then it is possible that both the incantation and the vial of nitroglycerine are essential to saving Couz's life. Believing in both, doubting neither is the refrain of cohabitation that runs throughout Mars's text.

The term "cohabitation" is taken from the text's description of Couz's neighborhood and reflects the juxtaposition of affluence and misery at work in present day Port-au-Prince: "Jalousie est un paysage de troglodytes. Des milliers de cubes en béton au flanc des mornes, avec une ou deux fenêtres en façade et des escaliers abrupts pour y circuler. La rue de Couz est une passerelle entre deux mondes, entre deux univers qui *cohabitent* sans se connaître" (Mars 2018a, 223; emphasis added) [Jalousie is a land of troglodytes. Thousands of concrete cubes line the hillside each with a couple of windows in front and crude stairs to navigate the slum. Couz's street is a gateway between the two worlds, between to universes that co-exist without interacting]. The text offers several such examples: for instance, the character of J-M-B, whose existence mirrors the life of the Haitian-American painter Jean-Michel Basquiat, and his relationship with Vanika in which each oscillates on a spectrum of masculine and feminine (200 and 201). The text is replete with other such examples, but the domain in which this cohabitation seems the strongest is in that of the religious syncretism and the mutability of spirits in the novel. For instance, toward the end of the novel, Vanika, the young woman who is the illegitimate child of Emmanuela's husband and who now seeks vengeance on the family, sees a vision of a *lwa*, *Bouk kabri*, in the stained-glass window of *l'Eglise St. Pierre* in Port-au-Prince. The image in the stained glass is *at once* a flaming bird (symbol of the Holy Spirit in Christian iconography) and *Bouk kabri*, *lwa* of fertility and, in the novel, a promoter of incestuous impulses (266). That Vanika perceives the latter evokes the vulnerability of cohabitation reminiscent of the abuses and misuses of the Bois-Caïman narrative.

The very nature of the haunting that takes place in the novel is emblematic of cohabitation. For instance, the text indicates that L'Ange Yvo is a *zanj* (52). This Kreyòl term may be read as a synonym for *lwa*, the spirits with whom Vodouisants interact, and, as Dayan explains, derives from an internalization of Christian language: "The practitioner [of Vodou] has internalized the language of Christian demonization, taught to him by the priest or pastor in order to wean him from belief, but usually reinforcing the presence of the gods" (1995, 104). Dayan goes on to list other terms that might be used as synonyms for the lwa: "The devotee refers to his lwa not only as angels (*zanj*), mysteries (*mistè*), saints (*sens*), or the invisibles (*envizib*), but also as devils (*djab*). As we have seen, the crossing of languages and terms is very much a part of the transformative and adaptive processes of vodou" (104). This reinforces the notion that, within the context of Vodou, many words can mean a single thing and, conversely, a single word can mean both demon and angel.

However, it would seem the pantheon of *lwa* is not so homogeneous. While Dayan emphasizes the mutability of the term *lwa*, regional difference may occur. As Mimerose Beaubrun (2013) explains in *Nan Domi: An Initiates Journey into Haitian Vodou*, "In the north of Haiti, especially, Vodouisants tend to distinguish between *lwa* and *zanj*" (19). She explains that *lwa* are more malevolent forces people call on for help with money, power, and love. Her explanation of *lwa* in Northern Haiti evokes the pact made by Emmanuela's great-grandfather: "These transactions do tend to involve harm to others, an exercise of force and constraint on the assisting *lwa*, and a resemblance to deals with the Devil as they appear in the Judeo-Christian tradition" (Beaubrun 19). Beaubrun explains that *zanj* have a more benevolent role and occur spontaneously (19). While Beaubrun asserts a distinction between *zanj* and *lwa* that resembles the angel/devil division traditionally associated with Judeo-Christian beliefs, Mars employs the more syncretic vision of spirits that Dayan observes. In fact, it may be that Mars intentionally uses the term *zanj* instead of *lwa* to get away from a "deal with the devil" example that planes over the Bois-Caïman ceremony.

Emmanuela's Transformation

To understand the significance of the rupture with Serge, one must first consider Emmanuela's initial attitude toward spirits. Early on, she disdains the spiritual activity of those close to her making a point to never get involved with Couz's demon-chasing (Mars 2018a, 45). Even as her life is being altered by spirits, she attributes the effects to possibly having Zika (46).

Yet, she cannot deny the changes taking place in her life: "[…] elle a le sentiment d'un déplacement subtil dans l'ordre physique des choses, comme si chaque objet autour d'elle bougeait, se déplaçait ou penchait juste un peu, un centimètre ou deux, lui enlevant le sentiment de sécurité que lui prodigue le fait de savoir chaque chose strictement à la place qu'elle lui a assignée" (43) [[…]She senses a subtle displacement in the physical order of things, as if each object around her were moving, shifting or leaning just a little, a centimeter or two, removing all sense of security she felt from knowing each thing was in its assigned place]. Not knowing that things are in their proper place is what, according to the citation, affects Emmanuela. This initial resistance invokes the rational circumstance of history to which Serge adheres. As the novel progresses, Emmanuela learns to be inhabited by this inability to categorize, an openness to ambiguity, that is cohabitation. Initially, amid characters like Couz and Patricia (adherents to Christianity and Vodou respectively) and, on the other side, Serge (secularism), Emmanuela exists within a dialectic of idealism and materialism. But cohabitation does not mean being at ease with all sides. For Emmanuela, the transition is full of tension. As she explains, while she was raised as a Christian and can cite passages from the Bible, Vodou is a strong part of her as well. Hearing drums from a distant peristyle, she feels at home: "dans une résonance qui lui est naturelle et instinctive" (98) [in a resonance that is natural and instinctive to her]. Yet, her Christian background creates a rift in this cohabitation. She reminds herself that, according to the book of Matthew, one cannot serve both God and Baal (98). For Emmanuela, existing at the crossroads of Vodou and Christianity does not mean embracing them equally but thoroughly questioning both. Even after the rupture with Serge, Emmanuela remains skeptical of the story of demons and *lwa* that Couz tries to tell her: "Elle commence à accepter cette Paula [Couz] qu'elle découvre même si son esprit reçoit ses mots avec encore un certain scepticisme" (141) [She slowly accepts what Paula tells her even though her mind receives the words with a certain skepticism]. As her encounters with spirits become more profound, Emmanuela inhabits a space beyond time, between dream and reality (211). At one point, when confronted by a spirit, Emmanuela slides into what she calls an intermediary space (213).

As the demonic presence in her life grows stronger, Emmanuela's experience of spacetime is altered. After a particularly visceral scene of possession, she loses all sense of time: "Elle ignore combien de temps elle a perdu, combien de temps ils l'ont retenue dans la maison pour tenter de boire son lait, voler sa sève et son âme" (292) [She has no idea how much time has passed, how long they kept her in the house in order to drink her milk, to steal her essence and her soul]. As she opens herself up to Couz's view of spirit, so her perception of spacetime, her awareness of time passing, deteriorates to the point that it becomes illusory. The disruption of spacetime, caused by possession that Emmanuela experiences late in the novel, mirrors an earlier scene in which Couz is simultaneously having a heart attack and under attack by evil spirits. Lying on the floor of her house, she asks, "Combien de temps s'est-il écoulé depuis qu'elle est tombée? Trois minutes, quatre, cinq peut-être. Une éternité" (39) [How much time had passed since she fell? Three minutes, four, five perhaps. An eternity]. Now, it would seem, Emmanuela has attained an openness to spirits that Couz previously embodied. In both instances, the proximity to spirits (both women are under attack by L'Ange Yvo) provokes an alteration in the perception of spacetime in which the borders of past and present are porous, if not altogether absent. Interestingly, for Emmanuela this contraction of spacetime only serves to heighten her awareness of its impact on her life: "Chaque seconde, chaque minute qui passe trace leur histoire avec le fil d'un rasoir, un rasoir qui peut les saigner à mort ou bien détacher de leurs corps la gangrène du passé, elle en est persuadée" (299) [Each second, each minute that passes traces their story like a razor's edge, a razor that can bleed them to death or expunge from their bodies the gangrenous past, of that she is sure]. As she embraces the idea of spirits from the past influencing her present, she becomes acutely aware of each moment's significance for her future. This cohabitation of contradictions and contraction of spacetime occurs not only as Emmanuela alters her stance toward history. In the last scene, Emmanuela, in full conversion as she prepares to take on the role Couz has left vacant, speaks to Patricia evoking the nature of cohabitation in the novel. She tells Patricia that she will enter Couz's sanctuary, the representation of the church in Jerusalem she had built in her basement, to which Patricia says: "Ginen yo avè w" (303), which roughly translates, "the *lwa* and those who serve the *lwa* are with you."[6] The idea that, as she enters this place that for Couz, a practicing Christian, was sacred, she carries with her the supernatural realm of the *lwa* is emblematic of the cohabitation that Emmanuela represents. Even at the apotheosis of her transformation, Emmanuela is at the crossroads.

GUARDING THE MYSTERY

Kettly Mars understands the power of the past. Yet, *L'Ange du patriarche* is squarely situated in the present. Like James Baldwin, she recognizes that the history we make in the present is just as important as the history that we allow to define us. Insisting on the present as a lens through which to see the past, not tracing spirits directly back to an African ancestor,[7] but binding them to present-day Haiti in time and space, Mars envisions a means of transcending the ruptured dialectic of nature and culture that Glissant describes.

Furthermore, the same vengeful spirit is not limited to Haiti, but reaches family living in Chicago. Under possession of the *lwa* Marinette *pye chèch*, Couz's granddaughter, Samantha, kills her own twin sister, cutting her throat like the black pig at the Bois-Caiman ceremony. The fact that Couz senses the death before hearing about it offers a depiction of the Haitian Diaspora in which space and time are contracted. Neither the distance in time nor space can protect family members from the vengeful spirit of L'Ange Yvo. Using spirits, Mars conceives of the diaspora as an extension of the homeland that, despite distance in time and space, continues to haunt those who left. Through the character of Emmanuela, existing at the crossroads of past and present, Mars offers a means by which Haitians today might learn to live with the ghosts of the past: a skeptical acceptance of events like the Bois-Caiman ceremony that individuals may simultaneously doubt and accept as truth.

Reading Emmanuela at the crossroads of the mythical and the empirical offers a sharp contrast to the character of Serge, whose adherence to the provable facts of history and penchant for sexual domination offer a critique of a certain, oppressive, androcentric vision of history (all the historians Serge reads are men) that, as Myriam Chancy has observed, silences women. Citing the pioneering work of Dayan and more recent work by Karen Richman, Mimrose Beaubrun, and Karen McCarthy Brown, who foreground the role of women in the formation of Haitian society and history, Laurent Dubois (2016) affirms that "to write the history and anthropology of Haiti is necessarily to write a woman's history" (2016, 88).

Likewise, Mars foregrounds the role of women in Haitian history, shifting the emphasis of Bois-Caïman from Boukman to the lesser-known woman said to have assisted at the ritual. She names her and renders her so ferocious that at least two characters are murdered by individuals under her control. But also, through the figure of Emmanuela, Mars offers a praxis through which one might overcome the dominant imposition of history that Serge represents. Likewise, the eponymous patriarchal angel underscores the oppressive, inescapable aspect of history against which Emmanuela positions herself. Cohabitation, for Emmanuela, means resistance. Through the figure of Emmanuela and other examples of cohabitation, the text allows the dialectic to retain the tension of its ambivalence, maintaining the mystery. This is epitomized in the novel's conclusion.

From the beginning, Couz has told Emmanuela that to stop L'Ange Yvo she must recover a lost message from the Archangel Michael. Finally, in a dispatch from beyond the grave, Couz recovers the lost text and transmits it to Emmanuela. Yet, this message, the only force that can stand up to the evil spirits, is withheld from the reader. In guarding the mystery, Mars leaves the story, much like the understanding of the Bois-Caïman ceremony, beyond the finality of history. Ending the novel in this way,

14 AT THE CROSSROADS OF HISTORY: THE COHABITATION... 267

intentionally withholding the message that the reader craves, may be read as Emmanuela's own approach to history, an equal appreciation for what is known and what is unknown, what is provable and what is speculative. Like Emmanuela, Mars is comfortable guarding the mystery.

NOTES

1. "C'est aussi un roman féministe, qui parle de trois femmes, de leur complicité pour se donner de la force dans une épreuve" (Le Point January 26, 2018) [It is also a feminist novel that disucusses three women and their complicity in strengthening each other during a crisis]*; all translation are my own.
2. For a more thorough discussion of uncovering silenced voices from the past in contemporary Haitian authors Marie-Célie Agnant and Yanick Lahens, see Sapp (2019).
3. Marx writes in The German Ideology, "History is nothing but the succession of the separate generations, each of which exploits the materials [...] handed down to it by all preceding generations, and thus on the one hand, continues the traditional activity in completely changed circumstances and, on the other hand, modifies the old circumstances with a completely changed activity" (in Tucker 1989, 172).
4. "Various accounts describe him officiating alongside an old African woman 'with strange eyes and bristling hair' or else a green-eyed woman of African and Corsican descent named Cécile Fatiman" (Dubois 29–30).
5. Ironically, despite his materialist reading of the circumstances of history, Serge's family name, Destin, suggests a fatalistic view of the future.
6. Further examination of the term Ginen reveals the mutable aspect of certain terms understood by Vodouisants that Dayan originally cites (1995, 33). The term itself derives from the French word for Guinée, which, in the seventeenth century, referred to the coastal region of Africa from where many men, women, and children were taken to be enslaved in St. Domingue. Yet, for a vodouisant it also refers the underwater realm of the spirits (the *lwas* as well as the souls of those who have died). So, *Ginen* evokes at once, the severed past with continental Africa, a present engagement with spirits of the dead, and the hope of reconciliation in a future where souls reside. It may refer to this realm but also to a single Vodouisant. The term *fran ginen*, for example, refers to a "Vodouisant pratiquant dans la tradition familiale et rejetant la sorcellerie" (Mars 2018a 50n2).
7. Here, Mars distinguishes herself from the works of other contemporary Haitian women authors. Consider, for example, Lahens's *Bain de Lune* and Agnant's *Le Livre d'Emma* in which a direct lineage with an African ancestor is established.

REFERENCES

Baldwin, James. 1985. "White Man's Guilt." *The Price of the Ticket: Collected Non-fiction 1948–1985*, New York: St. Martin's Press, pp. 409–414.

Chancy, Myriam J.A. 1997. *Framing Silence: Revolutionary Novels by Haitian women*. New Brunswick: Rutgers UP.

Baugh, Edward. 2012. The West Indian Writer and His Quarrel with History. *Small Axe* 38: 60–74.

Beaubrun, Mimerose. 2013. *Nan Domi: An Initiates Journey into Haitian Vodou*. Trans. D.J. Walker, San Francisco: City Light Books.

Dayan, Colin. 1995. *Haiti, History and the Gods*. Berkeley: University of California Press.

Dubois, Laurent. 2004. *Avengers of the New World: The Story of the Haitian Revolution*. Cambridge: Harvard University Press.

———. 2016. Haiti, Gender and Anthrohistory: A Mintzian Journey. In *The Haiti Exception: Anthropology and the Predicament of Narrative*, ed. Alessandra Benedicty-Kokken et al., 74–90. Liverpool: Liverpool University Press.

Glissant, Edouard. 1989. *Caribbean Discourse: Selected Essays*, Trans. J. Michael Dash, Charlottesville: University of Virginia Press.

Mars, Kettly. 2018a. *L'Ange du patriarche*. Paris: Mercure de France.

———. 2018b. *Interviewed by Valérie Marin La Meslée. "Je me suis fait peur en écrivant ce roman"* Le Point, 26 January. www.lepoint.fr/culture/kettly-mars-je-me-suis-fait-peur-en-ecrivant-ce-roman-26-01-2018-2189988_3.php. Accessed 19 August 2020.

Munro, Martin. 2006. Petrifying Myths: Lack and Excess in Caribbean and Haitian History. In *Reinterpreting the Haitian Revolution and Its Cultural Aftershocks*, ed. Martin Munro and Elizabeth Walcott-Hackshaw, 20–37. Kingston: University of West Indies Press.

Sapp, Robert. 2019. Hearing Haunted Voices: Voicing the Past in Contemporary Haitian Fiction. *Women in French Studies* 8: 225–235.

Tucker, Robert C. 1989. *The Marx-Engels Reader*. Norton & Company Incorporated.

Trouillot, Michel-Rolph. 1990. The Odd and the Ordinary: Haiti, the Caribbean and the World. *Cimarron* 2: 3–12.

Walcott, Derek. 1998. *What the Twilight Says: Essays*. New York: Farrar, Straus and Giroux.

Open Access This chapter is licensed under the terms of the Creative Commons Attribution 4.0 International License (http://creativecommons.org/licenses/by/4.0/), which permits use, sharing, adaptation, distribution and reproduction in any medium or format, as long as you give appropriate credit to the original author(s) and the source, provide a link to the Creative Commons licence and indicate if changes were made.

The images or other third party material in this chapter are included in the chapter's Creative Commons licence, unless indicated otherwise in a credit line to the material. If material is not included in the chapter's Creative Commons licence and your intended use is not permitted by statutory regulation or exceeds the permitted use, you will need to obtain permission directly from the copyright holder.

CHAPTER 15

Fiction as a Spider's Web? Ananse and Gender in Karen Lord's Speculative Folktale *Redemption in Indigo*

Tegan Zimmerman

While it is true that trickster figures pervade her fantastical tale, the true trickster in *Redemption in Indigo* (2010) is Barbadian storyteller Karen Lord. Substantiating that which Pascale de Souza calls "African continuities" with the New World (2003, 341), Lord's debut and award-winning speculative novel *Redemption in Indigo* skillfully merges familiar folk gods and hero(ines) from different African traditions, for example Akan, Ashanti, Xhosa, and Karamba. Ananse, the spider-trickster and African god of stories, and Ananse texts such as "The Gluttonous Ansige" (1996) are particular concentrations. This chapter argues, however, that *Redemption* challenges masculinist versions of Ananse and traditionally male-dominated Anansesem; Lord's antipatriarchal, anticolonial Ananse story by contrast employs a feminocentric web paradigm of concentric patterns, interweaving the past with the present, the ancestral African homeland with the Caribbean diaspora, to foreground feminine qualities

---

T. Zimmerman (✉)
Saint Mary's University, Halifax, NS, Canada
e-mail: tegan.zimmerman@smu.ca

© The Author(s) 2023
O. Ferly, T. Zimmerman (eds.), *Chronotropics*,
https://doi.org/10.1007/978-3-031-32111-5_15

271

and empowered female figures—the nonbinary storyteller, the heroine Paama, and the Indigenous goddess/djombi Atabey.

Though literary scholar Bibi Burger (2020) rightly suggests that African folktales and contemporary science fiction, Afrofuturism, and Africanfuturism (2) all fall under the rubric of speculative fiction, here I use the somewhat tautological term "speculative folktale" to better encapsulate the specific anticolonial, antipatriarchal vision of Lord's Caribbean text.[1] In the Foreword to her edited anthology, *New Worlds, Old Ways: Speculative Tales from the Caribbean* (2016), Lord indicates that Eurocentric definitions of speculative fiction problematically often overlook Caribbean literary "icons," like Erna Brodber and Nalo Hopkinson, despite the "richness of folklore, myth, parable and satire" found within their works (1). Scholar Linden Lewis (1990) likewise signals the political value of Caribbean folktales because they reveal the "ideological tricks" of conventional Western society, which erroneously claims "universality" and hegemonic status as "the official culture's concepts of the world of life" in the region (Lombardi-Satriani as qtd by Lewis 1990, 86). Texts like that of Lord's therefore productively expand the canon of speculative fiction while "transform[ing] ideas about what is considered valid knowledge" (Onoura 2015, 11) and laying claim to an alternative literary lineage, grounded primarily in Caribbean women's writing. In recognizing the folktale as "resistant to any subordination by the culture of the mainstream" (Lewis 1990, 85) and as an important vehicle for combatting colonialism and patriarchy, Lord's *Redemption* uses familiar genre features like "'supernatural, fantastical, or futuristic elements'…[to] wonder about the future, the present, and the past, as well as the not-quite-real or-realised" (Burger 2020, 2) in relation to women's lives. Specifically reworking the traditional Ananse folktales, Lord's text speculates on a feminocentric future, an as yet to come, that might have been.

At the same time, Lord's speculative folktale draws on earlier Caribbean women's writing utilizing the framework of the web to convey the complexity of spacetime and women's identities—especially the relation between enslaved foremothers and their female descendants, for example Simone Schwarz-Bart's *Pluie et vent sur Télumée Miracle* (1972/2015) and Paule Marshall's *Praisesong for the Window* (1983).[2] A web is not linear, rhizomatic, or chaotic (three male-dominated theories of chronotopes in the region, e.g. Garvey, Glissant, and Benítez-Rojo, respectively) but rather an impermanent organic silk structure, which as Kathleen Gyssels suggests is a more "feminine paradigm" (2002, 178).[3] Studying

Schwarz-Bart's and Marshall's aforementioned novels, Gyssels (2002) confirms that "the thread and the canvas of Anancy … signify the need to constantly weave and reweave the Caribbean identity" (178). Like Lord, these Caribbean authors revitalize "the myth of Anancy," (178) and "elect the horizontality and lateral and concentric character of the spider's web" (178) to inform their gender-inflected narratives. *Redemption*'s femino-centric web approach therefore also moves away from privileging traditional masculinist notions of singularity, individualism, and linearity to emphasize multiplicity, reciprocity, and interconnectedness, for connection is necessary for the "survival of the individual, the family, the community, the nation, the region, and the world or worlds that we inhabit. Survival is more than mere living. We need to relate: to connect, to identify, to tell our stories, to draw lines from past to present and from each to each," argues Lord (2016, 2). Lord's speculative folktale, interwoven with several tale-tellers and simultaneously occurring plotlines, envisions a socially just and sustainable future from empowered women's perspectives.

Redemption's gendered approach is of course informed by the traditional spidery folk-teller Ananse—a simultaneous "hero, object of hatred, and scapegoat," he is often "selfish, mean, hypocritical, vulgar, and sexually exuberant," though he "helps focus attention on the nature and limits of the taboos he breaks, thus creatively regenerating them" ("Ananse" 2008, 84)—and the traditional African story, "Ansige the Glutton." In this folktale, Paama, a chef-par-excellence, leaves Ansige, the eponymous gluttonous husband. After Ansige orders his servants to retrieve his wife, she quips: "don't act as though I didn't know you [Ansige]" ("The Gluttonous Ansige" 1996, 85). The text leaves a woman at a significant crossroads: whether or not to leave her domineering husband. Does Paama obey Ansige's order to return home? The story concludes ambiguously, or rather ambivalently, thereby allowing the writer to seize the opportunity to reimagine the heroine's life anew.

Accordingly, Lord adds a fantastical, supernatural storyline that foregrounds Paama's post-Ansige life in a fictive Caribbean setting. In Lord's alternative version, Paama encounters several djombis—Caribbean folkloric spirits unbeholden to space and time (e.g., Trickster, Taran, and Atabey)—and even comes to experience some of their power, before remarrying a tracker named Kwame (who is not a character in the original tale) and giving birth to twin sons (Yao and Ajit). The ingenuity of Lord's text thus lies, in part, in its critique of Ananse's worst qualities (violence,

274 T. ZIMMERMAN

selfishness, greed, arrogance, and anti-social) as distinctly hypermasculine, evidenced by their correlation to male characters such as Ansige and Taran. Meanwhile, feminine characteristics (reciprocity, care, generosity, forgiveness, and communality), associated primarily with Paama, are privileged for their ability to transform phallocentric characters and to act as catalysts for social change. The respinning of Ananse folklore functions as a distinct antipatriarchal, Afra-Caribbean storytelling strategy in this postcolonial speculative folktale.

THE AFRICAN FOLKTALE IN THE CARIBBEAN

Lord's novel joins an increasing number of contemporary texts offering antipatriarchal and anticolonial interpretations of Anansesem by Caribbean and African thinkers. Similar to Benjamin Kwakye's Ghanaian novel, *The Clothes of Nakedness* (1998), for instance, Lord's "art...goes beyond the intertextual incorporation of oral forms into...[her] novel and the appropriation of the structure of the African folktale...to re-enact the folkloric trickster as a metaphor of the web of social complexities in [a] postcolonial" setting, for example the Caribbean (Mwinlaaru and Nkansah 2018, 251). *Redemption* reminds us that in the late twentieth century in countries such as Ghana, Ananse not only regained importance "when the national policy of recovering traditional cultures led many... to include African culture in their" works ("Ananse" 2008, 84), but also "the disillusionment of the following historical phase" which used Ananse to symbolize a consumptive greed that undermined "the ideals of independence" ("Ananse" 2008, 84); this strengthens my reading of Ansige as a dangerous version of Ananse; he functions as a warning sign for when insatiability, masculinity, and individuality spirals out of control. Linking Ananse, literature, and consumption/corruption relates directly back to Lord's Caribbean retelling of "Ansige the Glutton" and *Redemption*'s explicit inclusion of feminine qualities, epitomized by Paama, as necessary to achieving social justice in the region.

While African tales describe both storytellers as male and Ananse as a male trickster deity (Mwinlaaru and Nkansah 2018, 265; de Souza 2003, 344), New World depictions, such as Lord's, play with the slipperiness of gender.[4] For example, in his collection *Mother Poem*, fellow Barbadian poet, Kamau Brathwaite, "identifies the mother figure with Ananse" (Mackey 2018, 45); likewise, Caribbean critic Adwoa Onoura (2015) stresses the importance of mothers as tale-tellers. In *Anansesem: Telling*

Stories and Storytelling African Maternal Pedagogies, Onoura highlights that though "Anancy stories are part of the historical memory of formerly enslaved Africans brought to the 'new world,'" they rely on a skilled teller like Jamaican folklorist Louise-Bennett Coverly to transmit their living energy (4). Reading this chronotope through a gendered lens, Onoura argues that Caribbean accounts of Ananse's crossing should be considered "as motherline stories to the extent that they allow the African child to tap into his/her African ancestral memory" (23). Onoura therefore hopes that her own daughter will "locate herself firmly within this motherline of storytellers and storytelling so that later she will, in learning about the herstory of Africans crossing the Atlantic, develop a sense of self and connectedness to her African identity" (23). *Redemption's* metafictional web-like narrative taps into the power of (re)telling Ananse stories that Onoura identifies while reimagining the traditional African folktales through an antipatriarchal lens and challenging male-dominated scholarship on African-Caribbean storytelling and folktales.

Accordingly, the novel begins with the asynchronistic, nonbinary Ananse narrator preparing the reader for a novel that will indeed break the rules, challenge masculine authority, and defy conventional literary expectations. The narrator announces, "A rival of mine once complained that my stories begin awkwardly and end untidily. ... All my tales are true, drawn from life, and a life story is not a tidy thing" (Lord 2010, 1). This statement directly contradicts African folk scholar Christopher Vecsey's claims that "Before the narrator begins his tale, he will say that the story is not true" (1981, 162) and "All Anansesem, whether they deal with Ananse or not, are considered to be untrue stories" (1981, 162). Three important points should be noted: first, Lord's narrator is never designated as a "he"; second, the narrator does not, as per the masculine tradition, absolve themself from responsibility for the text but rather implicates themself in constructing a narrative that, like life, is organic, complex, and weblike. Third, the narrator alludes indirectly to the original Karamba folktale of "Ansige the Glutton," which in fact ends rather untidily.

The nonbinary Ananse narrator's controversial and confrontational nature likewise suggests the suitability of the speculative folktale as the foundation of a contemporary anticolonial, Caribbean work that rejects the plot conventions of the novel, a literary form often claimed to have Western origins. As "an unpredictable liar who throws doubt on the concept of truth itself" (Vecsey 1981, 161), however, the Ananse narrator's ability to subvert or expose seemingly immutable categories like gender

276   T. ZIMMERMAN

proves invaluable. For in casting doubt on truth, the narrator, as do other radical Ananse figures like Paama, evidences that not only the traditional Anansesem but also patriarchal, colonial culture are fabrications designed to privilege maleness and/or Europeanness, and thus are subject to change. For instance, Lord's narrator claims to have included an Epilogue to "round off the story according to my own rules" (2010, 182). The narrator declares the power of their voice to not simply regurgitate the old tales but meaningfully transform them. The narrator's pen/spinneret therefore takes the original text(s) not as being static or linear (masculine, Western) but as fluid and reticular (feminine, Caribbean); hence, Anansesem must be rewritten or rewoven to better express the lives and voices of marginalized communities.

Lord's self-aware narrator further alerts one to the social construction of texts *and* genders. An historical link between women and textile arts concretizes the feminine-spider-web metaphor: "Weaving threads, embroidering or sewing quilts was a household occupation in which women ... put all their soul and all their ingenuity. The collection of small pieces, rags and tangled threads that constitute the patchwork metaphorizes the female artist-maroon," writes Gyssels (2002, 178). These materials became an important mode for expressing knowledge and life experiences. Caribbean women have recrafted their artwork, like maroons, like Ananse, to subvert the phallocentric plantocracy in covert ways. Twenty-first-century Caribbean women writers, such as Lord, echo this undervalued textual work through reviving various pieces from different folk mediums as the narratological fabrics of their novels.

One of the most striking features of African-Caribbean storytelling methods that Lord adopts for antipatriarchal purposes, however, is the role of the Ananse narrator as an active participant in the telling. Contrary to the Western intellectual tradition, which has privileged disembodied masculine individualism or the omniscient third-person narrator, in *Redemption* there is a real sense of embodiment and collective solidarity. *Redemption*'s nonbinary narrator also manifests as the singular (I) in the plural (Ananses): "i is spiders weaving/away" (Brathwaite 1977, 99). The spider is in their own web, not outside of it; there is no outside of the text/web/world, so to speak. De Souza (2003) confirms that "as a masterful trickster," and "[d]weller at the crossroads, inhabitant of nooks and crannies, Anancy is never in a specific enclosure yet never out" (340). Forgoing a typical linear metanarrative or master narrative, the reader, as if she were caught in the narrator's "web of probabilities" (Lord 2010,

131), experiences the novel as an untangling of fragments or threads. In weaving a tangential tale, the teller, however, buttresses their position as an anticolonial Ananse, a spidery figure who embraces sexual-textual, as well as spatiotemporal, liminality.

The teller's adoption of Ananse-like narratological indeterminacy as an anticolonial strategy is demonstrated again in these lines: "While Kwame is sniffing out the trail of Ansige's wife, let us run ahead and meet her for ourselves" (Lord 2010, 3), and "I can hear some of you complaining already" (2010, 6). The narration shifts between subject/singular and object/plural pronouns (I and us) and first- and second-person pronouns (I and you). Such comingling instills both a false sense of readerly control or choice over the tale and a sense of readerly helplessness that draws from Ananse's paradoxical qualities as potential perpetrator and victim. Likewise, that the Ananse-narrator's playful interjections and indirections throughout the novel routinely ensnare the reader into the telling make the reader an accomplice trickster figure-teller. This approach mimics the style of African-Caribbean folktales in which a binary between I/you, teller/listener, subject/object is nonsensical (Pelton 1989, 21). Referencing the Akan tradition, Vecsey (1981) also notes, "Before there is 'I' there is 'we.' In short, the Akan person derives his identity from his people; without them he does not exist, he has no reality, no being, no meaning" (165). The implication for Lord's text is that the presence of African folktales and figures, the "we" precedes and serves as a foundation for her Caribbean narrator. She also ontologically grounds her teller's "I" as not only a "he" but also a "she or they" to recognize other genders, and thus productively expands the lexicon of tale-tellers.

Lord's approach to gender inclusivity dialogues with the region's storytelling tradition, in which fluidity is not only encouraged but so too is "embroidering on the part of the teller" (Lewis 1990, 86)—that nook and cranny of the imagination where "spiders make patterns in her mind" (Brathwaite 1977, 25). Such a veritable "weaving of voices" (Gyssels 2002, 178) is demonstrated again by the narrator's use of antiphony, an African and Caribbean call-and-response storytelling technique/pattern historically linked with resisting slavery (de Souza 2003, 345). For example, *Redemption*'s narrator asks themself and then replies, "Do I have more stories to tell? There are always more stories" (Lord 2010, 181). Antiphony functions as an antipatriarchal narrative strategy because the updated Paama and Ananse stories speak back to their African-Caribbean folkloric roots and to the European colonialism, which attempted to

278 T. ZIMMERMAN

suppress and cut those ties. The outer-layers of the narrative-web thus symbolize the historical (dis)placement of African stories to the Caribbean diaspora and Lord's attempt, via polyphonic and antiphonic feminocentrism, to reinvent those folktales for a contemporary audience committed to social equity.

THE WESTERN ASSAULT ON THE FOLKTALE

To this extent, *Redemption* suggests that Western epistemologies of science and secularism (history) are problematically replacing or converging with beliefs in the Afro-Caribbean pantheon and its folk heroes/heroines, including Ananse and Paama. For example, the teller asserts:

> Once upon a time—but whether a time that was, or a time that is, or a time that is to come, I may not tell—there was a man, a tracker by occupation called Kwame. He had been born in a certain country in a certain year when history had reached that grey twilight in which fables of true love, the power of princes, and deeds of honour are told only to children. (Lord 2010, 1)

Lord's revising of Ananse stories within an indeterminate spacetime therefore directly pushes back against de Souza's claim that unlike European tales "African and Afro-American tales did not take place 'once upon a time' but rather unravel here and now with an ongoing call for response ... to ensure full audience participation" (2003, 345). The lack of audience engagement in this time and place, however, is markedly present when Kwame, who internalizes a denigration of his Afro-Caribbean heritage, dismisses so-called Anansesem as nothing but figments of the imagination.

Prior to setting out on his quest to retrieve Paama for Ansige, Kwame comments to himself: "*Fairy tales and nancy stories*" (Lord 2010, 1). Lewis (1990) explains that in Barbados, folk culture nowadays causes some to "become embarrassed by [it], because of its unpretentiousness. Folk culture is the culture of the common people, the unlettered and unsung people" (85). The novel thus implicitly critiques contemporary Caribbean thought (when echoing a Western treatment of time and space as separate dimensions), in which such stories are no longer believed or recited: an occurrence directly linked with the history of exploitation—slavery-colonialism-imperialism—in the region. As scholars note, Ananse metamorphosized when he came to the Caribbean via the Middle Passage:

"In the ruthless context of Caribbean plantations, Ananse sheds his god-like qualities and acquires more earthly features. His subtle cunning, the art of the weak, is used not only to ensure sheer survival, but also to deceive and overthrow the powerful" ("Ananse" 2008, 84). If in the African tradition Ananse tested and mocked but never dissolved the social order, then in the Caribbean he directly confronts oppression and seeks to overthrow plantation society (Maiser 2014, 31). Ananse's historical association with resisting slavery through cunning and wisdom, in the Caribbean context, further marks him as a dangerous figure and explains his value to a twenty-first-century writer like Lord. Lord's revival of the trickster-maroon-embroiderer as her anonymous, nonbinary narrator is therefore particularly fitting for an anticolonial, antipatriarchal novel. *Redemption* suggests that turning toward Ananse's lesser-valued feminine qualities, in addition to his variance, trickery, and indeterminacy, offers a path to confront the West's legacy of destruction including its hegemonic literatures and languages.

While slavery and colonialism attempted to eradicate and condemn alternative epistemologies and cosmologies, for example African stories like "The Gluttonous Ansige" (1996) or "The Story of the Glutton" (1886)—who, when transposed to a Caribbean setting, might be read as an allegory for greedy, insatiable European slavers/colonizers—analyzing the role of patriarchy reveals a nuanced attempt to specifically silence women's knowledges and voices. The metaphor of the narrator as either a skillful mother or a nonbinary spider spinning an elaborate new narrative/web/world further strategically undermines the more familiar androcentric master narratives—both African (traditional folktales) and European (historiography), found in the region. Lewis elaborates:

> The Barbadian male has, for sometime now, acquired a reputation for craftiness ... Though this behaviour has more to do with Barbadian thriftiness than stealth, the identification of the male as a "smart man" is widely accepted in Caribbean circles. The phenomenon of the clever male is not a characteristic unique to Barbadian men. Each Caribbean island has within its lore a male "smart man" or a "con artist" around which several folk tales are developed. In a sense these add to the store of patriarchal myths and myth making which soothes the collective male ego of the region and offers the illusion of men taking charge of their own affairs. (1990, 87)

Lord's spiderlike-narrator challenges these hypermasculine conceptions of identity by drawing on and updating African-Caribbean storytelling methods. *Redemption* relies on an African and Caribbean oral tradition, both folktales of the Gluttonous Ansige, and ones featuring Ananse, to not only undermine Western storytelling (e.g., masculine, chronological, progress, and teleological) but also centralize the smart woman and subvert the Caribbean's traditional/cultural canon from a gendered perspective.

Spring-boarding off the Ansige and Ananse tales allows Lord to explore new possibilities for Caribbean gender dynamics. This explains the narrator's preemptive interjection to imagined criticisms that her character Paama may not fulfil certain readerly expectations. One assumes that these comments are directed toward white Western feminists' problematic tendency to universalize women and claim to be the dominant referent for which all women, including those in the Caribbean and in Africa, should be compared. For example, Lord writes: "Paama will be too tepid and mild a heroine for some, they will criticize her for dutifully caring for her estranged husband in his last days" (2010, 181). Paama emphasizes the power of maternal qualities for the good of humanity, the many as opposed to the one, rather than reinforcing allegedly stereotypical female behavior such as sacrifice and selflessness. Likewise, Paama's kindness rejects a definition of the stereotypical, individualistic male hero who forgoes his path alone. *Redemption*'s African-Caribbean folk heroine shows compassion toward others, even those who have wronged her. Paama's communing with and dependence on others is essential to her survival and is depicted as a moral strength and social good. Onoura argues that if African and Caribbean women or girls can "uncover [the] key survival tools and strategies used by their female ancestors" like Paama, then they can use those models to help them "navigate issues such as racism, classism and sexism" (2015, 22–23) in a contemporary context.

That Paama initially finds herself trapped in a marriage/web drives the novel's plot and its insistence that toxic masculinity must be subverted. Consider the claim that the Ananse trickster figure can be duped: "his portrayal as a gullible glutton whose insatiable desire for food and meat blocks his sense of judgment and this gluttony leads him to become the victim of another trickster" (Mwinlaaru and Nkansah 2018, 251). Gluttony, as de Souza's (2003) research shows, connects with the enforced food shortages those enslaved in the New World experienced (and possibly Western food colonialism in the region today), but it also functions rhetorically to refer to Ansige's sexual appetite. Paama, in this context, symbolizes meat. The irony that an accomplished chef cannot satiate her husband's desire is not lost on the reader. As a patriarchal figure concerned with his virility, Ansige objectifies and consumes his wife. Ansige therefore literally embodies corruption in different societal power structures, particularly marriage, in which husbands too often abuse their power. That Paama rejects her husband's and society's sexist ideologies toward women is at the heart of *Redemption*. Thus, Lord's speculative folktale fully takes up the opportunities afforded by Ananse's multifaceted aspects to challenge rigid gender norms and expectations that denigrate the feminine and/or maternal not only in the imagined past but also in its future foretold.

LORD RECLAIMS AND REWORKS THE FOLKTALE

Inspired by African-Caribbean folktales and cosmologies, Lord's novel, in true trickster fashion, confounds common Western binaries and boundaries for example fiction/fact, religion/science, and male/female. Yet, equally important to Lord's postcolonial reimagining is that Ananse takes the shape of animals and/or humans; interactions between these facile categories happen unproblematically (Mwinlaaru and Nkansah 2018, 251) as do the blurring of ontologies and species. *Redemption* depicts these exchanges primarily through the presence of djombis, called undying ones, who resemble lwas or orishas. Like the narrator, the djombis disrupt the main folktale narrative. Described as "discorporate entit[ies] standing at the interstices of time and space" (Lord 2010, 47), "beings outside of time" (69) for whom "time means nothing" (167), djombis appear to humans in three ways: "they may take the shadow of an animal or borrow the shadow of a human, or they may make their own shape from matter and illusion" (Lord 2019, 70). Lord reminds us that with respect to binaries and hierarchies such as time and space or corporeality "never assume that these categories represent boundaries that are never crossed or lines that cannot be re-drawn" (2010, 58). In fact, this claim encapsulates perfectly this trickster text's aims: to promote an Ananse (African-Caribbean) and Anansesem that is feminine, complex, organic, and spiritual, that is to say weblike.

Lord reinforces her feminine weblike narratological strategy by including an unsavory Ananse protagonist named Trickster—"the spider of Ahani," and "the godfather of the troublemakers" (Lord 2010, 61).

Trickster lurks in dark, shadowy places such as bars and markets. Signifying Ananse's diminished presence in twenty-first-century folk/mainstream culture, he infamously appears, like a cobweb, in corners and abandoned, out-of-reach spaces: "The trickster's web is symbolically constructed in the novel as liminal spaces, a number of locations associated with the socioeconomically marginalized .... Ananse ... finds spaces at the edges of society that grants him easy access to his victims while allowing him a safe distance" (Mwinlaaru and Nkansah 2018, 256). Lord's Trickster-Ananse protagonist thus begins by preying on the vulnerable and abusing his power; for example, from afar, Trickster observes Ansige traveling to apprehend Paama. From Trickster, we also learn that Paama has received a special Chaos Stick that once belonged to Trickster's brother, Chance, another powerfully arrogant djombi. Capable of controlling "different possibilities in the universe" and "quantum fluctuations" (Lord 2010, 52) the stick is cleverly disguised as a domestic item—a stirring stick for cou cou, Barbados' national dish.

The novel hones in on Chance's attempt, with Trickster's help, to retrieve his rightful property from Paama (echoing Ansige's attempt to take back his wife, i.e., his property). The maternal goddess Patience, emblematic of Atabey, stripped Chance of his powers, however, because he became increasingly cynical and ruthless toward humans. The mark of Chance's disdain for humanity and his hubris culminated when "he set his form and features to the zenith of perfection, and then, instead of choosing a subtle mark, he made his skin deep indigo" (Lord 2010, 58). The historical connotations of indigo resonate throughout this postcolonial text.[5] For instance, the indigo plant, used for dye, was harvested on slave plantations in the United States and in the Caribbean (Fairbanks 1994).[6] That Chance adopts the cash-crop's color shows his heightened insensitivity toward human life and the legacy of slavery. Drawing on this important aspect of the Ananse-trickster figure, Lord's novel brings attention to how "In the entertaining storytelling sessions among enslaved Africans, Ananse's outwitting of bigger animals could be seen as a vicarious rebellion against slave-owners and overseers. ...[yet] he also outwits weaker creatures; his cruelty could occasionally end up being identified with the overseer's" ("Ananse" 2008, 84). The indigo lord, likened to a plantation master, is marked literally by the colour of slavery, and thus is unworthy of the spirituality, wisdom, intuition, and perception also associated with the color.

That the word "indigo" stems from the Greek word for India, where the crop was originally grown by Europeans, further emphasizes Lord's syncretic approach, which combines Indigenous, Afro and Indo cosmologies, epistemologies, and the histories of slavery and indentured servitude in the region. The importance of other religions such as Hinduism is evident in Chance's renaming of himself as Taran, which in Hindi means heaven or Lord Vishnu. In human guise, Taran is a composite of Hinduism's blue-skinned, multilimbed Supreme Gods Vishnu and Shiva—the latter being often portrayed as a trickster figure tasked with destroying the world/web/text—whose numerous avatars visit earth in the guise of animals, humans, or a hybrid of the two. As a "nomad merchant prince" (Lord 2010, 76), "veiled and robed in ivory linen" (Lord 2010, 94), the apostate Taran arrives in Paama's village in his Vishnu-Krishna avatar. By including Hindu elements alongside those from African cultures, Lord's web marks a creolized approach to understanding Barbados' past and present but simultaneously critiques these religions and leaders for their corrupted masculinity, arrogance, and violence.

Originally tasked with "the protection and improvement of humankind," the indigo lord, for example, finds "himself dismayed and disillusioned by humans and their flaws" (Lord 2010, 102). Emphasizing Ananse's hypermasculine, destructive aspects, the narrator cautions: "Remember what we mentioned to you before. This is a dangerous person. He [Taran] enjoys lulling the prey into a feeling of safety before killing it" (Lord 2010, 67). The spiderlike imagery is reinforced by extrapolating Taran to be a shortened form of tarantula. When Taran and Trickster meet Paama, however, the novel advances its venture into alternative epistemologies by introducing a theory of quantum physics, whereby other worlds and times can coexist outside of and in relation to human ones. For instance, Lord writes, "A bizarrely shaped figure loomed out of the stilled outside world and casually tore open their little bubble of time, holding the edges apart carefully with sharp-tipped, multiple, hairy legs. ...It was half Bini [Taran's human servant], half the trickster spider" (Lord 2010, 99). Trickster, the spiderman, intervenes when Taran cannot physically reclaim the stick from Paama's outstretched hands because he is morally bankrupt.

Lewis explains such otherworldliness: "This is yet another level of the complexity of the [Barbadian] folk culture – its ability simultaneously to separate and homogenize the present with the past, and to incorporate the future into a dialectical unity which gives shape and direction to the lived experiences of a people" (1990, 94). The ability for djombis to simultaneously exist in more than one space and time again demonstrates the text's gender-centric web-motif as capable of breaking free from a Western master narrative of linearity. That Paama is attuned to the djombi's existence and their special abilities to bend spacetime further lends evidence that Lord places immense importance upon the agency of women and their ability to envision another society. For example, when Taran kidnaps Paama and takes her to alternative tragic pasts/presents, for example witnessing a plague-ridden town or a coffle of slaves, three Catholic nuns follow their movements. In fact, the sisters play a pivotal role in utilizing advanced technology to help Paama transform Taran from a vengeful, abusive djombi to a humble, kind deity.[7] Paama's engagements with the djombis, however, also mark her and other maternal figures' unique ability to embody "Ananse...[who] assumes a role as link between the physical and the supernatural dimensions" ("Ananse" 2008, 84), for she communes with, transforms, and redeems both the divine and the earthly.

By outwitting and defying her husband, Paama echoes Ananse again: she takes "the opportunity to mock society's authority. He [She] is able to do what the ordinary Akan cannot: act unscrupulously with relative impunity. By so doing he [she] calls the most sacrosanct of Akan institutions into question" (Vecsey 1981, 172). In Lord's version, Paama not only breaks the societal rules/duties of marriage by leaving Ansige but also remarries. This antipatriarchal text thus imagines three new male characters, Chance, Trickster, and Kwame, who, in addition to the original Ansige, are lured into seeking out the cunning heroine, Paama. The spider's web thus functions as a network of reciprocity, which connects its heroine with others: "The advent of West Indian femininity therefore consists of placing oneself in a network of two-way relationships: Caribbeanness implies going towards others, at the same time as welcoming one to the other," explains Gyssels (2002, 189). Lord's speculative folktale therefore revises Ananse protagonists like Paama to propose an antipatriarchal, spiritual path that embraces mutuality, empathy, and community; the collective in *Redemption* is the village of Makendha and Paama's supportive family, prior to and after Ansige.

By reinventing the African folktale heroine for a contemporary Caribbean audience, Lord thus contributes to reconceptualizing gender identity in the region. Consider again the novel in relation to Gyssels' reading of maternal imagery in Schwarz-Bart and Marshall:

[An] [u]mbilical cord connecting the African-Caribbean … to her mother earth, Africa, the spider's thread is a marvelous realistic motif emphasizing the importance, for the quest for female identity, of a communication/communion with known and unknown, living and dead, people from here and there. It conveys the idea of a cunning resistance, barely visible, of a woven identity, that is to say, never fixed, but which must be patiently weaved, taking into account new contacts and exchanges. (190)

The narrator thus disentangles Paama from her marginalized position in both patriarchal storytelling traditions, for example African and Western, and emphasizes her critical pedagogical role in the new Anansesem.

After meeting Paama, for instance, Kwame's thinking is transformed. Kwame tells the Trickster, "I am trying to find a part of myself, something that I lost on the way from childhood" (Lord 2010, 139). Presumably, this lost part is his belief in nancy stories, a belief in African-Caribbean derived religions, which can be interpreted as a loss of knowledge of his heritage. The novel, once more echoing the folkloric wisdom found in Schwarz-Bart's *Pluie et vent sur Télumée Miracle* and Marshall's *Praisesong for the Widow*, suggests that knowing one's history, knowing one's ancestry, is critical to knowing one's self, and that women play an essential role in contributing to and sharing this knowledge. The world of Ahani and its surrounding villages is increasingly turning away from its Afro-centric religious, folkloric roots to a more Western, secular, scientific urban society (e.g., the crime-ridden underbelly of the city, the setting of Lord's sequel, *Unraveling*). A renewed belief in the Ananse stories and the divine is possible, however, as Kwame, under Paama's guidance, comes to perceive Trickster as a good omen: "finding out that someone like you is at the start of it [journey to self-community knowledge] is oddly encouraging" (Lord 2010, 139). The novel emphasizes that it is not so much that African-Caribbean deities do not exist so much as that most humans have stopped believing in them and their power. Backtracking to the old ways and embracing the feminine thus become part of the protagonists' journeys to locating the sacred within themselves and their world(s)/web(s).

Concretizing the power of female figures in this novel, the superior djombi, Patience ushers in the path toward spiritual redemption that the male djombis, Trickster and Taran, embark upon. While little is known of Patience in *Redemption*, in *Unraveling* Lord gives explicit clues to reading her as the mother earth goddess Atabey: "progenitor of the supreme being of the Tainos, mother of the Taino lakes and rivers, protector of feminine

286 T. ZIMMERMAN

ebbs and flows, of the great mysteries of the blood that women experience" (Benítez-Rojo 1997, 14). Exhibiting her formidable power, Patience exclaims: "I am Earth, the Eldest and First-born of all that walks here. I make my children, I destroy them, and I remake them again'" (Lord 2010, 271). Atabey notably shares affinities with the Akan Mother Earth goddess Asase Yaa, Ananse's mother. Ananse (the Trickster brought from Africa via slavery) and Vishnu-Shiva (Chance, the indigo lord brought from India via indentured servitude), as well as three Catholic nuns (also brought by/as European colonizers) are all subordinate to this precolonial indigenous Caribbean goddess. In this henotheistic divinity, the ultimate God is Caribbean and a woman. Lord's novel therefore insists that indigenous women and indigenous cosmologies must play an invaluable role in reconceiving the anticolonial, antipatriarchal Caribbean future.

In this light, one can see how the novel's title draws on its metafictional qualities and its African-Caribbean theological connotations: like the silk which the spider uses to spin their web, so too does the narrator write with their indigo ink. The redemption applies as much to the narrator and reader as it does to the divine who has been redeemed from ruinous error/ evil by three powerful maternal figures: first, the Ananse narrator, whose labour respins Anansesem; second, Atabey/Patience, Taran's immediate superior djombi, who punishes and exiles him but later forgives his transgressions; and third, Paama, who educates and mothers Taran—afterward he is reborn as her human son Yao. While, according to de Souza, "disharmony and disorder" (2003, 343) characterize the endings of Ananse trickster stories, and indeed the African Karamba story is inconclusive, Lord's feminocentric *Redemption* continues to break the rules: it ends more or less happily: Ansige dies, Chance/Taran earns back his Chaos power, and Paama marries Kwame, with whom she has twin sons, Yao and Ajit (fulfilling the Glutton tale). That Paama as human mother to Yao and Ajit (respectively incarnations of Trickster and Chance) parallels the senior djombi Patience as divine mother to Trickster/Ananse and Chance/Shiva-Vishnu is no coincidence either: *Redemption* insists that the potential for feminine qualities such as care, solidarity, and compassion toward others to subvert patriarchal society cannot be overestimated.

Lord's novel concludes with the narrator playfully asking readers to purchase the book, (which, of course they already have if they are reading it): "ladies and gentlemen, if you have at all enjoyed my story, be generous as the pot goes around, and do come back again soon" (2010, 181). The return, of course, will be the sequel, *Unraveling*, which like *Redemption* ends with an image of hope: mother and sons, on two different ontological planes, as human and as undying, demonstrating the powerful potential of trickster figures as capable of countering patriarchal-colonial discourses by offering feminine concentric retellings of African-Caribbean (folk) her story.[8] Lord's speculative folktale thus employs several Ananse trickster storytellers qua spiders spinning (a)synchronistic webs/texts. Centralizing a nonbinary Ananse-narrator, a female folk-figure, Paama, and an indigenous goddess, the power of marginalized figures to weave their own tales emerges. For Paama, it means bravely ending an unhappy marriage to an undeserving husband and becoming that folk-Ananse-heroine who survives: "one who relieves" not "his" but her "community … from power abuse and, in the process, brings new knowledge" (Mwinlaaru and Nkansah 2018, 253). Paama stands up to not only her husband but also a powerful male deity, both of whom exert violence and control over others. Colonial and patriarchal spaces and figures in *Redemption* are therefore inextricably transformed by female-maroon protagonists committed to social justice. As such, Lord's text speculates that if the fabric of Caribbean society is to change, then women and gender must be prioritized: the old Indigenous, Indo- and African-Caribbean folktales must be rewoven in novel form.

Notes

1. In *Engaged Queerness in African Speculative Fiction*, Edgar Fred Nabutanyi argues that "African folktales are truly sci-fi texts … [T]he very concept of African sci-fi is queer, because it destabilises the popular conceptions of African literature as realistic" (qtd. by Burger 2020, 2).
2. In her notes, Gyssels likens the mangrove framework used by Maryse Condé in her novel Traversée de la mangrove (1989) to a web and suggests it constitutes another woman writer's fruitful (re)consideration of Caribbean identity; the mangrove paradigm is also central to Odile Ferly's work A Poetics of Relation: Caribbean Women Writing at the Millennium (2012).
3. English translations of Gyssels' article are my own.
4. Also resonating with Aunt Nancy in the African American context ("Ananse," 2008, 84).
5. Marina Warner's novel Indigo (1992) links the dye with the deceased witch, Sycorax, in Shakespeare's play The Tempest. Resonating with Lord's version of Miranda in Unraveling, Warner's Miranda character lives in the twentieth century.

288   T. ZIMMERMAN

6. Jesslyn Shields (2020) discusses Moses Lindo, inspector general of indigo and importer of enslaved people from Barbados to Charleston. Lawrence Hill's novel The Book of Negroes (2007) depicts Lindo and the indigo slave trade.
7. The nuns cannot be exonerated from their historical role in perpetuating slavery in the region, and this is a missed opportunity in the novel.
8. That Paama's fraternal twins, Yao and Ajit, are human forms of the undying ones, respectively Trickster (Ananse) and Chance (Vishnu-Shiva), harkens to another African tale, a Xhosa one, called "The Story of the Glutton," (1886) which ends with the heroine's two sons killing the glutton and freeing the villagers trapped inside him.

REFERENCES

Ananse. 2008. In *Encyclopedia of the African Diaspora: Origins, Experiences, and Culture*. Vol. 2, ed. Carole Boyce Davies. 84. Santa Barbara: ABC-CLIO.

Benítez-Rojo, Antonio. 1997. *The Repeating Island: The Caribbean and the Postmodern Perspective*. Durham: Duke University Press.

Brathwaite, Kamau. 1977. *Mother Poem*. Oxford University Press.

Burger, Bibi. 2020. Engaged Queerness in African Speculative Fiction. *Scrutiny 2* 25 (2): 1–12. https://doi.org/10.1080/18125441.2020.1859772.

De Souza, Pascale. 2003. Creolizing Anancy: Signifyin(g) Processes in New World Spider Tales. In *A Pepper-Pot of Cultures: Aspects of Creolization in the Caribbean*, ed. Gordon Collier and Ulrich Fleisghmann, 339–363. Amsterdam: Rodopi Press.

Fairbanks, Virgil F. 1994. Blue gods, blue oil, and blue people. *Mayo Clinic Proceedings* 69: 889–892.

Gyssels, Kathleen. 2002. Fils et filles d'Anancy: exil diasporique et identité métissée chez Schwarz-Bart et Marshall. *Revue de littérature comparée* 302 (2): 178–190. https://doi.org/10.3917/rlc.302.0178.

Lewis, Linden. 1990. Exploring the folk culture of Barbados through the medium of the folk tale. *Caribbean Studies* 23 (3/4): 85–94. http://www.jstor.org/stable/25613006.

Lord, Karen. 2016. Foreword. In *New World, Old Ways: Speculative Tales from the Caribbean*, ed. Karen Lord, 1–3. New York: Peekash Press.

———. 2010. *Redemption in Indigo*. Northampton: Small Beer Press.

———. 2019. *Unraveling*. New York: DAW Books, Inc.

Mackey, Nathaniel. 2018. *Paracritical Hinge: Essay, Talks, Notes, Interviews*. Iowa City, University of Iowa Press.

Maiser, Véronique. 2014. Teaching the Caribbean Across Borders: The Web Approach. In *Reimagining the Caribbean: Conversations Among the Creole, English, French, and Spanish Caribbean*, ed. Valérie K. Orlando and Sandra Cypress, 23–42. Lanham: Lexington Books.

Marshall, Paule. 1983. *Praisesong for the Widow*. New York: Plume.

Mwinlaaru, Isaac N., and Samuel K. Nkansah. 2018. The trickster as a semiotic figure for construing postcolonial experience: Kwakye's 'The Clothes of Nakedness'. *Journal of the African Literature Association* 12 (3): 250–268. https://doi.org/10.1080/21674736.2018.1526030.

Onoura, Adwoa. 2015. *Anansesem: Telling Stories and Storytelling African Maternal Pedagogies*. Toronto: Demeter Press.

Pelton, Robert D. 1989. *The Trickster in West Africa: A Study of Mythic Irony and Sacred Delight*. Berkeley: University of California Press.

Schwarz-Bart, Simone. [1972] 2015. *Pluie et Vent sur Télumée Miracle*, ed. Alfred Fralin & Christiane Szeps. New York: Bloomsbury.

Shields, Jesslyn. 2020, Feb. 7. *The Dark History of Indigo, Slavery's Other Cash Crop*. https://people.howstuffworks.com/culture-traditions/world-history/indigo.htm. Accessed 27 June 2022.

The Gluttonous Ansige. 1996. In *A Treasury of African Folklore*, ed. Harold Courlander, 82–85. New York: Marlowe & Company.

The Story of the Glutton. 1886. https://www.sacred-texts.com/afr/xft/xft23.htm. Accessed 27 June 2022.

Vecsey, Christopher. 1981. The Exception Who Proves the Rules: Ananse the Akan Trickster. *Journal of Religion in Africa* 12 (3): 161–177. https://doi.org/10.2307/1581431.

Open Access This chapter is licensed under the terms of the Creative Commons Attribution 4.0 International License (http://creativecommons.org/licenses/by/4.0/), which permits use, sharing, adaptation, distribution and reproduction in any medium or format, as long as you give appropriate credit to the original author(s) and the source, provide a link to the Creative Commons licence and indicate if changes were made.

The images or other third party material in this chapter are included in the chapter's Creative Commons licence, unless indicated otherwise in a credit line to the material. If material is not included in the chapter's Creative Commons licence and your intended use is not permitted by statutory regulation or exceeds the permitted use, you will need to obtain permission directly from the copyright holder.

CHAPTER 16

Chronotropic Visions: Conclusion

Odile Ferly and Tegan Zimmerman

The twenty-first-century Caribbean women writers featured in *Chronotropics: Caribbean Women Writing Spacetime* deconstruct androcentric approaches to spacetime inherited from Western modernity. They turn to Hindu, Indigenous, Yoruba myths or West African folktales to restore a temporal connection and expand conceptions of space within and beyond the region. They promote social justice and collective healing through literary acts of archival disruption, radical remapping, and epistemic *marronnage*. We name this the chronotropics. Our volume connects the literary trajectories towards non-Western ontologies and epistemologies laid out by Julia Alvarez, Yolanda Arroyo Pizarro, Vashti Bowlah, Dionne Brand, Erna Brodber, Maryse Condé, Nalo Hopkinson, Rita Indiana, Fabienne Kanor, Karen Lord, Kettly Mars, Pauline Melville, Mayra Montero, Shani Mootoo, Elizabeth Nunez, Ingrid Persaud, Gisèle Pineau, Krystal M. Ramroop, and Mayra Santos Febres.

O. Ferly (✉)
Clark University, Worcester, MA, USA
e-mail: oferly@clarku.edu

T. Zimmerman
Saint Mary's University, Halifax, NS, Canada
e-mail: tegan.zimmerman@smu.ca

© The Author(s) 2023
O. Ferly, T. Zimmerman (eds.), *Chronotropics*,
https://doi.org/10.1007/978-3-031-32111-5_16

Part I: Archival Disruption revisits the colonial archive and its systemic practice of exclusion. As Odile Ferly contends in relation to Yolanda Arroyo Pizarro (2013) and Fabienne Kanor (2006), archival disruption ought to be regarded as an act of epistemic *marronnage*. The literary endeavours of the writers that make up Part II: Radical Remapping equally seek to break the thick chain of linearity (a matrix of colonialism, race, gender, and capitalism) by reconceiving territorial boundaries. Parts I and II thus validate Edouard Glissant's claim that "Place is the seam of Time" (Glissant 2000, 233). The narratives examined in Part III: Epistemic *Marronnage* go beyond retrospective examination and territorial interrogation to promote forms of *marronnage* intimately connected to ways of knowing, in particular science and spirituality. These subversive works propose the "quantum level" (da Silva 2017, 110) in their revival of the roots of ancestral communities. The alternative Caribbean women's spacetimes gathered in *Chronotropics* embrace metaphysical pluralism and the multiverse.

In her philosophical poem *The Blue Clerk*, Dionne Brand expresses a desire to live "in time like this, several and simultaneous" instead of "weighted" by the specificity and singularity of place (Brand 2018, 135). Echoing Santos Febres's "uno y múltiple" (Santos Febres 2021), Brand's "several and simultaneous" pertains to a chronotropic vision. Thus, upon visiting an Inca exhibit in Peru, Brand reflects on spatialities and temporalities underpinned by distinct epistemologies: "Conquest makes the life of the conquered seem brief ... those the Incas conquered must have felt the shortening of their existences too." Nevertheless, Brand implies, modern Euro-imperialism operates on a different scale: "When the Spanish arrived the thousands of years of the Inca collapsed into one earthen bowl. All their lives collapsed into one life. A summary" (199). The steamroller of Western expansion seems to flatten everything it encounters, just like the Peruvian museum (founded in 1926 at the height of the age of modernity) reduces pre-Columbian life to a collection of earthen bowls. Clearly, in its design and intent, the museum, the ultimate archive, is imbued with coloniality.

Many of the texts studied in *Chronotropics* likewise "violate" what Denise da Silva calls "the three onto-epistemological pillars (the theory of knowing, theory of being, and a theory of practice)—namely, separability, determinacy, and sequentiality—that sustain linear temporality" (2017, 83). Referencing Octavia Butler, da Silva (2017) echoes Erna Brodber (2014) and Mayra Santos Febres by proposing "a fractal figuring" (92).

This approach to spacetime illuminates how linear temporality served to justify enslavement and the appropriation of Indigenous lands and how it further obscured "the creation of capital" through its entanglement with the colonial and the racial (95). The writers examined herein revisit the past or alternatively conjure up futuristic worlds precisely to break these patterns, to challenge such laws, and to demand reparations that can positively impact Caribbean realities, actual and anticipated.

A timely reflection on contemporary migration can be found in Megan Jeanette Myers' contribution to this volume. Myers demonstrates that Julia Alvarez's in-transit narrative *Afterlife* (Alvarez 2020), coupled with her position on Haitian Dominicans and their descendants' right to citizenship, evince a pan-insular perspective on Hispaniola. This constitutes a radical shift in an intellectual tradition that has been dominated by ethnonationalism since the mid-nineteenth century. Alvarez's literary and grassroots engagement destabilizes Hispaniola (and U.S.) spacetime, insofar as it advocates for territorial elasticity and for solidarity across borders, race, nationality, and the diaspora: this is a clear manifestation of the chronotropics. Furthermore, contrary to scholarship that interprets works like *Afterlife* as intending to extend "the temporality of the dictatorship by exploring its afterlife" in the diaspora of the United States (Harford Vargas 2018, 10), Myers contends that the novel belongs to a new literary phase that moves beyond the *trujillato*. *Afterlife* thereby inaugurates a turning point in Dominican thought, a coming to an awareness, perhaps a new archipelagic mindset with an openness to the immediate neighbour and the rest of the region.

Erna Brodber's fiction, scholarship, and activism, examined in A. Marie Sairsingh's chapter, likewise prompt us to expand our notion of the nation by more fully embracing the diaspora (see Brodber 2020). Indeed, nationhood is frequently rooted in a narrow conception of spacetime; Brodber's entire oeuvre reads as a meditation on how the two diasporic components, the African and the Jamaican, or the temporal and spatial dimensions, are fundamentally constitutive of both Jamaica (and by extension, the Caribbean) and the black people. Maryse Condé's corpus, with its emphasis on the African and Caribbean diasporas, similarly posits rethinking spacetime as a precondition for equity and justice, an impulse that animates Fabienne Kanor's writing too. As Valérie K. Orlando shows, the hyper globalized world of Condé's later period has a very different tenor from the optimism of the earlier works, or from Brodber's later fiction. In *Les belles ténébreuses* (Condé 2008) and *Le fabuleux et triste destin d'Ivan et Ivana* (Condé 2017), the Guadeloupean author cautions against the dire consequences of being disconnected from one's spacetime, origins, birthplace, and history, especially for Afro-diasporic subjects. According to Orlando, it is precisely their ignorance and outright disinterest in Caribbean spacetime, both historical and geographical, that makes the young protagonists vulnerable and leads to their ultimate downfall. Sharing this palpable skepticism, the narratives by Rita Indiana (2015), Mayra Montero (1997), Pauline Melville (1997), and Elizabeth Nunez (2006) point to the destructive impact of the prevailing approaches to spacetime, as discussed by Joshua R. Deckman, Carine M. Mardorossian and Angela Veronica Wong, and Elaine Savory, respectively.

Several texts experiment with the chronotropics through spacetime travel. In Kettly Mars's *L'Ange du patriarche* (2018), the physical and metaphysical worlds collide when the characters meet the spirit. Lethal as it may be (all characters except one meet their ends there), this collision site or spacetime corridor offers the protagonists an opportunity to radically remap the present and alter the future: Thus, a scene towards the end of the novel is recounted twice, with one change leading to a different outcome. According to Mars, embracing *cohabitation*, that is, remaining fully receptive to the coexistence of spiritual and ideological beliefs that are ostensibly contradictory or seemingly at odds with each other, empowers the protagonists Emmanuela and Couz to take full ownership of the past; as Robert Sapp argues, this enables them to have an impact on their present and future. As an ethical stance, cohabitation is applicable beyond Haiti: attesting to this are several of the authors studied here, notably Hopkinson, Indiana, Melville, and Montero.

For her part, in *Fe in disfraz*, Mayra Santos Febres (2009) resorts to a spacetime travelling machine that doubles up as a site of memory: the iconic dress that the eponymous character puts on every year at Halloween. Tailored for a free woman of partial African ancestry striving to assimilate into Brazilian white society, this dress encapsulates the structural barriers that Afrodescendants, especially women, have invariably encountered across space and time in the Americas. And yet Santos Febres suggests that a mask or disguise can only grant the illusion of achievement; it cannot truly attain it. Perhaps one of the most innovative approaches to spacetime, however, is found in Indiana's *La mucama de Omicunlé*, where Alcide's spiritual initiation to *santería* opens, in Deckman's words, "a breach in the temporal fabric of Caribbean imaginaries," a passage along which the reader can freely travel in time along with the protagonist. The use of multiple timelines in the novel underscores the reproduction of the pattern of exploitation, abuse, and violence at the inception of Caribbean coloniality; at the same time, as Deckman contends, the repetition of the pattern and the prominence of the theme of betrayal illustrate the missed opportunities to break the pernicious cycle.

A similar effect is produced by the chronotropic device deployed in Gisèle Pineau: the memory jail where asynchronous characters are thrown together and where "time is abolished" (Pineau 2007, 7). Here distinct eras are merged to underline social stagnation: things have changed and yet remain the same. The striking commonalities in the plights of these four women whose lives span over two centuries insinuate that for Guadeloupe's black women of humble or modest extraction, progress has always been accompanied by setbacks. And indeed, several authors examined here show that, despite expansions of space, time seems to stand still. Literal and metaphorical imprisonment in Pineau's memoir reifies the urgency of a chronotropic vision that addresses the sociopolitical spaces women do or do not occupy. Additionally, as Renée Larrier notes in her chapter, the psychescape of the memory jail, an archive of its own kind replete with the author's foremothers' memories and voices, begs the question of whether writing can free her and her ancestors from past and present violence. This resonates with what Outar identifies as "the tentacles of traumatic pasts that continue to haunt Caribbean peoples and their descendants" in Ingrid Persaud's *Love After Love*. Undoubtedly, writing is a form of catharsis that empowers the Caribbean women in this volume to assume their traumatic history, as most evident in Pineau, Arroyo Pizarro, and Kanor.

Arguably, *rewriting* is another form of time travelling.[1] It is especially effective with plays. Thus, the community play performed yearly in Woodside, Jamaica can be seen as a constant collective rewriting of the 1838 Emancipation by Brodber and the Blackspace participants. It stands as a living text whose adaptations and shifting interpretations are tuned in to the contemporary context every year. Through the play and other annual Blackspace commemorations, the continued relevance of history becomes real to the audience, as the link between past, present, and future is highlighted. The rewriting of Shakespeare's *The Tempest* by writers across the Caribbean and the way each version speaks to the moment of its inception and various productions is likewise a form of time travelling; Elizabeth Nunez's novel *Prospero's Daughter* belongs to this long line of palimpsest. The originality of Nunez's version, Elaine Savory argues, lies in the couple Virginia and Carlos (Miranda and Caliban) whose alliance and respect for the environment undermine colonial dynamics (Prospero). Nunez intimates that these are two necessary preconditions to overcome the colonial predicament.

Its inherent flexibility should likewise grant the oral tradition timelessness and the ability to always speak to the moment; and yet, as demonstrated by Lisa Outar, it almost invariably reinforces social conservatism and patriarchal norms. Re/writing folktales such as Ti-Marie and the Devil and adapting figures from Indo-Caribbean folklore and Hindu legends allows Krystal Ramroop (2020), Vashti Bowlah (2015), and Ingrid Persaud (2020) to interrogate the sexism, outright misogyny, and gender normativity that characterizes the oral tradition and most religions. Because stories and elements of folklore serve a pedagogical function, it is imperative to revise them. Similarly, Zimmerman shows how in *Redemption in Indigo* Karen Lord (2010) *puts her own spin* on a Senegalese folktale, Hindu legends, and more broadly the conventions of Afro-Caribbean storytelling to push towards social change, notably regarding gender norms.

As Erica L. Johnson's discussion of *The Blue Clerk* demonstrates, the preoccupation with the records found in many writers and artists such as Dionne Brand is another form of constant rewriting. Archival institutions as conventionally conceived in the logocentric tradition of the West are places dedicated to marking time. Consequently, to engage with them, to question their omissions, silences, or outright absence is to reconstruct spacetime. Each in her own way, Arroyo Pizarro, Kanor, Brand, Pineau, and Santos Febres, redefines the archive as the Afro-diasporic body and collective/family memory. In these authors (and in Brodber too), writing, researching, or simply remembering becomes a way to elaborate a counterarchive. Time ravages the physical records as much as the immaterial ones. The authors' insistence on the ephemeral or the impermanent both reflects the absence of black Atlantic registers and artefacts and stands as an invitation to constant rewriting, to put the past, present, and future in *Relation*. As Kanor puts it: "Not knowing everything allows us, the heirs, to reinvent history [and to avoid being] in a state of eternal resentment" (Herbeck 2013, 975, translation Ferly's). While the official record is taken to task by each of these authors, its fragmented nature still holds immense practical and symbolic value. Kanor, for instance, can reimagine her protagonists jumping ship in solidarity, thereby preemptively foreclosing a future of enslavement through their deaths. The text speculates what world-archive, geographies, and temporalities would we be inhabiting had there never been a Middle Passage.

A chronotropics paradigm thus insists on rupturing and breaking open the present through dismantling the master's house of colonial records across several, interconnected geopolitical locations. Undertaking this knowledge translation work, Brand's clerk, in a performative gesture, looks for History within its blank pages. Similarly, the Afro-Venezuelan researcher in Santos Febres's novel tirelessly sifts through incomplete annals in Chicago to connect the disparate stories of women enslaved across the Americas. Santos Febres collapses the present and past, the diaspora, island, and continent, into a single spacetime, as Nicole Roberts' chapter makes clear. Reflecting on these connections across decades and generations, Melville's elusive narrator poignantly asks: "Do you think a man's life is slung between two dates like a hammock? ... It takes more than one life to make a person" (Melville 1997, 6). This recognition of interconnections leads Melville's unconventional anthropologist Rosa Mendelson to defend racial and cultural hybridity between the Wapisiana Amerindians of Guyana and others. In fact, as a form of counter-discourse, she comes to ventriloquize the narrator's belief that "disguise is the only truth and desire the only true measure of time" (10). Through unearthing the fragments of untold stories that echo each other, these authors evidence not only the sexual-textual politics of the archive but also the ethical stakes of rewriting the region's historical and historiographic discourses.

Caribbean women's writing therefore stresses the artificiality of Man's time by reminding us that nature operates according to its own schedule. To the consternation of "measurers, collectors or enumerators" like Charles Darwin, "in the tropics ... [s]ooner or later everything falls to the glorious spirit of rot" which, accompanied by "its herald angel, smell, announce most events" (Melville 1997, 7). In the same vein, texts by Hopkinson (2013), Mootoo (2005), and Nunez (2006) depict an overflowing, overgrowing tropical topography of multiplicity and fecundity intent on ruining and rebelling against the structured modern world. Hopkinson offers a particularly effective critique with her invasive kudzu plant, spreading out and across the urban landscape of Toronto. The fear of an untameable, alien plant/species not only implies hypersexuality or vulgarity but also calls to mind a specific kind of xenophobia. Alternative spiritualities and newcomers (construed as hyper-consumerists inattentive to the proper respect for nature) purportedly pose a threat to the Canadian landscape and the nation's Eurocentric approach to ecology.

Supposedly degrading the wilderness and introducing poisonous ways of thinking, immigrants must be effectively assimilated or contained lest they should destroy the chaste, Western subject like Darwin. This brings to the forefront Canada's fear for its pristine image, that is, space spiralling out of control when allegedly unchecked, unregulated immigration jeopardizes the nation/environment with irreparable loss and contamination. Vivian Nun Halloran's chapter notes that writing by Hopkinson, like Mootoo, directly addresses the hypocrisy of a country seemingly forgetful of its own diasporic origins, as its nationalism is entangled with sexuality, race, migration, and environmentalism.

A mirror to the unruly vegetation in Hopkinson's novel, Nunez's Prospero protagonist deeply desires to dominate others (including sexually) and master spacetime, hence his unethical experiments on the flora of the island. His eventual failure underlines his out-of-placeness. For Savory, however, the patriarch's destructive behavior is offset by the budding relationship between the mixed-race couple. Virginia and Carlos gesture towards another way of being-with-others. Instead of dominance, coercion, artificiality, division, and force, the pair propose an alternative mode, between singularity and duality, to (re)map spacetime, a mode that entails a shared exchange or sympoeisis between species, people, and cultures; only this renewed relation of reciprocity and respect can offer a pathway for a sustainable future.

This lesson, however, is lost on Mayra Montero's two male biologists in *Tú, la oscuridad* (*In the Palm of Darkness*) as Carine M. Mardorossian and Angela Veronica Wong's chapter highlights. While the fatal conclusion of their insatiable quest for power at the expense of others, human and non-human alike, could offer a glimmer of hope, Montero's novel is in fact suffused by a sense of doom that contrasts in tone with Nunez but resonates with Melville's depiction of the ever-encroaching foreign oil companies in Guyana. Likewise, Rita Indiana's *La mucama de Omicunlé* (*Tentacle*) ends on a pessimistic note. Given the irreversible damage done to "the kingdom of this world," Caribbean and South American metaphysical spacetime—that is, Afro-Caribbean and Amerindian syncretic cosmogonies—appears to be the only source of comfort for Indiana, Melville, and Montero. Their respective use of *santería*, Wapisiana spirituality, and Vodou seek to reestablish the sacred link between humans, nature, animals, and gods. These writers together with Lord, Persaud and Mars further link their contemporary protagonists back to mythical and spiritual ancestors (such as Ananse and the kali mai cult) and to pivotal moments in history (such as the Bois Caïman ceremony) to remap not only gender but also the area and its intellectual traditions.

Finally, other writers in this volume return to powerful chronotopes (Olokún, churile, ladjablesse, Paama, Mayotte) from across the archipelago that signal the desire to confront and move on from the personal and political wounds of the past. This may manifest in revenge against perpetrators' violence, as Lisa Outar's work on Vashti Bowlah and Krystal Ramroop recognizes. Outar's claim that "Folklore thus serves as an archive of women's suffering" can be extended to many, if not most, of the writers included in this volume: domestic violence and abuse that cut across different axes of identity such as race, sexuality, and class are recurring motifs. Meanwhile, Kettly Mars's novel, amongst others, reveals the long shadow of the fallible patriarch to indicate that we must find new ways to structure family and society; Tegan Zimmerman suggests that for Karen Lord, the feminocentric web of Ananse does exactly this: The web brings people together to disrupt traditional arbolic, patriarchal familial trees and lineages. As also illustrated in A. Marie Sairsingh's reading of Brodber, nonlinear imaginings of kinship are not confined to a single spacetime but rather branch out in multiplicity and heterogeneity. While Indiana's and Mars's novels exemplify that destruction is certainly one aspect that may lead to radical change, a more hopeful side can be gleaned through a return to the spiritual and the powerful call of ancestors. Speculative spacetime or the anticipated land thus holds immense political potential in these texts.

Chronotropics brings to the forefront the gender-inflected multiverse with its epistemological and metaphysical pluralism. The chronotropic frameworks adopted by the women writers in this collection seek to carve out new spacetimes in which multiple worlds exist simultaneously, the one-in-the-many is possible, and the isolated, disembodied subject is toppled and banished once and for all. For some, a more just future can be achieved through creative acts that entail more openings, that is, more movement and fluidity, more *Relation*, as Glissant might put it, while for others it means respecting the borders or boundaries of an Other as a legitimate entity—a goddess, an island, a frog—independent of human being. While no single, definitive answer can be given, the political activism and literary endeavors pursued by each writer signal that in order to find a way towards an ethical future, we must collectively reject the old frameworks, the old worlds, and not only decenter Man but go beyond the human as Sylvia Wynter (2003) conceives it. We must instead elaborate/create other spacetimes. This is the imperative of a chronotropics that foregrounds women's lives and voices in concert with, not in opposition to, the natural-spiritual worlds that we inhabit.

NOTE

1. This borrows from the argument Rachel Douglas (2022) makes in relation to CLR James as a historiographer of the Haitian revolution in his multiple versions of *The Black Jacobins*, both in the various editions of the history and in the different play adaptations.

REFERENCES

Alvarez, Julia. 2020. *Afterlife*. Chapel Hill: Algonquin Books.

Arroyo Pizarro, Yolanda. 2013 [2012]. *las Negras*. Cabo Rojo: Editora Educación Emergente. Original edition: Boreales.

Brand, Dionne. 2018. *The Blue Clerk: Ars Poetica in 59 Versos*. Durham: Duke University Press.

Brodber, Erna. 2014. *Nothing's Mat*. Kingston: University of the West Indies Press.

———. 2020. The Pathless Harbourless Spade. *The Sociological Review* 68.3 (May): 461–475.

Bowlah, Vashti. 2015. The Churile of Sugarcane Valley. Akashic Books. www.akashicbooks.com/the-churile-of-sugarcane-valley-by-vashti-bowlah/

Condé, Maryse. 2017. *Le fabuleux et triste destin d'Ivan et Ivana*. Paris: JC Lattès.

———. 2008. *Les belles ténébreuses*. Paris: Mercure de France.

Da Silva, Denise Ferreira. 2017. Unpayable Debt: Reading Scenes of Value against the Arrow of Time. In *The documenta 14 reader*, ed. Quinn Latimer, 81–112. Munich: Prestel Press.

Douglas, Rachel, 2022. Futures in the Present: Decolonial Visions of the Haitian Revolution. *Interventions: International Journal of Francophone Studies*, published online 08 June 2022, n.p. https://doi.org/10.1080/1369801X.2022.2080574. Accessed 28 July 2022.

Glissant, Edouard. 2000. *Faulkner, Mississippi*. Translated by Barbara Lewis and Thomas C. Spear, Chicago: University of Chicago Press.

Herbeck, Jason. 2013. Entretien avec Fabienne Kanor. *The French Review* 86.5 (April): 964–976.

Hopkinson, Nalo. 2013. *Sister Mine*. New York: Grand Central Publishing.

Indiana, Rita. 2015. *La mucama de Omicunlé*. Editorial Periférica.

Kanor, Fabienne. 2006. *Humus*. Paris: Gallimard.

Lord, Karen. 2010. *Redemption in Indigo*. Northampton: Small Beer Press.

Mars, Kettly. 2018. *L'Ange du patriarche*. Paris: Mercure de France.

Melville, Pauline. [1997] 2014. *The Ventriloquist's Tale*. London: Bloomsbury Publishing Plc. E-book.
Montero, Mayra. 1997. *In the Palm of Darkness*. New York: HarperCollins.
Mootoo, Shani. 2005. *He Drown She in the Sea*. New York: Grove Press.
Nunez, Elizabeth. 2006. *Prospero's Daughter*. New York: Ballantine.
Persaud, Ingrid. 2020. *Love after Love*. New York: Penguin Random House.
Pineau, Gisèle. 2007. *Mes quatre femmes: récit*. Paris: Philippe Rey.
Ramroop, Krystal M. 2020. *Midnight's Mischievous Mistress*. Brown Geeks.the-browngeeks.com/midnights-mischievous-mistress-a-short-horror-story/
Santos Febres, Mayra. 2009. *Fe en disfraz*. Doral, FL: Alfaguara/Santillana USA.
———. 2021. Afroepistemologías: Fractalidad vs fragmentación en las identidades afrolatinoamericanas y caribeñas. *Aproximaciones Teóricas* 12.
Vargas, Jennifer Harford. 2018. *Forms of Dictatorship: Power, Narrative, and Authoritarianism in the Latina/o Novel*. New York: Oxford University Press.
Wynter, Sylvia. 2003. Unsettling the Coloniality of Being/Power/Truth/Freedom: Towards the Human, After Man, Its Overrepresentation--An Argument. *CR: The New Centennial Review* 3 (3): 257–337. https://doi.org/10.1353/ncr.2004.0015.

Open Access This chapter is licensed under the terms of the Creative Commons Attribution 4.0 International License (http://creativecommons.org/licenses/by/4.0/), which permits use, sharing, adaptation, distribution and reproduction in any medium or format, as long as you give appropriate credit to the original author(s) and the source, provide a link to the Creative Commons licence and indicate if changes were made.

The images or other third party material in this chapter are included in the chapter's Creative Commons licence, unless indicated otherwise in a credit line to the material. If material is not included in the chapter's Creative Commons licence and your intended use is not permitted by statutory regulation or exceeds the permitted use, you will need to obtain permission directly from the copyright holder.

INDEX[1]

A
Abolition (from enslavement), 86, 93
   See also Emancipation (from enslavement)
Absence, 48–51
Abuse, 87
Activism, 123, 133–134
   community (ies), communal, 3, 5, 8, 10, 11, 13, 15, 17–19, 30, 33, 41n11, 42n14, 50, 56, 86, 105–107, 109, 122, 124, 126, 131, 146, 149, 150, 187, 196, 200–201, 203, 207–209, 210n1, 210n4, 225, 234–237, 244–246, 273, 274, 276, 284, 287, 292, 295
   grassroots, 18, 293
   resistance, 7
   revolution, 4
   social justice, 4

Africa, 141, 146, 149–151, 153
Africa, Congo, 90
African diaspora, 27, 29, 34, 37–39, 103–119, 196, 197, 199
African folktales/folk hero, 272, 274–278, 284, 287
African fractal theory/fractal, 103–119
African knowledge systems, 107–109
African legacy/African diaspora/ Africanness/blackness in Latin America, 69
African worldviews, 104
Afro-Caribbean, 159, 164
Afro-diasporic, *see* Diaspora/diasporic
Afrodiasporic space, 104
Afrofuturistic divine systems, 12
Afterlife, 121–134, 293
Agency/choice/responsibility, 140, 145, 146, 151, 153
   of blacks, 74
   of black women, 74

---

[1] Note: Page numbers followed by 'n' refer to notes.

© The Author(s) 2023
O. Ferly, T. Zimmerman (eds.), *Chronotropics*,
https://doi.org/10.1007/978-3-031-32111-5

303

304 INDEX

Akan tradition, 277
Alexander, M. Jacqui, 200, 201
Alterity, *see* Otherness/alterity/
  othering
Alternative archives/counter
  archives, 80
Alvarez, Julia, 2, 11, 15, 121–134,
  291, 293
Amerindian tradition, 185
Ananse, 271–287
Anansesem, 271, 274–276, 278, 281,
  285, 286
Anatol, Giselle Liza, 235, 239, 240
Ancestral knowledge/spiritual
  dimension, 3, 7–14
Anchor, *see* Roots, rootedness
Anthropocene, 11
Anti-Haitianism, 125
Apatrida, see Stateless/statelessness
Aphids, 53, 54
Aporia, 33, 35, 36
Appadurai, Arjun, 141, 143, 145, 154
Archival disruption, 19, 32, 291, 292
Archival Ruins, 47–59
Archive(s), 27, 28, 32, 34, 35, 38–39,
  83–89, 95, 48–59, 198, 208,
  260, 297, 298
  alternative, 27–39, 42, 50, 52–53,
    55, 56, 61n3, 70, 78, 80, 105,
    113, 238, 296–297
  body archive (*see* Archive, corporeal
    archive/body archive)
  body language, 34
  corporeal archive/body archive,
    27–39, 292, 295–297, 299
  and erasure, 28
  historical records, 7–12, 18, 27, 28,
    32–37, 48, 73, 76, 105, 115,
    117, 118, 198, 208, 260
  immaterial, 27–39
  museums, 58, 67, 71, 73, 75, 76,
    80, 260, 292
  official/colonial, 28, 105

records/official history, 7–12, 18,
  28, 105, 260, 297, 298
  See also Archival disruptions;
    Corporeal geography; Fossil-
    body (*corps-fossile*); History,
    historical records; Museum/
    exhibition
Arroyo Pizarro, Yolanda,
  2, 3, 7, 8, 11, 14, 18, 19,
  19n3, 27–39, 291, 292,
  295, 296
Atabey, 272, 282, 285, 286
Atlantic Ocean, 158, 162, 163
Atlantic, *see* Black Atlantic;
  Transatlantic enslavement
Atwood, Margaret, 164
Author, the, 48, 51–59

B
Bakhtin, Mikhail, 3, 4, 19
Baldwin, James, 251–253, 265
Barbados, 278, 282, 283, 288
Bastide, Roger, 34, 37, 41
Baugh, Edward, 252–254, 260, 261
Belief systems, 219, 224
  See also Cosmogonies/cosmology/
    cosmological; Epistemology
Belonging, 122, 123, 126, 130, 132,
  133, 135
  un-belonging, 106, 109
Beloved (Toni Morrison), 165
Bernabé, Jean, 141
Betrayal, 196, 201, 202, 206, 209
Black Atlantic, 4, 8, 14, 28, 29,
  31–41, 41n9, 42n15
Black female subjectivity, 80
Black ontology, 103, 104
  See also Selfhood, smadditization;
    Selfhood, subjectivity
Black women, 28, 34
  bodies, 197
  epistemologies, 202

Bodyscape, 73
  inscription of historical violence, 79
Blue Clerk, The, 47–59
Bois Caïman Vodou ceremony, 8, 252, 256–258, 263, 266
Border
  border crossing, border control, 124, 130, 132, 133
  border relations (Haitian-Dominican), 125 (*see also* Haitian-Dominican/intra-island relations)
  border relations (Mexican-US), 132
Botany (botanical, botanist), 180, 182
Boukman, Dutty, 256, 257, 266
Bowlah, Vashti, 2, 233–237, 240, 241, 243, 248, 291, 296, 299
Boyce Davies, Carole, 3, 20, 177, 188n4
Brand, Dionne, 2, 3, 12, 14, 17, 18, 47–59, 291, 292, 296, 297
Brathwaite, (Edward) Kamau, 4, 12, 158, 162, 163, 175, 186, 187n2, 274, 276, 277
Brodber, Erna, 2, 3, 5, 7–13, 18, 20, 103–119, 291–293, 295, 296, 299

C
Cabrera, Lydia, 3, 8–10, 175, 198, 199, 202, 204–206
Canada, 159, 160, 168, 170
Canadian Gothic, 164, 165
Capitalism, 2, 6, 14, 18
Caribbean Canadian, Caribbean-Canadian, 157, 164, 165
Caribbean Gothic, 157–171
Caribbean Sea, 158, 160
Caribbean Women Writing Spacetime, 2
Carpentier, Alejo, 12

Catholicism, Christianity, Christian, 186, 197, 216, 217, 244, 252, 262–265, 284, 286
Chacachacare, 178
Chamoiseau, Patrick, 141, 142
Chancy, Myriam, 254, 266
Childbirth, 236
Chronos, 1
Chronotope/chronotopal, 3, 4, 8, 10, 13, 14, 19, 27–41
Chronotropics/chronotropic, 1–19, 39, 198, 291–300
Churile, 234–237
"The Churile of Sugarcane Valley," 234, 235
Circularity/circular/concentric/recursiveness, 109, 111
Citizenship, 122, 126, 131–135
Cliff, Michelle, 47, 49
Cohabitation, 251–267, 294
Colonial matrix of power, 200, 207
Colonialism/coloniality, 6, 7, 53, 85–87, 91, 292
  colonial violence, 203
  imperialism, 201, 211n7
Colorism/racial hierarchies, 85, 87, 92
  See also Social hierarchies
Community (ies), communal, 3, 5, 8, 10, 11, 13, 15, 17–19, 30, 33, 41n11, 42n14, 50, 56, 86, 105–107, 109, 122, 124, 126, 131, 146, 149, 150, 187, 196, 200–201, 203, 207–209, 210n1, 210n4, 225, 234–237, 244–246, 274, 276, 284, 287, 292, 295
Condé, Maryse, 2, 3, 15, 17, 41n9, 139–154, 291, 293
Confiant, Raphaël, 141, 142
Confinement, 30, 34, 37
Corporeal archive, *see* Archive, corporeal archive
Corporeal geography, 34

306 INDEX

Corps-fossile, *see* Fossil body
Cosmogonies/cosmology/
cosmological, 2, 3, 9–13, 15, 19
Counter-narrative(s), counter
discourse, alternative histories,
2–6, 12, 14, 16, 18, 32, 50, 105,
124, 201–202, 297
COVID-19 pandemic, 143
Creole/creolizing, 213–229
Créolisation/creolization, 141,
147, 150
Créolité, 141
Crossing(s)
border, 124, 130–132, 134, 140,
141, 150, 195, 198–199, 210,
211, 245, 293
gender/transgender/queer/
androgynous, 9, 16–17, 180,
188, 196–200, 204–205,
210n1, 215, 242, 272, 275,
276, 279, 287 (*see also* Gender,
non-binary; Transgender)
pedagogical, 200–204 (*see
also* Pataki)
spiritual, 195–210
Crossroads, 174–177, 187n1, 187n2
Cultural and racial hybridity, 183

D
Da Silva, Denise Ferreira, 292
Danticat, Edwidge, 7, 21, 124,
125, 134
De Souza, Pascale, 271, 274,
276–278, 280, 286
Decolonial, 196–198, 200
Delany, Samuel R. (*Driftglass*),
169, 171
Deleuze, Gilles, 41n8, 126,
129, 130
DeLoughrey, Elizabeth, 163
Demigods (Afro-Caribbean), 159

Denationalization, *see* Stateless/
statelessness
Depression/mental health, 85,
90, 93
Desire/erotics, 158, 159, 162, 163,
171, 180–182, 185
Devil, she-devil, 237–239
Devoir de mémoire, 27–39
Diablesse, 234, 237–240, 246
Diaspora/diasporic, 1, 4, 6, 12, 13,
16, 17, 27, 39, 103–119,
157–159, 165–167, 171,
293, 297
African diaspora, 27, 29, 34,
37–39, 103–119, 196,
197, 199
Afro-diasporic, 27, 39
moorings, 112
Díaz, Junot, 124
Digenesis, 29, 34, 35, 38, 39
See also Glissant, Edouard
Digital records, 72
Disguise/mask and assimilating/
passing, 67, 68, 70
Displacement, 106
Domestic violence, 238, 239
Dominican Republic, 122–126,
129, 131
Douglas, Rachel, 300
Dress, 14, 67–68, 79
Driftglass/driftglass, 169, 171
See also Delany, Samuel
R. (*Driftglass*)
Dystopia/dystopian, 18, 30, 198–199,
207, 208
dyschronotopia, 30

E
Ecocritics/ecofeminist, 215
Ecological trauma, 11, 174, 176, 178,
180, 183, 186

Ecology/environment/nature, 11,
  141, 174, 176–178, 183, 186,
  188, 214–215, 218–223, 228n3,
  229n5, 296–299
  climate change/environmental
    disaster, 213, 214
  destruction of, 208
  environmental awareness/
    consciousness, 176, 177,
    183, 216
  environment (destruction of),
    climate change, 1, 9, 11, 18,
    140, 176, 180, 188n5, 199,
    208–209, 213, 214, 220, 223,
    225, 297
  See also Ecological trauma
Emancipation (from
  enslavement), 86, 93
  See also Abolition (from
    enslavement)
Empire, 178, 180, 185
Endangered species, 216
Enslavement/slavery, 1, 14, 17, 18,
  86, 87, 91, 293, 296
  Code noir, 91, 95
  transatlantic, 27, 28, 36–38,
    39n2, 40n5
Epistemic erasure (resistance to), 39
Epistemic *marronnage*, 2, 6, 19, 27,
  36, 39, 291, 292
  epistemic/intellectual maroon, 39
Epistemology, epistemologies,
  epistemological
  African, 104
  Caribbean epistemologies/
    knowledge/ways of knowing,
    3, 5–14, 18, 40n5, 103–119,
    197, 200–205, 207, 209,
    213, 216–223, 225–229,
    278–279, 283, 291, 292,
    297, 299
  medicinal knowledge/plants, herbal
    medicine, 175, 178, 179, 183,

186, 187, 188n7, 197, 205 (*see
  also* Healing)
spiritual (knowledge/
  understanding), 3, 8–13, 107,
  117, 196, 199–204, 217, 219,
  221–222, 245, 248, 263, 281,
  285, 292, 294, 298
Erotics/masochism, 240–248
Errantry, 126
Evil/good and evil, 144, 145, 151–154
Exploitation (of people, of resources),
  exploited, exploitative, 1, 15, 65,
  68, 77, 80, 84, 91, 92, 140, 148,
  162, 176, 181, 210, 233, 237,
  244, 259, 267, 278, 295

F
Family
  histories, 105, 109–112, 252–259
  tree, 96
  See also Rhizome
Fate, 145, 147
Fe en disfraz, 65–80
Femininity, 213–216, 218, 222, 225,
  228, 234, 238, 240, 246
Feminist/feminism, 115, 117,
  118, 233–248
Feminocentric future, 272
Ferly 2012, 27
*Folie, aller simple: Journée ordinaire
  d'une infirmière*, 95
Folklore, 233–240, 246, 248
Folktales, 3, 238, 248n1, 272–275,
  277–281, 284, 287, 296
Food, 89
  as repository/site of memory,
    88, 94, 95
Fossil-body (*corps-fossile*), 13, 34, 36
Foucault, Michel, 30, 35, 39
Fractal/fractality, 5, 9, 11, 12, 19,
  103–104, 106–111, 114,
  117–119, 210n2, 292

308 INDEX

France, 83, 89, 90, 97, 146,
149–151, 153
Freire, Paolo, 200
Frog/*grenouille du sang*,
213–217, 219–228
as species, 213, 216, 219, 228
as symbol, 215, 228
Future/futuristic, 173–187, 195–210

G
Galtung, Johan, 41, 42
Ganesha, 224, 225
Gender/the body/sexuality/
corporeality, 2–6, 8–10, 13, 14,
17, 27–29, 31, 39, 40n5, 51–52,
66, 74–75, 80, 86, 87, 90, 103,
117–118, 124, 133, 134n4,
135n6, 140, 146, 152, 154,
155n7, 174, 178, 182, 185, 187,
204, 215, 216, 222–225, 227,
228n3, 233–239, 242, 244, 247,
248, 271–277, 279–281, 284,
287, 292, 296, 298, 299
gay (homosexuality)/homosocial,
214, 222, 225, 242
gender (-based) violence, 34, 91,
233–234, 238–239, 242
heteronormativity, 224
homosocial/homosociality, 214,
222, 225
non-binary, 9, 10, 196–199,
204–205, 210n1, 272, 275,
276, 279, 287
Queer/queerness/queer theory, 9,
16–17, 180, 188n3, 198, 213,
215, 238, 281n1
See also Crossing(s), gender/
transgender/queer/
androgynous; Non-binary
gender; Queer/queerness/

queer theory; Sexuality;
Sexuality, gay/homosexuality;
Transgender, non-binary
gender, queer
Genealogy/generations/bloodlines,
104, 105, 108–111, 116,
117, 235
"Geôle obscure de la mémoire,"
83, 84, 96
Geopolitical boundaries/landscape/
deterritorialization/terripelagoes/
mapping/bordes, 2, 5, 12, 15–18
Ghost, haint, spirit, 38, 83, 95–98,
108, 117, 158, 161, 165–166,
169, 235, 237–241, 244, 250,
252, 254, 257–267, 292,
297, 298
phantom, spectre, haunting, 31, 38,
42, 165, 186, 196, 241, 244,
253, 259, 266
Gilroy, Paul, 28, 30, 31, 33,
40, 41
Glissant, Edouard, 4, 8, 12, 27, 29,
33, 40–42, 126, 139–144, 146,
147, 154, 155, 218, 253, 254,
256, 265, 292, 299
Globalization, 145, 147, 150
"The Gluttonous Ansige," 271, 273,
279, 280
"Goblin Market" (Christina
Rossetti), 171
Gods/deities/djombis, 271, 272, 274,
281, 282, 284–287
Gothic, 159–161, 164, 171, 297
Governance, 141
Guadeloupe, 86, 87, 89, 90, 143, 145,
149–151, 153
Guattari, Félix, *see* Deleuze, Gilles
Guyana, 177, 184, 186
Gyssels, Kathleen, 272, 273, 276, 277,
284, 287

INDEX   309

H

Haiti/Haitians, 122–128, 131, 134,
135, 195, 199, 210, 211,
213, 216, 220, 221, 223,
225, 228
cosmology, 216, 220, 226 (*see also*
Vodou/Vodun)
Massacre/1937 Massacre/Parsley
Massacre, 124, 125, 199
mythology, 216
Haitian Revolution, 252,
253, 256–260
impact of, 252, 253, 256–259
outsider's narrative, 258
Haitian-Dominican border, 124
Haitian-Dominican/intra-island
relations, 124, 125, 128,
131, 199
See also Anti-Haitianism; Haitian-
Dominican border; Haitian
Massacre/1937 Massacre
Hamilton, Njelle, 4, 85, 86, 88
Haraway, Donna, 173
Hartman, Saidiya, 29, 40, 48, 49,
51, 53, 57
He Drown She in the Sea, 157–171
Healing, 84, 94, 95, 196, 197,
199–203, 205–208
Herbert, Anne, 164
Heterotopia, 4, 30, 35
See also Foucault, Michel
Hinduism, Hindu, 245, 248, 283
Hispaniola, 121, 122, 124, 126, 131,
133, 134
Historical/transgenerational
trauma, 80
Historiography/gaps in historical
accounts/historical erasure,
66, 76, 77
History, 2, 3, 5, 6, 8, 10–12, 14,
16–18, 28, 32–35, 37–39, 41, 42,
84–86, 88–93, 95

Caribbean writers and the quarrel
with, 112, 252–253, 260
counter-history/counter-narrative,
alternative narratives, 32, 39,
105, 124, 201–202
dominant/hegemonic/official
narrative, historical discourse,
historiography, 3, 8, 14, 18, 28,
32, 37, 39, 50, 69, 107, 114,
115, 174, 176, 254, 256, 259,
260, 272, 279, 297
family history, 105,
109–112, 252–260
ghost of, 38, 253, 266
historical erasure/gaps in historical
accounts/historiography, 12,
27, 32–33, 35, 37, 39, 48–51,
55, 66, 69–70, 73, 76, 77
historical records, archives, 7–12,
18, 27, 28, 32–37, 39, 48–51,
61n3, 62n11, 66, 70, 73, 76,
78, 80, 96, 105, 115, 117,
118, 198, 208, 256, 260, 296
historical/transgenerational trauma,
30, 33–34, 80
linearity, 106
rewriting of history by Haitian
women writers, 256
See also Archive(s), alternative;
Haitian Revolution
Homosocial bonding, homosociality,
214, 216, 222, 225
Hopkinson, Nalo, 2, 8, 9, 12,
157–171, 291, 294, 297, 298
Humus, 27–39
Hypermasculinity/patriarchy, 272,
274, 279, 280, 283

I

Identity as performance, 73
Ignorance, 147, 150–151

310   INDEX

Imaginary/utopia/dreams, 4, 5, 10
Im(migration)/migrant worker, 121,
    128–131, 133
Imperialism, 214, 222
Incest, 145, 182, 185, 262
Indentured servitude, 42
Indiana, Rita, 2, 3, 8–10, 12, 17, 19,
    291, 294, 298, 299
Indigo, 282, 283, 286
Indo-Caribbean, 160, 166,
    171, 233–248
Interisland relations, 125
Interspecies, 216
    nonhuman/other-than-human
    relations, 215
In the Palm of Darkness, 213,
    214, 216–218, 220, 224,
    228, 229
Intimacy/erotics/desire, 9, 67, 74,
    77, 79, 80, 154, 158, 159,
    171, 181, 185, 215,
    242–243, 248, 260, 281,
    292, 297–299
In transit
    invisibility, 122
    narratives, 122, 123, 126–128,
        130–132, 134, 135
    in suspension, 123
    temporary admission, 126
Islamophobia, 149

J

Jahaji Bahin/Jahaji Bhai, 30, 31
    See also Solidarity/female
        solidarity/*Jahaji Bahin,
        Jahaji Bhai*
Jamaica, 104–106, 108, 109,
    111, 116
Jus solis, 126
Justice/injustice, 234, 235, 237, 238,
    240, 242, 248

K

Kala Pani, 31, 118, 158, 165–167, 170
Kali mai worship, 244, 246, 247
Kanor, Fabienne, 2, 3, 8, 9, 13, 14,
    19, 27–39, 291–293, 295, 296

L

Lake Ontario, 159, 166, 168, 170
Lakes (Canadian mountain), 168
Lamming, George, 130
La mucama de Omicunlé, 195–210
(La Mulâtresse) Solitude, 84
L'Ange du patriarche, 251–267
La sentencia/ TC-0168, 122–124,
    126, 127, 130, 133–135
Las Negras, 27–39
Latin America, 66, 68, 69, 71, 72
*Le fabuleux et triste destin d'Ivan et
    Ivana*, 139–154
Leprosy/disease, 178, 179, 188n5,
    188n6, 188n7
Les belles ténébreuses, 139–154
Lewis, Linden, 272, 277–279, 283
Lieux de mémoire/sites of memory, 32, 95
    creole as, 89
    food as, 89
    jail as, 95
Linearity/linear, 106, 109, 111, 114,
    116, 119
    See also "Time, linear"
Link between past and present/
    impact of the past (slavery) on the
    present, 72
Literacy/literature/reading, 88, 90,
    91, 95, 96
Living present, 106, 119
Loa, lwa, 225, 257–258, 262–264, 281
Lord, Karen, 2, 8, 10, 12, 271–287,
    291, 296, 298, 299
Love after Love, 234, 240, 241,
    244, 245

M

Macunaima, 183, 184
Madness/folie, 84, 223, 224
Magic, 159, 161
Mali, 146, 149–151
Man, 297, 299
"Man" (Sylvia Wynter), 6, 11, 14, 18, 175, 177, 178, 186
Mangrove, 18–19, 27, 31–32, 39, 41n9, 287n2
Mangrove poetics, 27
A Map to the Door of No Return: Notes on Belonging, 53, 54, 59
Marassas/twins, 145, 146, 149, 151–153
Marinette pye chèch/Marinette-bwa-chèch, 257
Marronnage intellectuel, 39
Mars, Kettly, 2, 8, 10, 251–267, 291, 294, 298, 299
Masculinist, 104, 114, 216, 225, 271, 273
Masculinity, 204, 214, 215, 222, 238, 243, 244, 274, 280, 283
  See also Hypermasculinity/patriarchy
Mask, 68, 79
Mat, 105, 107–109, 111, 113, 114, 117
Maternal/mother, 274, 279–282, 284–287
McKittrick, Katherine, 176
Melville, Pauline, 2, 9, 173–187, 291, 294, 297, 298
Memory, 7–9, 12–15, 32, 48, 50, 52, 54–58, 65, 67, 70, 79, 80, 83–96, 108–110, 117
  collective, 29, 32–34, 37, 39, 41, 85
  holes, 37
  lieu(x) de mémoire (site(s)/realm(s) of memory), 14, 32, 34, 67, 94–95, 99
  postmemory, 34, 38

transgenerational, 34, 94
  See also Memory jail; Site(s)/realm(s) of memory
Memory jail, 83–86, 88–91, 93
  as refuge/womb, 84, 86, 89
  as site of memory/archive, 83, 94
Mental health, depression, *folie*, madness, 75, 84, 85, 90, 93, 95, 153, 223–225, 229n7, 255, 256
Mes quatre femmes, 83–96
Metaphysical/metaphysics, 6, 8, 12, 292, 294, 298, 299
Mexico, 132
Middle Passage, 13, 28, 31, 33, 37, 39, 40, 42, 112, 117, 118, 158, 162, 165, 166, 199, 209, 253, 278, 297
"Midnight's Mischievous Mistress," 234, 237
Migration, 90, 163
Militarization/extremism, 15
Mind/body dichotomy, 9
Misogyny, 143
Mobility, 140–142
Mohammed, Patricia, 237, 239, 240
Monstrous, 233–248
Montero, Mayra, 2, 3, 8–11, 213–228, 291, 294, 298
Mooring, *see* Roots, rootedness
Mootoo, Shani, 2, 3, 16, 17, 19, 157–171, 291, 297, 298
Morant Bay rebellion, 114, 115, 117
Morrison, Toni, 95, 165
Museum/exhibition, 58, 67, 71, 73, 75, 76, 80, 260, 292
Muslim, 144, 152
Myth/mythologies, 233, 236

N

Naiveté, 147
Nationalism, 123, 126, 133

312 INDEX

Nature, 175, 180–183, 185, 186
Neo-gothic/gothic/Canadian
    gothic, 157–171
Newspaper, 89, 91, 92
Newtonian/quantum physics, 3, 4,
    282, 283, 292
1937 (Parsley) Massacre, 199
Nomadic subjectivity/nomadism/
    nomadology, 122, 126, 128–130
Non-binary gender, 9, 10, 272, 275,
    276, 287
Nothing's Mat, 103–119
Nothingness, 108, 112, 117, 118
Nunez, Elizabeth, 2, 173–187,
    291, 294–298

O
Olokun, 195–210
    See also Yemaya, Yemaya-Olokun
Onoura, Adwoa, 272, 274, 275, 280
Ontology/ontological (Caribbean), 3,
    5, 7, 9, 291
Oraliture, 83, 86, 94, 95
    See also Storytelling
Oricha(s), orisha(s), 98, 200, 202,
    203, 205–207, 209, 210, 281
Otero, Solimar, 197, 198, 200
Otherness/alterity/othering, 214,
    215, 222, 223, 225
Otherworlds, 283

P
Page(s)
    blank pages, 47, 48, 51
    left-hand pages, 47, 48,
        51–53, 55, 58
    right-hand, 47, 48, 51, 55
Pan-Africanism, 104
Panama Canal Zone, 131, 135
Pan-Caribbean/pan-Caribbeanism, 2,
    3, 9, 18, 198, 254

Pan-insular, 293
Pan-insular relations, *see* Haitian-
    Dominican/intra-island relations
Paper, 48, 51, 54, 58
Paravisini-Gebert, Lizabeth, 179, 186
Parsley Massacre (1937 Massacre),
    124, 125, 199
Past
    link between past and
        present, 251–267
    link with the/redeeming the, 197
    resurgence of the past, 254
Pataki, 196, 198, 200–205, 209–210
Patriarch/Patriarchy, 1, 7, 73, 75, 85,
    87, 92, 124, 146, 147, 158, 164,
    183, 198, 209, 210, 222, 236,
    237, 243, 247, 254, 266, 272,
    276, 279, 281, 285–287,
    296, 299
    antipatriarchal (anti-patriarchal),
        240, 246, 274–276, 279, 284
    heteropatriarchy, 6, 224, 234, 240
    heteronormativity, 7, 68, 224,
        243, 248
Pedagogy, 197, 200–204
    santeria/spiritual teachings, 196,
        199–204 (*see also* Pataki)
Persaud, Ingrid, 2, 16, 233–235,
    240–248, 291, 295, 296, 298
Philip, M. NourbeSe, 47
Philosophy, 3, 5, 6, 11, 13, 103–105,
    107, 113, 118, 129, 140, 141
Pineau, Gisèle, 2, 8, 14, 17, 83–96,
    291, 295, 296
Pirates/piracy, 202, 207, 208
Plantation/enslavement/indentured
    servitude, 279, 282, 283, 286
Poem/verso, 47, 51–57
*A Poetics of Relation: Caribbean
    Women Writing at the
    Millennium*, 19, 287n2
    See also Ferly 2012
Polyphony/antiphony, 277

INDEX 313

Pouchet Paquet, Sandra, 122, 123, 126–130
Powerlessness, 92, 144, 147, 148, 151, 153
Pregnancy (pregnant), 75, 91, 112, 123, 132, 227, 236
Prospero's Daughter, 173–187, 295
Psyche/psychic, 104, 106
Puerto Rico, 7, 9, 18–19, 66–70, 73, 76, 79, 80, 159, 163, 168–170, 210n1, 228n1
Pulitano, Elvira, 163

Q
Queer/queerness/queer theory, 215
  See also Gender; Non-binary gender; Transgender, non-binary gender, queer

R
Race/racial hierarchies, 5, 8, 14, 30, 52, 66, 72, 74, 80, 85, 87, 90, 92, 105, 118, 127, 133, 135, 144, 152, 174, 182–184, 186, 187, 235, 292, 298, 299
  See also Colorism/racial hierarchies; Social hierarchies
Racism, 52, 77, 83, 124, 125, 134, 143, 175, 178, 187, 188n3, 253, 259, 280
Radicalism (political, religious)/ radicalization, 140, 149, 153
Radical remapping, 2, 19, 291, 292, 298
Rafael Leónidas Trujillo Molina, 124–125, 134, 199, 293
Ramroop, Krystal M., 2, 233–235, 237–241, 243, 248, 291, 296, 299

Re/writing
  folktales, 291, 296
  history, 295, 296
  righting history, 70
Records
  historical (*see* History, historical records)
  scientific records, 219, 221, 226
Redemption in Indigo, 271–287
Re-engineering, 13, 18–19, 80
Religion, cosmologies, 2, 9, 10, 13, 15, 19, 241, 245–248, 281, 283, 285, 298
  See also Catholicism, Christianity, Christian; Hinduism, Hindu; Kali mai worship; Santeria/*santería*; Spirituality/ spiritual beliefs; Vodou/Vodun
Religious extremism, radicalism/ radicalization, fundamentalism, 15, 140, 146, 149
Repository (of history), 88, 95, 112, 113
Responsibility/agency/choice, 140, 145, 146, 151, 153
Reyes-Santos, Alaí, 201, 209
Rhizome, 31, 41n9, 86–87, 96, 142–143, 155n4, 199, 272
  family tree, 96
Rodaway, Paul, 158
Roots, 5, 31, 37, 41n9, 73, 79, 86, 130, 142, 148, 155n4, 158, 199, 240, 246, 277, 285, 292, 293
  anchor, 108
  grounded-ness, 108
  mooring, 112
  rootedness, 108, 142
Rossetti, Christina, 171
Ruin/ruination, 32, 47–59

314 INDEX

S

Santeria/*santería*, 198, 205, 294, 298
  rituals, 205–206
  teachings, 200–204 (*see also* Pataki)
Santos Febres, Mayra, 2, 3, 5–8, 13,
  14, 18, 19, 65–80, 291, 292,
  294, 296, 297
Science/scientists, 213–228
  critique of modern Western, 4, 34,
    181, 216–221, 227, 228, 278,
    281, 292
Scientific experiments, 177, 179, 180
Sedgwick, Eve, 214, 216, 225
Self-awareness/self-knowledge, 75,
    78, 92, 107, 108, 111, 112, 117,
    118, 147, 150–151,
    245, 264–265
Selfhood
  smadditization, 113
  subjectivity, 106
Sensuous geography, 158, 159
Sexual abuse/sexual exploitation,
    65, 68, 77
Sexuality, 8, 66, 74–75, 80, 154, 182,
    185, 222, 224–225, 236, 237,
    242, 246, 298, 299
  desire, 74
  erotics, 67, 74, 77, 79, 158, 159,
    162, 163, 171, 180–182, 185,
    240, 243, 248
  homosexuality/gay, 241, 242
  power relations, 72, 74, 79, 178
  sexual violence, 34, 91, 233–234,
    238–239, 242
  See also Gender; Non-binary gender;
    Queer/queerness/queer
    theory; Transgender, non-
    binary gender, queer
Shakespeare, William (*The Tempest*),
    178, 181, 183, 188n8,
    189n9, 295
Ship crossing, 30–31, 84
  See also Ship, slave ship

Ship, slave ship, 8, 14, 18, 27–35,
    38–39, 40n5, 40n8,
    41n9, 84, 296
  belly of, 29, 40
  as chronotope, 8, 14, 28
  crossing, ship crossing, 30–31
  hold of the, ship hold, 29, 40, 84
  as matrix, 29
  as womb, 29
Sisal mat, 12, 105, 107–109,
    111–114, 117
  concentric circular patterns, 111–114
  weaving, 107–109
Sister Mine, 157–171
Site(s)/realm(s) of memory, 13, 14,
    32, 34, 67, 83–96, 99
  See also Memory
Slavery/enslavement, 49, 56, 293, 296
  and brutality, 66
  and pain, 69
  slave trade (*see* Enslavement;
    Transatlantic enslavement;
    Transatlantic trade)
Smadditization, personhood, 113
Smith, Cauleen, 58, 59
Social hierarchies, 87
Solidarity/female solidarity/*Jahaji
    Bahin, Jahaji Bhai*, 31, 32, 39
Solitude (*La Mulâtresse*), 84
Soucouyant, 234, 239
Sovereignty/sovereign acts, 121–134
Space, 195–198, 200–202, 205–208,
    210, 291, 294, 295, 298
  delimited, 2
  privatized, 2
  tamed, 2
  and time, 253, 266
  See also Ecology/environment/
    nature, destruction of
Spacetime, 2, 3, 6, 7, 14–19, 28–30,
    35, 37, 39, 40, 198, 210,
    213–215, 253, 264, 265,
    291–294, 296–300

INDEX

Spacetime travel, 294
Species, 213, 215, 221
Speculative fiction/speculative
 folktale, 271–287
Spider, 271–287
Spirits, 5, 7–10, 35, 68, 108, 117,
 175, 185, 196, 225, 228, 235,
 241, 245, 247, 252, 254–255,
 257–267, 267n6, 273, 294,
 297, 298
 See also Loa, *lwa*; Oricha(s),
 orisha(s)
Spirituality/spiritual beliefs, 3, 8–13,
 107, 108, 117, 175, 195–210,
 210n2, 215, 217, 219, 221–222,
 224, 241, 245, 248, 258, 260,
 262–264, 281, 282, 284, 285,
 292, 294, 297–300
 African/Afro-Caribbean/Afro-
  diasporic spirituality, 11, 169,
  196 (*see also* Santeria/*santería*;
  Spirituality/spiritual beliefs;
  Vodou/Vodun)
 Caribbean, 11
 crossing(s), 195–210
 See also Santeria/*santería*
State, 124, 126, 128, 129
Stateless/statelessness, 123, 127, 135
Stoler, Ann Laura, 48
Storytelling, 10, 86, 94–96, 274–277,
 280, 282, 285
 belief-systems, philosophies,
  wisdom, folktales, oral
  histories, 3
Structural violence, 42
 See also Aporia; Confinement;
  Galtung, Johan
Sujet global (global subject), 143
Supernatural, 157–159, 161, 162,
 165, 170
Sympoesis/sympoetic, 174, 177–187

T

TC-0168/ *La sentencia*,
 122–124, 126, 127,
 130, 133–135
The Tempest, 178, 181, 188n8,
 189n9, 295
Terrorism, 149, 153
Thomas, Bonnie, 85
Tidalectics, 158, 162–164
Ti-Marie, 238, 296
Time, 292, 294–297
 alternative temporality, 106, 119
 arbitrarily standardized, 2
 linear, 2, 5, 10, 106, 119
 measured, 2, 4
 singular, 2
 and space, 195, 198, 200, 201, 206,
  207, 265, 266
 and teleological, 2
 time travel, 8, 14, 67–68, 79,
  201, 206, 294–296 (*see
  also* Dress)
Toronto, 159, 170, 171
Tout-Monde, 139–154
Trade, transatlantic slave, 49, 56
Transatlantic enslavement,
 27–29, 31–41
Transatlantic trade, 34
Transgenerational trauma, 13, 34, 38,
 80, 85, 96
 See also Trauma/pain,
  traumatic memory
Transgender, non-binary gender,
 queer, 9, 16, 17, 180, 188n3,
 196–200, 204–205, 210n1, 215,
 242, 272, 275, 276, 279,
 287, 287n1
 See also Crossing(s), gender/
  transgender/queer/
  androgynous; Non-
  binary gender

316 INDEX

Transit, *see* In transit
Transnational Hispaniola, 9, 121–123, 125, 128, 131, 133–134, 293
   See also Crossing(s), border; Pan-Caribbean/pan-Caribbeanism; Pan-insular
Transnationalism, 140
Trauma/pain, 233, 234, 241–244
   traumatic memory, 30, 34
Trickster, 271, 273, 274, 276, 277, 280–287
Trinidad and Tobago, 177, 187
Tropos, 1
Trujillo regime, 124
   See also Rafael Leónidas Trujillo Molina
Tú, la oscuridad, 228
Twins, 159, 168, 169

U
Undocumented, 123, 127, 128, 132, 133
United States (US), 121, 126, 128–130, 132, 135
Uno múltiple, the many-in-one, 5, 9, 18
Unraveling, 285, 286, 287n5

V
Vancouver, 160, 167, 170, 171
The Ventriloquist's Tale, 173–187
Vété-Congolo, Hanétha, 29, 32, 34, 35, 41
Veteran/World War II, 85, 89, 90
Violence/revenge/spousal abuse/trauma, 2, 8, 13, 15, 16, 91, 93, 141, 142, 145–147, 153, 234, 236, 238–248
   domestic, 299

Vodou/Vodun, 214, 216, 217, 226, 228, 229, 252, 256, 259–264

W
Walcott, Derek, 12, 27, 32, 33, 48, 119, 182, 244, 252, 253
Wapisiana, 183, 184, 186
Wayward index, 53–55, 57, 59
Web, 12, 18, 31, 108, 110, 134, 173, 271–287
   webbed network, 31, 41n9
Western modernity/logic/ideology, 2–4, 6, 13, 19
Western science, 216, 218, 219
White geology, 176
Wilson, Betty, 84, 86
World-in-motion, 139–154
Wreckognition, 47–59
Wynter, Sylvia, 3, 6, 7, 175–178, 181, 186, 299

X
Xenophobia, 143

Y
Yanique, Tiphanie, 224
Yemaya, Yemaya-Olokun, 198, 199, 202–206
   See also Olokun
Yoruba, 5, 9, 175, 196, 200, 291
Yusoff, Kathryn, 176

Z
Zien, Katherine, 122, 123, 127, 130–133, 135
Zong! (M. NourbeSe Philip), 47

Printed in the United States
by Baker & Taylor Publisher Services